BROTHERS
AND FRIENDS

BROTHERS AND FRIENDS

The Diaries of Major Warren Hamilton Lewis

Edited by Clyde S. Kilby and Marjorie Lamp Mead

1817

HARPER & ROW, PUBLISHERS, SAN FRANCISCO

Cambridge, Hagerstown, New York, Philadelphia
London, Mexico City, São Paulo, Sydney

FIRST EDITION

Designer: Jim Mennick

Library of Congress Cataloging in Publication Data

Lewis, W. H. (Warren Hamilton), 1895–1973
  BROTHERS AND FRIENDS.

  Selections from the previously unpublished diaries of the author.
  Includes index.
  1. Lewis, C. S. (Clive Staples), 1898–1963—Biography. 2. Lewis, W. H. (Warren Hamilton), 1895–1973. 3. Authors, English—20th century—Biography. 4. England—Social life and customs—20th century. I. Kilby, Clyde S. II. Mead, Marjorie Lamp. III. Title.
  PR6023.E926Z77 1982   828'.91209 [B]   80-7756
  ISBN 0-06-064575-X   AACR2

82 83 84 85 86 10 9 8 7 6 5 4 3 2 1

CONTENTS

ACKNOWLEGEMENTS

The editors would like to express their sincere appreciation to the following for their valuable assistance: Elmhurst Public Library Readers Service Department; the librarians of Wheaton College Library, especially Miss Ivy Olson; Roy M. Carlisle, Kathy Reigstad, and Melissa Stoker of Harper & Row, San Francisco; Naomi Lucks; Barbara Sloan Hendershott; Cheri Bedell Peters; Evelyn L. Brace, Ruth James Cording, Stephen G. Parker, and Brenda Blount Phillips of the Wade Collection.

A special note of debt and appreciation must also be extended to Professor George Sayer of Malvern, England, without whose friendship and help this book would not have been possible.

Appreciation is also due to Clifford Morris for permission to quote his poem "In Memory of Clive Staples Lewis"; and to Harold Shaw Publishers, Wheaton, Illinois, for permission to quote from J. B. Phillips's *Ring of Truth*.

INTRODUCTION

"A book, a good chair, my pipe and a good bed to go to when night falls, and I'm as happy as one can be in this very trying world."* So Major Warren Hamilton Lewis described his simple wants three years before his death, wants that accurately detailed the greater part of his life. He loved ships and slow trains, "bathing" in the ocean, a good symphony, small parish churches and large solemn cathedrals, a pint at the village pub, a quiet evening walk with a companionable dog, the smell of the sea, and talk with good friends. But chief among these pleasures was his delight in the companionship of a book.

This delight was superseded by only one other aspect of his full life: the friendship of his brother, C. S. Lewis ("Jack" to his family and friends). Rare as true friendship between brothers is, it was the integral element in the lives of the Lewis brothers. The sons of a Belfast solicitor and a mathematically practical mother, the two boys chose widely diverse careers. Jack pursued the life of a scholar, becoming a widely respected Oxford don and a best-selling author. Warren, meanwhile, chose the more obscurely quiet profession of a career army officer.

As close as the two brothers were, there were great differences in their personalities. Jack, a brilliant debator, delighted in pursuing a verbal opponent; Warren preferred the exchange (rather than a triumph) of ideas. Both enjoyed diverse weather, but only Jack relished the coming of snow, a "white curse" Warren never could quite accept. While an eager Warren owned several motorbikes in his lifetime, eventually purchasing a small boat, Jack never could even learn to drive a car. Both brothers were intelligent, but Jack the more brilliant.

But if there were differences, there were also intense similarities. Both brothers vigorously pursued the maintenance of sameness in their everyday lives—a sincere love of monotony, as they cheerfully described it. Both loved the solitude of long walks in the British countryside. Neither appreciated the music of hymns nor the "bustle" of the high ecclesiastical calendar, though both enjoyed the beauty of

---

*Unpublished letter to Dorothy Thibaut from Warren Lewis, June 23, 1970.

classical music and the quiet significance of "two or three gathered together." A shared legacy from their father was their almost irrational fear of poverty—though both gave conscientiously to those they saw in need. The silence of a sunset, the comfortable security of the fog, and the crystal exactness of a single flower were pleasures increased when enjoyed in the other's company. Perhaps above all, there were the shared memories of their boyhood in Ireland.

In spite of their diverse careers, both brothers were accomplished authors. The writings of Jack Lewis are well known, and do not need to be catalogued here. Warren's efforts began after his retirement at the young age of thirty-seven, when he turned first to the recording of Lewis family history (resulting in eleven bound volumes, never published), and then to the development of seven books on the history of seventeenth-century France. Perhaps Warren's most significant literary accomplishment is one that during his lifetime was a private pleasure shared only with his brother, Jack: the patient keeping of a lifetime diary.

With a style light, quick, and perceptive, Warren writes in the pages of his journal with the sensitive eye of the novelist—and yet his is a record of fact, not fiction. A keen reader of published diaries, Warren valued the insights he gained through such works. Even as a historian he was unafraid—and often preferred—to find the truth of history in these accounts.

Consequently, it is most appropriate that the life of Warren Lewis should be told in such a way—through the words of his own diary. His is not a simple story—perhaps no one's ever is—but it is a true one. It is a life filled with much happiness, and a life of great sorrows. While the supreme tragedy of his life was certainly the premature loss of Jack, Warren Lewis also struggled mightily with the disease of alcoholism.

He was to battle this agony for over forty years. A man of integrity, and of strength even in his weakness, he knew that his occasional though intense fits of depression left him sadly ill-fitted to cope with the attractions of alcohol. Nevertheless, Warren continued to face this reality courageously—and, more often than not, successfully—for the rest of his life.

The diary of Major Warren Hamilton Lewis is the record of a sensitive, loving man, a gentleman above all, who struggled honestly with the temptations of human life. He was no hero, no saint, and yet he was a good man—devout in his attempts to live a Christian life. Just an ordinary man. And just as extraordinary.

CHRONOLOGY: MAJOR WARREN HAMILTON LEWIS

1894	August 29	Marriage of Florence (Flora) Augusta Hamilton and Albert James Lewis at St. Mark's Church, Dundela (suburb of Belfast), Northern Ireland
1895	June 16	Birth of Warren Hamilton Lewis at home, in Dundela Villas (one of a pair of semidetached houses rented by the Lewis family from a relative, Thomas Keown); this home was located on the outskirts of Belfast
1898	November 29	Birth of Clive Staples Lewis at home, in Dundela Villas
1900	August 6–27	Flora (with the assistance of a nurse) takes her two sons on a vacation to Ballycastle, County Antrim (a seaside resort north of Belfast)
1901	June–July	Flora, Warren, and Clive (with nurse/housemaid Lizzie Endicott) vacation at Bath Villa at the seaside resort of Castlerock
	September	Flora and Albert visit Scotland
1903	May	Flora, Warren, and Clive (now known as "Jacksie") vacation at Spar Hotel at the seaside resort of Ballynahinch, County Down
1904	June–August	Flora, Warren, and Jack vacation at Castlerock
	August	Construction of the family home, Little Lea, is begun a short distance north of Dundela Villas
1905	April 21	Lewis family moves to Little Lea
	May 10	Warren is enrolled by his mother at Wynyard School, Watford, Hertfordshire, England

	September	Flora, Warren, and Jack vacation at the seaside resort of Killough, County Down
1906	September	Flora, Warren, and Jack vacation at Castlerock
1907	August–September	Flora, Warren, and Jack vacation at Berneval, Northern France
1908	February 15	Flora undergoes major cancer surgery
	April 2	Death of Richard Lewis (grandfather)
	May 20	Flora and Jack at Larne Harbour for a convalescent visit; Warren away at Wynyard School
	July 8	Warren comes home early in term from Wynyard due to Flora's illness
	August 23	Death of Florence Augusta Hamilton Lewis (on Albert's forty-fifth birthday)
	September	Warren and Jack are sent off to Wynyard School together
	September 3	Death of Joseph Lewis (Albert's brother)
1909	May	Albert, Warren, and Jack visit Dublin
	September	Warren becomes a student at Malvern College, Malvern, England
1910	July 12	Jack's last day as student at Wynyard
	August 19	Albert, Warren, and Jack visit William Lewis (Albert's brother) in Scotland
	September	Jack is enrolled as student at Campbell College, Belfast
1911	January	Warren continues as student at Malvern; Jack is enrolled as student at neighboring Cherbourg Preparatory School
	August	Albert, Warren, and Jack visit Dunbar, Scotland, for a joint vacation with the Richard Lewis family (Albert's brother)
1912	January	Warren begins to keep a diary
	March	Warren is confirmed at Malvern College
	December	Warren asks his father for permission to smoke (though, as early as spring of 1911, Warren

records that both he and Jack were "confirmed smokers")

1913	May 24	Warren decides on the Royal Army Service Corps (RASC) as a career
	July	Warren completes his education at Malvern College
	September	Warren begins private studies with his father's former teacher, W. T. Kirkpatrick, in Great Bookham, Surrey, in preparation for the entrance exam to the Royal Military Academy at Sandhurst
	September 18	Jack is enrolled at Malvern College
	November	Warren takes the Army entrance exam
	December	Warren finishes his studies with Kirkpatrick and visits Jack at Malvern before both brothers return home to Little Lea for Christmas
1914	January	Results of the Army exam place Warren twenty-first out of 201 candidates. As one of the top twenty-five candidates, Warren is awarded a "prize cadetship" to Sandhurst
	February 3	Warren enters the Royal Military Academy at Sandhurst
	August 5	While home in Ireland on leave, Warren is recalled to Sandhurst when Britain declares war on Germany
	September 19	Jack begins his studies with Kirkpatrick
	September 30	Warren is appointed a commission as a second lieutenant in the RASC (due to wartime need, his accelerated officers' training was only nine months instead of the usual two years)
	November 4	Warren is sent to France, where he serves with the 4th Company 7th Divisional Train BEF (British Expeditionary Force)
1915	February	Warren's first leave from France; Jack is allowed "leave" by Kirkpatrick to travel home to Little Lea with Warren

	September	Warren is transferred to 3rd Company 7th Divisional Train, France
1916	September 24	Warren is promoted to lieutenant
	October 1	Warren is promoted to the rank of temporary captain
	November 13	Warren is appointed officer commanding 4th Company 7th Divisional Train, France
	November 21	Warren is transferred to 32nd Divisional Train, France
	December 13	Jack receives a scholarship to University College, Oxford
1917	April 28	Jack begins his studies at Oxford
	May	Jack is drafted into a cadet battalion and housed at Keble College, Oxford, while in training to obtain a commission; his Keble College roommate is an Irishman, E. F. C. ("Paddy") Moore
	September	Jack is appointed a temporary commission as a second lieutenant in the 3rd Battalion of the Somerset Light Infantry
	November 17	Jack serves in France
	November 29	Warren is promoted to substantive rank of captain
	December 23	Warren is sent to Mechanical Transport School of Instruction (France)
1918	March 4	Warren graduates from Mechanical Transport School (first in class)
	April 15	Jack is wounded by English shell on Mount Bernenchon during Battle of Arras (near Lillers, France)
	April 24	Warren visits Jack in Liverpool Merchant's Mobile Hospital, Etaples, France
	May	Warren serves with 31st Divisional Mechanical Transport Company, France
	May 25	Jack is transferred to Endsleigh Palace Hospital, London

	July	Jack is transferred to Ashton Court Hospital, Bristol
	July 16	Warren learns to type
	September	Paddy Moore (Keble College cadet roommate) is officially declared dead
	November 11	Armistice is signed
1919	January	Jack is demobilized and back at Oxford as student
	January 22	Warren returns from Christmas leave at home in Belfast to duty in France
	March	*Spirits in Bondage* (Jack's first book) is published by Wm. Heinemann
	April	Warren is transferred to the 6th Pontoon Park, Namur, Belgium
	August	Jack and Albert have serious quarrel
	November 19	Warren is reassigned to service in England
1920	March	Warren purchases a motorbike with sidecar
	March 1	Warren begins training courses at Aldershot Military Garrison, England
	June 1	While enrolled in the second of four courses, Warren is assigned to 487th Company (later 15th Company) Army Service Corps
	November	Albert still considers himself estranged from Jack
1921	March 9	Warren sails in the *Appam* for service in Sierra Leone, West Africa
	March 22	Death of W. T. Kirkpatrick
	Summer	Jack has by now moved out of college housing and into an Oxford household with Mrs. Janie King Moore and her daughter, Maureen (the mother and sister of Paddy Moore). A year before, Jack had assisted the Moores in moving from Bristol to a rented house on Warneford Road in Oxford
	July	Albert visits Jack at Oxford (Jack's living ar-

rangements with the Moores remain a secret from Albert)

1922	April 7	Warren arrives home in Liverpool from his service on the West Coast of Africa
	August 1	Jack and the Moores move to Hillsboro, Western Road, Headington (a suburb of Oxford)
	August 5	Warren meets Maureen and Mrs. Moore for the first time
	October 4	Warren's six-month leave (earned for his service in Sierra Leone) expires, and he is assigned as assistant to the officer in charge of the RASC at Colchester, England (where he serves as officer in charge of suppliers)
1924	June	Warren asks Albert to supplement his army pay by £6 per quarter; Albert agrees
1925	May 20	Jack is elected to a Fellowship in English Language and Literature at Magdalen College, Oxford (for five years, from June 25, 1925)
	December	Warren completes his service at Colchester
1926	January	Warren is assigned to duty as officer commanding No. 17 M.T. Company, RASC, Woolwich, England (just east of London)
	October 4	Warren begins six-month Economics course at London University
	December	Christmas holidays of 1926 were the last time that Albert, Warren, and Jack were to be together
1927	April 11	Warren sails on the *Derbyshire* for China
	June	Warren serves as second in command of the base supply depot, Kowloon, South China (15th Infantry Brigade)
	July	Warren is hospitalized with boils and high fever
	September	Warren is transferred to Wei-Hei-Wei convalescent camp
	November	Warren is assigned to duty as officer in command of the supply depot, Shanghai, China

1928 May 2   Albert retires with an annual pension of £550 as Belfast Corporation County Solicitor (a position held since 1889)

October   Warren is no longer officer commanding Shanghai supply depot—superseded by incoming officer; Warren meets Major Herbert Denis (H. D.) Parkin, officer commanding RASC Shanghai, who becomes a lifelong friend

1929 July 25   Albert goes to Belfast nursing home for X-rays

August 6   Albert returns to nursing home for additional X-rays

August 13   Jack returns to Belfast because of Albert's illness

August 25   Jack writes Warren of their father's illness (letter not received by Warren until October 9)

September 25 Death of Albert James Lewis

September 27 Jack sends Warren a telegram advising him of their father's death

1930 February 24 Warren sails from Shanghai on the freighter *Tai-Yin*; he visits the United States on this voyage home

April 17   Warren arrives in Liverpool after a three-year absence from home

April 22–25   Warren and Jack visit Little Lea

May 10   Warren decides to edit and arrange the Lewis family papers, which had been brought back from Little Lea; this plan, which is intended for Warren's retirement, is encouraged and approved by Jack

May 15   Warren is assigned as assistant to the officer in charge of supplies and transport at Bulford, England

May 25   Warren decides to accept Jack and Mrs. Moore's invitation to make his home with them upon his retirement

July 7   Warren, Jack, Mrs. Moore, and Maureen inspect an Oxford house and garden—The Kilns

	July 16	Offer to purchase The Kilns is accepted
	October 10–11	Warren assists Jack, Maureen, and Mrs. Moore in the move from Hillsboro to their new home, The Kilns
	December	Warren begins the task of editing the Lewis family papers while home at The Kilns on leave
1931	January 1–4	Warren and Jack take their first walking tour (54 miles along the Wye Valley)
	May 9	Warren returns to belief in Christianity
	September 19	Jack has an important late-night discussion with J. R. R. Tolkien and Hugo Dyson about myth, truth, and Christianity
	September 28	Jack returns to belief in Christianity while riding to Whipsnade Zoo in the sidecar of Warren's motorbike
	October 1	Jack writes to Arthur Greeves that he now believes in Christ and Christianity
	October 9	Warren leaves on the *Neuralia* for his second tour of duty in China
	November	Warren serves as officer commanding the RASC, Shanghai
1932	January 19	Warren receives a letter from Jack informing him that both brothers share in the return to Christianity
	January 29	Japanese attack Chinese Shanghai
	April	Warren serves as officer commanding the supply depot, Shanghai
	July	Warren applies for retirement from the RASC
	October 22	Warren sails from Shanghai on the cargo liner *Automadon*
	December 14	Warren arrives home at Liverpool
	December 21	Warren retires from the RASC after eighteen years, two months, and twenty days of service; he moves permanently into The Kilns with Jack and the Moores

1933		Probable beginning of the Inklings
	January 3–6	Warren and Jack take their second walking tour (continuing their ascent of the Wye Valley)
	mid-January	Warren returns to the editing of the Lewis family papers
	March 30	Warren purchases a gramophone, which is used to give family "concerts"
	April	Warren, Jack, Maureen, and Mrs. Moore vacation for two weeks at Flint Hall, Hambleden, a farmhouse in the Chilterns
	April	Warren begins to learn the piano from Maureen
	June 1	The first volume of the Lewis family papers returns from the binders (now officially titled *Memoirs of the Lewis Family: 1850–1930*)
	August 3–15	Warren and Jack visit relatives in Scotland and then sail for London (from Glasgow) on the Clyde's Shipping Company tour cruise
1934	January 1–6	Warren and Jack take their third annual walking tour (continuing along the Wye Valley into Wales)
1935	January 3–5	Warren and Jack take their fourth annual walking tour (in the Chiltern Hills)
1936	January 13–16	Warren and Jack take their fifth annual walking tour (Derbyshire)
		Warren has a twenty-foot motor boat built, the *Bosphorus*, which he uses for inland cruising on rivers and canals
1937	January 5–9	Warren and Jack take their sixth annual walking tour (in Dulverton, Somerset)
1938	January 10–14	Warren and Jack take their seventh annual walking tour (in Wiltshire, 51½ miles)
1939	January 2–6	Warren and Jack take their eighth annual walking tour (in the Welsh marshes, 42 miles); they visit Malvern as well
	September	Oxford University Press is relocated to Oxford

		(from London); Charles Williams begins to attend the Inklings
	September 2	Evacuee children from London arrive at The Kilns
	September 4	Warren is recalled to active service for World War II, and posted to Catterick, Yorkshire; Jack begins volunteer service as religious lecturer to the RAF
	October	Warren is assigned to serve with No. 3 base supply depot, Havre, France
1940	January 27	Warren is granted temporary rank of major
	February	Warren is hospitalized with fever (second time since October)
	April	First weekly Thursday evening Inklings
	May	Warren is evacuated with his unit from Dunkirk to Wenvoe Camp, Cardiff, Wales
	August 16	Warren is transferred to Reserve of Officers (and sent home to Oxford); he serves as a private soldier with the 6th Oxford City Home Guard Battalion. During the summer months, Warren serves as part of the "floating" Home Guard from his motor boat
	August 27	Maureen marries Leonard J. Blake, Director of Music at Worksop College
1942		Warren writes his first book, *The Splendid Century: Some Aspects of French Life in the Reign of Louis XIV* (not published until 1953)
1943	February 22– 26	Warren accompanies Jack to Durham, where he gives the Riddell Memorial Lectures (later to be published as the *Abolition of Man*)
		Warren begins to act as secretary for Jack
1945	January 8	Birth of a son, Richard Francis, to Maureen and Leonard Blake
	May 9	End of World War II
	May 15	Death of Charles Williams

	December 11–14	"Victory" Inklings holiday at The Bull, Fairford
	December 24	Death of Augustus Hamilton (uncle—brother of Flora Lewis)
1946	January 16	Death of William Lewis (uncle)
	March 18–22	Warren, Jack, and Hugo Dyson take a short holiday in Liverpool; Jack is there to participate in a Brains Trust
	June 26–29	Jack receives honorary Doctorate of Divinity from St. Andrew's University; Warren accompanies Jack on this trip to Scotland
1947		Warren sells his boat, the *Bosphorus*
	March 29	Warren ceases to belong to the Reserve of Officers
	April 4–17	Warren and Jack take a brief holiday at Malvern; Hugo Dyson is present for a portion of the vacation
	June 20	Warren is taken seriously ill while on vacation in Drogheda, Ireland—an illness resulting from alcohol abuse
	August 4–18	Warren, Jack, and J. R. R. Tolkien vacation in Malvern (Tolkien is present only through August 9)
1948	March	Jack is working on his autobiography, *Surprised by Joy* (not published until 1955)
1949	October 20	Last recorded meeting of the Thursday night Inklings; Tuesday mornings at The Bird and the Baby continue
1950	January 10	Jack receives a letter from an American, Joy Davidman Gresham
	April 29	Mrs. Moore is admitted to Restholme (a nursing home)
	September 20	Warren and Jack walk from Dorchester Abbey to Oxford (16 miles on the old Roman Road)
1951	January 12	Death of Janie King Moore (in Restholme)
1952	June	Warren and Jack vacation in Ireland

[xxi]

	September	Jack meets his correspondent, Joy Davidman Gresham
1953		Warren publishes *The Splendid Century: Some Aspects of French Life in the Reign of Louis XIV* (London: Eyre & Spottiswoode)
	January	Joy Gresham returns home to the United States
	December	Joy Gresham returns to England with her two sons, David and Douglas; they visit The Kilns for four days
1954	December 3	Jack completes his last tutorial at Magdalen College, Oxford, leaving the University to accept the chair of Medieval and Renaissance English, Magdalene College, Cambridge
1955		Warren publishes *The Sunset of the Splendid Century: The Life and Times of Louis Auguste de Bourbon, Duc de Maine, 1670–1736* (London: Eyre & Spottiswoode)
	Summer	Joy, David, and Douglas Gresham rent No. 10, Old High Street, Headington (a house one mile from The Kilns)
		Joy Gresham publishes *Smoke on the Mountain* (with a foreword by C. S. Lewis)
1956	April 23	Jack and Joy are married at the Oxford registry office
	November 14	Joy is seriously ill, and Jack determines to give her an ecclesiastical marriage ceremony
1957	March 21	Jack and Joy married by Reverend Peter Bide in her room in Churchill Hospital, Oxford
	September	Joy's health is improving
	December 10	Joy is walking
1958		Warren publishes *Assault on Olympus: The Rise of the House of Gramont between 1604 and 1678* (London: Andre Deutsch)
	June	Joy's cancer is diagnosed as arrested
	July	Joy and Jack honeymoon in Ireland
	November 11	Death of Lt. Col. Herbert Denis Parkin

[xxii]

1959		Warren publishes *Louis XIV: An Informal Portrait* (London: Andre Deutsch)
	October	X-rays show the return of Joy's cancer
1960	April 3–14	Jack and Joy, with Roger Lancelyn Green and his wife, June, visit Greece
	May 20	Joy undergoes further cancer surgery
	June	Joy is seriously ill in the Acland Nursing Home
	late June	Joy is able to return home to The Kilns
	July 13	Death of Joy Davidman Gresham Lewis
1961		Warren publishes *The Scandalous Regent: A Life of Philippe, Duc d'Orleans, 1674–1723, and of his family* (London: Andre Deutsch)
1962		Warren publishes *Levantine Adventurer: The Travels and Missions of the Chevalier d'Arvieux, 1653–1697* (London: Andre Deutsch)
1963	June 15	Jack is admitted to Acland Nursing Home following a heart attack
	August	Jack returns to The Kilns
	September	Warren returns home to The Kilns from Ireland
	November 22	Death of Clive Staples Lewis—Jack—at home at The Kilns
1964		Warren publishes *Memoirs of the Duc de Saint-Simon* (London: B. T. Batsford)
	May 19	Warren moves from The Kilns to 51 Ringwood Road, Oxford
1965		Warren suffers a minor stroke that leaves his right hand slightly paralyzed (he also experiences a temporary speech impairment)
1966		Warren publishes *Letters of C. S. Lewis* (London: Geoffrey Bles Ltd.)
	May	Warren and Mollie and Len Miller take a fortnight holiday at June Flewett Freud's cottage in Walberswick, Suffolk
	August 29	Death of Arthur Greeves
1967	April 18	Warren moves back into The Kilns from 51

Ringwood Road; Len and Mollie Miller move into The Kilns with him

	July	ATV adaption of *The Lion, the Witch, and the Wardrobe* begins to be broadcast in installments on British television
	September	Warren purchases a new typewriter after his thirty-five-year-old machine breaks down
1969	June	While on holiday with Len and Mollie Miller, Warren celebrates his seventy-fourth birthday at a party given by the nuns at Our Lady of Lourdes Hospital in Drogheda, Ireland
1970	August 8	Warren is told by a specialist-surgeon that poor circulation in his right leg will prohibit any future "walks"
1972	January	Warren has a pacemaker installed
	February	Warren experiences recurring dizziness as a result of his pacemaker
	August	Warren is admitted (at his request) for what is intended to be a month of rest at Our Lady of Lourdes Hospital, Drogheda, Ireland; circulation difficulties result in the development of gangrene in both feet (which requires minor surgery)
1973	April	Warren returns home to The Kilns from the hospital in Ireland
	April 9	Death of Warren Hamilton Lewis peacefully at home in The Kilns, while reading a book

LEWIS FAMILY GENEALOGY

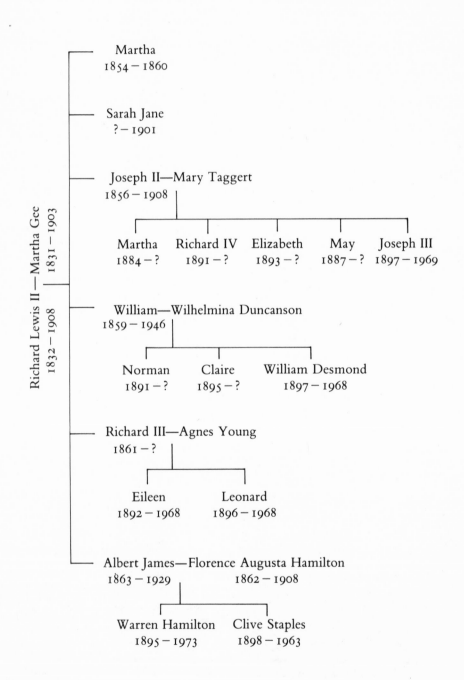

Martha
1854 – 1860

Sarah Jane
? – 1901

Joseph II—Mary Taggert
1856 – 1908

Martha   Richard IV   Elizabeth   May   Joseph III
1884 – ?   1891 – ?   1893 – ?   1887 – ?   1897 – 1969

William—Wilhelmina Duncanson
1859 – 1946

Norman   Claire   William Desmond
1891 – ?   1895 – ?   1897 – 1968

Richard III—Agnes Young
1861 – ?

Eileen   Leonard
1892 – 1968   1896 – 1968

Albert James—Florence Augusta Hamilton
1863 – 1929   1862 – 1908

Warren Hamilton   Clive Staples
1895 – 1973   1898 – 1963

Richard Lewis II—Martha Gee
1832 – 1908   1831 – 1903

WARREN, HAMILTON, AND EWART FAMILY GENEALOGY

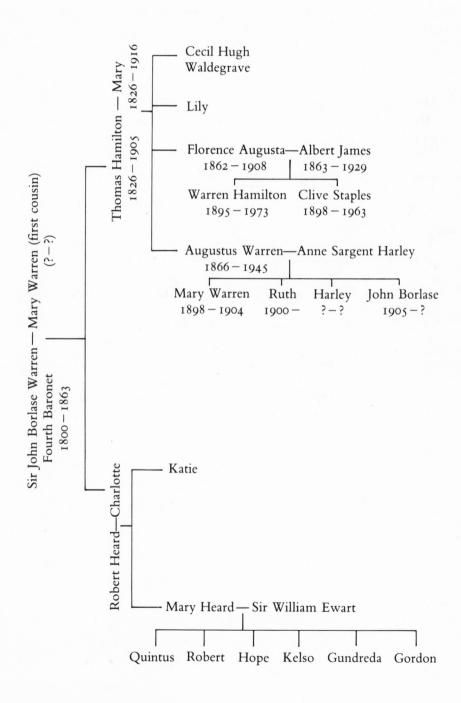

EDITORIAL NOTE

The diaries of Major Warren Hamilton Lewis encompass a span of fifty years, fill twenty-three handwritten volumes, and consist of more than a million and a quarter words. From this vast record of a lifetime, the editors have been forced to choose fewer than one hundred and forty thousand words, a task both agonizing and challenging.

In this process of selection, the attempt has been made to be representative, above all, of the character of Warren Lewis, while still concentrating on his relationship with his brother, and their mutual circle of friends, the Inklings. Copy editing within each diary entry has been held to a minimum, with corrections of punctuation and spelling made only when necessitated by clarity. All British idioms and spelling have been retained. It should be remembered, however, that (in the words of Warren Hamilton Lewis) "no Hamilton can spell," and such standards should be applied lightly, if at all. All additions within entries are indicated by [ ]'s, with the bracketed insertions frequently phrased in the words of Warren Lewis. It should also be noted that certain passages in this manuscript were deleted at the request of and as a courtesy to the C. S. Lewis Estate.

For the reader who has an interest in the origin of this volume, the diaries of Warren Lewis were willed to the Marion E. Wade Collection, Wheaton College, by Major Lewis himself, along with a variety of other manuscript material, at his death in April 1973.

PART I
1912-1929

When he was sixteen years old and a third-year student at Malvern College, Warren Hamilton Lewis made his first attempt at keeping a diary. In a "tiny 'Collin's Pearl Diary for 1912', measuring only 2 X 3-1/2 inches, bound in dark green leather" ("presumably . . . one of his Christmas presents"),[1] Warren Lewis recorded the events of daily life—school assignments, dances, the purchase of gramophone records, visits to Grundy (a Malvern pub) and more. The final entry in this volume is dated Wednesday, March 13, 1912.

It was not until January 1918, after a silence of over five years, that Warren Lewis once again resumed his efforts as a diarist. On June 8, 1919, he described this beginning in his diary: "It is on record that Boswell once asked Dr. Johnson what he thought of the marriage of a mutual friend, a widower. 'Sir, it is the triumph of optimism over experience' was the reply. Allowing for the difference between a serious and a trivial subject, the same might be said of my recommencing my attempt to keep a diary. My 1918 one had its origin in a casual excursion from Peselhoek to Hazebrouck which Collins and I made in the early part of December '17. The town was being shelled and the civilians were clearing off their stocks at bargain prices: among other things which caught my eye was the aforesaid diary—how often have I cursed it since! I imagine there was nothing peculiar about the way in which my diary was kept. It was begun enthusiastically, carried on mechanically, then doggedly, and finally died of exhaustion during the time I was on leave in December of last year. Now comes the question: what is the reason for the 'triumph of optimism'? Well, there is not one reason but several. Firstly, I have had a strong and prolonged injection of diarists: I have just finished *St. Simon*,[2] I am

---

1. Warren H. Lewis, ed., *Memoirs of the Lewis Family: 1850-1930,* Volume III (Oxford: Leeborough Press, 1933; privately "printed"), p. 259.
2. *The Memoirs of the Duke of St. Simon,* an unidentified abridgement. Warren

[1]

half way through Boswell's *Tour of the Hebrides*,[3] and Pepys[4] awaits me on my bedroom mantelpiece. This I have no doubt has had some influence on my actions, but it is not the really important reason. My real reason is that I am astonished at the pleasure which I get from browsing over my last year's notes—the book itself is nothing: in fact an outsider, in the words of a celebrated book critic, would find it 'like eating sawdust' but the bare statement of facts enables me to remember accurately ALL that happened on each individual day: I read a few lines and I remember that I was at such a place—I remember how the sunlight looked on the trees, the whine of a shell, the voices of friends, the rubber of bridge after mess—a thousand little things which are of no interest to anyone but myself. This has proved to me such an unanticipated source of pleasure that I am going to make an effort to stick doggedly to the drudgery of writing for another few months. At any rate I start with some experience: I know not to expect any sparkle or wit in a daily account which one forces oneself to write: I know that it is fatal to put off the job until tomorrow: and I know that all I write is going to be a cinematograph which can be seen at will in the years to come."

Writing as he was during the waning months of World War I and from the battlefields of France, Warren recorded his gradually improving situation as the German Army drew closer to defeat. He had first entered the war in November 1914, as a young second lieutenant of only nineteen; now, a captain in the Royal Army Service Corps

---

Lewis later dated the beginning of his interest in seventeenth century France to this volume, which he had purchased several months earlier from a St. Omer bookstore. "[I] bought it [originally] as a change from French novels, and became a life-addict to the period." (Publishers biographical note, dust jacket of W. H. Lewis's *Levantine Adventurer* [New York: Harcourt, Brace & World, 1963]). However, in a letter to his father dated March 3, 1919, Warren indicates that his interest in this period actually predates this purchase: "I have waiting for me . . . St. Simon's *Memoires* in French. I hope the language won't be too difficult for me, as it is a book which I particularly want to read. Did you ever make the acquaintance of St. Simon? He was a genial old waster who left behind him an account of everything worth noting which happened during his life and records all the people he knew. As his period is Louis Quatorze [Louis XIV] and he was never happy away from the Court of the Grand Monarque, you will see that he knew some very interesting people. The period as you know, is one of, or perhaps IS my favourite in History, so I anticipate a lot of enjoyment from the memoirs." (Warren H. Lewis, ed., *Memoirs of the Lewis Family: 1850-1930*, Volume VI [Oxford: Leeborough Press, 1934]: pp. 94-95.)

3. *A Journal of a Tour of the Hebrides* (1785), by eighteenth-century author James Boswell, records the Scottish tour he took in the company of Dr. Johnson.

4. The *Diaries* of seventeenth-century diarist Samuel Pepys, which cover the period from January 1, 1660 to May 31, 1669, were edited by Lord Braybrooke in 1825; numerous subsequent editions have followed.

with nearly five years war experience, Warren Lewis was responsible for the supply and transport of several thousand men, horses, and equipment. Still, in spite of hard work accentuated by wartime shortages, Warren found his circumstances not entirely unpleasant. Writing to his father, Albert Lewis, on July 16, 1918 while "in the field," Warren comments: "I am getting quite fit now. A unit near here lends me a horse and I go for a hard trot from 7 a.m. to 9 a.m. daily. Then I have breakfast. One boiled egg and a piece of toast. I also generally get a couple of hours walking before dinner: so you see I am not doing badly. Can you send me Boswell's *Life of Johnson* in a cheap edition? I have often meant to read it but have never done so."[5]

Although the Service Corps was of necessity required to operate behind the front lines, the safety of its men was only relative and there were times when planes strafed them and bombs landed close by. Nonetheless, Warren's chief concern at this time was the welfare of his younger brother, Jacks.[6] Wounded severely in April 1918, Jack was still convalescing in a Bristol hospital in July. Both Warren and Albert hoped that Jack's injury would prevent him from returning to active duty; their hopes were realized.

In his entry of September 30, 1918, Warren writes: "In personal matters things continue to go well. Jacks is still at home at a time when some very fierce fighting is being done. Then there is the matter of his book.[7] Even if it is a failure, he has achieved something—and I am confident that such will not be the case."

Warren's diary entries continued. "Vendredi 8 [Friday, 8 November].[8] The end is I think very near now. The delegates have passed through the French lines to arrange the terms of an armistice.

"Samedi 9 [Saturday, 9 November]. Up at the usual time. Nasty raw morning, but not too cold. Cleared up later. News today of the abdication of the Kaiser and Crown Prince is confirmed. In the afternoon went for a walk around the town. Everyone very excited. Great things expected shortly.

"Dimanche 10 [Sunday, 10 November]. A day which I shall not forget in a hurry. I was in the office at about 9 p.m. and suddenly

---

5. Warren H. Lewis, ed., *Memoirs of the Lewis Family: 1850-1930,* Volume VI, pp. 8-9.

6. "Jack" or "Jacks" was C. S. Lewis's self-designated nickname. For an explanation of this, see the Introduction to *Letters of C. S. Lewis,* edited by W. H. Lewis (New York: Harcourt Brace, 1966), p. 2.

7. C. S. Lewis's first published work was a book of poems, *Spirits in Bondage: A Cycle of Lyrics* (London, William Heinemann, 1919).

8. While stationed in France, Warren Lewis dated his diary entries in French.

there was an outburst of syrens, rockets, Verey lights, hooters, searchlights and all sorts of things. Hurried back to the mess and found everyone dancing round the room! Everyone off their heads. Cars with people sitting all over them. Australians firing Verey pistols in the square. There were about six bonfires going with Belgians dancing and shouting round them with our lads. Cathedral and Church bells pealed most of the night. Got home and to bed about 2.30 a.m. A very great day indeed. So ends the war.

"Lundi 11 [Monday, 11 November]. It seems wonderful to think that the war is really over at last. Thank God Jacks has come through it safely, and that nightmare is now lifted from my mind.

"Mardi 12 [Tuesday, 12 November]. Much speculation and talk today about when we are likely to get home. Rumour has it that our Division is not going to Germany: most annoying. After all this time out here, I should have liked to cross the Rhine.

"Jeudi 14 [Thursday, 14 November]. All the people who are going up to Germany very pleased with life, and those who aren't, including ourselves, trying to pretend they don't want to go."

Though allowed leave to return home[9] for Christmas, Warren Lewis remained stationed in France until mid-April of 1919. He was then posted to the 6th, Pontoon Park, Namur, Belgium. When this company was demobilized in July, Warren was again granted leave, arriving in Oxford on the twenty-third: "Went up to Univ. to let J [Jack] know that I had arrived. He turned up about a hour later. I was delighted to see him again. After dinner we went for a stroll, and so to bed, Jacks coming up to my room for a chat. Fine to think that I am back for a real holiday at last."

This holiday included a visit by both brothers to the home of their former tutor, W. T. Kirkpatrick, in Great Bookham, and thence, to Little Lea. Here, except for spending time with their father and other relatives and friends, they led an enjoyably idle existence.

Warren's entry for August 4, 1919, reads: "I find it impossible to keep a daily record of our doings: one day is so like another. Here one forgets that time exists, or at the most one remembers it as an arbitrary measure for the use of less favoured mortals. We read, smoke,

---

9. Home for Warren Lewis was Leeborough ("Little Lea"), the house of his widowed father, in Belfast, Northern Ireland. In spite of its vast size, Albert Lewis had continued to maintain the family home, with the help of a housekeeper, in anticipation of visits from his two sons. Such visits were to be irregular, however, as Jack Lewis was to return to his studies at Oxford in January 1920, while Warren continued to pursue his career as a professional soldier.

argue, walk, talk nonsense and play the gramophone in the garden
when it is fine. It is in times like these that one envies the rich. If only
we had enough money to shut ourselves off from the world and live
our own lotus life!" Among the books which Warren read during this
period were the *Memoirs of Count Gramont*[10] and *Ascendency of France in
the 17th Century*.

Exactly one month after his arrival in England, Warren sailed once
more for Belgium. Here his diary breaks off, not resuming again until
nearly a year and a half later. During the interim, Warren completed
his service abroad and was posted to Aldershot (military headquarters
in England) for the "2nd. Regular Officer's Course," which he described as a "most unpleasant experience. The cost of living had at
this time about reached its zenith: we had to work, and work hard,
and in the evenings a lot of drink was consumed and one way and
another I finished the year, having spent all the money I had saved
during the war, and rather heavily in debt into the bargain."

However, all was not unsatisfactory: "About this time [I bought a]
Triumph and side car for £130 paid in installments [and I] began to
take week ends to Oxford to see Jacks. . . . 'The joy of the open road'
is a very hackneyed phrase, but it is none the less true for all that: let
a man provide himself with a reliable bike and sidecar, a congenial
companion, and a pocket full of money, and if he doesn't enjoy himself
it would be doing him a kindness to poleaxe him."[11]

Upon successful completion of his Aldershot course, Warren
Lewis was granted leave pending his posting to his next overseas tour
of duty at Sierra Leone, West Africa. In December 1920, he and Jack
travelled home to Little Lea for the holidays.

Sunday, 9th January, 1921.
A wet and rather miserable morning. P[12] having decided that he

---

10. Count Anthony Hamilton, ed., *Memoirs of Count Gramont,* 2 volumes (London: Goodwin, 1903). This work, recommended to Warren Lewis by Jack in a letter
of April 1919, was part of Albert Lewis's vast library at Little Lea.

11. Undated summary from the diary of Warren H. Lewis recorded on the first
eight pages of his 1921 volume.

12. "P" in Warren's diaries refers either to Papy or "Pudaita," their father's nickname. The Lewis family excelled in the creation and enjoyment of nicknames. Warren
was known as "Badge" to his father, while Jack (already a nickname) was alternately
noted in family records as "Babs," "Babbins," "Baby," "Klicks," "Binks," and "It"
(the contribution of a rather condescending older brother). Their mother, Flora, was
simply "Mammy"; but Albert Lewis did not escape his sons' invention so easily.
"Papy" was his "official title," and, according to an unpublished letter from Warren
Lewis to Clyde S. Kilby on December 12, 1966, it was the "usual way for child to
address father 60 years ago in Ireland (and perhaps today)." However, it was seldom

has a cold, J and I went to church by ourselves, where a stranger preached a dull, lazy sermon, full of vague, muddy thoughts about the earlier history of the world.

Wednesday 12th January.

J and I unearthed some old drawings which we did years ago—judged by internal evidence to be about 1905—and pasted them into our collection.[13] . . . In the afternoon J packed. He is taking a trunk with him this time when he returns to Oxford.

Saturday 15th January.

Was wakened by Annie[14] at twenty minutes past nine who told me that P was not getting up. Went in and saw him. He has a bad cold and a touch of fever. . . . Today I was promoted to the acting rank of butler and provided with the cellar key. P—in the interests of his health—had me bring some soda water and a bottle of whiskey up to his room! In the evening I read some more Mlle. de Montpensier[15] with interludes of going in to see P. Having the cellar key I made the

---

used between the two brothers. Products of the English public school system, both boys soon learned to despise dialects that differed from the King's English; this of course particularly applied to the strong Northern Irish accent of their youth. One day, when Albert accidentally slipped from his normally dignified manner of speech into a working class pronunciation of potatoes ("pudaitas"), his delighted sons discovered a new name: "Pudaita" or alternately, "Pudaitabird."

13. As young boys, Jack and Warren Lewis created the imaginary world of "Boxen," a land of dressed animals, "knights-in-armour" (devised by Jack), and steamships and trains (the work of Warren). Jack Lewis recorded the history and geography of this land, while Warren carefully drew maps of "India" and Animal-Land (which together comprised Boxen). Both boys drew pictures of their favorite aspects of Boxonian life; some of Jack's were illustrations to accompany the stories he wrote about the adventures of his dressed animals. Boxen provided both Jack and Warren with an additional outlet for their delight in "naming." This common language did not expire with adulthood, however, for as Warren noted: "Neither of us ever made any attempt to keep that vanished world alive but we found that its language had become a common heritage of which we could not rid ourselves. Almost up to the very end, "Boxonian" remained for Jack a treasured tongue in which he could communicate with me, and with me only. The Harley street specialist of that world had been a small china salmon, by name Dr. Arrabudda; and Jack, during the closing weeks of his life, on the days when his specialist was due to visit him, would say to me with a smile, 'I'll be seeing that fellow Arrabudda this morning.'" (C. S. Lewis: A Biography, p. 222, an unpublished biography written by Warren, later revised and adapted into The Letters of C. S. Lewis, ed. W. H. Lewis [New York: Harcourt Brace, 1966].) The originals of the Boxen stories and drawings were carefully preserved by the Lewis brothers during their lifetime. These twelve volumes were willed by Warren Lewis to the Marion E. Wade Collection, Wheaton College, Wheaton, Illinois.

14. Annie Mulligan, housemaid at Little Lea from 1919 to 1928.

15. Mémoires de Mademoiselle de Montpensier, notes by A. Chéruel (Paris: Charpentier, 1858-1859).

most of it by standing myself a large whiskey and soda before going to bed. Before turning in I read a few favorite Lamb essays. That illustrated Dent edition which J has got is really beautiful. To bed at half past eleven.

Thursday 20th January.

Today I received a letter which said "that I was in orders as having sailed on the *Appam* from Liverpool on the 12th. I have had no orders altho Ainslie says in his letter that they were sent direct by the W.O. As I left my address at Aldershot I don't see how any blame can attach itself to me in the matter, but still the whole thing is very disquieting. . . . I sent off a telegram to the W.O. asking for instructions.

Saturday 22nd January.

P is worrying himself into a fever about my [failure to sail for West Africa on the twelfth, as posted, lest I be blamed for disobeying orders] and I am very worried about it myself too although I would not let him see it.

Wednesday 26th January.

Having had my tea, I sneaked downstairs to see if there was any letter for me: there wasn't, and careful as I had been, there was the P'bird waiting for me at the head of the stairs with that most irritating "Well?" Took a turn in the garden after breakfast: the snowdrops are coming up and the birds are beginning to sing again, which always makes me feel enormously light hearted, although goodness knows there is no reason for it.

Friday 28th January.

As a day it was uneventful but pleasant although the fact of there being no news for me is becoming very worrying.

Monday 31st January.

For dinner tonight there was an excellent piece of cold boiled bacon: but the fuss which P made was simply ridiculous. He broke off in the middle of a remark and gazed at it as if it had been something unclean: then before Annie had left the room—"I'm sorry Badge." I do hate being used as a medium for talking AT the servants!

Sunday 13th February.

The P'bird has been rather irritating all day: I don't mean sulky, but an obstinate inability to grasp the sense of any remark addressed to him. In fact I often find myself saying with Browning:

> Oh. to be in England
> Now P'daita's here.

Or words to that effect.

Tuesday 15th February.
My orders HAVE been sent to Sierra Leone and a fresh passage is now being engaged for me: I should expect to sail in from four to six weeks.

Monday 21st February.
P came home in a very bad temper this evening re the servants. There was an excellent dinner: vegetable soup and fricassee of chicken: when the latter appeared, P's rage and grief were quite alarming: I ventured to ask if he didn't like fricassee. "I do NOT like" he thundered "to be given this dirty rubbish while they keep the remains of the good mutton for themselves."

Saturday 26th February.
By the midday post I got my long expected orders. I am to sail from Liverpool by the *S.S. Appam* on the 9th of next month.

Monday 28th February.
I realize what a curious life mine is: my army life and my home life are two absolutely watertight compartments, and any junction between them always has a sense of unreality.

Tuesday 8th March.
Finished packing after lunch. . . . [P] made me a present of five pounds . . . which was jolly decent of him I thought. Gillespie's taxi came at 7.30 and so into town: I was very glad when P left me on the quay: these partings are always most infernally painful things. A calm night which I hope, is a good omen. Now that I have really started on the great adventure, I feel that haunting suspicion that I may be doing a foolish thing. But the die is cast.

Captain Warren Lewis's one year tour of duty on the West Coast of Africa was completed on March 23, 1922. His year there was largely one of boredom, as his diary entry for Monday, May 16 indicates: "A whole holiday today but so far from being grateful I must admit that whole holidays bore me in this dead alive place." Nonetheless, what time was not occupied with official duties he attempted to use profitably. Reading (including a resolution made on March 27, 1921 to "read the Bible during my tour out here. I calculate that if I get through five pages daily, I should finish it. It is extraordinary how little the average layman knows of the Bible: I anticipate being able to floor the P'bird in great style when and if I get back again"), a pet monkey named George, letters from home, walks, "bathes" (swimming), badminton, drinks at the "Officer's Club," and the keeping of a diary comprised Warren's daily leisure routine. However, none of these activities served completely to eliminate his dislike for the tropical heat and insects which were so much a part of life in Sierra Leone. It was with great relief and happiness that he arrived home in Belfast the first week of April 1922.

The first four months of Warren's leave (earned for his twelve month service in Sierra Leone) are unrecorded, as he was not keeping a diary during this period. He resumed his diary August 14, 1922, while in Oxford visiting Jack.

Monday 14th August.

A fine day which we decided to spend on the river. After breakfast J and I went into Oxford by bus, stopping at Magdalen Bridge to book a punt for 12 o'c. We then went on to the Union where I returned the Life of Anne of Austria[16] and took out *Social France in the XVII Century* by Cecile Hugon of Somerville.[17] And so back to Headington where we collected Andree and Maureen[18] and the chop boxes and bussed back to Magdalen Bridge: there we were joined by Miss Wibelin ("Smudge").[19] J and I sat on the poop or stern locker and paddled: I found it a very pleasant way of taking exercise and not so difficult as I had anticipated. After we had rounded Parson's Pleasure—the men's bathing place, Smudge did a spell with the punt pole: this I should judge to be a very difficult accomplishment, from some of the attempts I have seen. I forgot to mention that boats

16. Madame Langlois de Motteville, *Memoires pour servir a l'histoire d'Anne d'Autriche* (Anne of Austria was Queen Consort to Louis XIII).

17. Cecile Hugon, *Social France in the Seventeenth Century* (London: Methuen & Co., 1911).

18. In 1917, Jack Lewis's roommate in the army billets at Keble College, Oxford had been E. F. C. ("Paddy") Moore. Through his friendship with Paddy, Jack became acquainted with Paddy's mother, Janie King Moore, and his sister, Maureen. When Paddy was killed in the war, Jack honored a promise to care for Paddy's family in his stead. This promise, coupled with Jack's own loneliness since the death of his mother, involved him in a commitment which was to last until 1951 with the death of Mrs. Moore. In the summer of 1920, Mrs. Moore and Maureen moved to Headington (a suburb of Oxford), where they rented a house with Jack's help; a year later, Jack moved permanently out of College rooms and into this household. For a further explanation of this relationship, see the Introduction to *Letters of C. S. Lewis,* pp. 8-10, 12-13. Warren Lewis met Mrs. Moore and Maureen for the first time just a few days prior to this, on August 5th, over tea at Headington.

19. "Smudge" and Andree were two of Mrs. Moore's (and consequently Jack's) friends. Smudge was studying at this time for a Music Baccalaureate Degree.

proceeding up river have to be hauled across a piece of land on steel rollers just before Parson's Pleasure is reached: here women folk must land and walk round the outside of the men's bathing place, and are picked up by their boats about sixty yards further on: what happens with a boat load of women I don't know. The stretch of river above P.P. is much more beautiful than that below: I enjoyed myself greatly: in fact the day would have been nearly perfect had it not been for the presence of Maureen—a noisy and irritating child of fifteen. J and I were lured into paddling up to a place called Slay's tea gardens by what may be described as the "just round the corner" method: here we landed and lunched gratefully off sandwiches and ginger beer.

Tuesday 15th August.

A bright crisp morning with a distinct flavour of frost: in fact a perfect autumn day, but ridiculous for the middle of August. After breakfast I volunteered to go into Oxford to buy two pork pies for Mrs. Moore: had a very pleasant walk in through Mesopotamia: this is the name given to an island in the Cherwell which is joined to opposite banks of the river at each of its extremities and forms the recognized foot passenger route from this part of the world to Oxford. J spent the earlier part of the afternoon in writing to the OAB[20] but readily abandoned this amusement in order to play croquet with me.

Friday 18th August.

The Pasleys[21] came for tennis this afternoon and after tea they decided that a shower which had just fallen would make the court too soft for tennis and that they would play ping pong instead: so we organized a tournament. I played astonishingly well for me, and beat

20. The exact translation of this initialled designation for Albert is not to be found in any of Warren's recorded family history: nor is there an available definition for Jack's acronym, SPB. Only in the case of Warren, do we know that the APB represents "Archpigibotian." Though the source of these nicknames is not known, they undoubtedly were created in very early childhood—perhaps related to the world of Boxen. It is known, however, that "pigiebotianism" (and its many derivations, "pigiebotian," "pigiebotie," "pigibudda," etc.) came to represent both the close relationship of the brothers and their early philosophy of life. While a "pudaita" (Albert) continually fretted about the most trivial of daily concerns, "pigibotians" (Jack and Warren) were equally committed to maintain a life of complacent contentment—idlers who both approved and enjoyed their idleness.

21. Mr. and Mrs. Rodney Pasley. Pasley was an Oxford friend and classmate of Jack Lewis. When Albert visited Oxford in July 1921, Pasley assisted Jack in the fabrication of temporary undergraduate "digs." This subterfuge was necessary since Albert Lewis was unaware that Jack had moved out of College housing and now maintained a separate household with Mrs. Moore and Maureen in Headington.

everyone except Pasley. When they had all gone, J and I walked down to the village pub and had a drink and so back to supper. After supper Smudge, Andree, J and myself played bridge until about 11 o'c. when Smudge had to go, and we co-opted Mrs. Moore in her place. We had just won our first rubber when back came Smudge in a state of great alarm, having been shadowed on her bicycle by a village Don Juan: J and I volunteered to see her part of the way home. Mrs. Moore did not mend matters by telling S "that it was probably only a mad man who lived in the next street"! Having turned out, we found it pitch dark with a fine penetrating rain: there was a bus, but it was simply returning to Oxford, so we walked down as far as the White Horse and waited until we saw Smudge out of sight. Fortunately she was in no way molested, as both J and I admitted to each other afterwards that we would have been sadly at a loss what to do if anything of the sort had happened. I hope this is the concluding chapter in the adventures of Smudge.

Saturday 19th August.

Maureen's sixteenth birthday today. In the morning J and I walked into Oxford through Mesopotamia and having enquired for my books which are now promised for Tuesday, went on to the photographers where we got the prints of my films. J bought a new pipe. After lunch Mrs. Moore asked me what I was going to do. "Oh" says Smudge "he's going to sleep with me"! However, Smudge retired chastely up stairs and I took a chair out under the apple tree and read Louis XIV,[22] finishing the first volume. Maisie Hawes[23] came round this afternoon and I started to play a single of croquet with her, but J coming in about this time, took one of her balls for her. Maisie Hawes stayed to supper and afterwards danced for us: as far as I could judge she will be very good: it was a most enjoyable performance. After she finished dancing we played hide and seek in the garden, and then had some piano music. I was requested by Mrs. M to see Maisie home, while J performed the like office for Smudge. My way was not without peril and I very nearly fell into [an] abysmal ditch, but finally I struggled safely home at about half past eleven and went to bed soon after. Very thirsty this evening, owing to having eaten boiled ham for supper.

22. *Oeuvres de Louis XIV* (6 volumes) (Paris: Treutel & Wertz, 1806).

23. Another friend of Mrs. Moore's and a frequent visitor to the Headington household.

Sunday 20th August.

In the afternoon J and I played a single at croquet which had to be abandoned as J had to "do a Mugger". (Anglice "call on the Master of Univ.") By the way, I find that the name "Mugger" is not peculiar to McCann[24] but is Oxford slang for "Master".

Monday 21st August.

A dull autumn morning. After breakfast J, Andree and I bussed into Oxford. We then went to Univ. to see the College chapel which I had never seen before. It is a small dimly lit building with some excellent sixteenth century Dutch windows. I took a time exposure in the chapel, while J held the sightseers at bay. We then went to [Merton College Chapel]. As we were leaving the chapel the porter told us that we should not miss seeing their library, dating from the 13th Century. This is a splendid L shaped gallery with rows of bookcases set at right angles to the walls between each two bookcases runs a narrow oaken bench placed there because in the old days the books were chained in their cases and had to be read in situ: we saw a couple of the old chained books over which was a notice something as follows "Do not disturb us: there is nothing interesting about us except these bonds".

Wednesday 23rd August.

After I had finished my diary I played a single of croquet with J. I was off my game and he was playing really well: he beat me by six hoops and thoroughly deserved his win. After tea J, Andree and Smudge went for a walk, but instead of going with them I stayed in and read Kipling.

Friday 29th September.

My long neglect of my diary has its origin in the fact that my father spent a week at home after my return from Oxford on the 25th of August. He had been, he told me, sick for three weeks: he was first afflicted the morning after I left home and his convalescence dates from the 24th, i.e. the day he received my telegram: in answer to my questions he admitted that he had neither been confined to his bed or to the house but "he had been VERY sick". Humph! The trip to Oxford was one of the most enjoyable holidays I have ever had. I am glad to have met Mrs. M and Maureen, not only intrinsically but because it gives me a larger share in J's real life: happy though I think we can be together at Leeborough, there cannot in the nature of things

---

24. Reginald R. Macan, Master of University College, Oxford.

be any return to the old days, nor indeed is it to be desired. J was at home from the 11th to the 21st of this month and I think enjoyed himself: I know I had a splendid time. The weather on the whole was not too bad, and the Daudel[25] showed off all of its virtues and none of its vices. Despite the shortness of the time we managed three decent runs. Having heard that mess kit[26] has been reintroduced at home, I decided to take the opportunity of J's crossing to Oxford to go with him, and we had an excellent trip. We arrived at St. Pancras [London] at 12.15 and taxied together to Euston where I booked a room while J went to secure theatre tickets. The piece which we had decided to see was Galsworthy's *Loyalties* at the St. Martins. There was no particular star in the caste, but the level of the acting was extremely high and the play, although we had some criticisms to make, was unconventional and interesting. After the show we tubed to the Euston where we collected J's bag and took [a] taxi for Paddington: I gave him a whiskey and soda and sandwiches in the refreshment room as he would be rather late at Oxford. Although the train was crowded he managed to get a corner seat, and so we parted at 6.45 p.m. For some time I wandered round the Paddington area, a prey to the depression which I have never outgrown at parting from J. However, I cheered myself up by reflecting that we ought to get a couple of days together at Xmas when he is on his way back from Little Lea. Little Lea as usual has seemed dull now that J is not here: however, as the OAB would say "The holiday is nearly over anyway". A feature of this holiday which I have not touched upon I find, is "Pudaita Pie"[27]: I had suggested to J that it would be a good thing to keep a written record of the more amusing remarks of the OAB and he took up the idea very keenly: between us we harvested more than forty of his historic utterances, which J has written up with a very excellent little preface.

Saturday 30th September.

At about half past one P came back from town and announced in the triumphant voice he reserves for national disasters that we had declared war on Turkey.

---

25. Warren Lewis's most recent motorbike and sidecar. (He had sold his earlier bike when he was posted to Sierra Leone.)

26. A derogatory comment on the meals at Little Lea. Warren and Jack Lewis frequently differed with their father's choice of menu.

27. Warren and Jack continued to collect their father's sayings in *Pudaita Pie,* which today stands at exactly 100 anecdotes. This small, handwritten notebook is a part of the Marion E. Wade Collection, Wheaton College, Wheaton, Illinois.

Sunday 1st October.

A fine autumn morning with the sun struggling through banks of mist and fog. The whole household was rather late in getting up, which threw the OAB in to a twitter of excitement about being late for church. (I may mention that we were in our pew nearly a quarter of an hour before the service started.)

Monday 2nd October.

A typical north of Ireland wet day. I spent a long and uncomfortable morning collecting my uniform for packing. . . . After lunch I found out that I was expected to play bridge at Janie's[28] tonight: I'm afraid this will be a cause of offense to the Pudaitabird, but it will spare me that terrible ordeal "the last night at home".

The next day, Warren Lewis left Belfast for Colchester, England, where he was to serve until December 1925 as officer in charge of suppliers. (On October 5, 1933, he wrote in his diary that it was this "station where the happiest years of my service were spent.") From Colchester, Warren was reassigned to Woolwich and the position of officer commanding No. 17 Military Transport Company Army Service Corps. He remained at Woolwich until April 1927, when he sailed for the Far East and his first of two tours of duty in China.

China was a mixed tour of service for Warren—much more intense in both its pleasures and its liabilities. The first five months of duty were nearly intolerable, as Warren had the misfortune to serve under the command of Colonel G. E. Badcock. In a letter to his father (written April 14 from the troopship *Derbyshire* enroute to China), Warren speculated: "My own C.O. is Colonel Badcock: I know little about him except that he is very clever and is one of the best hated men in the Army Service Corps. So far however he has been very pleasant indeed to me. I am in hopes that like other men I have served under, I shall find that his conduct is better than his reputation."[29]

On April 23, Warren wrote: "I had a long chat with Badcock before going to bed. . . . I hope I manage to serve under him satisfactorily, but I am doubtful about it. He is so Aldershot, and so interested in the service, whereas, to be quite frank, I am neither."

---

28. Jane A. MacNeill (1889-1959), a close family friend and neighbor, and daughter of the Headmaster at Campbell College, Belfast. Jack Lewis dedicated *That Hideous Strength* (London: John Lane the Bodley Head, 1945) to her; she was also the dedicatee for Warren's *The Sunset of the Splendid Century* (London: Eyre & Spottiswoode, 1953).

29. Warren H. Lewis, ed., *Memoirs of the Lewis Family: 1850-1930*, Volume IX (Oxford: Leeborough Press, 1934), p. 184.

This hope was not to be realized as this summary of Badcock's influence on Warren clearly details: "Colonel Badcock is the most tremendous personality I have ever met: in almost any company he dominates, not by the power of his intellect, which is of the second class, but by sheer force of ego. . . . Had he a better brain, he might very well pass for an earthly replica of H. G. Wells' Martians—a comparison which is suggested as much by the inhumanity of his appearance as by his character. . . . If his treatment of officers was bad, that which he meted out to the men made a spectator's blood boil. We had a clerk with a stutter on board the *Derbyshire:* Badcock held a conference of his clerks every day on board, at the end of which everyone present had to ask 'one intelligent question'. This unfortunate was generally encouraged to do so with the invitation, 'And now, poor stuttering fool, what imbecility have you got for us today?' On a parade one day, a Sergeant collapsed in a faint and was carried to the hospital: I took the news to Badcock. 'Ah' he said quietly, 'pity he's not dead. I've made up my mind about that man: he's no use to me'. And he really meant it."[30]

An opportune, though serious, illness allowed Warren Lewis to escape temporarily from Badcock's command, his two-month hospital stay lengthening into a one-month convalescent leave to Wei-Hei-Wei bay. This escape was made permanent in November of 1927 when Warren was transferred to Command of the Supply Depot at Shanghai.

Warren's service in Shanghai was basically a happy one, filled both with hard work and vigorous recreation. During this time, he met Major H. D. Parkin, an equally fun-loving career soldier, who was to be a lifelong friend. Together with other officers, Parkin and Warren developed a steady schedule of Shanghai nightlife—moving from club to club in a torrent of merriment and drink. This routine, both "very happy and very demoralizing",[31] was broken only by one very sobering and painful event.

On August 25, 1929, Jack Lewis wrote his brother that their father had been taken rather suddenly and seriously ill. This letter, sent by sea route, was not to reach Warren in Shanghai until October 9. Thus, without any preparation, and after being absent from home for over two years, Warren's diary entry for September 27 records the following.

"The Pudaitabird is dead. When I got down to the office at quarter

30. Warren H. Lewis, ed., *Memoirs of the Lewis Family: 1850-1930*, pp. 172, 174.
31. The diary entry of Warren H. Lewis for February 6, 1967.

to nine, Lee handed me a cable: it was from J, handed in at Belfast at 4.20 p.m. yesterday—'Sorry report father died painless twenty fifth September. Jack'. In a dull nagging way it is hurting me more than I should ever have imagined it would have done. For one thing, my relations with him on paper have been friendly and intimate ever since I was unexpectedly ordered abroad, and by mere lapse of time I was perhaps more affectionately disposed to him than I would have been had I been in frequent contact with him. And now that the blow has at last fallen so unexpectedly I find that his many irritating and objectionable characteristics fade from my mind. All day I have been seeing pictures of him at his best, jumbled up in no chronological sequence— Saturday evening tram rides and visits to the Hippodrome with late supper afterwards in Malvern days: earlier days of 'where do you want to go to' in the study . . . the 'Well boys, this is grand' at the beginning of the holiday: walks over the hills: his generosity in gifts of money and clothes: his little drop of whiskey: his fund of 'wheezes'.[32] I am glad that it is these things that I remember. Most of all, I am glad that the last time we spent together was also one of the happiest we ever had—the first week of April 1927—unclouded by the emotionalism with which he would have spoilt it had he known that I would be half way to China before the month was out. I suppose it is cowardly to be glad that I was not at home for the final scene: saying goodbye is almost unendurable: at times Mammy's is still a horribly vivid memory. Perhaps however there was no final scene—tho' I do not think J would normally be at Leeborough so late in the year as this. . . . Mixed, perhaps rather callously, with my feelings about P, is the wrench of losing Leeborough, the Leeborough of the little end room and the attics, and of our room, and rare warm summer afternoons in the garden with the gramophone. And worst of all, being pulled up by the roots—worse for me than for J, for Leeborough has always been my base whereas his real home has been Hillsboro for some years now. The thought that there will never be any "going home" for me, is hard to bear. I'd give a lot at this minute for a talk with J."

---

32. Jokes or humorous anecdotes; Albert Lewis loved both to hear and share his favorite "wheezes." When overseas, Warren always made a special effort to send home in his letters any special story which he thought might qualify as a "wheeze."

PART II
1930·1939

Five months later, after numerous letters and much preparation, Captain Warren Lewis sailed for home, his Chinese tour of duty complete. With the permission of the War Office, Warren arranged to travel home on a commercial freighter, the Tai-Yin, *in order to have the opportunity to visit other countries. This itinerary was to include both Japan and the United States.*

Monday 24th February.
Started for home at last, but found it undefinably flat, as I think usual with all long anticipated emotions.

Tuesday 25th February.
Ship sailed about 7 a.m. I woke up feeling very sick and shaky. It may be seasickness but I'm afraid it's too much whiskey.

Wednesday 26th February.
Woke up this morning feeling very much better, but not quite all right yet. . . . Now that I begin to take stock of my surroundings I find to my horror that out of a total of eleven passengers, six are women. As in British cargo boats it is the invariable rule that "unaccompanied females" are not carried it had never occurred to me to consider this snag: of course it goes a long way towards ruining the trip, but it is too late to complain now. . . . About teatime today a woman I have never seen before came to the smoking room and asked each of us to a "karktail poity" in her suite at 5.30: resistance being obviously impossible, we all went: I've never spent a more appalling hour. . . . The whole thing was such a nightmare of vulgarity as one had thought was only to be seen in stage burlesques of American gin parties. (The conversation by the way was exclusively on the subject of alcohol.) The sort of remarks I remember are "Does this baby love to throw one bug grand gin poity? Well I should say!". . . However the last supper gong put an end to our miseries: but the thought of

this sort of thing the whole way to New York simply freezes me with horror.

Thursday 27th February.

[I] was rather late for breakfast. Had a pleasant meal though, as mercifully none of the Americans turned up: the two Englishwomen —a Mrs. Ross and her daughter, seem pleasant folk although of course one wishes them elsewhere. . . . About eleven o.c. we began to close in with the land. . . . One's first glimpse of Japan . . . is almost exactly like the coast of North China: the same receding layers of sharply serrated mountains and general sense of desolation and dim blue perspective: the chief differences being that there were far more trees to be seen and that some of the peaks were snow covered.

Friday 28th February.

After breakfast Barton, Dakin[33] and I set out to visit Kyoto, the old capital of Japan. . . . I only [stipulated] that whatever was missed, I must see the Dibutsu Buddha, this being the object of my pilgrimage. Firstly we drove through the Park of the Imperial Palace: one cannot of course go through the Palace itself, but right up to the walls the park is open a la Kensington Palace and Kensington Gardens. . . . Of the palace there is nothing to be seen except the wall, and I was very surprised to find this roofed with the tubular tiles which I always thought peculiar to China: except that they were greenish black in colour and stamped with a chrysanthemum plaque, they seemed to me identical. After this we drove round the most interesting parts of the old town, but time was so short that we really saw little except that the place was very beautiful: I'm no believer in this sort of sight seeing a l'Americain, and think we would have done better to have concentrated on one or two places. All I retained of the drive was a vision of dripping pine trees with little temples and monasteries and rushing green water in stone canals and one large stream and some pretty houses. . . . Next we drove a short distance to the Dibutsu Buddha temple. . . . I very nearly missed the Dibutsu I had come to see, as he sits on a lotus leaf at the base of a gigantic wooden head of a Buddha, which is the main feature of the temple and quite dwarfs the bronze one. Having found him I was loath to leave him—he is so exquisitely serene and unruffled. . . . The difference between Chinese and Japanese temples is very remarkable:

---

33. Leonard H. Barton and Dakin were Shanghai friends of Warren Lewis who accompanied him on the *Tai-Yin*.

the spotless condition and excellent repair of the latter show that the thing obviously means something. [Tonight I] sat up in the smoking room and finished *The Warden*,[34] which reads as well as ever. To bed at about 11 o.c.

Sunday 2nd March.

About 10 o.c. we made out Yokkaichi harbour and turned towards it. . . . A tug brought out our cargo as soon as we anchored and work started immediately: it was all china, for which the port is famous, and I noticed that most of it was consigned to Woolworths, New York. The Japanese coolie is a picturesque person: most of them were wearing stiff flat looking coats with lettered facings—rather like a stole—and big characters on the back, with legs encased in cotton tights: they looked exactly like the gardener in *Alice in Wonderland*.

Monday 3rd March.

[This evening, I made arrangements] to go out to Kamakura to-morrow morning, where I now find the *real* Dibutsu Buddha is—the one I saw at Kyoto being only a small copy: the real one is becoming as elusive as the Holy Grail.

Tuesday 4th March.

A fine chill morning with rainclouds still about, but a fair promise of a decent day, so Barton and I decided to make the trip to Kamakura and left the ship by taxi soon after nine. Dakin, who had some shopping to do, stayed in Yokohama, and we arranged that he should buy us three cases of Japanese beer as some provision against the coming hot weather. We caught an electric train from another and more distant station than the one we used yesterday, [and we] emerged at Kamakura where we took a taxi and drove through the village to the Dibutsu shrine: on the way we picked up that rara avis, an American gentleman, who had been in the same carriage in the train with us, and gave him a lift. On our arrival at our destination we found a big red gate, guarded by rather Chinese looking guardian statues, on which was posted the following notice in both English and Japanese:

N O T I C E.
Kotoku In Monastery.
Kamakura.

STRANGER WHOSOEVER THOU ART and whatsoever thy creed, when

---

34. *The Warden* (1855) was the first of six novels in the Chronicles of Barset series written by Victorian novelist Anthony Trollope.

thou enterest this sanctuary, remember that thou treadest upon ground hallowed by the worship of ages. This is the temple of BUDDHA and the gate of the ETERNAL and should therefore be entered with reverence.

By order of the Prior.

A broad tree lined avenue led up to the Buddha which we had come to see, and there it was, huge and aloof even at two hundred yards distance. This is certainly one of the few things worthy to rank with the Temple of Heaven. Though it is enormous—about 50 to 60 feet high I should say—mere size is not its attraction—or rather that it should have been possible to cast and carve a master piece of such a size is what gives it its fascination: there is something uncanny in staring up into that huge face which looks down under half closed eyelids with an expression which seems to say "I have always known everything and have always been here, and anything you may do or say in your little life is mere futility". I would like to stop in this place for a few days and come back and look at this statue at various times —early morning and evening—but not on a moonlight night. I must have looked up, into his face, for nearly ten minutes. . . . In the grounds near the foot of the image I bought a fairly good bronze model of the statue for Y20.[35] . . . We travelled back with our pleasant American who has had the courage and good sense to go on an individual world tour: he warned us earnestly against thinking that New York was in any way representative of America.

Wednesday 5th March.

[The] new Americaine installed herself in the smoking room immediately after breakfast and having announced that it was the most comfortable place in the ship, spent the day there—so that cosy little haven is apparently out of bounds until we leave Frisco. It is useless even trying to use the room jointly with her, for the minute anyone goes in she puts down her book, opens her mouth, and lets out a non-stop cascade of bosh.

Thursday 6th March.

After my morning beer I read in the saloon till lunch time; the smoking room has already become quite unfamiliar territory to us. I am re-reading *Doctor Thorne*[36] with much enjoyment. It was certainly

---

35. This significant moment in the life of Warren Lewis was similar to his brother Jack's experiences with the numinous. Warren was to remember this encounter for the rest of his life, even to the point of preserving his souvenir statue of the Dibutsu Buddha.

36. *Dr. Thorne* (1858) is the third novel in Trollope's Chronicles of Barset.

a happy idea to keep the Barsetshire saga for this trip: I cannot think of anything I would change it for, with the possible exception of an equivalent quantity of Scott, and even of this I am doubtful.

Friday 7th March.

[This] morning I was talking to the Ross girl who told me with great glee that she had been button-holed by that old harridan who has annexed the smoking room, thus "Say d'ye think I have frightened those boys away by sleepin' in here?—they don't seem to come around now"—to which Miss R simply replied "Yes, I think you have".... I finished *Doctor Thorne* today and read a couple of plays of Moliere in my new Everyman translation.

Saturday 8th March.

Coming on deck, I found it much the same sort of day as yesterday—almost black sea, a grey sky, and the ship pretty steady, with very little water coming on board. In fact it was so dry that Dakin and I were able to take our walk round the main deck and enjoy it: we did 22 laps which I reckon to be the equivalent of four miles. Nothing in sight for the fourth day in succession, except for our escorting squadron of albatrosses—they are magnificent birds, and it is amazing the way they manage to overtake us with the slightest movement, not of the whole wing, but of the tips only: they are certainly more graceful than seagulls.... In the afternoon I did another 22 laps around the deck, making eight miles in all today, and felt quite tired when I had finished. ... When I had finished my walk I read in the saloon until supper time, and also glanced into Wells' *Outline of History*[37] which Dakin is reading. Having tried him on the Grand Siecle, the Ulster crisis, the war, and the position in the Far East, I came to the conclusion that he is inaccurate, superficial and deliberately misleading.

Sunday 9th March.

Absolutely nothing in sight all day, not even the albatrosses, which seem to have deserted us.... Wrote my diary after supper.

Extra day. On the 2nd 10th March or whatever one likes to call it, this being the day the Captain has elected to make up the 24 hours gained on the Eastbound passage.... In the afternoon I read in the

---

37. *Outline of History* (1920) by H(erbert) G(eorge) Wells was a popular approach to the development of man from creation to modern times.

saloon: after finishing *Framley Parsonage*[38] I borrowed Vol. III of Dakin's *Outline of Literature*[39] which, though it does not contain anything particularly new, is an eminently dippable book, generously supplied with quotations. There is a good chapter on Dickens and Thackeray, supplied by Chesterton: I also got a lot of pleasure out of the *Victorian Poets*. Reading poetry is with me at any rate, a chancy business: when I open a volume which I have read before, I never know whether it is going to give me keen pleasure or fall absolutely flat: today was however one of my poetical days, and I browsed very contentedly, making a resolution to re-read Tennyson when I got home. There are worse ways of spending a cold afternoon than sitting in a warm cuddy with a pipe and a book, the comfort being accentuated by the periodic "whoosh" of a sea coming aboard, followed a few seconds later by the crash of the remnants against the scuttles at one's back.

Friday 14th March.

I was amused at supper by Mrs. Ross who in reply to Mrs. La Hache's contention that it is best to sleep whenever one feels like it, replied that that was to reduce oneself to the level of a dog or a cat. This was not well received. When I went on deck after supper, the ship was pitching and the wind freshening: there was an impressive view forward—a clear yellow moon, gleaming on a restless sea, and under the moon a queer mass of black cloud resting on the sea and having the shape of a vast bird in flight.

Saturday 15th March.

Some talk of taking Miss Ross to a show in San Francisco on Monday night, but she says that her mother doesn't allow it.

Monday 17th March.

Many more seagulls than usual this morning, and they are begin-ning to scream (why do seagulls scream only when near land, and how do they know that they are near land?). . . . San Francisco lies on the right side of the bay as you go in, the left being undeveloped (and naturally much prettier). . . . In front, in the middle of the harbour, is the local Chateau d'If—a rocky island with a big grey walled prison in the middle of it,[40] and a factory and other auxiliary buildings outside

38. *Framley Parsonage* (1861) is the fourth novel in Trollope's Barsetshire series.

39. *The Outline of Literature* (1923) was edited by John Drinkwater and published in London by George Newnes.

40. Alcatraz Federal Prison, located on Alcatraz Island in San Francisco Bay, was until 1962 a maximum-security, "escape-proof" penitentiary.

the wall. . . . The first thing which struck me was that the skyscraper is a legitimate and attractive contribution to architecture: the effect of the mass of tall oblong clean lined buildings is really rather fine: in brick or stone they would I think be rather monstrous but the effect of unbroken sweep which is obtained by concrete carries the thing off. . . . Getting ashore at this port is a very tedious business: first we dropped anchor and a tender came off from the shore which after a good deal of manoeuvring was rather clumsily brought alongside: from this emerged a fat elderly U.S. Army doctor in uniform, accompanied by an Immigration Officer, and the two of them proceeded to count the passengers and crew. . . . But this was only the beginning of our troubles: the next order was "All passengers to the saloon", and there was the doctor enthroned at one table and the Immigration man at the other. The former unfortunately suffered from the impression that he was a wag, but was in point of fact merely rude, e.g. pretending to mistake Mrs. Ross's passport for Miss Ross's and asking the latter if she was really 66 years of age etc. With me his hilarity took the form of addressing me in French for some reason. . . . The Immigration man, to whom we were next handed over, was an elderly unshaven spectacled person, and almost I think the stupidest man I have ever met: very few ideas penetrated until the matter had been explained twice, and sometimes three times: when I had at last convinced him that I wasn't disembarking at San Francisco, he stamped my passport—curse his insolence—"permitted shore leave", and then explained, to my absolute bewilderment, that I needn't take the passport ashore with me. The whole business was an eyeopener in American "efficiency". At last Barton, Dakin and I got ashore lateish in the afternoon. . . . First we had a "shoe shine"—until it was too late to retract it had not occurred to me what an infernal fool one would feel sitting on an elevated chair in a busy street having one's shoes polished: but of course this was pure self consciousness, as no one took any notice whatever. Crossing streets in San Francisco is a perilous adventure partly because all traffic keeps to the right, and partly because there does not seem to be any system of traffic control—at least if there is, I never grasped it, and I frequently saw cars miss each other by inches at cross roads. . . . The American policeman produces an unexpected repercussion of having developed the film habit—there he is, with his peaked cap, metal star, and club: what is missing? And then you realize that he is neither (a) threatening someone with a pistol or, (b) having buckets of whitewash emptied over him. The gradients in this town are terrifying—in places quite as steep as the Wych cutting at Malvern, and to go up one of them in a taxi sets you wondering what kind of brakes the car is fitted with. . . . Having had a look round we met Dunkley[41] by appointment at "Herbert's Batchelor Grill" to give it its full title. . . . [Along] the grill side of the room were the "short order" customers eating for dear life on high stools in the counter: we however chose the more conventional table: the food was good, but the prices, judged by our standard, were outrageous. For four steaks, chipped potatoes, asparagus, four bottles of "Nearbeer" and four cups of coffee, we paid eight dollars, which works out at 33/4, English money! This teetotal beer is a remarkable achievement: it was called "Busch Lager". It looked like beer, it smelt like beer, and what's more it tasted like beer: Barton, who understands these things, says that it *is* beer, the only difference being that after it has been brewed something is added to precipitate the alcohol, which is then extracted. This raised an argument as to whether a teetotal generation would drink this beer for its flavour alone: I said "yes", but the others were against me.

Tuesday 18th March.

I rarely notice the air of any place, but one cannot miss the bracingness of San Francisco: I have not felt so fit for ages. Arrived at the hotel, I scribbled a note to J, telling him of my safe arrival on this side of the Pacific. . . . We then had another "shoe shine" as naturally as if we had been doing this all our lives and set out for the Hong Kong and Shanghai Bank where Dakin had a letter of credit to cash. On the way I discovered something that is cheap in San Francisco—tobacco: I bought 3-1/2 ounces for 50 cents. I also bought a tube of Pepsodent. After this we adjourned to our haven of refuge, Herbert's, where we had some imitation beer. . . . We lunched at the "Sir Francis Drake" where we had a good meal at a much more reasonable cost than our supper at Herbert's: it began with an extraordinary concoction called a mixed salad, and it certainly was mixed—lettuce, cucumber, pears, pineapples, crystallised fruits, gherkins and tomato: it wasn't very nice, but it didn't taste anything like as unpleasant as it sounds. The porcelain was green, which was rather effective: after tiffin[42] Barton and I sat in the lounge for half an hour or so watching the passers by: I haven't seen so many plain women for a long time. . . . We sailed at 4.40 and got out without any incident. . . . Very busy all evening

---

41. A fellow passenger on the *Tai-Yin*.
42. A British colonial term for a light midday meal—lunch.

jotting down these impressions of my first American port. To bed about 11 o.c. The Captain tells me that two of the engine room crowd deserted today: we sailed two short.

Wednesday 19th March.

During the morning two sea lions came up to port, and later on a school of black and white porpoises which we watched from the forecastle head for some time. . . . The water today has frequently been discoloured by large patches of scummy brown oil: presumably the tankers clean out their tanks on the run down to San Pedro. [At the San Pedro Harbour] I had arranged to go on shore with Barton and Dakin but shortly after we were alongside I was told that a gentleman wished to see me in the saloon, who proved to be that Mr. Hanson to whom Huck Longfellow[43] had given me a letter of introduction, and who had a cut and dried programme all ready for me. At first I was somewhat put out, as one prefers to retain the initiative in these matters, and to be committed to an unknown programme in a strange town is somewhat of a pig in a poke: he had with him a Mr. Churchill. . . . Hanson luckily turned out a very pleasant fellow—clean shaven, taciturn, but with a distinct humour of his own, and like all Americans of the better sort, almost embarrassingly hospitable: I liked his friend too. Hanson began by announcing in a tone which did not admit of any argument that he was carrying me in his car to see some wrestling matches: that I had been made an honorary member of the Johnathan Club of Los Angeles where I would spend the night: that he was sorry I had not wired him that I had friends (Barton and Dakin were present at this time) as he would have got them tickets for the wrestling too: but that he hopes they would join me tomorrow morning when he had arranged a visit to a film studio at Hollywood for us—which needless to say they were delighted to do. . . . The drive into Los Angeles took about an hour, which made me very glad that I had agreed to the stopping ashore part of the programme: I found my two companions easy to talk to, so the drive passed off without any awkwardness. . . . The wrestling is the nearest thing to gladiatorial combat which I have seen, and though brutal, is undoubtedly very exciting—much more so than boxing. . . . The excitement among the audience was tremendous—much more so than at a boxing match in Shanghai. I must admit that I was rather bored with it before the finish, and also very

---

43. A fellow officer Warren had known in Shanghai.

hungry, having had nothing since my tiffin, and was very glad when the last fight ended at about half past ten.

Thursday 20th March.

I had some difficulty in getting off to sleep in my strange bed, but once I did so, slept very well, the room being quite cool for an American one when I had opened both the windows. . . . Was in some doubt about the question of tipping, and finally left two half dollars so disposed that if I was ever challenged with doing the wrong thing I could claim to have forgotten them. I had a quick look round the club premises when I had dressed and found it more like a very good hotel than the English conception of a club—that peculiar hotel like look about the public rooms, and page boys in pill box hats and so forth. I had an excellent breakfast, beginning with grape fruit (served by the way by an English waiter), after which I went back to my room and "packed my grip". . . . It was a glorious morning, like one of those rare perfect English summer days, and with a clear bracing tang in the air: cleanliness by the way (and the alert fitness of the people) is the first thing that strikes one about Los Angeles: not only are the streets and trees and vehicles clean, but there is a cleanness which amounted to an austere beauty about these tall buildings: I like the sheer soaring sweep of them. One which impressed me particularly was the offices of the Richfield Oil Co. . . . As we approached Hollywood, the town became cleaner if possible, and there was more grass about. . . . I was at first surprised at the number of palm trees I saw everywhere, until I came to think of how far south we have got. In the suburbs proper we passed a succession of delightful houses, all in various styles. . . . Many had their own swimming pools in the garden. One thing which looks odd to English eyes is that none of these houses have any hedge or railing separating them from the road —their front lawn simply ends on the public footpath. Though it happened later in the day, I might as well put in here that we inspected two of these houses which were for sale, and the arrangements inside are as good as those out. Both had beautiful pegged wooden floors, and in one there was a very fine raftered ceiling: but the glory of the American house evidently lies in its bathrooms: these were most sumptuously got up, each in a different colour scheme, and elaborately equipped. Of the smaller of the two, which had perhaps five rooms upstairs, four down, and half an acre of ground, we enquired the price—125,000 dollars, or £25,000 English money! . . . We next drove into what looked very like a model factory, but was in fact the film studio we were to be shown over—that of United Artists, run by Mary Pickford and Douglas Fairbanks. These studios are really a little town in themselves and appear to be almost self contained, and, like everything else I have seen here, are most scrupulously clean and tidy. It is by the way for obvious reasons very difficult to get permission to see over a studio, and Hanson plumed himself not a little on having managed it for us: we pulled up outside the garage where stage cars are faked up, which was placarded with the characteristic American notice: "No private work done here: No, not even for you". In the first place we came to (a four walled building open to the sky) an Arctic "set" was in course of preparation: the whole floor was covered with "snow drifts" of white sand, and in a corner was a fine model about 4 feet long of an icebound steamer in a frozen river with all its tackle frozen up, and a model village of log huts. . . . We then wandered outside and looked at some more of the life size scenery, and I was extraordinarily impressed with its absolute realism and solidity: we walked through a "street" remaining from the *Taming of the Shrew*[44] and one could go and touch the stones of the houses without realizing that it was all lath and plaster. . . . After seeing the outdoor tank where "sea battles" take place, we got back into the car and set out for the Los Angeles Country Club for lunch. Once again we passed an endless succession of attractive houses (the wealthy suburbs extend for 15 miles in this direction), but I was not so pleased with them as I was before, and it was some time before I realized why: the answer is that they have no atmosphere or soul, if such a word can be applied to a house: none of them are anyone's home and they never will be: beautiful they certainly are, but one admires and passes on. They are not houses to live in. . . . We stopped for a few minutes in [San Pedro] to lay in a stock of oranges and grape fruit and then drove down to the ship, which we reached at 3 o.c., where I said good bye to Hanson and thanked him for my most interesting visit, as indeed it truly has been. We went to sea at six o.c. From supper until now (11.15 p.m.) I have been busy putting down as much as I can remember of the last two days.

Sunday 23rd March.

I sat on deck for a little after supper, but Mrs. La Hache came on deck looking somewhat amourous, so Barton and I fled to the main deck where we walked for some time and watched the phosphorescence glinting and sparkling in the ships bow wave.

---

44. The first sound film version of William Shakespeare's play *The Taming of the Shrew* was made in 1929 and costarred Douglas Fairbanks and Mary Pickford.

Monday 24th March.

This afternoon I went to my cabin and very reluctantly tackled the job of washing an accumulation of dirty linen: with cold water and no scrubbing board, it is uncommonly hard work. . . . Miss Ross . . . has undertaken to give me a lesson in ironing tomorrow.

Tuesday 25th March.

One month out from Shanghai at 6 a.m. this morning. . . . Throughout the day many turtles have been swimming past, one carrying a bird on his back: also in the morning a school of porpoises was frolicking round the ship. While they were at play, a turtle bound the other direction passed slowly through the school, glancing to right and left of him, for all the world like a dignified and nervous old gentleman passing through an urchin's snowball fight. There was also a large number of very small flying fish. . . . Miss Ross came to my cabin this morning and there initiated me into the mysteries of "damping" linen, which is apparently a necessary preliminary to ironing: I then got the ship's electric iron against ironing with Miss Ross this afternoon. . . . An annoying incident occurred this afternoon: Miss Ross got everything ready for ironing in the saloon and then I found the iron gone out of my cabin: after searching high and low I found Jacob looking very hangdog, who muttered that Mrs. La Hache had taken it: so there was nothing to do but give up: I did send Jacob to get it from her, but either he didn't ask at all or else she wouldn't give it up: at supper she had the damned impudence to say— "Cap'n, I'm a-fraid I cheated you out of your iron". What is one to do with a woman of this sort? Now I hear the damping process has to be done again tomorrow.

Wednesday 26th March.

During the morning I "damped" my clothes again and ordered Jacob to have the iron ready for me at four o.c.—and this time it actually was. Miss Ross did a couple of shirts for me while I watched, and one collar, after which I did the rest myself, finding it a much hotter job than I imagined: but I was very proud of the finished result, done entirely with my own hands. I was very glad to have the shirts done for me, as I find there is quite a science in ironing.

Tuesday 1st April.

When I came on deck after dinner I surprised Dakin and Miss Ross in the act of moving my deck chair and installing Mrs. R's in its place in the only useable position on the starboard side, so as to leave the port side available for their tete a tete: they looked sheepish and tried to laugh it off. As I had been going to move my chair anyway, I did not protest, but the scheme was a failure anyway: Barton, who is a Communist where chairs are concerned, came on deck later on, and seeing the chair invitingly prepared for Mrs. R, flopped into it and promptly went to sleep, with the result that when the old lady came on deck, she minced over to the other side and spoilt the party.

Wednesday 2nd April.

Up about seven o'clock and found that we are back to English summer day latitude, clear and sunny with a chill breeze from the north. I dressed in my ordinary European rig of a blue blazer and flannel trousers, in which I was just pleasantly warm. . . . I spent the time between dinner and four o'clock alternately dozing and reading *Pride and Prejudice:*[45] I don't think anything shows it such a masterpiece as Darcy and Collins: so long as one is actually reading one is hypnotized into thinking them entirely plausible, and it needs several minutes calm thought to convince you that they are preposterous and quite impossible characters. There is tremendous last minute scrubbing and painting going on all over the ship today in anticipation of the grand entry to New York, and certainly we look as spick and span as many yachts. . . . On going to the smoking room for the evening whiskey I found to my disgust that there is another long complicated form to be filled in before we can land in New York: I do not regret this trip—far from it—but I don't know how anyone is persuaded to face the U.S. Government formalities twice in a lifetime.

Friday 4th April.

Dressed in my shore going clothes and as I finished with each thing I packed it. . . . It is difficult to explain what makes a last morning at sea so different from all others, but no one ever seems able to settle down to anything: the others just hung about, but I at least had an hours walk on the after well deck. . . . We sighted the American coast about eleven o.c.—low flat uninteresting country. . . . When we came on deck after dinner we were steaming up the estuary of the Hudson . . . on the right a long steep embankment of yellow sand called "The Pallisades": Mrs. La Hache told me proudly that here more murders are done every year than in the whole of the rest of New York put together—the modus operandi being to take your friend for an evening drive, shoot him, and roll the corpse down the

45. *Pride and Prejudice* (1813), a novel by Jane Austen.

Pallisades. After passing through this neck we hugged the left hand side which was covered with country houses, very much more home-like and permanent looking than those we saw in California—in fact in better taste, judged by our standards: a cluster of them stood round a church which might have been transplanted from an English vil-lage. . . . I was much surprised at my first view of New York proper: I had expected to see a huge mass of skyscrapers, but the skyscraper area is a very small portion of the whole. . . . The central or sky-scraper part of New York, as seen from the river, is remarkably fine: all these huge buildings are built on a very narrow base, and no two are of the same shape or height: as the sun strikes them they gleam in various greys and yellows and look like some fantastic faery city—an illustration of Avalon[46] perhaps, in a modern edition. [When] at last the Immigration people showed up, things went quite rapidly. The Customs too were very friendly and gave no trouble, only getting me to open three boxes. . . . I was very sorry to leave *Tai Yin* which I have come to look on almost as a home: also I shall miss our companions—or some of them at any rate. [At the Cunard pier] we waited for the lorry which was bringing our kit, and found to our disgust that all work ceases on the pier from six to seven p.m. There was nothing to do but while away the time as patiently as might be. Our lorry arrived all right about 6.15, and much of the subsequent wait I spent in talking to the "truckman" (Eng. "lorry driver"). I found that the New Yorker of this stratum really does talk as represented in funny books, i.e. says "de" for "the", and substitutes "i" for "r" in words of one syllable, thus: "woik", "goil", "Yoik" for "work", "girl", "York". . . . We then got another taxi, and keeping out our suitcases only, drove to the Hotel Seville on Fifth Avenue and 29th Street . . . and booked a room apiece with bathrooms, for three dollars each.

Saturday 5th April.

Was called by telephone—a detestable custom—at seven o.c., after a restless night, mainly owing to the heat, which was infernal al-though before going to bed I turned off the heater and opened the windows. I packed before breakfast and found Barton in the lounge when I got downstairs, and we had breakfast together: he too had had a bad night. [Last] night he and Dakin took a stroll down the far famed Broadway to see the electric sky signs in which they were very

46. Avalon was the island to which King Arthur is traditionally said to have been taken after he was mortally wounded.

disappointed—they were not half as good(!) as Piccadilly.[47] . . . Having tipped the chambermaid (a Londoner by the way), paid our bills, and said goodbye to Dakin, we set out with our bags in a taxi. . . . The traffic in the business part of New York is denser than anywhere I have ever seen and rather alarming: also, one sees very little as most of the time one is driving under the lattice work steel arcade on top of which runs the overhead railway. I noticed that there is still a large amount of horse traffic here. . . . Railway Stations are one thing in which New York is definitely ahead of London . . . who could resist the temptation to travel in an "all parlor car" train rejoicing in the ridiculous name of "The Knickerboker Limited"! . . . At one o'clock punctually we pulled out, shaking the dust of New York off our feet very thankfully: in no part of the world have I ever felt before in the same degree, an alien in an alien land.

Sunday 6th April.

Wakened up, by telephone of course, after a very comfortable nights sleep and found it a beautiful sunny morning and dressed and packed with such despatch that I was down to breakfast by eight o'clock. Barton did not show up until quarter to nine: I had a Club Breakfast (Eng. "table d'hote") of grape fruit, ham and eggs, marmalade and coffee for 75 cents, which is extraordinarily cheap judged by the standards of this country. Having had a shoe shine and wasted two ten cent pieces in attempts to get into a more than usually complex pattern of privy, I finally went to my room in despair and used the one up there. Damn this Robot like country which no one except a mechanic can understand! B had by this time finished breakfast, and, after sending a cable to J giving the date of my arrival at Liverpool, and cashing a cheque, he and I set out on foot to see something of the town: apropos of this they have an excellent idea here which I wish home hotels would copy—in each bedroom is a folder with an excellent sketch map of the town, which you are invited to take with you on your wanderings. Boston, superficially at any rate, is simply a very pleasant English city which has had the misfortune to be dumped down on the Eastern American seaboard. I felt as instantly at home in it as I had felt the opposite in New York. Within a few minutes of leaving the hotel we found ourselves crossing an unwalled public garden called Boston Common, and it was not America at all, but the first breath of home—loafers and respectable Sunday idlers sat in the

---

47. Piccadilly Circus, a famous entertainment center in the West End of London, was famed for its brilliant neon and electric advertising signs.

same way as homeside on the same sort of benches—fat pigeons strut-
ted and cooed and squirrels came begging for nuts, the surrounding
streets were quiet and cat frequented, and mellow church bells tolled
lazily from the same dingy city churches as in London. . . . [At] a
Cafeteria, I rounded off my American experiences by having an ice
cream soda—a disgusting mess consisting of a partially submerged
globe of ice cream, floating in an opaque well of some fizzy stuff,
with a muddly bottom of strawberry jam. After this sacrifice to the
instinct of adventure, we got back to the Hotel through the same park
where we had started, and had a lobster mayonnaise for lunch and a
bottle of imitation beer. . . . After this we paid our bills and took a
taxi down to the Cunard pier. . . . [On board the ship] I was both
surprised and disappointed by her appearance: the public rooms and
cabins are clean enough, but the ship in general is disgustingly
dirty. . . . We were late in getting away (5.30 p.m.) owing to loading
the scenery of the Stratford-on-Avon Players[48] who are returning
from a tour, and indeed constitute the bulk of the First Class
passengers. . . . I have made one disastrous discovery namely that the
ship is now calling at Belfast and not at Queenstown: there is irony in
plenty in this happening on the first occasion when there is no
Pudaitaheim.[49] I hope the Queenstown people have the sense to
forward J's letter to the Belfast office. . . . I wrote up the days doings
in my diary in the library. I am very glad that my last recollection of
the United States is Boston, a place I should like to see again.

Monday 7th April.
Speaking generally, there seem to be a rather unpleasant lot of
passengers on board. The actors, actorlike, keep together and talk
loudly, nominally to each other, but actually to the rest of the ship,
about their triumphs in the past, and how they insisted on the manager doing so and so etc. They have three pretty women with them,
who seem to be of a better type than the men: at any rate they are
quieter. The rest of the men seem to be commercial travellers and the
women are unidentifiable. . . . By the afternoon the sea was really awe
inspiring and the ship was rolling heavily, it being described in the
weather report as "moderate gale". During the afternoon two or three
people got upset, chair and all, in the smoking room, and tables,

48. The Shakespearean touring company from Stratford, England.
49. Pudaitaheim was Warren's expression for his father's home (Pudaita is Albert
Lewis, heim is German for home). However, though Warren understandably considered that his father's home no longer existed since the death of Albert Lewis in
1929, the actual house, Little Lea, had not yet been sold.

palms and tea things were crashing all over the place. I was wedged on a heavy sofa which slid backwards and forwards with monotonous regularity, hitting first the piano and then the bulkhead with a thud. This sort of thing becomes exceedingly tedious after a time. . . . After dinner I attempted to walk on the deck on the veranda side, but not with much success, and later in the evening I looked into Francis Thompson,[50] a man of whom I know nothing. I liked his stuff, particularly "Hound of Heaven" and "Ode to the Setting Sun". In places he is extraordinarily seventeenth century.

Tuesday 8th April.

Had a very disturbed night, being rolled and banged about my bunk, and woke up to find it another perfectly beastly day—heavy sea running, with patchy fog, surprisingly and unpleasantly warm, and the syren going at intervals. Racks on the table at breakfast, and with all curtains drawn (presumably for the benefit of the squeamish) the saloon was very foggy. . . . This morning I started Gosse's *Short History of English Literature*,[51] a most readable book, and almost worth buying I think as a work of reference. The only thing worth reading of the earlier works is said to be an anonymous poem called *Sir Gawain and the Green Knight*,[52] which I must look into. It had never occurred to me before looking into this book that English literature for several centuries is English poetry, and poetry alone. Roughly speaking, prose begins with Bacon. Every time I read a book of this sort I am annoyed at my inability to appreciate Shakespeare: if I had no literary taste, it would not matter, but here is [a] man about whom the whole world is agreed, and yet I would part with everything that [Shakespeare] ever wrote sooner than lose, say, *Endymion*[53]—to say nothing of greater things. . . . If opportunity offers when I am at home this time, I will make an effort to hear a play and see what is the result.

Friday 11th April.

Three years ago this morning I left Southampton for China, and, leaving out the ghastly Hong Kong episode,[54] they have been good

---

50. Francis Thompson was a late-nineteenth-century Roman Catholic poet.

51. *A Short History of Modern English Literature* (1897), by Sir Edmund William Gosse.

52. *Sir Gawain and the Green Knight* is an anonymous middle-English poem written around 1400.

53. *Endymion* (1818), a long poem in heroic couplets by John Keats.

54. Warren Lewis's difficult tour of service under the command of Colonel G. E. Badcock. See pp. 14–15.

years. I got up feeling remarkably fit and took a turn on deck before breakfast. . . . All our table musters at 6.40 in the smoking room before going by invitation to the Captain's cabin for a cocktail, Mrs. W and I having one each before we started, in case of mishaps. . . . During the cocktail the inevitable photo of his wife was passed round for scrutiny: I have never yet discovered on these occasions how to produce the correct blend of admiration and intellegent interest: fortunately the women were able to coo about it a bit. We were in the Captain's suite until about 7.30 and then went below to an excellent dinner, after which I strolled about on deck until bed time: it was a glorious night—a calm sea gleaming and sparkling under a full moon and little pools of damp light in the heavy deck dew. Even the Stratford-on-Avon players were affected by its beauty, and, coming unexpectedly round a lifeboat, I found the odd mixture of Hamlet having a hugging match with the Queen of the Fairies.

Saturday 12th April.

For the first time today I had a drink with one of the actors, who proved to be a very pleasant fellow: of their tour, he told me how surprised they all were at the success of their show in the little "wild west" places such as Moose Jaw and Medicine Hat. These fellows certainly have a hard time of it—they get thirty six hours leave on arrival in England (having been playing for six months) and then start in again.

Sunday 13th April.

Went to the cabin after lunch and spent an hour between sleeping and waking, watching the reflection of the sea passing like clouds on the cabin ceiling. . . . We are now due to get to Liverpool Landing Stage about 7 p.m. on Tuesday.

Tuesday 15th April.

A day which has redeemed the dullness of this long crossing, and to me one of the most interesting of the whole trip. I was washed and dressed and on deck by 7.30, to find it a lovely sunny morning with a chill wind and gentle foamy sea. . . . With such a fine morning I had thought that in true Irish fashion it would turn to rain before midday, but the weather held and about 10.30, hugging the Antrim coast, we crept into the Lough[55] and let go our anchor, just past and near to Whitehead, where the tender met us, bringing among others a typical

---

55. Belfast Lough, the bay off of the North Channel that leads to the port of Belfast, Warren's boyhood home.

Belfast newsboy with his papers: it was delightful to hear the old familiar accent again. . . . On the Co. Down side the view stretched from the Coplands to Holywood Point, with every detail clear cut and vividly coloured, though still with that soft grey coating over the colours which I think is the essence of the Ulster scenery. . . . To see the fields and roads of all that familiar country so near and yet so far was a tantalizing experience. . . . We will not disembark until 8 a.m. tomorrow morning [at Liverpool].

Wednesday 16th April.

I stepped ashore punctually at 8 a.m., having been out of England three years and five days, and after a journey of fifty days from Shanghai: just before leaving the ship I got a telegram from J saying he was surprised not to have heard from me, so presumably he did write to Queenstown after all and the fools did not send the letter to Belfast. The customs formalities at Liverpool are easy and expeditious and, having said goodbye to Barton on the dock, I was at Lime Street by twenty to nine: it was good to taste the old friendly smell of an English railway station again. . . . What struck me most on the journey was the intense, almost unnatural green of the fields and the settled look of everything—woods and ploughland and old grey churches standing up out of trim villages and copses and streams: I felt I was no longer looking at scenery merely, but at a system of life totally different to what I have grown accustomed to. I spent the night at the Euston Hotel [London] where the coal fire laid in the bedroom grate and the old fashioned furniture felt most friendly after the slick inhuman efficiency of America. In the evening rang up Minto,[56] who, with J is coming up to town tomorrow. Arranged to meet them at Waterloo [Station] at noon. Posted my arrival report to the War Office.

Thursday 17th April.

In the morning chartered a couple of taxis and transported my baggage to Paddington, and then, it being a bright sunny morning, walked across [Hyde] Park, stopping to look at my old friend the Peter Pan statue [in Kensington Gardens], and so on past the Guner War Memorial to Victoria from where I took tube to Waterloo, and in due course met Minto and J, both looking in good health and spirits. . . . After some discussion it was agreed that J and I should go

---

56. Warren and Jack's nickname for Mrs. Moore was derived from Nuttaoo's Peppermint Candy—Mintos. The exact reason for this association is not clear, though it appears likely that this candy was a favorite of Mrs. Moore's.

to Oxford tonight and join Minto and Maureen at Southbourne tomorrow, after having arranged for any orders which arrived for me to be sent on to my temporary address. When this had been fixed I was carried by taxi to the Ideal Homes Exhibition at Olympia, M and J being very full of the scheme of building their own home near Oxford. . . . During the afternoon I managed to have a good deal of talk with J. On the way back we got ourselves into the wrong tube, and in an effort to make up for lost time took a taxi from Victoria, which turned out to be the worst thing we could have done, as we got into a bad traffic block on Westminster bridge: Minto damned it very heartily but eventually, more by luck than management, we got her into her train and off to Bournemouth.[57] J and I then took a tube to Paddington and caught the dining car train to Oxford, travelling 1st [class] in view of the amount of luggage which I had. Having left my heavy baggage at the station, we went up to Magdalen:[58] it was good to get the damp keen feel of Oxford again and hear the bells and see its mouldering stones: pleasant too to find myself once more in J's rooms with their white panels, inspecting his books and his two new Medici prints. I was billetted for the night below him on the same staircase in a dank closet belonging to one Sideway.

Friday 18th April.

A chill bright morning with sunshine. Breakfasted with J in common room, a dark panelled room decorated with oil portraits and having much more the appearance of a sitting room than a mess room: while we were eating, a man came in to whom J did not speak, and to whom I was not introduced. I heard afterwards that his name is Weldon[59] and that he is the leader of the Magdalen "Junto", which is a rather dirtier and less efficient edition of our "shilling ring".[60] After breakfast we bussed out to Hillsboro. . . . Having dumped some

57. Jack and the Moores were vacationing at Christchurch, a seaside resort near Bournemouth, Hampshire, southwest of London.

58. Magdalen College, Oxford, where Jack was a Fellow in English Language and Literature. He was elected to this Fellowship in May of 1925, while Warren was serving at Colchester, England. Jack Lewis remained at Oxford until December 1954.

59. T. D. ("Harry") Weldon, Philosophy tutor at Magdalen College. A militant atheist, Weldon was a leader of the "progressives," and in frequent opposition to Jack Lewis. According to Humphrey Carpenter in *The Inklings* (Boston: Houghton Mifflin Company, 1979), the character of Lord Feverstone in Lewis's *That Hideous Strength* (1945) and consequently of Dick Devine in *Out of the Silent Planet* (1938), was based on Weldon.

60. A derogatory horse-racing term derived from the enclosure where nonmembers were allowed to observe the races after the payment of a fee; admission to this lower-class area was originally one shilling.

kit there we went back into town and . . . set out on a leisurely and surprisingly enjoyable cross country journey (J read the last volume of my diary) . . . and so on through the gathering dusk to Christchurch, our destination, passing through Southhampton en route, whereby I was able, literally to complete my journey round the world. From Christchurch we finished the journey on foot, J losing his way. . . . However, after walking for some time, J finally hit off the scent. Minto, Maureen, and last but not least, Mr. Papworth,[61] were all waiting to welcome me when we got to "the Rest", and our landlady, Miss Weston, had a supper ready for us. . . . J and I shared a comfortable room.

Sunday 20th April.

A beautiful day, bright and sunny and quite warm, with a pale blue sea—or so at least I called it, but J tells me I have forgotten my homeside colours. To the left as we stood on the beach, the Isle of Wight and the Needles are plainly visible, and to the right the Dorset-shire coast. . . . In the afternoon J and I went for a country walk . . . we had a glorious ramble, talking of many things, but mainly of books. J tells me that the new edition of the *Encyclopedia Britannica* is "popularised", and the standard of its scholarship is indicated by the fact that one of his friends was offered the writing of the article on Dante "provided that he took such and such a view": this led us to agree to keeping the Leeborough edition, which J had previously set aside for disposal. In order to let Miss Weston take in some more people today, J and I have moved into a tiny room, and after supper all merry making up a bed for Minto on the drawing room sofa: it looked to me very uncomfortable, but she was firm in saying it was alright. Our party breaks up tomorrow, Minto and Maureen going to Bristol, and J and I returning to Oxford enroute for Belfast.

Wednesday 23rd April.

Before breakfast I took a turn on deck, enjoying the sights and sounds and smells of the Lagan again, but with an undercurrent of depression and hating the thought of seeing Leeborough again under the altered circumstances. We breakfasted in the ship, and . . . walked in the bright sunshine to the Belfast S.S. offices, where we booked our return berths for tomorrow night, and then on to 83 Royal Ave-

---

61. Mr. Papworth, the family dog, was a black, curly-haired mixed breed (pre-dominately a terrier). In keeping with Jack and Warren's penchant for nicknames, Mr. Papworth was alternately known as "Tykes," "Baron Papworth," and "Pat." Mr. Papworth died in 1937.

nue (which still has the old brass plate on the door) for our talk with Condlin.[62] J's conversation had in some sort prepared me for him, but even so he was more nearly the novelists idea of a lawyer's chief clerk than I had thought existed: I understood very little of what he had to tell us, but came away with the impression that he had been genuinely fond of the Pudaitabird and that we could rely on this protection of our interests. To get him to commit himself to any definite statements proved impossible, and J hazarded the theory afterwards that P's studied vagueness about money matters was as much due to his inability to understand his own affairs in Condlin's hands as to any innate secretiveness. So far as I could make out, the investments of the estate will only yield about £190 a year net, which is a very considerable disappointment: but, on asking Condlin if this were the case, he replied in his soft dreamy way—"Oh it will be more than that for sure". I asked him to let me have, as soon as possible, a simple list of the investments and their approximate annual yield, which he promised to do. We also arranged that C should supervise the packing and despatch of the keeps in the study to Oxford: that the remaining contents of the house should be advertised for sale: and that the house itself should be advertised in the press and by notice boards for sale or to let. As regards the sale of the house Condlin says "It is worth £3,000 to a man that wants it"—a singularly useless bit of information in view of the fact that we can't get an offer. Having arranged this business and got the location of the grave from him, we set out for the cemetery by tram. . . . The cemetery was much less oppressive than I had expected to find it—under bright sunlight it seemed rather an oasis of quiet in the middle of the city, backed by the foothills of Divis: but there was something unpleasantly intimate about seeing familiar names wherever one wandered. Our own family graves (of which I had not the faintest recollection, though J had) are on a circular plot of grass at the meeting of two paths: there are all of us who have died in Belfast, both Lewises and Hamiltons. . . . The sight of P's grave with its fresh turned earth, and a handful of withered daffodils at its head, alongside Mammy's, was perfectly beastly, and I was very glad to get away after deciding with J to duplicate Mammy's inscription on his side and reserving the question of a suitable text for further discussion. [From the cemetery, we took a taxi through] a much altered Strandtown to Little Lea. There was a chill about the rank untended garden, but inside, at first, the house seemed much less strange than I had expected it to be, in spite

---

62. J. W. A. Condlin, Albert Lewis's managing clerk since 1917.

of J's labours—superficially it was as if a spring cleaning was in progress: but its utter lifelessness: silent it has of course been for many years during most of the day, but this was something new and horrible. It brought home to me as nothing else could have done, the tremendous personality of the Pudaitabird—the whole place is as blank as a frame from which a picture has been stripped. It was both pleasant and painful to renew something of the old life in chatting with Mary[63] who was I think really glad to see us again. But had J not been with me, and without plenty of work to do, I would have had one of my worst fits of depression. As soon as we had had a light lunch we got to work, beginning with taking up and stowing in the study the drawing room and hall carpets—a pretty heavy job—after which we revised the list of books which we were going to keep, including the Encyclopedia, and after some hesitation keeping the Dumas[64] as well. . . . Next we took turn about in digging a hole in the vegetable garden in which to put our toys—also a heavy job—and then carried the old attic trunk down and buried them: what struck us most was the scantiness of the material out of which that remarkable imaginary world was constructed: by tacit mutual consent the boxes of characters were buried unopened.[65] . . . After dinner we started to make some pretence of going through the playbox, but it soon degenerated into a random reading of our old treasures and J wrote some twenty or thirty new couplets to his parody of Pope. We had a fire in our room tonight, which is the only unchanged part of the house, and it was very pleasant to shut out the still gloom of the rest.

Thursday 24th April.

Again a fine day, and after breakfast we once more got to our work, packing the contents of the playbox and as much of the family documents from the chest which formerly stood in the attic as would fit into my tin box. . . . We also sorted a large collection of photos of ourselves and various members of the family, keeping the best to be sent across with the study stuff. We gave Mary her choice of the photos of the Pudaitabird, she having asked for one. [Later] we walked down to Uncle Gussie's[66] by the High Holywood Road: this is

---

63. Mary Cullen was the cook-housekeeper at Little Lea from 1917 until 1930; the Lewis brothers nicknamed her the Witch of Endor.

64. Alexandre Dumas, nineteenth-century French novelist and dramatist, author of one of Warren Lewis's favorite works—*The Three Musketeers* (1844).

65. These stuffed animals and china figures were the characters who peopled the Lewis brothers' imaginary world of Boxen.

66. Augustus ("Gussie") Warren Hamilton (1866-1945) was the brother of Flora

little changed and very pleasant, though tinged with sadness, it was to do this old familiar walk through the bright green foliage of a spring evening. . . . Aunt Annie was not well and looks much older than she did when I saw her last. In manner and appearance Uncle Gussie was what he has always been, and as youthful as ever. Ruth and John have changed little. . . . Uncle Gussie produced whiskey for dinner—the first time I can remember anyone ever being offered a drink in his house. Later he drove us back to Leeborough in his car and on arrival I made him a present of the contents of the cellar: nothing brought home to me the finality of the old life as did the carrying out of those bottles and the putting them in his car—to see the mysteries of that jealously guarded secret room emerge as plain matter of fact bottles, and the cellar stand revealed as an ordinary empty cupboard was an unpleasant feeling—and again, to be sitting with them in the dining room chatting, without the thudding impact of "Well Gussie, how are things at the yard?", brought the position home with a stab. We left for Donegall Quay a few minutes after them in Gillespie's taxi, leaving the same untidy dining room table and saying goodbye in the kitchen as I have been doing for the last twenty five years. I was glad to be away from it as it is now. We sailed by daylight, a thing I don't remember ever to have done before.

Saturday 26th April.

An awful shock while I was at breakfast this morning: J rang up to say that there was a letter from the W.O. which he had opened to say that I was granted leave until the 15th of next month and was posted to Aldershot. . . . Though I had been expecting Aldershot, the confirmation of my fears was none the less unpleasant, and I walked into Oxford in a very gloomy state of mind, via Cuckoo Lane and Mesopotamia. . . . When I got to Magdalen and read the fatal letter, I was much relieved to find that J had misread it: there is unfortunately no mistake about the extremely stingy period of leave which I have been granted, but the posting is merely an attachment to "Y" Depot Company for the period of my leave: so the horror is at any rate postponed. . . . I put in an hours delightful pottering at Blackwells,

Hamilton Lewis. He married Anne Sargent Harley (1866-1930) in 1897, and had four children: Mary Warren ("Molly," 1898-1904), Ruth (1900-   ), Harley (dates unknown; born after Ruth), and John Borlase (1905-?). Aunt Annie, in particular, had a special place in the affections of Warren and Jack; her closeness to their mother—both in friendship and in temperament—helped to assuage ever so slightly some of their emptiness at Flora's death. Warren continued to correspond with his cousin Ruth (Mrs. Desmond Parker) until his death.

whose premises have greatly extended since I was there last: there is now an extra room upstairs at the front of the shop, and a big new basement opening off the second hand room: here I had a find—a two volume edition of *Guy Joli*.[67] . . . I also bought an "Everyman" edition of Wordsworth's longer poems. After lunch J and I walked up Shotover with Mr. Papworth, it being a most glorious spring afternoon, quite hot: I never saw so many rabbits in a warren before—sunning themselves, scampering in and out of their burrows, and fighting: somehow one never visualizes the rabbit as a fighter: Mr. Papworth watched them quite unmoved. We came back through a bottom on the Cowley side of the hill which was delightful—fresh green trees and grass, and the music of the birds clear and echoing round the confined space, and so past a grey stone house with purple flowers and home across the common. . . . J went into College after supper and slept there as I gather he does every night in term time. During the evening I started re-reading *The Prelude*[68]—grand stuff.

Tuesday 29th April.

At breakfast it was arranged that M, Maureen, and I, and J, if he could get away, should go to Vaughan Williams' *Sir John in Love*[69] on Saturday night, I to ask J his plans when I got into College. . . . J had pupils continuously all morning, which was rather a bad snag from my point of view as I was consequently unable to get any more boxes upstairs: so I sorted out such of my records as I have unpacked and was glad to find that so far there are very few breakages. After doing this I was brought to a full stop and spent the rest of the morning pottering among his books until twelve o.c. He has a beautiful little library, both qua books, (contents) and also pleasing to the eye and touch and smell: it is especially rich in leather bindings: in addition to his folios I noticed particularly a fine Johnson and a Pope. J's twelve o.c. pupil failed him so I impressed him for the horrid job of helping to manoeuvre my remaining three boxes upstairs. . . . while we were doing it, Maureen came in to confirm the arrangements for Saturday night: J is able to go and will spend the night with us at Hillsboro.

Wednesday 30th April.

Much talk at tea about the proposed new house, and I told J that so far as I was concerned there was no objection to his drawing on the

67. *Mémoires de Guy Joli,* 2 vols., Paris, 1677.

68. *The Prelude* (written 1798-1805), an autobiographical poem by William Wordsworth.

69. British composer Ralph Vaughan Williams's third opera, *Sir John in Love* (1929), dealt with the character of Falstaff.

estate for £500 if that sum was needed. After supper I bussed into
College taking a large suitcase with me so as to bring out some more
tropical stuff tomorrow. J was not in when I arrived, and I sat for about
an hour in his front sitting room reading Gray's letters[70]—a very entertaining book. After he came across we had some talk about the fitting
up of his front room with Leeborough stuff, he having very decently
conferred upon it the title of "our" room. When my books are set up
and the curtains and pictures hung, it ought to be a very comfortable
library. After a drink, and having made a thermos of tea against the
morning, I went off to the guest room.

Thursday 1st May.

Woke before the scout came to call me at 5 a.m., as I find I generally do if I set my mind to it, and began the summer well by hearing
the birds very loud and clear and beautiful. J was up earlier and came
in while I was dressing. It was pale daylight with a clear windless sky
when we got out into the quad. After a cup of tea, we set out for the
Tower, J in hood and surplice, the cloisters looking dim and still in
the early light.[71] Many people were arriving, and the journey up the
circular stone stair to the tower roof was a tiresome one, ending in a
short ladder, and emerging on to the ridged and duckboarded roof
through a low narrow door. The sun had not yet risen when we got
out, and the wide pale view was beautiful—all still and clean, with a
powdering of heavy dew on the eastern hills, and across the unruffled
Cherwell a splendid Cotswold stone house standing in motionless
poplars. As the sun rose the whole picture lit up and the hedges and
trees started to throw their morning shadows, while from all the
chimneys below us, smoke started to float up almost simultaneously:
I wonder was it on a tower that Milton thought of "the smoke and
stir of this dim spot which men call earth"? By this time the top of the
tower was closely packed, but I managed to get a good place near the
rope cutting off the College noblesse from the town bourgoisie, and
heard the choir sing a Latin hymn which was very effective and a

---

70. Thomas Gray, an eighteenth-century poet, was known as one of the greatest
of English letter-writers. Jack Lewis owned three volumes of his letters (published
1912). These books are now part of the C. S. Lewis Library at Wroxton College,
Wroxton, Oxfordshire, England.

71. On May Day morning at 6 A.M., the choir of Magdalen College gather at the
top of Magdalen College tower and sing a Latin carol, "Te Deum Patrem Colinus."
Then the Chapel bells are rung, and the Morris men dance in the streets of Oxford
amongst great frivolity. This May Day celebration has been a tradition in Oxford
since Elizabethan times.

beautiful tune: why on earth don't they sing these hymns in church? After the hymn the chimes were played at intervals, and every time this was done the tower swayed and shook quite perceptibly: by looking over the edge and taking a point on the ground, one could *see* it shaking. Just about then we saw a crowd of ridiculous little figures running over Magdalen Bridge, being hustled on by a fool with his bladder, and in their wake the rest of the Morris Dancers dressed in white. It was some time before we were able to get down off the tower, as everyone was apparently struck with the idea of "waiting for the crowd to thin", but it was not time wasted: I have never seen Oxford look better than it did with its cluster of stone buildings gleaming in the morning sunlight. Finally we got down, passing the deafening peal of bells and the solemn looking ringers on the floor below, and made our way up the High and into the Broad, following the crowd to outside Balliol where we found the Morris dancers: en route a hag screeched to a friend "*They* 'aven't got any work ter do—*they* don't 'ave ter get up early every morning like you and I". I liked the Morris dancers, there being something very fresh and simple about their dances which really expressed some joy at the summer's coming. The troupe consisted of seven dressed in white shirts and trousers with green cross belts and rosettes, and bells at their knees, one oldish man also in white, but with red cross belts, who did a solo, and a couple of Fools: one of the men played a concertina: the dancers had a white handkerchief in each hand, I thought the effect would have been much better if they had worn boots or hard soled shoes instead of gym shoes. . . . When they had finished J and I went for a walk round Christchurch meadows where we saw an extraordinary tree, formed apparently of three trees planted too close together: and so to the Eastgate Hotel about ten to eight, very sharp set, where I had force, haddock, sausage and bacon, toast and marmalade and talked about India and Governments in general. . . . When I got back to Magdalen I found that Minto had rung up with the inevitable commission, so set out again for Grimbly Hughes where I bought a pie, and then after the devil of a search found a shop called Taphouses where I had to collect some music for Maureen.

Friday 2nd May.

While lunch was getting ready I read a little in Minto's copy of *Aurora Leigh*[72] and found it such good stuff that I shall get a copy of it

---

72. *Aurora Leigh* (1856), a romance in blank verse of the life of nineteenth-century poet Elizabeth Barrett Browning.

tomorrow: I read a few lines to J whom I was surprised to find did not know it either. . . . Had a long evening with Wordsworth . . . and read in a diary of J's[73] for half an hour. Was stupefied to find him noting after my departure at the end of the Clevedon holiday that he was restless, it being bad for him to associate with "people with money and leisure", i.e. *me!*

Saturday 3rd May.

Barfield,[74] a friend of J's, was expected for lunch but did not turn up. . . . Supper tonight was not [a] very pleasant meal, there being a tension of some sort between Minto and J—I suppose about this house problem. After supper J and I argued about some passages in *The Prelude* before settling down to our books, and later in the evening were in labour for a new opening line for a poem written by his friend Barfield—rather a good one too. Finished *The Prelude* this evening, being particularly struck with the passage in which he describes his feelings as a child when he looked at the road passing over the crest of the hill out of his known world—our "green hills"[75] in fact, perfectly expressed. J went into College about 10 p.m.

Wednesday 7th May.

Woke some time before I was called and read a little in Tilley[76] before getting up. It was a dull chill morning and after breakfast I felt none too warm walking into Oxford with a coat on. I took Tykes with me, who behaved very well, though terrified at meeting an enormous Irish wolfhound in Cuckoo Lane. . . . Went first to College

---

73. It was common practice for Jack and Warren to exchange and read each other's diary; note for example, Warren's entry of April 18, 1930.

74. Arthur Owen Barfield (1898-) met Jack Lewis when he was reading English at Wadham College, Oxford, where he took a First Class. In 1931, after seven years as a freelance writer, Barfield was forced to enter his father's legal firm in order to support his wife and children. This alteration in career direction largely prevented Barfield from pursuing his literary ambitions, but a partial retirement beginning in the 1950s did allow him to publish several significant works; among them are *Saving the Appearances* (1957), *Worlds Apart* (1963), and *Speaker's Meaning* (1967). An earlier volume, *Poetic Diction,* was published in 1928. Jack Lewis and Owen Barfield were to continue as firm and lifelong friends. For a more personal view of this relationship, see C. S. Lewis, *Surprised by Joy: The Shape of My Early Life,* (New York: Harcourt, Brace & World, Inc. 1955), pp. 199-200.

75. The "green hills" of Warren and Jack's childhood were the distant Castlereagh Hills seen from the nursery windows of Little Lea. The brothers shared a common feeling that these soft, green hills were both unreachable and desirable—objects of longing. See also, C. S. Lewis, *Surprised by Joy,* p. 7.

76. A. Tilley, *Decline of the Age of Louis XIV* (Cambridge: Cambridge University Press, 1929).

where Tykes was all in favour of joining J's tutorial, but I manoeuvred him into the bed room where he blew disconsolately under the door while I wrapped the photo of *Tai-Yin* and two little pictures with broken glass, which I took to a shop opposite Christchurch to be framed. A dog on a lead in town is a nuisance: his idea of points of interest and likely turnings never agrees with that of his leader. . . . I also bought a box of sticky labels and when I got in pasted one on the cover of each volume of my diary and worked out the dates and venue to be written on each. . . . Minto and Maureen arrived at 1.15 for lunch by appointment as a preliminary to witnessing the deeds. J gave us an excellent feed—a sole, chicken, new potatoes and beans, a currant tart, and a bottle of Graves: the latter nearly led to disaster, poor M complaining after two glasses that she felt quite overcome and would not be able to complete the business of the afternoon! However, she came to after her coffee. . . . The Mr. Langley to whom we had been directed was out, and we had some difficulty in finding a solicitor. On the way I knocked over a girl's bicycle propped against the kerb in the High Street and wasn't able to set it up again, to the vast amusement of the other who heartlessly walked on and laughed at me from a safe distance. When we did find a solicitor, the actual witnessing of the deeds was a matter of a few minutes (fee 5/-), and we then split up, Minto and Maureen going to pay calls whilst J and I took a protesting Mr. Papworth home via Mesopotamia. We talked of editing the family papers and think of having them typed by sections so as to spread the expenses over a long period.

Thursday 8th May.

After book hunting I looked into the National Gallery [London]: it was a bad day to go, as there were numbers of students copying and one cannot help looking from the original to the copy instead of con-centrating on the original. However, I renewed my acquaintance with a lot of old favourites—*The Avenue, Middelharnuis, Lady at the Virgin-als, The Little Street in Delft,* and the Claudes and Poussins: I also wandered rather vaguely through some of the other rooms, enjoying particularly a Judgement of Paris which I don't remember to have seen before: I also had a look at *Vigee le Brun,* the uncanny freshness of which always fascinates me.

Saturday 10th May.

On getting back to Magdalen [from my morning's errands] I spent the rest of the morning in drawing up a scheme for the editing and arrangement of our family papers: this I discussed with J at lunch time and he approves of it: there will be a lot of work in it, and I expect it will occupy the first year of my leisure, if and when it comes.[77] ... Supper was at half past six this evening against our going to the opera—Vaughan Williams's *Sir John in Love*. Getting the party under weigh was something of a business, and we just missed our bus by the fraction of a minute, but had not long to wait for another, and all very merry on the way in: M left her umbrella in the bus and J got overcarried a stage in retrieving it.... Vaughan Williams was present—a large, rather pleasant looking, sleepy grey haired man. *Sir John in Love* is more or less founded on *The Merry Wives of Windsor* tho' J tells me it bears little resemblance to it. The fun was good and the music delicious and very English, including a lot of traditional stuff—"Greensleeves", and the music of the May morning Morris dancers among other things. All of it was most infectious and tingling.

Tuesday 13th May.

[I] went straight to College where I found my posting orders awaiting me. I took them into the front room and stood for a moment like a bather contemplating a particularly uninviting sea—then broke the seal and saw the word "Bulford":[78] so whatever happens I have avoided the most evil fate which can befall a man. I shall like the surrounding country, and it is a station of which all my friends speak well: I do not know who is serving there however, and on that of course depends the comfort or otherwise of a station in a far greater degree than on its physical attributes. Still, I went to my packing with a much lighter heart than might have been the case. ... I broke the good news to J at the Eastgate, and on the way out we discussed the

---

77. In December of 1930, Warren began to arrange the Lewis family papers while home at The Kilns on leave. These papers consisted of numerous diaries, letters, photographs, and miscellaneous documents that had been brought back from Little Lea by the brothers after their father's death. After his retirement in January 1933, Warren returned to this task, arranging, excerpting, and typing the materials he chose to illustrate the recent history of his family. Once the papers had been entered into the typed volumes, Warren disposed (with his brother's permission) of all the original materials—with the exception of his own diaries. On June 1, 1933, the first volume of these papers was returned from the binders, now with the official title, *Memoirs of the Lewis Family: 1850-1930, Volume I: From October 17th., 1850 to September 23rd., 1881.* The final and eleventh volume was completed in 1935. The originals of the Lewis family papers were willed to the Marion E. Wade Collection by Warren Lewis.

78. Bulford, Wiltshire is located on the Salisbury Plain, forty-eight miles from Oxford. While stationed at Bulford, Warren was able to arrange frequent weekend leaves to visit Jack and the Moores in Oxford.

feasibility of a walk from Bulford to Southbourne at Christmas, which is an attractive proposition.

Wednesday 14th May.

[After lunch, J and I] walked through the fields on the far side of the road, including the dandelion field which was ablaze, with a grand view of the valley to the left, and so on until we came to a fallen tree in the shade where we sat down and ate apples and discussed public schools in general and of course the Coll. in particular. Arising out of this, J told me on the way back that mathematicians are nearly always educated men, and chemists etc., hardly ever. . . . J came out late for supper and we took Tykes for a stroll afterwards. I love the time about nine o.c. in summer when the sky begins to pale and the trees turn dark and the swallows very black and clear cut, especially if it is still. I find that familiarity has not spoilt Headington for me—a delightful village with its stone walled lanes and irregular houses of all sorts: the church too is good, especially in twilight. As I was going to bed tonight M said she thought I was proving myself well suited to domesticity, which encourages me: apropos of domesticity, forgot to say in its proper place that I got J to agree after some difficulty to accepting my £200 towards the new house. Upstairs at 11 o.c. to my diary. So ends a very pleasant holiday.

Thursday 15th May.

Woke up with that end of leave feeling which, though but a pale ghost of the Wynyard feeling, is not pleasant. . . . At 2.15 J, Tykes, and I set out for College in King's taxi and separated there, Tykes as usual being very reluctant to break up the party (which reminds me that this is the third anniversary of my landing in Hong Kong). I left by the 3.2 in misty rain. . . . [There] are many worse amusements than having a First Class compartment to oneself in a slow train on a summers afternoon and I enjoyed the run greatly. It was delightful country—a long spacious vista of rolling plough and grass lands broken with bright green woods carpeted with blue bells, and ribboned with very white roads: once we rang along a very old wall with wallflowers growing out of its sides, and just after leaving Basingstoke we passed a ruined church of which all that remained was a curious octagonal tower and some arches. It was also a country of streams and lush water meadows. I arrived at Salisbury a few minutes before six and having an hour and twenty minutes to wait, set out to walk in the Close. . . . I ate some sandwiches and then caught a train at 7.30 for Bulford. . . . As we trundled out on to the open plain with its vast expanse of sky, the insignificance and incongruousness of this little train became more and more pronounced. The Plain is even better than I remember it and looked very solemn and beautiful in the evening sun. Whenever we stopped at wayside stations the voices of people in the next compartment sounded startlingly loud in the evening hush, which was only broken by the larks and the "baa" of folded sheep. I don't think even an unpleasant station could poison this country for me. When we got to Bulford I was met by an M.T. [mechanical transport] driver with a curious 6 wheeled car, and a very courteous note from the acting P.M.C. apologizing for not meeting me, as it was guest night, and saying that dinner was waiting for me in the mess office, which was a pleasant surprise. What little I saw of the place during the evening I liked: I have quite a good room looking across a lawn to the mess, and so far as I can judge, a five minutes walk takes one on to the solitude of the Plain.

Friday 16th May.

When I got across to the mess I was pleased to find that this is a "silent breakfast" mess, and I read my paper in comfort. . . . At ten o'clock I was taken in and introduced to Inflefield, the C.O. . . . [He told me] that I was to be assistant to Major Lowdell, the O i/c [Officer in Charge of] Supplies and Transport. [After] a very dull morning, spent mainly in smoking cigarettes, I got back to the mess at one o'clock and was regaled with a tough bit of stewed steak—I find Minto's cookery has unfitted me for the "luxuries" of mess life. Lowdell went on week end leave after lunch, leaving me in charge. Having changed and unpacked my books, I went down to the office and was assured that there was nothing to do, so struck out past the camp railway station and on to the plain, across a ford in a pool of very clear water, full of minnows, which formed part of a bubbling stream overgrown with weeds. The plain is wonderful—an apparently endless expanse of rolling grassland sprinkled with dandelions and daisies, with thick villages of trees at intervals, the dark green of the firs setting off the light green of the newly foliaged trees, and overhead the huge sweep of blue sky with slow white clouds: larks were everywhere, and the occasional rattle of a farm cart was a pleasing noise. I walked to the top of the nearest ridge, which was crowned by a big clump of fir, and when I got to it found that the curious white discs which I had seen from a distance were solid masses of white chalk on the roots of uprooted trees. Here I sat for some time, and for the first time for years really saw a daisy: they are exquisite, with a beauty one associates with enamel or cloisonne flower work: presumably the inventor of "enammeled fields" was thinking of this.

Thursday 22nd May.

I am just recovering from having my whole routine thrown out of gear by a most exasperating accident: on Tuesday afternoon I was coming back in a W.D. Austin 7 from the hamlet of Tilshead about ten miles away, where I had been inspecting the camp supply arrangements of an artillery practice camp. The driver struck me as being a most reckless youth, but it is so long since I have been in a Govt. car that I thought perhaps it was my imagination and said nothing to him, but sat on tenterhooks all the way: as we were taking the last crossroads (a blind one) at a brisk 30 m.p.h., I caught sight of the head of a cyclist coming at right angles to us, and next minute— CRASH!—and we bumped to a standstill in an ominous silence. I got out feeling like someone in a dream (or else very drunk) and saw the cyclist lying in the road behind the wreck of a bike. We got him to the side of the road, badly injured, poor fellow, and then, to my horror, big blotches and smears came over the landscape: I sat down and had a vague idea of a crowd chattering, and—most insolent of all—people talking about me as if I wasn't there—"This fellow's got concussion— look at his eyes". Myself (indignantly) "Not at all! Not at all! Perfectly all right". A Doctor (taking my arm and still ignoring my entity) "Help me to get him into the car please". (Is helped) Self. (peevishly) "I assure you this is quite unnecessary". "Mind his head against the hood" (this from the Doctor). This beastly feeling of seeing people and the landscape only in bits wore off on the way back to the hospital, and by the time I got there I was more or less normal, and tried to persuade the M.O. to let me go back to the mess, but he would have none of it. . . . Having had my head dressed (it was now aching severely) I was popped into an ambulance and taken off to the officer's hospital at Tidworth and made to go to bed at once and of course stuffed with calomel, given a "bottle" and endured all the other beastlinesses and indignities of a Hospital. I however avoided a bed pan by dint of waiting until the lights had gone out for the night and then finding the privy. On this expedition I found, to my great relief, that except for the headache, I was feeling normal (i.e. not windy or restless), but on the physical side I had a sore jaw and two front teeth chipped, damn it. I had a very good nights sleep. I spent all Wednesday in hospital and it was one of the longest days I can remember. It began with my being wakened up at 6.30 and told to wash in a basin, as I was too ill to get up and wash—two hrs. later the M.O. told me I could get up and dress as soon as I liked! . . . [Though] on "full diet" I was nearly starved: (I wonder what on earth "light diet" would have been like?). If I had been there another day I would have written to the mess to try and smuggle in some food. However luckily I had my bottle of aspirin with me and with that improved my head to such a point that I was spritely enough at evening rounds to convince the M.O. that I was well enough to come out today, and made my escape in an ambulance at 12 o.c. (a very cold morning) and got back to the mess in time to eat an enormous lunch. Whilst I was in the place I read three books by Edgar Wallace: they are just better than merely doing nothing, but how any free man could read such stuff, and what's more, pay for it, is to me an insoluble mystery. . . . When I got back to the mess today I heard that the civilian with whom we collided, though in a nasty mess, is not in any danger. I also find that my driver, with admirable presence of mind, when the collision became inevitable, decided to use me as a buffer to take the shock and put his helm down: the result being that he escaped with a slight cut on one of his hands. All afternoon I was busy in my own room unpacking my heavy boxes, arranging things, and hanging pictures, and at last have the satisfaction of being completely dug in. It is very pleasant to have my Buddha installed again. . . . This evening I tried my gramophone and found it again broken down: I was so furious that I considered—seriously—beating the damned thing to pieces with a poker, and was only stopped by the thought that this would be altogether too Lewisian a thing to do: but then it is a Lewisian grievance: these days, I don't suppose there is one machine in 10,000 is a dud, and I must needs go and buy that one. I don't know what on earth to do with the thing, for it is apparent that I shall have to get a new one. To bed at midnight.

Friday 23rd May.

[Tonight] while I was changing for dinner I heard the strains of Beethoven's Fifth Symphony coming from Newmarch's[79] room, so later in the evening I challenged him on the subject and find [that] he is an enthusiast on Beethoven and Bach. After dinner I lent him my Ninth Symphony and Bach's Fugues. He has come here straight from Aldershot and his surprise at being treated as homo sapiens by a captain is an illuminating commentary on that station.

---

79. Second Lieutenant Newmarch was a fellow officer in Warren's mess.

Saturday 24th May.

A most annoying letter from J by the first post to say that the first vanload of keeps has arrived from Leeborough and that it is all wrong —things done which should have been left undone and vice versa— and asking me to stand by to go over to Belfast and clear up the mess: so on my way down to the office I dropped in on Seymour and found out from him that there would be no difficulty in getting three or four days C.O.'s leave at short notice: later in the morning I wrote to J telling him that I proposed to run over after the arrival of the last vanload to make sure that everything was clear. . . . I caught a bus to Salisbury about half past two and on arrival set out to reconnoitre the town from a book point of view: I found two good bookshops and overhauled them pretty thoroughly, spending an interesting after- noon, though I drew a blank. . . . I find one has to be very much on one's guard against the tendency to buy a book through sheer reluc- tance to come home empty handed. After this I walked for a long time in the Close which was gloriously still and restful, and a wonder- ful blend of colour—the old grey houses, the green of the trees, a lot of lilac, and splendid flaming beds of tulips in many of the gardens: at the bottom of the Close were some magnificent horse chestnuts in bloom. The Cathedral was all I remembered it and more: it is won- derful the way its perfect symmetry leads the eye upwards by front and roof and flying buttress to that soaring spire.

Sunday 25th May.

Our little garden [at Bulford] is a delight these days—a rectangle of turf, walled with pink white apple blossom and in its centre a grey sundial surrounded by tulips. . . . While I was out I considered very seriously the pros and cons of Hillsboro life as a permanency, in the light of (a) My recent very pleasant leave, and (b) my life in what is apparently one of the pleasantest home stations. I finally envisaged the case for and against the Hillsboro scheme something as follows: against it in general there is a loss of liberty which in the particular manifests itself in the impossibility or at any rate extreme difficulty of doing any reading: but this could I think be adequately met, given full membership of the household, by doing the bulk of my reading in College and for the rest, turning my bedroom into a bed sitting room, and reading at night: and in any case in mess life, one's reading, even in one's room, may be considerably interfered with by the mess bore. Secondly there is the substitution of a scheme of life under which ones day is woven into the general stuff of a communal day in contradiction to the army scheme of a day which consists of periods of rigidly defined duty alternating with periods of absolute liberty: e.g. situated as I am at present, if I am at a certain place at a certain hour, my outgoings and incomings before and after that hour are nobody's business but my own: for instance this evening I am going into Salisbury for supper, and providing I am at the office by nine o.c. tomorrow, no one has the least interest in the fact: at Hillsboro I should have to explain when I was going and when I was coming back, and if I did not come back by the bus I had named there would be uneasiness: further, I should almost certainly be given a shopping commission to do, or asked to change busses at Amesbury to leave a note for Mrs. Pumpernickel. To this point which raises issue in its clearest cut form, the answer seems to be that just as the discomforts of my "lone wolf" existence are inseparable from its luxuries, so one cannot expect to have the good of domesticity without the bad. Finally there is the consideration of the assets of Hillsboro life to which the army can show not only no corresponding assets but actual debits—a closer intimacy with J and a correspondingly fuller intellectual life: a healthier life too, by the cutting out of those hours spent in social and ceremonial drinking, and if a poorer life financially (which is by no means certain) at any rate one which such income as I have will be spent to much better advantage. I came home more than ever convinced that I have made a wise decision and should throw in my fortunes with Hillsboro as soon as it becomes economically possible. . . . After supper I strolled in the mess garden for a long time and watched the daylight fade over the Plain: "It was a beauteous evening, calm and free" and I felt a great peace and content come on me, as it sometimes does for no very obvious reason.

Monday 26th May.

I had intended to inspect Tilshead as being the least Mondayish job available, but Lowdell forestalled me by deciding to go there himself. . . . After lunch Booth and Newmarch constituted themselves a board on my gramophone and put it right for me within ten minutes. I wish I had been taught to use my hands like that. . . . This evening I played Schubert in C Major with a great deal of enjoyment, and afterwards went across to the billiard room for a night cap, and asked Newmarch about Beethoven 1 and 2. . . . A very autumnal night with heavy dews and a white ground mist.

Tuesday 27th May.

Before dinner I read most of the third book of *The Excursion*[80] with considerable enjoyment: it is the best book so far. I learnt from this that I can no longer be reproached with having no philosophy ergo a bad philosophy—I am an Epicurean: that is if Wordsworth's definition of an epicurean philosophy is correct: I am certainly in sympathy with those who,

> yield up their souls
> To a voluptuous unconcern, preferring
> Tranquility to all things.

and a little later on he describes them as,

> those who did, by system, rank
> As the prime object of a wise man's aim
> Security from shock of accident,
> Release from fear; and cherished peaceful days
> For their own sakes, as mortal life's chief good.

After dinner I played Brahms' piano quintet in a very receptive mood.

Wednesday 28th May.

After dinner I played my two new symphonies [Beethoven's First and Second Symphonies], and liked them very much. Both were fresh and delicate without being weak. Wonder what a musician would say to such a remark?

Thursday 29th May.

Daubeny as usual was full of grievances about how overworked he is: actually he potters round barracks between drinks, holding confused conversations with such officers and N.C.O's as come his way. . . . All very amusing. In fact it is amazing how little real work anyone does in this station. Lowdell too manages to give an atmosphere of work while doing, so far as I can see, practically nothing.

As arranged with Jack on May 24, Warren travelled home to Little Lea in order to ensure that the brothers' instructions (on which items they wished to keep) were properly executed.

Saturday 31st May.

I like travelling to and from Bulford by rail: the fact that so few people use this line, and the miniature scale of everything, gives me the feeling that it is "my" railway, and I already rather resent other

---

80. *The Excursion* (1814), a poem by William Wordsworth.

passengers travelling on it at all. . . . [The] earlier part of the run was delightful, through Farnsborough and seeing Aldershot spread out like a caged reptile, at a safe distance. . . . For reading on the journey I had Rose Macaulay's *Casual Commentary*[81] which gives me great amusement: it is worthy of better treatment than Railway literature, and shall have a place among my bedside books. . . . We did not sail until after midnight.

Sunday 1st June.

Even in the short time I have been away, the place has changed enormously, everything having sprouted to Gargantuan heights. . . . The sale notices and the board in the garden gave me a twinge, though I was expecting them: the only other bad moment I have had was when I heard St. Mark's bell tolling morning service—odd that one can get a pang from the unpleasantest of associations at times like this! Otherwise I am finding much less depression than I expected, perhaps because it has been a beautiful day. Having greeted Mary (who is doing me like the trump she is) I went upstairs, unpacked, made up my bed, changed into knockabouts, and got to work with such good will that though I had to unstack most of the books, I was finished by lunch time: I have set myself a very stern standard over the additional books, setting aside only 14 "yellowback" Trollopes, Motley's *Dutch Republic,* Johnson's *Lives, Cyrano de Bergerac, Pilgrim's Progress,* and *Great Short Novels of the World.* I am also keeping my hymn and prayer books in leather case, given me by Grandfather Hamilton at Xmas 1899: the existence of such a gift to a child of four is the measure of the nuisance he would have become if he had lived. . . . Whilst I was at work comes Mary with a breathless "Misther Arthur Greeves[82] wants ye on the telephone". Is there then *no* peace on this side of the grave or the lunatic asylum? I asked him how on earth he knew I was at home, but he would not tell me: I must say he was very reasonable, and said he did not want me to feel that I had *got* to come over and see him: but this of course is just what I do feel as a result of these unseasonable civilities. . . . After supper I wrote up

81. *A Casual Commentary* (1925), a book of essays by novelist, poet, and essayist Dame Rose Macaulay.

82. Joseph Arthur Greeves (1895-1966) was a Belfast neighbor and boyhood friend of Jack Lewis. Greeves was initially a minor source of annoyance for both Lewis brothers, and Jack never really made his acquaintance until early 1914. Immediate and intense friendship was the result. See also, C. S. Lewis, *Surprised by Joy,* pp. 46, 130-131; and Walter Hooper, ed. *They Stand Together: The Letters of C. S. Lewis to Arthur Greeves (1914-1963)* (New York: Macmillan, 1979).

my diary to this point, the birds singing very sweetly outside. From eight till twenty past nine, when the sun went down behind the Cave Hill, I walked in the garden: a fine sunset with almost a magenta tint in the afterglow. A garden in decay has a melancholy beauty of its own, and it raised many memories as I paced up and down the long grass of the lawn—but not sad ones, or rather the mild sadness one feels at inevitable change: at this distance only the happy times associated with the place stand out. After I came in I [read] in the little end room, where by the way is the only light in the house by which one can read with any comfort. Before going to bed I went down to the dining room and had my little drop of whiskey by the dim light of one gas jet—how it brought the whole thing back to me!

Monday 2nd June.

Woke up late after a good nights sleep to find the sunlight was streaming into the room and Mary just coming in with tea (and bread and butter) and a bundle of letters. One incoherent and almost entirely illegible from Minto from which I gather that I am to take Condlin's advice about the eligibility of some building society at Rickmansworth. Apparently she is still determined not to pay a lawyer for his advice and Condlin's remarks, transmitted through me of all people, are to serve as a substitute. I should imagine the proverbial house built on sand would be safe compared with this procedure.

Tuesday 3rd June.

Another perfect day: such a day as in retrospect one is apt to imagine one had at Leeborough throughout the summer hols., though I suspect in actual fact they were few and far between. While I was getting up I noticed how quickly and suddenly the process of decay has set in here—i.e. curtains with holes in them, cracked walls and ceilings, the leak in the bath—all have apparently come on in the last three years. . . . I did not finish breakfast until nearly ten o.c., and then set out for a walk. . . . [Later] I wrote out an inventory of the additional keeps to send to J and then read in a W. W. Jacobs[83] until seven o'clock when Mary insisted on my having a boiled egg and some tea to sustain me until I got my supper on the boat. . . . After this preliminary meal I strolled in the garden until 8 o.c.: another lovely evening and I could not dismiss the sort of thoughts which were I suppose natural to the time and place. I notice that the place

---

83. William Wymark Jacobs (1863-1943) was a writer of predominately humorous short stories.

where we buried the toys is already nearly overgrown with weeds. . . . Punctually at eight, Gillespie's taxi arrived and I settled up with Mary and said goodbye to her—a beastly business, especially when she thanked me for all my kindness to her—and then I got my luggage on board and drove off—the last of a succession of "last nights" which has spread over 25 years, and since the days of going back to Wynyard, I cannot remember feeling so depressed: as the taxi crunched down the gravel to the gate, it was impossible not to say "You will never again leave Little Lea in Gillespie's taxi for Donegall Quay".

Saturday 7th June [back in Bulford, having returned from Little Lea].

After lunch I went into Salisbury by bus. . . . The market was in full swing and while I was waiting a man turned on a gramophone at one of the stalls which played a medly of tunes which I have not heard or thought of these fifteen years—"We All Go the Same Way Home", "Follow the Footprints in the Snow", "Put Me Amongst the Girls": it's very odd to reflect that they once gave me the exact same thrill for which I now go to Beethoven or Brahms: another thing which struck me is how completely old fashioned and out of date they seemed.

Wednesday 11th June.

Just as I was settling down to my gramophone after dinner, in comes Daubeny to say that he had forgotten to warn me that the C.O. is touchy on the subject of officer's wine bills, a valuable bit of information for which I thanked him: this discloses an irritating state of affairs: not that one necessarily suffers any inconvenience from it, but at 35 it is intolerable to be supervised like a Sandhurst cadet. I played Mozart's clarinet quintet this evening, an ideal piece for the time of day and this season of the year. . . . At eleven I turned out the guard and visited the sentries, and so to bed, reading a paper on treasure trove found in an old desk, from *Essays of Today*.

Saturday 14th June.

[I had] a letter from J [who tells me] that Epicureanism is a bad philosophy, so my philosophic status remains as undistinguished as it was before I made the discovery.

Sunday 15 June.

Woke on a fine warm morning with a feeling that there was something wrong, and then seeing Fuller coming in with my jacket and medals on it, I suddenly remembered this bl—dy church parade, and pondered anew on the amazing out of dateness of such a performance, dispassionately considered. . . . Parade, though very unpleasant, was less of an ordeal than I had anticipated, i.e., I manouevred my troops into church if not with distinction, at any rate without disgrace. The interior of the garrison church is unexpectedly pleasing, done in a cool white stone with clean lines and pillars and plain light wooden furniture and fittings, giving something of the impression of one of the Lutheran interiors of the Dutch school: the only things I did not like were the parquet floor and the east window—a feeble Christ flanked by Sts. George, Patrick, David, and Andrew, topped by the gunner crest and grenades in yellow on a blue ground.

Monday 16th June.
My 35th birthday and another link with the past severed, it being the first on which I have received no note or telegram of good wishes.

Tuesday 1st July.
This evening Giles Daubeny introduced me to the officer's bathing place, a very pleasant spot which I hope to frequent regularly in future: having taken the Daudel through the village, we struck west up a rutty lane until we came to a locked gate in a wood, over which we climbed and wandered for perhaps a quarter of a mile down a lovely grassy ride with tall still trees on either side and the gleam of the Avon showing through on our right, and so out on to a cart track with a very sweet smelling hedge along its side and a field with a glorious smell of new mown hay: there were dozens of rabbits scuttling about which set Giles' fingers itching for a gun—extraordinary that the average Englishman cannot see a pretty animal without wanting to kill it—a few yards further on turned we right across a crazy plank bridge over a scummy backwater, and arrived at the bathing place — a set of sluice gates with a pent house over them, from which the water runs swiftly down between stone banks to the shallows below: the pent house is used as a ladies changing room and the men undress on the banks. The water looked to me remarkably fast and remarkably deep—so it did to Giles: we undressed and contemplated it thoughtfully; while we were still debating, whether to jump in or wade in, a girl arrived with what was evidently her small sister and both took the plunge in the most offhand way, so of course there was nothing for it but to follow suit: incidentally she was an attractive creature, about eighteen or so to judge from her delightful figure. This sluice gate bathing is a new and jolly kind which I have not tried before; one swims upstream close in to the bank and then crosses it

into the current which sweeps one down until you strand in the shallows and repeat the process—or as an alternative you can walk out along the stone supports of the sluice and fling yourself into the current—both very good fun. We were in for nearly half an hour, and I came out with a rare feeling of well being and content.

Monday 7th July.

I got back at 11 o.c. last night after spending a very pleasant week end at Headington where I found M more excited than I have ever seen her over the prospect of buying a house which has been offered to us, and J, though more cautious, equally enthusiastic. J and I went out and saw the place on Sunday morning, and I instantly caught the infection: we did not go inside the house, but the eight acre garden is such stuff as dreams are made of. I never imagined that for us any such garden would ever come within the sphere of discussion. The house (which has two more rooms than Hillsboro) stands at the entrance to its own grounds at the northern foot of Shotover at the end of a narrow lane, which in turn opens off a very bad and little used road, giving as great privacy as can reasonably be looked for near a large town: to the left of the house are the two brick kilns from which it takes its name—in front, a lawn and hard tennis court—then a large bathing pool, beautifully wooded, and with a delightful circular brick seat overlooking it: after that a steep wilderness broken with ravines and nooks of all kinds runs up to a little cliff topped by a thistly meadow, and then the property ends in a thick belt of fir trees, almost a wood: the view from the cliff over the dim blue distance of the plain is simply glorious. J and I spent an enthusiastic half hour building castles in Spain and rambling about the grounds, both agreeing that we simply must have the place if it is any way possible—and here I don't think there need be any difficulty, for the price is £3500 and we had already visualized spending that amount on building. In addition to this we want to build on two more rooms, which M calculates would cost another £100: this I consider an underestimate, so told J that he could count on my next £100 from the proceeds of the sale of the goodwill of the office, making £200 in all which I think will be nearer the mark. The more I considered the place and its possibilities, the keener I became on the plan: many a £10,000 house is worse situated and has a much poorer garden. The one drawback is the distance from Oxford. . . . In the afternoon M, J, and I had a committee of ways and means, J enacting the role of advocatus diaboli, but he was routed and the project successfully canonized. I really don't think we are doing anything very imprudent in committing ourselves to the bargain, for bargain it undoubtedly is. . . . I nearly forgot to record an admirable "Maureenism" on Saturday: on my way to Hillsboro I stopped at College and rang up to let them know that I had arrived: Maureen answered the phone. When I got to the house she greeted me thus:— "Oh Warnie, did you ring up just before you did?"

Monday 14th July.

I was able to spend the week end at Hillsboro: But though every Hillsboro week end is a plus quantity—by which I mean a happier week end than one spent elsewhere—this has been one of my dullest. To begin with, there was another guest in the house, and for one so awkward as I am, this always spoils things. The guest was M's sister, whose name I never discovered, as she was introduced simply as "Edie": she is much more Irish than Minto and altogether, mentally, physically, and in character, a much frailer woman, and with none of M's good looks. . . . Quite a pleasant woman none the less. I saw next to nothing of J who worked all Sunday Morning and in the afternoon had himself carried to some address in North Oxford where he remained until nearly seven o.c. working with some colleague on these wretched exams.

Tuesday 15th July.

Before going to bed last night I read the lessons for the day, and am in hopes, if I can make a regular practice of it, that in a twelve-month or so I shall have at least a nodding acquaintance with the Bible, of which I am grossly ignorant.

Friday 25th July.

I went by appointment to tea with the Turners[84] today, and in case I should have attempted to excuse my self at the last moment Tom was sent up to the mess to collect me in the car, which I thought a very insolent thing to do. On the way down he mentioned casually that "two of his children were at home": from his description I was quite unprepared to meet two cigarette smoking and powdered young women of eighteen or so. . . . The girls obviously put me down as a dull dog and the conversation was of the doubtful innuendo type at which I am no good. In addition, the room was stiflingly hot, so altogether I felt about as awkward and uncomfortable as possible. When tea was over, Mrs. took pity on me (or perhaps thought I had bored her daughters long enough) and led me into the drawing room

---

84. Tom Turner, a friend from Shanghai, was stationed with Warren at Bulford.

where she produced a big bundle of MSS by her dead brother . . . and asked me if I would look through them and give an opinion on their suitability for publication. . . . About five o'clock I escaped in Tom's car, carrying my bundle, and having given him a drink in the mess, set off northward for a walk over the downs. Oh, the glorious relief of being out in the wind and sun, and alone again. It was almost worth the tea party.

Sunday 27th July.

In the afternoon, under a Ruysdael sky I had the first real Daudel-spiel[85] which I have had for many a long day: such a jaunt as I love, working my way along by map and signpost through new country with no necessity or attempt to hurry: near a village called Alton Barnes I came upon some sort of fete or perhaps a service: several old men with silver instruments were sitting in a circle in the open with trees in the background, and a crowd stood watching them. After that I climbed a solemn lonely hill on which was a white horse,[86] and a barrow on the sky line, and so on through East Kennett to Avebury,[87] my destination. I was very disappointed in the famous ring, which so far as I can find, is merely two or three stones in a meadow: Newmarch tells me at supper that it used to be far bigger than Stonehenge, but that it was demolished by some goth in the reign of Charles II. Evelyn makes no mention of it in his account of his visit to these parts. At the further end of the village are more remains of the same sort, but much bigger, including two huge blocks of stone on the edge of a wooded gash.

Wednesday 30th July.

At breakfast today I got a note from J proposing himself for this week end, which has crossed with mine of yesterday putting him off and suggesting the 9th-10th. It also contains the maddeningly incomprehensible statement from Condlin that our credit balance at the Bank of Ireland is £1391, tho' according to J's reckoning it was only

---

85. Daudelspiel was Warren's term for short excursions on his motorbike—a Daudel.

86. The White Horse of Uffington (Berkshire) is a huge figure of a horse that has been created by cutting away the grass. The White Horse is 374 feet long, and is traditionally the symbol of the Saxons under Alfred the Great; it is thought that the symbol was carved in the hill in order to commemorate the Saxon victory over the Danes in 871. G. K. Chesterton writes of this symbol in his poem *The Ballad of the White Horse* (1911).

87. Avebury is the largest prehistoric monument in Europe. The stone circles, built around 1800 B.C., are thought to be religious in purpose.

about £500: where it has come from he does not know. I hope he has had the sense to put some of this elusive faerie gold into the new house before Merlin-Condlin waves his wand again.

Friday 8th August.

A letter from Ruth this morning. . . . I found that it was to say that Aunt Annie died on Tuesday 5th, at a quarter to seven in the evening. "We knew it was coming" says Ruth "and it was terribly hard, for she did so want to live". I have no single relative, or for the matter of that any four relatives whose loss I could not have borne better: like the Pudaitabird himself, she goes back to the beginnings of things and seemed a fixed and permanent point in the universe. Looking back, I cannot remember an occasion at any stage of my life when I was not glad to see her. . . . What a tower of strength she was to us in that seemingly vast space of time which intervened between Mammys death and my leaving Malvern! . . . I have remembered too, that for many years her presence, alone, in Leeborough signified that the holidays were at an end, for it was her habit to come over and supervise the packing of our trunks . . . and so thoughts flow on to the last time I was destined to see her—appropriately enough in the dining room at Leeborough where she had drunk so many glasses of Burgundy and listened with apparent acquiescence to so much emphatically enunciated dogma. . . . It gives me the feeling that not Leeborough alone but the whole familiar world of our youth is crumbling and vanishing.

Sunday 10th August.

I got back this evening from one of the best week ends I have spent for a long time, having managed at last to get off from Friday afternoon to Sunday evening. I began by going in to Salisbury by bus in the afternoon [and] thence to the second hand bookshop where I had a good look round. . . . Having finished my look round I wandered down to the station where I had a cup of tea and a bun while waiting for J, who arrived on the 5.55 in good spirits, wearing his curious hat, but having had his hair cut in honour of his visit. After buying a couple of bottles of whiskey and depositing them in the Red Lion we walked up to the Cathedral and admired it anew, J pointing out that the symmetry for which it is praised would have existed in all our Cathedrals had the money been available to finish them in the style in which they were begun: which led us to discuss whether lack of money really made much difference to church building in those days: J thought it did. After this I took him to my bookshop where he made a find—an old edition of one Du Bartas, a poet who had a strong influence on Milton. . . . At the same time I bought for 10/- a very early precursor of the *Michelin Guide*—a collection of the road maps of the English counties with mileages in the margin, and at the end the hackney coach, chairmen's and watermen's fares in London: it was published in 1742. It should be an interesting book to tour with. After finding this treasure trove and dumping it at the Lion, we went down to the County Hotel and had a drink and so back to an excellent mixed grill at the Lion, which J insisted on paying for, though I tried to argue the point with him. . . . J tells me by the way that he once stopped at this pub on a walking tour. . . . We set out for the station in the twilight, laden with our parcels . . . and I introduced J to "my" railroad: for a wonder, we were not the only passengers. . . . The trudge up to the mess was very hot and we were both glad to get our slippers on and sit down to a little drop of the whiskey, and spent a very pleasant evening with much good talk. I played my Beethoven Second Symphony, J being greatly impressed with the difference between electrical and non-electrical recording. He admired my Claude. He brought me a present—a presentable copy of *Aurora Leigh,* a thing I have been looking for for a long time, which he picked up in Oxford for 6d. On Saturday morning we were up betimes though not so early as I had intended; before breakfast I showed J our mess water colour of a heavy swell mashing a superb creature. The Daudel was on its worst behaviour and I really thought she had broken down: however, after about ten minutes I got her started and so away across the plain on a dull sticky morning with occasional smears of rain, making very good time. . . . [Once at Oxford, I] found both Minto and Maureen in good spirits, though M has been suffering from indigestion, poor thing. Much talk about the house, now finally purchased. . . . This morning after breakfast I ran J out to North Oxford . . . and then went on to College and spent almost an old "little end room"[88] morning: J dipped at random into the chest of family papers and I entered my new books in the catalogue . . . after which I read the first volume of *The Sailor,*[89] undoubtedly the best of that series. . . . In the afternoon J and I attempted to go for a walk . . . but the sticky heat today was so bad [that we] sat on a tree trunk where the sight of some

---

88. "The little end room" was Warren and Jack's favorite room in the attic of Little Lea, where they had been allowed to play, read, and write in complete privacy—their sanctuary from the intrusiveness of Albert in particular.

89. *The Sailor: A Study* (1913), written by Jack, was one of the Boxen manuscripts.

village louts aimlessly kicking a tennis ball led to a discussion of boredom in various classes of society. . . . The crown of a successful week end was to find Breughel's *Winter Landscape* waiting for me in my room when I got in. I immediately unpacked and hung it, and it is now on the opposite wall to me as I write, and is all that I had hoped it would be. There is always something very satisfying in the fulfillment of a plan made long ago: this particular picture I first saw in a bookshop in the Charing Cross road in January 1926 . . . now at long last I have it.

Monday 11th August.

Before changing for dinner I finished *The Story of the Glittering Plain*,[90] in some ways one of the best of Morris romances: plenty of movement, and the Land of the Undying such a faerie land as Spenser would have loved: but there is little or none of the usual sensuous love story which makes so much of the charm of the typical Morris romance.

Tuesday 12th August.

After dinner I read the first book of *Aurora Leigh* and a good part of the second. Undoubtedly poetry, and poetry of a high class, though not altogether my style: queer, bitter, smouldering, unhappy stuff, flaming suddenly into savage irony and sometimes beauty. . . . So far, the chief fault I have to find is that the poem is too abstract and intellectual, and in places very difficult: it does not flow smoothly onwards as poetry should do, and more then once I found myself having to read a passage twice before I understood. When one has to do this I consider that whatever merits the passage may have, it is at any rate not poetry.

Monday 18th August.

Another Hillsboro week end, with a flying start, for the Daudel was chuffing out of barracks at two minutes past one on Saturday, and I was in Oxford at twenty past three after a pleasant run, the country now having a harvest look and smell. . . . Some talk of Arthur Greeves coming over to stop for a while, or alternatively of J going over to stop at Bernagh: if I were J I would elect to do the latter, as I know the walks over Co. Down with Arthur would do him good. . . . Sunday morning we adjourned to Magdalen where we spent the morning very pleasantly, I cataloguing four of my French

---

90. *The Story of the Glittering Plain* (1891), a fantasy romance by late-nineteenth-century author William Morris.

books which I had forgotten to do last Sunday and afterwards finishing *The Sailor,* reading *Littera Scripta Manet*[91] and looking through the collected volume of drawings. [After] tea ... we went for a walk (admittedly in the rain in macs.). [We] watched the rabbits at play and afterwards sat against a gate and talked of many things—time as the chief "character" (J's phrase) in modern novels, and the distance we are now from the war as seen by people of varying ages, and thence to some unborn Gibbon's "Decline and Fall of the British Empire". We got home just before seven and I left at 8.10 and had on the whole an unpleasant journey.... I journeyed ... in rain of varying degrees of solidarity: out on the plain was grim and grand—sky black as pitch, lit by periodic lightening flashes, and the echoing crash of thunder drowning the roar of the engine, the rain stabbing down in glittering needles in the glare of the headlights: I opened the throttle and raced for home, more than half feeling that the frightful fiend did close behind me tread.

Sunday 24th August.

[On weekend leave at Oxford I] re-read J's fragment of his Ulster novel[92] and found it so good that I urged him to take it in hand again, and he did not at any rate turn down the suggestion: I have hopes that he may yet do something with it.... At tea ... the conversation turned on non-conformity and an extremely amusing argument followed between J and M, M being of the most uncompromising school of churchwoman.

Saturday 30 August.

Before going to bed I read the lessons for the day, the first of which was the twelfth chapter of Ecclesiastes—beyond all doubt the lovliest thing in the whole Bible. In reading it I heard the cadences of P's voice as plainly as if he had really been reading it. I wonder would "man goeth to his long home" do for his epitaph?

Sunday 31st August.

I am re-reading *Our Village:*[93] with the possible exception of Cowper, I don't know anything in the language which so vividly expresses the sheer joy there is to be got out of the little apparently

91. *Littera Scripta Manet,* a comedy in four acts written by Jack sometime between 1913 and 1916, was part of the Boxen manuscripts.

92. Jack Lewis probably began what Warren described as his brother's "only attempt at a modern novel" sometime in 1927. This fragment has been recorded in the *Memoirs of the Lewis Family: 1850-1930,* Volume IX, pp. 291-300.

93. *Our Village* (1832), a novel of rural village life by Mary Russell Mitford.

trivial things of life. . . . Any educated person can appreciate the "de luxe" in scenery or weather, but it is not so easy to keep tuned up to the Mitford pitch of finding beauty in the ordinary countryside on every day of the English year. I never read this book without acquiring a keener eye for the attractions of whatever part of the country I'm living in.

Thursday 4th September.

Work, eat, sleep and an hour to myself in the evening, looks like becoming my life until these accursed manoeuvres are over, and today has been particularly exasperating—pressed for time, worried out of my life, and making arrangements in the dark without sufficient information, with the foreknowledge that success will bring no kudos and that failure will probably entail exile to the penal settlement at Aldershot. I would give £50 at this moment to open my eyes and find I had dreemt it all over an after dinner cigar at the Shanghai Club: and at the back of it all is the appalling reflection that this is a "quiet" year from a training point of view.

Saturday 6th September.

After tea I enjoyed the unaccustomed luxury of changing into knockabouts and played myself a Mozart Quintet with great satisfaction. About seven o'clock I had the disturbing experience of being nearer to lightening than I have ever been before, even in West Africa: nor have I ever seen lightening under the same circumstances: slow heavy rain was falling out of low spongy grey cloud diffused equally over the whole sky, and I was sitting reading in my chair when suddenly between me and the fireplace flashed a sheet of violet flame, the lights went out, and there was an appalling crash of thunder. For some minutes afterwards my hands and arms as far as the elbows tingled just as if I had touched a live wire.

Sunday 7th September.

There is nearly a full moon tonight, and for a long time after supper I strolled in the garden with a pipe, drinking in the delicious quiet of the deserted mess. The garden with its roses and its sundial looks extraordinarily "stagey" in this light—a harlequin and columbine setting. I am writing this in my room where the absolute stillness (I am the only person in the building) forms a precious oasis between the bustle of today and the impending bustle of tomorrow.

Wednesday 10th September.

These weary days, varying solely in the intensity of their beastliness and the number of their problems, follow each other with a monotony of worry which provides little material for a diary. One wakes reluctantly with the knowledge of an interminable stretch of anxiety and hard work separating one from the only thing to be looked forward to—bed. No walks, no jaunts to Salisbury, no Daudelspiels: I have had no exercise of any kind now for eight days, and indeed have not been out of the camp, except once to go to the bank in a car. Today has been particularly bad with transport lost all over the country—everyone panicking, units stealing lorries, and a shortage all round, with which I have struggled with the hopelessness of a man trying to put out a fire—as soon as you smother it in one place, it breaks out in another.

Thursday 11th September.

Looking back over the last few entries I see my diary is acquiring a likeness to the medical bulletins published on distinguished invalids, and to continue in the language of the quacks, I can say of today "The S. & T. officer passed a restless day with frequent sudden rises of temperature: the position, though serious, is not critical".

Sunday 14th September.

After tea—ah! rare!—oh! brave!—I actually managed a walk: it was only the Beacon Hill one, but still it was grand. . . . I think autumn has now come in earnest: on top of the hills there was that keen choking wind which comes out of a hard cloudy sky and grips one by the throat. . . . I had a fire in my room when I came in, it being decidedly cold: one of the best of life's minor luxuries is the first fire of the season.

Saturday 27th September.

[Today I bought] a 2nd hand edition of *The Wallet of Kai Lung*[94] and spent most of the afternoon in reading it at the club: an inimitable book, as unique as *Alice in Wonderland,* and as completely hit or miss: either a man finds it completely unfunny or else it becomes one of his books for all time.

Wednesday 1st October.

Today I complete the seventeenth year of my sentence—sixteen from actual fact, but seventeen from the only point of view which interests me, i.e. that of pension, thanks to my year on the West

---

94. *The Wallet of Kai Lung* (1900), a witty fairy tale of ancient China as seen through the eyes of a Victorian Englishman, Ernest Bramah (a pseudonym of Ernest Bramah Smith). This volume, and other Kai Lung stories, are intended to be humorous, not authentic, interpretations of Chinese life.

Coast. How many more years to run I wonder? . . . Later in the day wrote to Minto who has appealed to me to be there on those days to help in the move to The Kilns, saying that this was the best I could do: my role is to be ferrying things to and fro in the Jowett which they have just bought and are *all* learning to drive: it must be a pretty sturdy car. Incidentally I haven't driven a car for ten years, and shall use the Daudel in preference if I am allowed to do so. J, the lucky dog, has apparently made good a claim to exemption from taking any part in the move, being too busy in College. I had hoped too, to do likewise, but I cannot in decency refuse to help if I can really get a long week end.

Thursday 2nd October.

A mixed bag of letters for me this morning [including] an amusing one from J saying that he has been made by Minto to adopt a prehistoric Leeborough Norfolk jacket as his daily wear: he gives a sketch reconstructing the monster in its own environment.

Saturday 4th October.

An amusing squib from J this morning in a burlesque tradesman style, enclosing a cheque for £7.2.6., being my share of the proceeds of the sale of some Leeborough books: I sent him an acknowledgement during the morning. . . . In the afternoon I had a most interesting walk: a blustering sunny day with falling brown leaves and big clouds and I set out feeling pretty near the top of my form. Going down under the railway arch into Bulford village I made my first stop at Bulford Church, a not very interesting old Norman building externally, but very pleasant inside, with rough hewn roof beams like a barn: I'm glad to see that I am beginning to have an eye for a church, for I picked on the chancel arch as the oldest part, and when I came to look round, sure enough there was a notice to say it dated from 1130. . . . From Bulford I walked on to Durrington. . . . Both here and at Bulford the church was decorated for the harvest festival, and there was a pleasant blend of church and garden smell. I forget in which of them it was I saw a tin basin of eggs in the window, which somehow looks more ridiculous than fruit or vegetables.

Monday 6th October.

I spent another long evening with Lockhart.[95] I was interested to find Scott saying in 1808 that the drawback to the Lake District was

---

95. *Life of Scott* (1838), a biography of Sir Walter Scott by novelist and biographer John Gibson Lockhart, who in 1820 married Sophia Scott, daughter of Sir Walter.

that "it attracted so many idle insipid and indolent gazers": I certainly did not imagine that the tourist nuisance extended back further than the 1850's—except for the Grand Tour of course. . . . At midnight I got myself dressed up and turned out the guard and visited the sentries: quite the coldest night we have had so far—cloudless, bright moonlight, and the trees all waving: just the night for a witches steeplechase or some such ghostly diversion.

Tuesday 7th October.

I enjoyed the walk in gentle steady autumn rain, smoke curling up slowing from the cottages, and the patter of the rain on the still brown trees: some people find this sort of thing depressing, but I don't: the fact of the matter is that unless one's liver is out of order, no sort of weather is depressing unless it is physically uncomfortable: and (though few people agree with me here) the country is beautiful at all seasons of the year.

Wednesday 8th October.

Before changing for dinner I read [Sir Walter] Scott's "Vision of Don Roderick", . . . It is odd that Scott, in spite of his penchant for the eerie and the supernatural, never realized that the secret of the thing is to suggest that there is a ghost round the corner, not to drag him out of his hiding place with a crash on the big drum and a red rocket or two: but perhaps his generation like to have their ghosts in the flesh so to speak. In this poem occurs the line:

> but in the middle path, a Lion lay.

This I presume is the origin of "There are lions in the path", with which P was so fond of vetoing any walk which did not suit his inclination.

Friday 10th October.

After a flustered morning I got away for Oxford at 1.30. [It] was a beautiful fine autumn afternoon and I made a two hour run to Magdalen. . . . I have never seen a more glorious bit of autumn colour than the trees in the deer park outside J's windows—a really wonderful picture. When I got out to Hillsboro I found the move in full swing and the house a complete chaos: most surprising spectacle of all J in the drivers seat of a Jowett car, about to drive up to The Kilns, which he proceeded to do, "navigating", as they say in the Navy, "with the greatest caution". The state of The Kilns proved to be rather worse than that of Hillsboro, there being considerably more furniture in it, and we were soon all busy on one job or another. . . . During the evening I . . . went through such of the family photos as we have kept—the first time I have really examined them, and I found them very interesting indeed: it is odd how P improved as the years mellowed him: from all the earlier photos one gets the impression of a man whom it must have been difficult to live with: I studied the Ballycastle beach photo for a long time (when he must have been about the age I am now) in the hope of detaching him from his surroundings and visualizing him as a contemporary, but I could make nothing of it: the Pudaita of 35 and myself would have had nothing in common.

Sunday 12th October.

Woke up to find it a glorious autumn morning, bright sunshine, and white dew on the grass. . . . The Armitages[96] turned up for tea this afternoon and there was a most amusing episode when Mrs. A insisted on J taking her out in the punt (we had been weeding and it was filthy). J, who is no expert punter, kept them gyrating in the middle of the pond helplessly, and suddenly Mrs. A sat down in an inch of black slime disclosing the unsuspected fact that she was wearing bright scarlet knickers: Tykes, who was of the party, showed his opinion of punting by jumping ashore the instant the boat was near enough to the bank to make the leap practicable. Mrs. Armitage is one of the best natured women I have ever met: though her skirt must have been ruined, she joined in the laugh as heartily as the rest of us. . . . After tea . . . J and I set out on foot through the Quarries past the lighted parish church, which we agreed that we must patronize now that we are landed gentry. Arising out of the new edit. advertised in the *Observer* we discussed Cobbett's *Rural Rides:*[97] I was surprised today to discover that J has never read *Our Village.* To bed very tired, and with a blister on the palm of my hand, caused by sawing logs for the fire, but very contented.

Monday 13th October.

Yet another lovely day: it is a great piece of luck that my first impression of the new house should be under these conditions and not in a grey weeping landscape. Immediately after breakfast [we] tackled the beastly job of getting the Leeborough wardrobes[98] upstairs: even

---

96. Mrs. Armitage and her daughter were neighbors, and friends of Mrs. Moore.

97. *Rural Rides* (1830), a description of English agriculture and politics by journalist and politician William Cobbett.

98. The wardrobe, which Warren Lewis said was the "inspiration" for the ward-

though dismembered they gave a considerable amount of trouble. . . . I put in a good mornings weeding on the lake. . . . A rather amusing thing occurred as we were unloading the last punt load of weeds: I pitchforked one on to my head and was as it were crowned with a skull cap of that evil smelling mud: needless to say J enjoyed the joke thoroughly, and I returned to my room for a wash.

Tuesday 14th October.

As usually happens to me on these occasions, I woke up shortly before five without the aid of my alarm clock, and found it still quite dark. I got up about quarter past five and dipped my head in the basin and dressed and crept downstairs where I found to my great annoyance that Minto had got up to make me some tea, in spite of my overnight prohibition on the subject. I was on the road by twenty to six, burning the precious remnant of my battery and with the red glimmerings of the dawn showing through the trees and the roads wet with dew. . . . It did not get really broad daylight until I was . . . climbing Wantage hill when the sun got up in real earnest and the whole landscape behind me came to life: a glorious feeling and I then and there decided that this early morning departure will become my normal procedure if I can devise some means of keeping Minto in bed.

Wednesday 15th October.

I love these wet autumn evenings when the trees sigh and the wet roads gleam whitely in the gathering dusk. (Query: why do such weather conditions remind me of Chopin?). . . . Dinner was much the same sort of meal as usual . . . what a blessed relief in army life is that moment when one shuts the door of one's room for the night!

---

robe in his brother's children's story *The Lion, the Witch, and the Wardrobe* (1950), was purchased at auction on October 30, 1973 by the Marion E. Wade Collection, Wheaton College, Wheaton, Illinois. This dark oak wardrobe, originally from the family home, Little Lea, in Belfast, was adzed, assembled, and carved by Warren and Jack's grandfather; the hinges and nails on the wardrobe were also handmade. When the family home was sold after the death of Albert Lewis, this wardrobe, along with other valued possessions, was transported by the Lewis brothers to Oxford; eventually, it came to stand in the main hallway of The Kilns. After receiving a photograph of this wardrobe, Mrs. Claire Clapperton (1895-   , cousin to Jack and Warren, and daughter of William Lewis—Albert's brother) wrote: "I am now 84 [and] I can remember Xmas visits to Little Lea and even sitting, when very small, in the wardrobe while Jacks told us his tales of adventure." (From an unpublished letter to Clyde S. Kilby, August 20, 1979.)

Monday 20th October.

A pleasant week end at The Kilns. . . . Sunday turned out a glorious autumn day and I enjoyed it thoroughly. We began by taking Tykes for a stroll before breakfast, and found the garden delicious: the gorse on the slope was matted and stayed with white ropes of cobweb with sparkles of dew to an extent I have never seen anywhere before and was a lovely sight. . . . After breakfast J and I biked in to College where he had to set an exam paper. . . . Our journey home was for me an amusing one—the Daudel, heavily freighted, going dead slow, with J sitting perched on the seat with his knees up to his chin, clutching one of the Medicis, which completely obscured his view. All the afternoon until tea time we were hard at work wheeling boxes of books from the garage and unpacking and shelving them. . . . We were ultimately interrupted by the arrival of a Mr. _____, a forestry expert, who had consented to give his advice on our wood, but was pronounced by J, after a cursory examination, to be a blockhead, he insisting on explaining what we should do to improve our timber for sale, in spite of assurances that there was no question of regarding it as a commercial speculation. . . . Supper this evening was not a pleasant meal, M being in a bad temper, brooding over her china [half of her "unmatchable tea things" having been broken earlier], whilst we had apparently given offence by being late for supper—a somewhat unreasonable attitude as supper has never in my experience of this household been before eight o.c. However, anyone who works as hard as Minto does is surely entitled to her off days. Under colour of a broken alarm clock Minto again insisted on giving me a five a.m. call, a kindness which embarrasses me considerably: I don't want to give up my plan of going back in the early mornings, but on the other hand I'm sure it cannot be good for her to get up at such an hour: I don't quite know what I am to do about it. . . . This morning, as last week, I acted as my own alarm clock, and woke up just a little before five, but early though I thought myself, Minto was still earlier, for I was hardly out of bed when she met me on the stair with a cup of tea and a plate of bread and butter: J was astir too and when I left at 5.30 the pair of them were sitting in the kitchen.

Sunday 26th October.

[At The Kilns, there] is another road making project on foot of which I by no means approve, viz. widening the avenue, which, it is alleged, is dangerously narrow: this would involve cutting down a pleasant row of trees. Apropos of my arguing against it, J afterwards told me that to argue against any proposition in domestic life at its first appearance is a waste of time, as nine out of ten are mooted and dropped immediately.

Thursday 30th October.

A very busy day . . . morning parade . . . mail . . . monthly stock-taking . . . at G. Company, I paid out the Company and then harangued the N.C.O.'s on their duty to become subscribers to the Corps Magazine: asked each in turn if he would subscribe: Jesty, with whom I sympathized replied—"Sir, I will do anything which will prevent me hearing any more about it for a year"! . . . I devoured about two thirds of Lockharts ninth volume before going to bed. Biographies (I suppose its the same with life) have a tendency to make dismal reading towards the close, and Scott's is no exception—money troubles, deaths of family and friends, failing health, melancholy pages from his diary—these are the motif of this volume: but there was rare courage and cheerfulness about the man, which keeps the book going.

Sunday 2nd November.

[On weekend leave at The Kilns, this morning I went into Oxford] in the Daudel, to bring out J and his friend Harwood.[99] . . . Harwood proved to be a pleasant, spectacled, young looking man, with a sense of humour of a whimsical kind, to whom I took at sight: he likened our meeting to that of Livingstone and Stanley in the jungle: he is an anthroposophist by conviction and a schoolmaster by trade, but with none of the caste marks of his calling. I wish I had seen more of him, and hope to do so on some future occasion: but the worse of these Kilns weekends is that it is impossible to have one's talk out with anyone, and already I find myself sighing after the peace and quiet of Hillsboro. I brought Harwood out and J drove the car. Before the others arrived I showed him the pond which needless to say he approved of: in fact we found ourselves seeing everything with much the same eye. . . . I hear this week end that our lake has quite distinguished literary associations, being known locally as "Shelley's pool" and there is a tradition that Shelley[100] used to meditate there: I suggested that this tradition might be turned to financial account

---

99. Alfred Cecil Harwood (1898-1975) first met Owen Barfield when Barfield was a scholar of Wadham College, and Harwood a scholar at Christ Church, Oxford. They were both introduced to Jack Lewis in 1919 through a mutual acquaintance, Leo Baker. Along with Barfield, Harwood was later to be appointed a Trustee of the C. S. Lewis Estate. See also, C. S. Lewis, *Surprised by Joy*, pp. 200-201.

100. Percy Bysshe Shelley (1792-1822), Romantic poet and dramatist.

during the American tourist season if ever we find ourselves more than usually hard up.

Saturday 8th November.

I begin to understand that it was probably no mere rhetoric when P used to say that he often wished he could just go to sleep and not wake up again. Of course one's own job is always worse than the other man's, but I don't honestly think that the *average* civilian's job can be quite so bloody as the army.

Friday 14th November.

Except abroad, the days have apparently gone forever when a man could be content to do the routine duties of his appointment and regard the remainder of the day as his own—so abroad I *must* get for one more tour, and then, unless anything goes wrong (which I think would in sober earnest drive me insane), I shall have served my sentence and the prison doors will open.

Saturday 15th November [on weekend leave at The Kilns].

I found J in our room [at the College] having a real "little end room" half hour, pouring over relics in the successor to the old playbox. . . . [We] adjourned to the High to await the arrival of J's friend Barfield, who was coming out to tea: having told him that J and I were going out to the house together, we left him to find his own way and set off in the Daudel, J anything but comfortable, it raining and he having lost his hat, beside which, my attache case was taking up most of the floor space. . . . Barfield and his wife found their way out just as we were finishing tea. . . . Barfield I liked from what I saw of him. . . . We all three had some talk together, mainly of books, while Mrs. B was undergoing the feminine ordeal of being shown over the house. I was consoled by B's remarking of the *Testament of Beauty*[101] that he had wondered if it could be understood by people who had not read certain books: there was some talk of modern poetry which neither J nor B are prepared to condemn out of hand. I was sorry to hear from J later on that B, having failed to get a job as editor of an American edition of Coleridge, is now going into the office of his father, who is a solicitor. . . . The Barfields left about six o'clock. . . . Minto started a hare this evening about our income from the estate being woefully below our expectations which at first alarmed me considerably until I realized that she was basing her assumption on the supposition that all dividends are paid quarterly.

---

101. *Testament of Beauty* (1929), a poem by Robert Seymour Bridges, O.M.

She has something of the same power which the Pudaitabird had of making the most unpleasant hypothesis ring true for a minute.

Sunday 16th November.

This is one of the sleepiest houses I know: I did not wake up till nearly nine o'clock, and I had been up for some time before J was awake. It was a glorious frosty morning with the birds in full swing as if it were spring, which was both odd and produced an extraordinary fine effect. After a delicious breakfast of sausage and bacon (Minto fries these better than I have ever tasted them anywhere else) we settled down to our morning tasks. . . . [This evening, J and I] went down to the pub for a whiskey and soda, and while talking there, J told me what I had not realized before, that the cause of P's death was a mystery: Joey[102] says it was something cerebral. On the way back we discussed Bookham days, which J tells me he still regards in many ways as being the happiest of his life. We also discussed the pity of P dying when every year was mellowing him into a more likeable figure.

Sunday 23rd November [on weekend leave at The Kilns].

As soon as I was dressed I hauled out the Daudel and set to work on the wheel—a job which the maker's hand book assures me can be done in 30 seconds, which I think must be a misprint for 30 minutes: however, with J's assistance, and a certain amount of blasphemy, I at last got it done. J has a theory, born of his recent painful contact with machinery, that engineers have second rate brains, rather than that there is anything very difficult in mechanical contrivances i.e. that the slovenly, unimaginative, and clumsy devices for tending machines are necessitated not by any intrinsic difficulties, but because the men who design them are incapable of thinking clearly enough to produce anything more efficient: I'm not sure but what he is right.

Friday 9th January, 1931.

I arrived back last night from a holiday which was so full and pleasant a one that I had neither time nor inclination to touch my journal, and must now attempt a summary of the interval. On [Saturday, 6th December], I met J in Salisbury as arranged, and after a grill at the "Red Lion" brought him on to Bulford, where we spent a cheerful evening in my sitting room. I forced him to recant his former

---

102. Joseph Lewis III, M.D. (1897-1969), cousin of Warren and Jack (and son of Albert's brother, Joseph). "Joey" had been especially close to Jack when they were young boys. See C. S. Lewis, *Surprised by Joy*, p. 43.

unfavourable opinion of Brahms by playing him the string sextet which he enjoyed immensely, and then gave him the *Sorceror's Apprentice,* and a snippet of de Falla, and so to bed all merry after much cheerful chat in anticipation of our holiday. . . . [We returned to Oxford on Sunday where] I was very glad to settle down again into the routine of our own menage, which has only one fault—there is too much of what Barfield has admirably named "Kafuffle"—a continuous bustle, which is most irritatingly manifested at meal times: J will be in the middle of an interesting story, which suddenly breaks off while he hunts for a saucepan—you start a telling rejoinder to some heresy he has propounded, but find yourself speaking to the air—he is in the larder getting the cat's fish: and so on. This would be quite understandable if there were no maid, but as it is it's maddening. . . . For the first ten days of my leave, J was busy all day correcting exam. papers at the house, and I saw little of him, except for half an hour each evening when we walked down to the "Chequers" for a drink—this is a cosy little pub., always with a roaring fire, and a very pleasant company of habitues. . . . During this period I spent my whole days in College working at the family papers. . . . It is one of the most engrossing tasks I have ever undertaken, and I am looking forward with more eagerness than ever to my days of retirement in order to finish it. We hope to raise enough money to have the results bound into a typewritten volume. . . . After J's spasm of examining was over, we usually spent our afternoons in working in the garden, and only went for walks on wet afternoons. . . . From tea time onwards, with the exception of our walk to the "Chequers" was devoted to reading, and here the holiday was memorable by my first hearing "the surge and thunder of the Odessy" in Morris' translation[103] which J says is the nearest thing to the original that there is. . . . I also read the very best ballad I ever came across in my life—Chesterton's "Ballad of the White Horse". . . . When J's other work permitted he was busy with the *Roman de la Rose* which he is reading for his medaeval book[104] . . . but he had to give it up some days ago and start working up his lectures for next term. I do wish he could get a fellowship which would relieve him from the necessity of taking

---

103. William Morris's verse translation of Homer's epic poem *The Odyssey* appeared in 1887.

104. *Roman de la Rose (Romance of the Rose),* a thirteenth-century French poem, written in two parts by two authors: Guillaume de Lorris and Jean de Meung. As early as 1923, Jack Lewis had envisioned a book on the development of the Romantic epic; other duties prevented the realization of this goal until 1936, with the publication of *The Allegory of Love: A Study in Medieval Tradition* (Oxford: Clarendon Press).

pupils: what between back work and domestic service at The Kilns he gets very little time for original work. . . . Twice during my leave, J and I went to the village church—not our own parish church which is at Forest Hill some couple of miles away, but Headington Quarry church: it is a plain little building of no architectural pretentions, but on both occasions we enjoyed the service, the music being excellent for a village church: we had a remarkable fine Te Deum, and the hymns are from a special book, which, with some real poetry in the verses. . . . On each occasion we heard a good sermon from the Vicar, an elderly very tall square shouldered man with a stoop and a long jaw. . . . He is of that rare and invaluable school of preachers who has something to say, says it, and then shuts up. . . . Altogether, we were glad to have discovered our village church and purpose to continue visiting it. . . . This leave I found a new pleasure in life by going on my first walking tour, an expedition with which J has been threatening me for two years or more. We left Oxford by train on *Thursday 1st January* . . . [and returned Sunday the 4th of January, after] a fifty four mile walk from Chepstow, which is one of the best holidays I have ever had in my life.

Tuesday 13th January.

This morning I got a catalogue from Blackwell which contained two memoirs wh. I thought were worth speculating on, so wrote them accordingly, tho with many misgivings, for my book bill is now very high. . . . I then posted the catalogue to J there being some Icelandic items in it which I thought might interest him.

Friday 16th January.

A letter from Condlin this morning, duplicating that wh. I received yesterday, and containing the great good news that Little Lea has been sold for £2300—a good deal less than we had once expected, but more than we had resigned ourselves to getting. It would be idle to deny that I feel a pang at the final parting with what has been my home for twenty six years, even tho' I should never have lived there again, and want the money for my new mode of life. I was often unhappy there, but also the memory of many happy times in Leeborough come back to me: if I could have controlled Fate, I would have wished it to catch fire and be burned to the ground when we had finished with it.

Sunday 18th January [on weekend leave at The Kilns].

[I slept] like a log until ten past nine then up and dressed, it being a bright sunny morning. Before having my breakfast I took Mr. Papworth for his walk, and after breakfast fed the fowls and the swans: the latter are now quite tame and make friendly or at least non committal noises when one approaches them: I live in hopes of being able to stroke them one of these days. Having done these jobs I byked into College where I found J at work on his papers and having had a look round, settled down to read a volume of my diary—that for 1922— and read a good deal of it with interest and enjoyment. After a drink, we set out for home, the Daudel being very wet, it having rained heavily during the morning. I forgot to mention a pleasant sight from J's windows—two cart horses sitting amongst the seated deer in the park and looking enormous by contrast with them. . . . Good story at dinner from M about our neighbor Mrs. Kreyer—she is very perturbed to hear that her bitch has been stealing old Phillips' eggs "because you know, the last time she did it, she had puppies". . . . After dinner J and I sawed wood and replenished the woodbaskets: I accused J of saving all the knotty bits for week ends but he denys it. . . . For the remainder of the day I read Keats' letters:[105] the astounding range of the man's interests is the most striking thing about them, next to the way in which he puts gems of poems casually in his letters, apparently thinking little of them himself: e.g. the only manuscript of "La Belle Dame" is that in a letter to his brother. When he writes, as he often does, in boisterous high spirits, he is capital fun. I wish though, he wasn't interested in such subject as "The Soul": an infallibly yawn raising topic, though J disagreed with me when I said so on our evening walk down to "The Chequers". He today, has been reading the life of one Gerard Manley Hopkins S.J.[106] who acquired some reputation as a poet; from the quotations given I should have thought him an illiterate: the book has his photograph as a frontispiece—a mean dishonest looking man. . . .

Sunday 1st March.

On the 17th of last month I joined at Aldershot for No. 6 War Course, and in the ensuing Kafuffle have not been able to give any attention to my diary: today however, we are half way through the course, and having just returned from week end leave at The Kilns I shall try to take stock. The course itself is by no means uninteresting and qua course I am enjoying myself. . . . It is the hours when we are not working which I find so insufferable: I could not live in this place:

---

105. The *Life, Letters, and Literary Remains* of John Keats (1795-1821) were edited by Lord Houghton in 1848.

106. Gerard Manley Hopkins was a late-nineteenth-century priest and poet.

it is possessed by some spirit which produces an unending furtive restlessness: an air of intrigue, spying and treachery seems to brood over it, masked in cocktails and over hearty good fellowship. I can settle down to nothing except my work—that done with, I pick up a book, read a few pages and throw it down and try another—then off to the anteroom to hear the latest news, for as in old Versailles, to be half an hour behind the current gossip may be to lose a point in the game. If I go for a walk, it is through evidence of the same sort of life spread all round me: and on the physical side, one must needs walk over what is one huge parade ground for all real purposes: right out in the country one comes on notices such as "This ground not to be used for Parades. By order. Aldershot Command". But when I was passing just such a place the other evening I took shelter under a bush from a flurry of snow: as it passed over a low gleam of setting sun flashed out across a little level heath and lit a row of tall beech trunks dazzling white against background of dull green. The beauty of it took my breath away, and as I walked on it occurred to me that the real asset of life is that beauty never dies, and is to be found anywhere and under any circumstances—even in Aldershot.

Wednesday 25th March.

Somehow it is more difficult to get going with this volume of my diary than it has been with previous ones: I must make a fresh start. The war course ended on the 17th at midday and by supper time I was at The Kilns in an entirely different world, and there stopped until the afternoon of the 23rd. . . . During the week we finished the 1931 tree planting programme, having put in a total of 43—a magnificent start. We also explored the lower wood pretty thoroughly, as a result of which we set to and cut a soaking machine out of the cliff or from the path up to it—a fact which was tested within an hour of its completion by Maureen and some of her friends. . . . Here we passed several pleasant hours of glorious spring weather, more like summer than March, perfectly sheltered, listening to the birds, and once watching a young rabbit on a hillock opposite. The catkins are out in the lower wood and already some trees are beginning to put on their spring green. I never remember a better place for birds: When in full choir just before dark they are simply glorious: once too, I woke very early in the morning and heard the first bird notes, and noticed for the first time that they then sound quite different to what they do later in the day. This garden is a perpetual joy to me. . . . Before dinner last night I wrote to four firms of stained glass makers in Dublin asking for rough estimates for a memorial window in St. Marks[107] to the Pudaitabird and Mammy: I do hope it will prove to be within our means.

Saturday 28th March.

In the evening I took bus into Salisbury and had a grill at the "Red Lion", somewhat inconvenienced by a football dinner which had reached the noisy state of drunkenness. There is a vicarious humiliation in seeing very young men getting drunk: you have presented to you in cold blood a picture of your self at the same age and are able to appreciate what a fool you looked at 19 or 20 when you were under the impression that you were doing something rather fine.

Tuesday 31st March.

At last I have got the written approval for my exchange, concluding with the words "Captain Lewis will be required to proceed for duty to Shanghai during the trooping season 1931-2". So unless something unforeseen happens I am in sight of the last stage on the stony road to retirement. I am sometimes frightened at the hold that this dream has got on me: not that I will be disappointed in my new mode of life, for I have no expectation of finding it roses all the way—but that some financial disaster may come to shatter the whole thing and leave me plodding on to old age—I really don't think I have any resources in myself capable of standing up to such a disaster.

Wednesday 13th May.

I am slowly recovering from a dose of flu: on the 2nd I went over to The Kilns for the week end and on the Sunday evening took to my bed with a temperature. . . . While I was convalescing, spring came at last, with a couple of perfect days, which I spent pottering in the garden, not being fit for anything else. The endless varieties of shades of young tender green, the bursts of colour of the wild flowers, and most of all, the birds, made me very happy. Our new trees are, on the whole, doing well, especially the mountain ashes, and the chestnuts: the young firs I am sorry to see have been nibbled by the rabbits, but I do not think they have been killed. . . . My most interesting personal experience while I was away was that on Saturday last, 9th, I started to say my prayers again after having discontinued doing so for more

---

107. St. Mark's Church, Dundela, Northern Ireland was the parish church of the Lewis family throughout Jack's and Warren's childhood. Their grandfather, Reverend Thomas Robert Hamilton (1826-1905) served as Rector of St. Mark's for over twenty years, retiring in 1900; Albert and Flora Lewis were married at St. Mark's Church on August 29, 1894.

years than I care to remember: this was no sudden impulse but the result of a conviction of the truth of Christianity which has been growing on me for a considerable time: a conviction for which I admit I should be hard put to find a logical proof, but which rests on the inherent improbability of the whole of existence being fortuitous, and the inability of the materialists to provide any convincing explanation of the origin of life. I feel happier for my return to the practice which is a fact that no material explanation will cover. When I have prepared myself a little further, I intend to go to Communion once again. So with me, the wheel has now made the full revolution—indifference, scepticism, atheism, agnosticism, and back again to Christianity. I hope I manage to retain my faith.

Sunday 17th May.

I tried very hard this morning to regard the garrison church as I would any other church and to take a real part in the service, but it was no good: it simply wouldn't come to life as Divine Service, but remained obstinately Church Parade. . . . In a real Church, where two or three are gathered together because they believe, the thing is easy enough: but when two or three hundred are gathered together in the name of the Army Council, it's a different proposition—all, or nearly all, there for the simple reason that if they refused to go, they would find themselves in the guard room.

Friday 22nd May.

This evening the wind dropped and for the first time this year I was able to stroll in the garden after supper, which I did with great enjoyment until nearly ten o'c. I know few pleasanter things than to watch night gradually fall over a garden when ones pipe is drawing well and all one's dreams for the future seem probabilities.

Tuesday 26th May [on a one day visit to The Kilns, due to a missed leave the previous weekend].

I was up earlier than I need have been and caught the 7.56 in what was ample time even judged by Lewis standards. A lovely sunny morning with the larks audible even above the rumble of the train, and quite hot as the day advanced. I got to Oxford at ten past eleven after a very enjoyable journey—the country was gorgeous especially between Basingstoke and Reading where there was an extraordinary variety of summer colour—quilts of buttercups and daisies, woods with a ground mist of bluebells, lilacs and laburnums in gardens, and masses of chestnuts in flower, all against a background of every possible shade of green: in one place I saw a mare and a foal. There is no doubt that (walking apart) the best possible way to see country is from a 1st Class Railway carriage. Arrived at Oxford, I walked up to Blackwells, finding it now really hot, and there gave in my two books to be bound, and then went on to the Eastgate where I drank some beer before going into College. I found J looking better than I had expected, but tired, and complaining of a perpetual feeling of limpness. . . . While we were talking, in came Arthur Greeves who is spending a week at The Kilns and who I was very glad to see again. Except that he has become completely bald, he does not appear to have changed, though J subsequently told me that if I knew him more intimately I would notice a difference. Amongst other things, Arthur told me spontaneously how very much P used to enjoy my letters from China, of which he was in the habit of reading A extracts. It is a great consolation to me now that I took as much trouble over them as I did: poor old chap, he had not very many pleasures in life. We bussed out to the house where I found Minto looking well. . . . The Kilns is looking a veritable garden of Eden, a lotus island, a faerie land, or any other term which will express sheer loveliness. . . . It was so hot in the afternoon that there was some talk of bathing, but we decided not to risk it, and instead sat in deck chairs on the edge of the top wood, watching the busy hum of men on the London road which gave a zest to our pleasure. Presently Arthur wandered away for a stroll, and J and I, apropos of P, talked of the muddy thinking which is indulged in on the subject of Omnipotence.

Saturday 6th June [on weekend leave at The Kilns].
I gave J my Marlborough essay to read this evening, and was much pleased when he afterwards urged me to try my hand at writing something. By the way he called my attention to a good thing I had missed in the easily earned bit of praise at the end of the paper. Knox says it is an "excellent peace (sic) of work". Not bad for an ex director of Military Training and present Divisional Commander.

Wednesday 10th June.
A chill, forlorn hopeless morning of moaning wind, impenetrable banked cloud, and drizzling rain. The sort of day to set one thinking of every stupid thing one had done this twenty years past, of death, disease, suffering and revolution.

Friday 14th August.
Today began our long anticipated jaunt to the North of Ireland— the most ambitious "sentimental journey" which we have so far un-

dertaken. . . . I never feel so completely at my best as when setting out on a trip with J—an experience which never fails to renew the sensations of coming home from the coll. in the old days—except that there is no longer any equivalent for the thrill of the first openly smoked cigarette. . . . At Liverpool we were sufficiently far north for it to be perceptibly colder, and on getting on board the ferry we found conditions to be as they so often were when coming home for the Xmas holidays—the Liver building shrouded in thin driving rain, and the yellow Mersey slapping sullenly into the piles of the pontoon. . . . There was some talk of going to have a look at the Cathedral but the weather was so beastly that we went straight to the hotel instead. On the way we saw a new idea in tailors wax models—instead of the usual man from a novellette illustration, three figures were grouped together—a very fat man, a very tall one, and a very short one. "Are you going to take an action against them?" enquired J on observing the first figure. . . . After our traditional mixed grill and pint of beer we took the tram back to the Landing. . . . We sailed late.

Saturday 15th August.

Awoke at half past six after a comfortable night and on looking out of the scuttle got the old never failing thrill at seeing "my own, my native land". . . . I don't know what the secret of Co. Down. landscape is: its essential quality is its restfulness, but whether this is due to colour, grouping or atmosphere, or a combination of the three, I am not artist enough to say. Or again it may be mere sentiment on my part. . . . On reaching Royal Avenue we found Condlin in [and] for the first time since P's death I found myself in what used to be his own office, where C installed us and we had a long chat. . . . C was very amusing about the sale of Little Lea, which appears to have been a most rascally proceeding on our part. In the most matter of fact way he explained that the house had no proper foundations and that he had had the dining room floor underpinned before the sale so that the real extent to which the place was rotten could not be discovered. [After] leaving Condlin we strolled down towards the Ulster Club. . . . We had a long wait for Uncle Gussie in a very bleak room of the club, and when he did appear—half an hour late—it was, characteristically, without any apology for keeping us waiting. He is a little greyer, and perhaps more inclined to substitute dogmatism for argument, but otherwise quite unchanged: he was very full of a recent motor trip which he and Harley made to Italy, during the course of wh. they went flying and met with a motor accident, to say nothing of descending the Alps with brakes wh. were out of order—not bad for a man in the middle sixties! . . . After inviting him and Harley to lunch with us at the Olderfleet tomorrow . . . we parted [and then] we caught the 5.20 to Larne. [Once there we] unpacked and dined, [and] set out for a stroll. . . . We took to the beach past Ty-na-mara and thus escaped observation. . . . and then continued along the shore as far as the mens bathing place, where disaster overtook us—"Hello, Jack" said a voice, and we found ourselves confronting Dick![108] To add to the agony he said he wd. never have recognized me if it had not been for J with me. We were pinned down to coming in for a drink after our stroll there being of course no way out of it. . . . It was strange to find oneself in Ty-na-mara again after so many years and I was glad to have been there if only to see that once very familiar view from the dining room windows. Mrs. Dick—Jean—I remembered having met before when I was introduced to her. Dick improves on acquaintance, and we spent a very pleasant hour with him: like his namesake, Uncle Dick, he has a tremendous fund of animal spirits and the gift of extracting genuine amusement from the simpler happenings of every day life. We had many a laugh over old family happenings. But the visit would have been worth while were it only for one capital story which he told us about the Pudaitabird: One day, on arriving for his weekly visit at Sandycroft, he nipped his forefinger rather badly in the front gate: in a fury, he went for Uncle Joe[109] who was in his potting shed, and attempted a dramatic entry with the bleeding finger held out in front of him: unfortunately however he overlooked the exceptionally low height of the door, and instead of a reproachful and telling entry he merely banged his head with stunning force against the lintel: this dispersed the last fragment of self control which he had been able to retain, and without a word, he left the premises and walked straight back to Little Lea from where he rang up to have it out with Uncle Joe. I'd have given a lot to have seen this happen.

Sunday 16th August.

[After church, we were off to Olderfleet for our luncheon engagement.] Soon after we got in, Uncle Gussie and Harley arrived. . . .

---

108. Richard ("Dick") Lewis (1891-?) and his wife, Jean Robinson Lewis, lived in a seaside home called Ty-na-mara in Larne Harbour, County Antrim, Northern Ireland. Cousin to Jack and Warren, Dick's namesake was his uncle and Albert's brother, Richard (1861-?).

109. Joseph Lewis (1856-1908), brother of Albert and father of Dick.

During the course of the afternoon, the Einstein theory cropped up—Uncle Gussie had of course anticipated Einstein—and he and J had a long metaphysical arguement about the nature of the atom: I of course could not follow it, but I remember being startled by Uncle G's assertion (agreed to by J) that there was remarkably little matter in the world. As the conversation retreated from me into the thickest of the metaphysical jungle, I felt very strongly a whimsical temptation to recall it by a method wh. never failed in the old days—a sharp bark of "How are things at the yard, Gussie?" . . . It was not until nearly six o'c. that Uncle G made a move and much though I enjoyed his company . . . I should have preferred it not to take up the whole of the afternoon. When he came to go, we found that his self starter was out of order, which entailed first cleaning the plugs and then swinging the engine in a rain storm: J rather cleverly evaded this part of the entertainment, and in some way which I didn't quite grasp, managed to ensconce himself in the back seat of the car under cover—to my great annoyance. After dinner, though it was raining, we decided that some exercise was essential. . . . It was a typical grim Northern evening, with waves breaking on black gleaming rocks and a grey sea: in some ways and in some moods a melancholy effect: J tells me that Arthur feels this grimness of the Antrim coast so acutely that he never visits it. I can understand such a feeling though I do not share it.

Monday 17th August.

We were awakened by our delightful red haired girl in green, who had both our teas on one tray—"Which of you is the laziest?" she enquired with a friendly smile, by way of finding out which was going to pour out the tea. It's only in Ulster that servants can adopt that attitude with a complete self respect on both sides. . . . We reached Castlerock[110] at 11.30. . . . My first impression . . . subsequently confirmed—was that it has changed very little in the twenty seven years which have passed since I was here last. . . . As soon as we were fairly installed, we changed into bathing things and slipped on macs. and went down to the beach, the tide being just on the turn. . . . It is just the sort of beach I love—firm gently shelving sand, with good breakers. I had however forgotten how cold the sea can be in the North of Ireland: it was simply icy and we needed no little resolution to get into it. But once in, how grand it was (after two years abstinence) to bury one's head in salt foaming water again, to

---

110. Warren and Jack frequently vacationed with their mother at the seaside resort of Castlerock when they were children.

taste it, and to be lifted on the crest of a wave! Of the physical pleasures of life, I don't think any surpass surf bathing. Unfortunately it was much too cold for me to stop in anything like as long as I had hoped to do, and when we were dressed again I was very glad of a whiskey and soda, while J had a rum. . . . [On our afternoon walk, we encountered] a little weed choked cemetery wh. we explored in the hope of finding some clue to the history of the Bruces,[111] but in this we were disappointed: there was one important looking tomb, but built with its back to the rest of the cemetery and shut off from it by high iron rails, so we left this grim and depressing place none the wiser. As J said of it, it's the sort of place where the ghosts wd. not defer to convention further than to knock off for a couple of hours in the middle of the day. . . . [The walk this evening in] the last of the day light in which the wet sand gleamed whitely was very pleasant. This talk about "strong" sea air is "not so ridiculous as you boys think" to quote P. I came in feeling almost drugged with it, and fell asleep almost as soon as I got to bed. Delightful to doze off to the murmur of the sea outside one's windows.

Tuesday 18th August.
After breakfast, J and I took a stroll round the village, finishing up by sitting down under a wall on the way to the bathing pool, where, cut off from the wind, it was pleasantly and unexpectedly hot. There the talk turned on systems of Government, I as usual urging the merits of a benevolent despotism, tho' forced to admit that the best autocracy the world had ever seen—the govt. of India—does not appear to be an unqualified success. Whether successful or unsuccessful, J pointed out that such a system was only workable in a country where the government is neither related by blood or class to any section of the governed. . . . Once again we had tea at the pub. in Downhill: on the walk there we discussed the Irish problem, J reproving me for the stupidity of my assertion that I hated the Irish and pointing out that one cannot possibly hate a race qua race but can only judge the individuals composing it on their individual merits—which led us on to a discussion on the causes of wars.

On August 26, Warren went on embarkation leave, pending his sailing in early October for his second tour of service in China.

---

111. The family of Sir Harvey Bruce, a local territorial magnate, now dead, whose deserted estate skirted the small cemetery.

Friday 28th August.

J returned from Ireland today, after spending a week at Bernagh with Arthur Greeves, they two having had the house to themselves, John and the old woman[112] being on leave. . . . One experience I envy J during his week was a dinner at Glenmachan: I should dearly have liked to have renewed my accquaintance with it again. On Sunday he and Arthur went to St. Marks which J tells me is just as deadly as we remember it to have been, and says that the acoustics are very bad indeed. Apropos of St. Marks, he saw Chavasse about the window and finds that it has now been (the design I mean) submitted to the Bishop for his approval.

Saturday 5th September.

I arranged today with J and Minto to take up £500 of the mortgage on The Kilns, they to pay me the same net interest as I would obtain if the money were invested in War Loan, until such time as I take up my permanent residence at The Kilns when it (the interest) will become an appropriation in favour of my mess bills. The result of this will be that the mortgage is now all held within the family, the position being as under:

Cost of The Kilns	£3300
Paid cash (I paid)	300
	3000
Mortgage held by J	1000
	2000
Mortgage held by me	500
Mortgage held by Askins trustees	1500

On Tuesday we are meeting Barfield at his office in town to see if this arrangement is a practicable one, and Minto is making a settlement whereby each of our shares is secured in the event of her death, she being the nominal owner of the property.

Monday 28th September.

Today the family paid its long projected visit to Whipsnade Zoo after the usual Kafuffle which seems inseparable from a family outing in our house. Maureen was at her sulkiest, and wrangled with Minto all breakfast time as to whether a rather heavy ground fog should or should not cause the cancellation of the whole plan. I decided quite

---

112. Arthur's brother John (1892–1969) and his mother, Mary Margretta Gribbon Greeves (1861–1949).

early on that if I regarded the day as a visit to the Zoo I should probably lose my temper, so, having given Maureen a sketch map of the route, washed my hands of the whole affair and settled down quietly in the common room with my book—Trevelyans *England Under the Stewarts*[113] which I am enjoying immensely. The plan worked capitally. At about quarter past eleven J told me that the plan now was that he and I should make a start in the Daudel[114] while Minto, Vera Henry,[115] Mr. Papworth and Maureen followed on the Singer: which we did. About Thame, the fog dispersed, and it became a glorious sunny day and we had a most enjoyable run, stopping on the way for beer and petrol. . . . Whipsnade itself must have been a lovely village before its approaches were "improved" to carry the traffic to the new Zoo: now many of the nicest cottages in it are to let, and small wonder. J and I got there shortly before one, and after reconnoitering the approaches, pulled up on the road outside, and spread out the Daudels waterproof on a slope of short turf, where we lay and chatted very comfortably in the sun and consumed one of our bottles of beer. As time wore on, and there were no signs of the others, we fell to considering the proposition and decided that if they had not arrived by 3 o'c. we would carry on on our own: however they turned up at about twenty past two, and glad we were to see them as we were by this time uncommonly peckish. Their delay had been caused by Lydiat[116] having played the same trick on them that he did on me last time I went over to Bulford—pumped the tyres up so iron hard that they could only do about 15 m.p.h. After a substantial sandwich lunch we parked our transport and went into the Zoo, J remaining outside with Tykes, whom Minto had insisted on bringing. As a park, Whipsnade is a triumphant success, but as a Zoo, rather a failure, owing to the comparatively few animals, and the lack of an intelligible guide book. The Dukes Walk is a handsome avenue, and

113. *England under the Stuarts* (1905) by historian George Macaulay Trevelyan, O.M.

114. "On Monday 28th September we had a family outing to Whipsnade Zoo, Jack making the journey in my sidecar; which at first sight may seem to be a singularly pointless bit of information. But in fact it records the most important day in Jack's life. It was during that trip that he made his decision to rejoin the Church. . . ." (*C. S. Lewis: A Biography* written by Warren, p. 231, later revised and adapted into *The Letters of C. S. Lewis*. See also C. S. Lewis, *Surprised by Joy*, p. 237.

115. Vera Henry was an Irish friend of Mrs. Moore, who periodically visited the Lewis-Moore household. For a time after World War II, she assisted as a maid at The Kilns. Still later, she ran a resort camp near Drogheda, Ireland, where the Lewis brothers were frequent summer guests.

116. Lydiat, a general handyman employed by The Kilns household.

on the right of it as you go in, is the most magnificent fir wood I have ever seen—tall clean trunks and a deep brown carpet underneath: here were American timber wolves—evil noiseless looking beasts grotesquely like the Alsatians of a nightmare: when one studies the wolf it is easy to understand the supernatural associations which have grown up around him. On the other side was a large enclosure full of bears—the best thing in the Zoo. Some—skinny black duck toed fellows with white noses—I did not care for, but there was one delightful brock brown plethoric one who sat up and saluted for buns. J is full of the dream of adding a pet bear to our private menagerie, which he intends to christen "Bultitude"[117]—a capital name. This park is on the top of a hill, and all round there glorious vistas through gaps cut in the woods, especially at the fellows pavilion: near here we saw the wombat—a poor relation of the bear's I should imagine. The Kangaroos were out of the enclosure, being hand fed by a Keeper, while another tried to photograph them —when one attempted to break away, he was caught by the tail and carried back upside down, apparently without its causing him any discomfort! I did not see half what I wanted to, as, after an hour inside, I had to go and relieve J at the gate, where he was holding Tykes. However I browsed on a bench there very comfortably, looking down the noble vista of Dukes Walk, and listening to a man at the gate who was selling "Whipsnade Rock".[118] I wonder which is the original of all these "rocks"? The others came out about half past five, and we then went home independently, J and I travelling via Oxford, on which route we made a fast run. Altogether an enjoyable day, even if we did not see much of Whipsnade.

Monday 5th October.

J and I went over to Whipsnade by ourselves and did the place thoroughly: foggy early in the morning but turned fine later on. Lunch in a cloister restaurant in the Zoo grounds, cheap and good. The whole layout in excellent taste. We both still consider Bultitude the bear the star turn of Whipsnade. Got back about six p.m. after a most enjoyable day.

---

117. Though Jack Lewis never actually acquired a pet bear, he did incorporate this favorite animal as a character in the third book of his space trilogy, *That Hideous Strength* (1945).

118. A sugar candy stick with a white center on which the word "Whipsnade" was continuously imprinted throughout the entire piece. This sugar "rock" had various names, depending on the particular locale where it was sold, and is still sold in areas of England today.

Warren's embarkation leave over, he was scheduled to depart on the Neuralia *for China from Southhampton on October 9.*

Wednesday 7th October.

I left on the 8.30 p.m. for Southampton after an early supper, J coming in in the taxi to the Station to see me off. Beastly these partings are, but please God, this will be the last of them.

Friday 9th October.

A comfortable night alongside: I am in a three berth cabin. . . . Parkin came down during the morning and we had a few drinks together followed by the usual chaotic sailing day lunch. We went to sea about 2 p.m.

Wednesday 14th October.

Went to sea before breakfast. Organized sports began today, but have managed to avoid being put on the committee. Started *Joseph Andrews*.[119]

Warren Lewis arrived in Shanghai on Tuesday, November 17.

Monday 23rd November.

I almost feel as if I had never left Shanghai—a feeling accentuated by the fact that I have bought back from Bill Wilson the identical pieces of furniture which I sold him when I went home. I am writing this at the same old desk, and in front of me are my own old curtains and mosquito windows. A good many of my gramophone records, I'm sorry to see, have got warped on the journey, but they are still playable. Now that I have got my pictures up, and bought a $30 Japanese rush carpet, unpacked all my books and the gramophone, I feel I can sit back and breathe.

Monday 30th November.

[After lunch, I] walked round to Kelly and Walsh to choose a calendar. Surprising the number of people to whom a calendar is just a calendar, whereas I think it needs nearly as careful selection as a picture: after all, one is going to look at it for 365 consecutive mornings, probably at that grimmest hour of the day which precedes shaving. I finally chose an East Anglian winter landscape.

Wednesday 2nd December.

On getting down to the office, I found a long letter from J waiting

---

119. *Joseph Andrews* (1742) by eighteenth-century novelist and playwright Henry Fielding.

for me: his chief item of news is that Maureen has been offered and has accepted a resident job at a girls boarding school at Monmouth. Minto complains of fancying she has the feelings which she imagines she ought to have in such circumstances. . . . In the evening I taxied down town and met Chunk Boxer and Charles Pennack by appointment at the Shanghai Club and spent with them a very pleasant evening: while we were drinking at the bar, comes Wilson Brand, who we co opted into our party. . . . After dinner we adjourned to the billiard room where we played a noisy game of pool until eleven o'c., and then set out in Chunks car, on the old Shanghai game of going round the town: first, with a great deal of difficulty, we found a new place of Chunks—"The Aquarium", up by the French Club—staffed entirely by Russians: there a Russian girl sang quite well, what was evidently a comic song. From there we went on to St. Georges where the others danced, and Wilson Brand got extremely enthusiastic over the beauty of a Chinese dancing girl, and treated us to a long discourse on a Chinese he had kept when he was out here last: this conversation soon languished however, for one's mistress like one's pass book is a subject which is very dull to anyone but the owner. . . . From St. Georges we went on to Del Monte which has been redecorated since I saw it last: it is still managed by "Satan" Hyde with whom I had a few words. I also met Shanghai Mary, looking the same as ever, who neatly took advantage of my reminiscent mood to tease me into buying her a bottle of champagne. After this it was proposed that we should go on somewhere else, but on looking at my watch I found it was four o'c., so amended the proposal to read that the party should now break up. Charles had already disappeared, so the amendment was accepted, and Chunk drove me home in his car. And so to bed, quite sober, and having thoroughly enjoyed my outing.

Thursday 3rd December.

[After breakfast] there was a letter waiting for me from Minto: it's a pity that my two correspondents cannot arrange to write by different mails as this embarras de richesse means that they both tell me much the same things. . . . Poor Tykes was apparently much affected by my departure, and I find his regret as flattering as that of any Christian. As soon as we had left the house for the station he climbed into his basket and refused to hold any communication with the household until the following morning. Minto goes on to say that whenever Lydiat starts up the Daudel, Papworth rushes down to the garage to see if it is me come back again.

Monday 14th December.

During the latter part of the day I read a good deal of Ponsonbys *Diaries:*[120] the best part is his own introduction in which he analyzes the motives which lead people to keep diaries, and discusses the two types of diary—the objective and the subjective: how anyone can be sufficiently unselfconscious to keep one of the latter kind, even for his own private use, is a mystery to me: and if the object of a diary is to provide pleasant reading for one's own old age an introspective one would I fancy make pretty depressing reading—at least any samples I have seen depress me. He emphasizes the facts that intercourse with the great does not necessarily or even usually imply an interesting diary, and that no literary talent is necessary to keep one: if by interesting, he means interesting to outsiders, I agree with him as regards the first point, but not the second: the outstanding diarists—Pepys, Burney[121] and Boswell—all had literary talent, while the excerpts he quotes from the lesser fry are on the whole, dull reading.

Wednesday 16th December.

After getting home I finished Ponsonbys *Diaries.* Throughout he insists that the interesting thing in a diary is not the diarists record of events, but the insight obtained of the psychology of the writer: this seems to me to go too far. If the diarist has an interesting personality, well and good, but his implication really amounts to this—that an objective diary cannot be an interesting diary, and with this I disagree entirely.

Sunday 20th December.

Bright, chilly, and sunny. Morning service was at 10 a.m. today instead of the usual 10.30 and although I was called at half past seven I had rather a rush to get there in time. Matins preceeded choral eucharist and there were exactly four people in the church—the Dean who read the service, an elderly man, an old woman and myself: at first I found the service embarrassing—the three members of the congregation were separated and one's voice sounded intolerably loud—but soon I found it both impressive and comforting: such a tiny congregation brings home the "two or three gathered together" idea in a

---

120. *English Diaries:* a review of English diaries from the sixteenth to twentieth centuries, with an introduction on diary reading (1923), and *More English Diaries* (1927), and *Scottish and Irish Diaries* (1927), by Baron Arthur Ponsonby.

121. Fanny Burney (Madame d'Arblay), novelist and author of *Diaries and Letters, 1778-1840* (published 1842-1848) and *Early Diary, 1768-1778* (published 1889).

way which the normal service does not. . . . After lunch I walked down to the Shanghai Club to change a book, and after pottering in the library for some time ultimately decided on Vol. VI of The Cambridge Modern History *The XVIIIth Century:* the year 1715 is beginning to have for me something of the quality of the green hills seen from the window of the nursery at the old house—what lies beyond?

Friday 25th December, Xmas day.

Called at half past six and got up in uniform, and carried Barnett with me to the eight o'c. celebration at Bubbling Well chapel. This is my fourth Christmas day in Shanghai, and oddly enough on each of them, the weather conditions have been identical—bright sun, frost on the ground and a faint keen wind. As we got to the chapel the congregation was just coming out from the seven o'c. Celebration and I was surprised at its size: and in view of that, even more surprised at the size of ours. I suppose the chapel holds about 100 people, and though we packed up tight at least a dozen had to stand throughout the service. . . . I attended the service with very mixed feeling, gladness predominating at once again finding myself a full member of the Church after so many years of indifference or worse: but the thought of when I last attended Communion brought with it sadness for those old Christmas mornings at Leeborough—the kafuffle of the early start, the hurried walk in the chill half light, Bartons beautiful voice, the dim lights of St. Marks and then the return home to the Gargantuan breakfast—how jolly it all seems in retrospect! I came away feeling profoundly thankful that I have once again become a communicant, and intend (D.V.) to go regularly at least four times a year in future—Christmas, Easter day, the Sunday nearest my birthday, and the Sunday midway between August 23rd and September 25th.

Wednesday 30th December.

I spent yesterday, and this morning in bed with this infernal cold —one of the worst I have had for a long time—and am still feeling miserable and depressed, tho' I cheered up on getting a long letter from J. Amongst other interesting news, he has been for a short walking tour with Barfield to the Barley Mow Inn and back: I'm glad I followed J's advice and brought my maps abroad with me this time: I was able to get out the Oxford sheet and follow the whole itinerary— almost a walking tour by proxy when one already knows the country. . . . There was also a letter from Minto enclosed from which I am sorry to see that they are still maidless: but from what I have seen of the way in which M handles servants, maidlessness will be our normal situation.

Monday 18th January, 1932.

The Japanese Admiral who prides himself on his command of English idiom was recently the guest of honour at a dinner at Government House, Hong Kong: during its course, the Governor turned to him and said "I hope, Admiral, you like champagne?" "Very much" replied the Jap., and of course champagne was immediately served to him. After a time the governor noticed that it was untasted and asked his guest if the wine was not to his taste—"Ah Excellency" replied the Admiral sadly, "it is not that, but just at present I am what you English call, on the water closet"! I cannot find out whether it was a mixed dinner party or not—but whatever the facts it will doubtless very soon become one in the telling. Even as I was laughing at the story, I felt a pang of regret that it would never be told to the Pudaita-bird: how he would have enjoyed it!

Tuesday 19th January.

A letter from J today containing the news that he too has once more started to go to Communion, at which I am delighted. Had he not done so, I, with my altered views would have found—hardly a bar between us, but a lack of a complete identity of interest which I should have regretted.

Tuesday 26th January.

When I got back from my walk this afternoon I heard from Mac. that orders had been issued for us to hold ourselves at the end of the telephone in case of an emergency arising: so it looks as if we may be drawn into this infernal Sino Japanese quarrel after all. The thing has been brewing for months, the real cause of the trouble being the very effective boycott of Japanese goods instituted by the local Chinese patriotic societies: this, Japan is determined to break and she got her chance the other day when a Chinese mob fell upon a Japanese Buddhist priest in the Northern District and playfully pounded him to death with concrete slabs. Then Jap consul promptly sent in an ultimatum—a public apology, punishment of the murderers, compensation, and the dissolution of all anti Japanese societies, failing which he will occupy Chapei. This ultimatum is said to expire at midnight on Saturday.

Saturday 13th February.

This weary war which is officially not a war still drags on, with a resultant boredom which is hard to imagine. . . . For four or five days after making my last entry I was too busy to write, and since then I have been too bored. . . . I hope we are through the worst of it. I must admit that in a way I have enjoyed it: there is a fearful joy in being on one's own in a crisis, unable to appeal to anyone for advice or orders, and dealing with almost hourly emergencies: but a little of it goes a long way. . . . Throughout these troublous times I have been rereading the *Faerie Queen*[122] and, as is generally the case when I reread, am finding it even better than I remembered: what a gorgeous, glittering, simmering world it is! The battles I find a great bore, but his endless lovely dawns and sunsets, and great houses and country side of Faerie Land are simply overwhelming in their sweetness and richness: and how his women fascinate one. I never remarked before that every woman of any importance (in the first three books at any rate) has yellow hair. . . . Tomorrow will be the third Sunday I have spent in the office instead of going to Church, but even in this, there is consolation: I am delighted to find how much I miss the Sunday service. I was afraid when the first emergency Sunday had passed that I might feel tempted to slip back into my old indifference.

Tuesday 23rd February.

I was woken up two or three times during the night by heavy shelling, nearer than it has been, or else very big stuff, for I could hear the whine of the shells—a sound which I'm sorry to observe one does not get any more reconciled to as one grows older. . . . A notice was sent out last night by the Consul General, whose lack of any sense of humour is causing many chuckles. The C.G. has, quite rightly, made plans for evacuating the women and children to Hong Kong if the worst comes to the worst, and has selected the Shanghai Club as their rendezvous. This is the last stronghold of bachelordom in the town, and, like all places to which women are not admitted is of course an object of intense curiousity to them, most of them firmly believing it to be a place of "nameless orgies": the message which every British matron and maid received yesterday, ran as follows: "On receipt of the message so and so, at any hour of the day or night, you will proceed at once to the Shanghai Club:—minimum of clothing".

Wednesday 24th February.

[Last] night we got the first batch of home papers with the Shang-

---

122. *The Faerie Queene* (published 1590-1596), an epic poem of medieval romance and chivalry by sixteenth-century poet Edmund Spenser.

hai news in them. It is very disconcerting to find how completely our press has become Americanized: the *Daily Sketch* has scare headlines about "night of terror in doomed city" which the sack of a European capital would hardly justify: it is also careful to conceal the vital difference between Chapei and the settlement so as to suggest that it is on the latter that the rain of the bombs has been descending: this suggestio falsi, coupled with downright lying—e.g. that there has been a Chinese attack on the settlement—must have caused intense suffering to thousands at home, and is the meanest way of earning money that I ever heard of. The Editor should be flogged. . . . A dirty cowardly trade this journalism. . . . I went for my usual walk this evening in a keen wind—masses of grey cloud about, and no birds singing: three Japanese planes were up bombing in the direction of Chapei, and in addition to the wallop of the bombs, the stutter of machine guns was to be heard everywhere. It appears to me that whenever the Japanese are disappointed at the lack of success of their military efforts, they ease their spleen by dropping a few more hundredweight of explosives on the helpless civilian population. As I walked, I withdrew my mind from the whole subject and thought of a cottage at Ardglass on a soft grey Co. Down evening, with a shallow foam flecked bottle green sea in front of the door—and came home feeling much better for the exercise both of body and mind.

Wednesday 21st December.

The long interval which has passed since I last wrote any thing in this diary, the better part of a year in fact, has been in every way so unpleasant that I don't propose to follow my usual custom of making a summary of the interval. . . . On arriving home [from Shanghai], I found The Kilns as beautiful as ever, and actually improved by the new wing which consists of a study, and beyond it, my bedroom, both capital rooms. Today, I got up early, and went to the hall door where I found *The Times* containing the announcement which I have been dreaming of for years—"Capt. W. H. Lewis retires on ret. pay. (Dec. 21.)." And so, after eighteen years, two months, and twenty days, my sentence comes to an end, and I am able to say, like Wordsworth, that I have "shaken off",

> The heavy weight of many a weary day
> Not mine, and such as were not made for me.

But so far from grousing, I am deeply, and I hope devoutly thankful. It has been a good bargain: how many men are there, who, before they are forty, can struggle free, and begin the business of living. To bed with many thoughts of Lamb.

On January 3 through 6, 1933, Warren and Jack took their second annual walking tour, continuing their ascent of the Wye Valley.

Wednesday 25th January, 1933.

Tolkien[123] carried J and I to dine with him at Pembroke. We were late for dinner—T's fault, he having said he wd. meet us in J's rooms, but being under the impression that he had fixed the rendezvous as outside the porters lodge. However, we were not very late. I was put on the left of the Master, called I think, Duddon—who looked almost too good to be true, i.e. more like the head of a house than most heads of houses ever succeed in looking—almost a theatrical likeness. He was a heavily built, clean shaven, firm lipped, aquiline nosed clergyman, with beautifully waved grey hair. I heard from Tolkien afterwards that he is persona non grata with the Queen and preaches at Sandringham. I was a little uneasy about the whole business, J having told me that in Colleges, it is not the custom to show any sort of attention to a mans guests: Pembroke however must be an exception, for everyone was most friendly and anxious to make one feel at home. . . . After dinner we went to the common room, taking our napkins with us, and there found a number of little tables to seat two people each, arranged in a semicircle round the fire. I was put at one with the vice president, whose name I forget—a pleasant man. What waiting was necessary, was done by the Chaplain. Conversation was general. This is a much better way of taking dessert and wine than the army habit of sitting round the mess table. . . . After we had had our wine, the circle broke up and we all stood round the fire chatting, mainly about Johnson, and from there the conversation drifted to Trollope—much to my relief for I had feared the talk would be entirely above my head. After this we went back to J's rooms where we sat until eleven o'c.

Friday 27th January.

The frost still showing no signs of breaking, stopped at Eaglestons on the way into town this morning and bought two pairs of skates,

---

123. John Ronald Reuel Tolkien (1892-1973), professor of Anglo-Saxon at Oxford until 1945, when he became Professor of English Literature at Merton College. He was a close friend of both Jack and Warren Lewis (who called him by the nickname "Tollers"), and a member of the Inklings. He is perhaps best known as author of *The Hobbit* (1937) and the fantasy trilogy, *The Lord of the Rings* (1954, 1955). See also, Humphrey Carpenter, *Tolkien: A Biography* (Boston: Houghton Mifflin Company, 1977); Humphrey Carpenter, *The Inklings* (Boston: Houghton Mifflin Company, 1979); and C. S. Lewis, *Surprised by Joy*, p. 216.

with which J and I experimented in the afternoon on the pond. This is the first time either of us have been on ice since the Easter term of 1912 when I was at the Coll. and he was at Cherbourg. We both found we had forgotten all about it, and the torture—no other word is adequate—to one's shins was very severe. I did not succeed in recapturing the old thrill but then I did not expect to. The best feature of it was the extraordinary beauty of the lower wood seen from this unaccustomed viewpoint: especially beautiful was the purplish colour of the tops of the young trees. We neither of us fell, but that is the most that can be said, for my skating at any rate. I was surprised to see that both the dogs realized at once that there was no use in trying to run on the ice. On Saturday and Sunday we also skated, I with diminished enthusiasm.

Monday 13th February.

I found some more material for the family papers this morning—a fragment of diary written by J in 1916. It is highly characteristic of him, that during the period in which he is recording walks with Arthur, visits to Glenmachan etc., I have reliable evidence that he was in England.

Saturday 18th February.

Magdalen tower looked very beautiful from J's windows this morning, with the right hand side, and pinnacles coated in snow, shown up by the grey of the stone and the lead blue cloud background. I finished typing Chap. III of Thomas and started to correct it. While I was so doing, in came J's friend Dyson[124] from Reading—a man who gives the impression of being made of quick silver: he pours himself into a room on a cataract of words and gestures, and you are caught up in the stream—but after the first plunge, it is exhilarating. I was swept along by him to the Mitre Tap, in the Turl (a distinct discovery this, by the way) where we had two glasses of Bristol milk a piece and discussed China, Japan, staff officers, Dickens, house property as an investment, and, most utterly unexpected "Your favourite readings *Orlando Furioso*[125] isn't it?" (deprecatory gesture as I get ready to deny this) "Sorry! Sorry! my mistake". As we left the

---

124. Hugo Dyson (1896-1975), Lecturer in English at Reading University until 1945, when he was elected a Fellow and Tutor in English Literature at Merton College, Oxford. He was a close friend of both Jack and Warren Lewis, and a member of the Inklings. See also, Humphrey Carpenter, *The Inklings;* and C. S. Lewis, *Surprised by Joy,* p. 216.

125. *Orlando Furioso* (published 1516 as 40 cantos; 1552 as 46 cantos), a romantic epic by Lodovico Ariosto.

pub., a boy came into the yard and fell on the cobbles. D (appealingly) "Don't do that my boy: it hurts you and distresses us". We parted outside, D inviting me to dine with him in Reading on the 18th of next month, and J to dine and spend the night. "We'll be delighted to have you for the night too, if you don't mind sleeping in the same bed as your brother". This part of the invitation I declined, but I think I shall dine. . . . [This evening] there was a beautiful feathery fall of snow in the fading light, while we were having tea, and J put me in mind of a thing which I had completely forgotten—that when we were children we used to be told of a snow fall, that "the old woman up in the sky was plucking her goose". Altogether a beautiful and satisfying day.

Friday 24th February.

J came out yesterday morning, this time with a temperature, and went straight to bed, where we intend to keep him until he is very definitely cured.

Saturday 25th February.

Still snowing, and the garden and lane very deep. The papers record that it is the worst storm we have had for thirty years. There are of course a crop of mishaps and inconveniences viz. wires down, busses suspended, charabancs lost, ships aground, Fishguard express and Flying Scotsman, fourteen and six hours late respectively. I went for a walk in the afternoon, but could not even pretend I was enjoying it. Minto and I much amused and irritated by J who lies in a warm bed, with roaring fire, in my room, lamenting missing this lovely weather.

Sunday 26th February.

Thaw and slush. Impossible to go to Church except in gum boots, and I still retain enough of the Irish Protestant leaven to regard that as a somewhat sacreligious proceeding. So stopped at home.

Wednesday 15th March.

I am reading *War and Peace*[126] a novel which seems to me to reduce all the so called "great" novels to the class of the second rate: and as regards its war scenes, it simply obliterates the whole of the war literature of the last war. Part of the secret is that whereas the moderns tell you what the horrors of war look like, Tolstoi tells you what they feel like.

---

126. *War and Peace* (1864-1869), novel by Count Leo Tolstoy.

Saturday 18th March.

J and I caught the 5.50 p.m. for Reading and arrived there at 6.30: a fine ruddy golden sunset tonight, with masses of metallic blue cloud to the east: the country still looking very flooded. Dyson met us at the station, and the manner of his greeting, though hearty, confirmed me in the uneasy suspicion started by Minto, that I had not been expected to accept his invitation. D himself said that J had so emphasized the "I" in saying "I will be arriving etc." that they had been in some doubt about my coming. I put up for the night at the "Great Western" a gloomy, but not uncomfortable pub., where we all three had a drink together before D carried J off to his house, leaving me to dress. I arrived at the house about quarter to eight, by taxi, with that sinking feeling which generally accompanies an entry to a strange house, and found J, D, and Mrs. D in the drawing room—the latter slim and very fair, rather pretty and pleasant, but too anxious to make one at home to be quite successful. There was also there a Polish girl, a lecturer at the university: good looking in the unusual style of grey eyes and black hair, with an unpronounceable name. She has been working on the CON section of the N.E.D.[127] She was boisterously greeted by D who proceeded to upset a glass of sherry over her frock without in the least impairing his own self confidence. . . . After dinner, things improved considerably: Dyson took us to a little book lined study, where we had coffee and he read an imitation of Pope which he has just written, and which I thought good, tho' here again I was rather handicapped by not understanding most of the allusions. . . . I was just getting comfortable when he uttered the fatal "Shall we join the ladies?" which put me out the more, as I had not been expecting it. (J afterwards said "I wonder what would happen if one just said Well, I think we're very comfortable where we are"). The rest of the evening passed in general chat. I walked home in the unsatisfactory state of having liked everyone I had met, without greatly enjoying the evening.

Sunday 19th March.

J turned up shortly before eleven, and we caught the 11.20 to town: a crowded train. On the way up, a curious thought struck me: what becomes of all the dead in this country? Not one in ten thousand of the people who have died even in the last two centuries can be buried in church or grave yards. It would be easier to understand if there were no graves in existence, say, more than fifty years old: but

---

127. *New English Dictionary*, the original name for the *Oxford English Dictionary*.

any churchyard I have ever looked at, contains a selection of graves, generally from the late XVII Cent. onwards. . . . We caught a steam train at 2.5 which got us to Watford about half past, and having put our things at the Clarendon we set out on what was now a cold wet afternoon to have a look at Wynyard.[128] . . . Wynyard (now the junior house of a girls school which has succeeded Corran) still has the power to bring back a flood of memories—and such memories! If there was anything in Kiplings theory of an abstract haunting—that is to say that a house where someone has experienced great misery is one in which no one will ever be happy again—Wynyard would be tenantless to this day, for no one could resist the accumulated weight of over twenty years of collective juvenile and adult suffering.

Thursday 30th March.

Before going to bed last night I finished an uncommonly interesting book—a war book quite out of the ordinary run: *The Land Locked Lake* by Hanbury Sparrow, the same who was garrison adjutant at Colchester in my time. He has now retired and is chicken farming in the country, I presume at Church Stretton, from where his preface is dated, and has apparently found a solution of the spiritual doubts which beset him in anthroposophy. This I found out from Barfield and not from his book. HS is to go on the walking tour this year—a strange bedfellow for J, Harwood, and above all, Barfield. . . . This afternoon my long expected new gramophone arrived by in charge of two men, who set it up in the study where we tested it with a Debussy, a bit of the Pastoral symphony, and a chorus from Beethovens Mass. I am delighted with it: it is that rare thing, an article which really does what is claimed for it in the advertisments. I had been afraid from its enormous size, that it would be too loud for the study, but it is actually quieter than the old machine. The beauty of the new one is that it really does differentiate the instruments, and completely does away with that "flat" composite effect that all other soundboxes give. . . . after supper J, Minto and I sat cozily in the study and I played them the Pastoral Symphony and a sonata of Bach.

In April, Warren, Jack, Maureen, and Mrs. Moore vacationed for two weeks at Flint Hall, Hambledon, a farmhouse in the Chilterns.

---

128. Wynyard School, Watford, Hertfordshire, a boarding school attended by both Warren and Jack when they were young boys. The brutality of the headmaster, Reverend Robert Capron (1851-1911), and the intellectual sterility of his teaching combined to create a nearly intolerable environment for the young boys under his care. See also, C. S. Lewis, *Surprised by Joy*, pp. 24-36.

Florence ("Flora") Augusta Hamilton Lewis, mother of Jack and Warren, ca. 1897.

Albert James Lewis, father of Jack and Warren, 1925.

Warren Hamilton Lewis, ca. 1898.

Family group in garden, 1899. From l. to r., first row: Agnes Young Lewis (aunt), Anne ("Annie") Harley Hamilton (aunt), *Warren Lewis*, Martha Gee Lewis (grandmother), Flora Hamilton Lewis (mother), and *Jack Lewis*, on mother's lap. Second row: Mary Warren Hamilton (cousin) in her father's arms, Augustus ("Gussie") Warren Hamilton (uncle), Leonard Lewis (cousin), Richard Lewis II (grandfather), Eileen Lewis (cousin), and Albert Lewis (father).

Family group on vacation at Larne Harbour, County Antrim, Northern Ireland, 1903. From l. to r., first row: Joseph ("Joey") Lewis III (cousin), *Jack Lewis*, Richard Lewis II (grandfather), Leonard Lewis (cousin), and standing, *Warren Lewis*. Second row: Eileen Lewis (cousin), Elizabeth ("Bessie") Lewis (cousin), May Lewis (cousin), Flora Hamilton Lewis (mother), Mary Taggert Lewis (aunt), Agnes Young Lewis (aunt), Martha Lewis (cousin). Third row: Albert Lewis (father)/ and Joseph Lewis II (uncle).

Family group on doorstep of Little Lea, Belfast, Northern Ireland, 1905. From l. to r., first row: *Warren Lewis, Jack Lewis*, Leonard Lewis (cousin), and Eileen Lewis (cousin). Second row: Agnes Young Lewis (aunt), maid, maid, Flora Hamilton Lewis (mother), and Albert Lewis (father), holding the dog Nero.

Jack and Warren with bicycles in front of the Ewart family home, Glenmachan, Belfast, Northern Ireland. This photograph was taken by Gundrede Ewart (distant cousin) in August 1908.

The Albert Lewis and Augustus Hamilton families posed on the staircase of Little Lea, Christmas 1909. From l. to r., first row: Mary Warren Hamilton (grandmother), Harley Hamilton (cousin), John Hamilton (cousin), and Anne ("Annie") Harley Hamilton (aunt). Second row: Ruth Hamilton (cousin) and, partially hidden behind grandmother, *Jack Lewis*. Third row: Albert Lewis (father) and *Warren Lewis*. Photo: Augustus Hamilton.

Neighbors and relatives at a tennis party at Glenmachan, the Ewart family home, summer 1910. From l. to r., first row: unidentified, unidentified, unidentified, Lily Greeves (Arthur's sister), and Robert Heard Ewart (distant cousin). Second row: Arthur Greeves (neighbor and friend of Jack Lewis), Gordon Ewart (distant cousin), and *Jack Lewis*.

Jack Lewis with fellow classmate-actors in theatrical costumes at Cherbourg Preparatory School, Malvern, 1911. Jack is seated on the front left.

A "water colour drawing of the Star Liner, 'Indian Star', by W. H. Lewis. (Circ.) 1911." This illustration is one of many drawings preserved by the Lewis brothers in a small orange paper notebook, *Leborough Studies: Ranging from 1905–1916*, collected by C. S. Lewis. This small watercolor (in shades of black, gray, white, salmon, and blue) was one of Warren's contributions to the world of Boxen. Photo: Robert Mead.

Warren Lewis with friend and classmate "Blodo" Hilton in Officers' Training Corps uniforms outside School House, Malvern College, Easter term 1913.

Warren Lewis with two Malvern classmates and friends, Easter term 1913. From l. to r.: F. C. C. B. Hichens and *Warren Lewis*. "Blodo" Hilton is seated on wall.

Second Lieutenant Warren Lewis, on leave from France, with his father and neighbors at a picnic in the field above Glenmachan, the Ewart family home, May 1916. From l. to r.: Mary Bradley (visitor at Glenmachan), Albert Lewis (father), Isabello Kelso ("Kelsie") Ewart (distant cousin), unidentified, and *Warren Lewis*.

Warren Lewis home on leave from France, seated on bench in grounds of the Ewart family home, Glenmachan, May 24, 1916.

Jack Lewis with Keble College cadet roommate, E. F. C. ("Paddy") Moore, in a punt in Oxford, 1917.

Captain Warren Lewis with fellow officers on the steps of the Officers' Mess, Villa Vista, Wepion, Belgium, May/June 1919. Warren Lewis is the officer on the right.

Thursday 13th April.

In whatever direction one explores, this county is uniformly lovely. Yesterday morning J and I set out north to Skermitt, the next village up the road, and then turned roughly east up a steep hill. . . . At the top of the hill is the village of Frieth, where was a pleasant little church, with a semicircular brass war memorial, clamped to a pillar by the lectern. They have a rather beautiful custom here that on Easter Sunday one gives a lily to decorate the altar, in memory of a dead friend. . . . While going through the village we saw a notice of a Passion Play to be performed on Good Friday in the church of Lane End, which we intend to go to: as J says, it will probably be very bad, but if one does not support such things on that account, there can be no possibility of a revival. . . . The rest of the day I spent in correcting the proof copy of *Pilgrims Regress*,[129] except for a short stroll with J after tea, and the usual visit to the pub. after supper. Supper by the way caused a certain amount of awkwardness last night: Minto and Maureen had gone shopping to London, and did not get back until 8 o'c. Supper, contrary to custom, was a hot meal, and our hostess, Mrs. King, kept it back, which I felt very hard on our two fellow boarders. . . . Our apologies on the whole went down fairly well. One doesn't so much mind M being late—it is her complete and obvious unconcern that one does mind. I'm afraid that along with her many good qualities, she has a good streak of selfishness in her make up. This morning was bright with a thin cold wind. After breakfast J and I and Mr. Papworth set out by the wood path running up the west side of our valley opposite the front gate. The wood was lovely with the morning sunlight dappling the stems of the big trees and putting life into the blossom. Of woods, particularly the woods on the top of the Holywood hills, J remarked that their beauty is only brought out when some effort is required to reach them: I agree with him. . . . We had a halt on the bare hill side above Turville, behind a hedge, with Fingest Church in the middle of the valley below us, and talked of childhood, more particularly of the time before we could read, and of our luck in being brought up in a house where there were plenty of good picture books to start us off on the right lines.

Good Friday 14th April.

Fine sunny morning after a frosty night. I woke up several times: no tea this morning, and a cold bath. In short, in spite of the beauty

---

129. *The Pilgrim's Regress: An Allegorical Apology for Christianity, Reason and Romanticism* by C. S. Lewis (London: J. M. Dent, 1933).

of this part of the world, I am beginning to wish very heartily that I was back at home. . . . But I must admit that any irritation which one feels indoors, is dissipated as soon as one gets out. This morning J and I took Maureen with us for our walk. Crossing the stream at the bottom of the farm yard, we walked up the side of the big grey chalky field which borders Hatchet Wood, and then made our way through the wood itself to the top of the hill: these woods are perhaps the best we have been in—fine straight gleaming stemmed trees, clear of undergrowth, floored with a rich soft carpet of dead leaves, violets and celandine, in which Mr. Papworth progresses like a ship, with a wash under his stern from his propellers. . . . Maureen made the sensible remark this morning that in summer with everything in full leaf, this country would be too rich to be comfortable. . . . We set off in the car after supper . . . we had some difficulty in finding the church: when we did, it was a plain little building pleasantly situated on a steep grassy slope, with organ music streaming out of it into the twilight, and a bustle of men and boys in cassocks about a heap of chairs in its yard. One of these sold us programmes and we went in. . . . The play was in five scenes, interspersed with hymns and the reading of the story of the Passion by the Vicar, all most reverentially carried out. I found it impressive and helpful: the acting was of course bad, but it was the badness of naivete—no ranting or anything of that kind: and they had avoided the pitfall of having a professional or a trained amateur in the anonymous caste "to help the show along". . . . Altogether I enjoyed my evening greatly.

Sunday 16th April.
Easter Sunday. . . . We had a Choral service, a thing which I don't remember ever to have met with at early Celebration before. . . . I cannot get to like the now almost universal practice of administering a prepared Wafer instead of the ordinary Bread: I can see its practical convenience, but there was a reality about the use of an actual daily food, which I do not find in this substance which could not conceivably have been used at the first Lords Supper, and I cannot help feeling that to emphasize the symbolic aspect is a mistake: I should almost prefer a movement in the opposite direction—something more like the actual *meal* of the Presbyterians. . . . J has a new idea for a religious work, based on the opinion of some of the Fathers, that while punishment for the damned is eternal, it is intermittent: he proposes to do

sort of an infernal day excursion to Paradise.[130] I shall be very interested to see how he handles it.

Friday 2nd June.

As soon as we got home from our Buckinghamshire jaunt, Maureen started to teach me the piano: I am making very slow headway, but I practise every day, and am getting a great deal of fun out of it: already I find I appreciate music more as a result of my study. The first volume of the Lewis papers arrived from the binders yesterday, and we both pronounce it a great success: I am delighted with it. Volume II is well under weigh, more than fifty pages of it being finished. Apropos of books, we are all eagerly awaiting the reviews of J's, which was published last week.[131] Since I wrote last, J and I have decided to go for a Clyde Shipping Co.'s cruise from Glasgow to London in the first week of August, combining it with a week end at Helensburgh.

Saturday 3rd June.

Another added to this long sequence of perfect days, and no signs of a change. From one of my bedroom windows I now look out on yellow roses, and from the other, on geraniums—a delightful beginning to the day. . . . I did a good morning's work in college on the family papers, getting very nearly to the end of my character sketch of P. J read through the four portraits last night and liked them, which pleases me much. We saw the first review of his book today, in the local paper—quite favourable, but of course the *Oxford Mail* ne vaut pas grand chose.

Saturday 17th June.

This evening we all, that is to say Minto, Maureen, her friend and fellow school marm Phyllis Wright, J and myself went to see the O.U.D.S. [Oxford University Dramatic Society] do *Midsummer Nights Dream* in Morrells park: my first Shakespeare play. It was produced by the great Max Reinhardt who was there in person and took a call at the end of the show. I went rather dubiously, but enjoyed it immensely, finding it, to my great surprise, amongst other things really funny. The open air setting was most effective—no attempt at scenery of any kind: the "stage" was a shallow bank with three or

---

130. This idea, which developed into *The Great Divorce* (London: Geoffrey Bles, 1945), was originally published in serial form in the *The Guardian* (November 1944-April 1945) under the title, "Who Goes Home? or The Grand Divorce."

131. *The Pilgrim's Regress,* see p. 101, diary entry for April 13, 1933.

four big trees on the top of the bank where it merged into a paddock. To hear over and between the actors speeches the soughing of the wind in these big trees as the dusk fell was delightful, and towards the end we had nightingales. . . . On the whole the faeries were better than the mortals I thought, although even the dim open air setting could not attenuate them enough to produce the shadow even of an illusion—with one exception: a slim, delightful, almost naked German girl called Nini Theilade did the first faery, and produced a low thin faery laugh which really carried conviction. J and I agreed on the way home that if faeries could laugh, that is just how they do it. All the women by the way were good looking. I thought the play very formless: what seemed artistically to be the finish, came about two thirds of the way through, after which followed a most amusing play within a play, which however had nothing to do with the main theme. But J tells me this is quite usual in Elizabethan plays. There was no control over the car park, and we had a difficult time getting out: Maureen drove very well and patiently under maddening conditions—forward six inches, and then stop close up against the car in front to prevent someone else jockeying you out of your place. Minto's selfishness is so colossal and so entirely naif that it can be very amusing or very irritating according to the mood one happens to be in: as soon as she realized that the two hundred or so other cars trying to get out were not going to give us a clear run through to the gate, she began railing in no uncertain tone at the "selfishness of people who thought of nothing but trying to push their way out without thinking about anyone else" . . . . I give Maureen full marks for saying nothing at all when the solid mass of slow moving traffic was pointed out to her with the gentle admonition "You'd have done better to have kept over there"! To bed tired after a very pleasant evening.

Tuesday 27th June.

J was looking tired and jaded. I wish he would give up all this examining, but I suppose he can't.

Sunday 2nd July.

On our way home from church J and I discussed the evidence, or rather the lack of evidence in support of the common assumption that Our Lord's family were extremely poor. On the contrary, remembering the structure of middle east society in general and the references to the Holy Family in particular, the village carpenter must have occupied a quite comfortable position. "Is not this the son of Joseph" etc. shows that Joseph was a well known person in his own neighborhood, and that they were able to travel argues at least a competence. I think the opposite view is held, largely from the dramatic instinct which makes one want the contrast to be as extreme as possible, and partly owing to the oversubtlety of reading "There was no room for THEM in the inn", instead of the quite ordinary travelling experience, "There was no room for them in the inn".

Monday 10th July.

This afternoon I bathed [in The Kilns' pond] in a very heavy shower, a thing which when seen from the level of the water, produces a very beautiful and unusual sight—difficult to describe, but rather like little diamonds jumping on a sheet of some opaque green material over which lies a belt of mist about two inches thick.

Tuesday 11th July.

While working on the family papers this morning, I came across a letter from Mammy to P which almost startled me. It was written in the summer of 1893 and contains this sentence: "Do you know it made me quite sad talking about your stained glass window. . . . I don't want there to be any stained glass window unless some one puts one up to both of us". I am perfectly certain I never read this letter in my life before, so it could not have suggested the window to me. It explains what I have often wondered at, and that is that P never put up a window to Mammy. Finding this letter has made me even gladder that we did this.

Sunday 23rd July.

Another hot morning. J and I went to early Celebration at eight o'c. . . . The Barfield's attended the 11 o'c. service; Alexander[132] greatly interested, and stood on the pew most of the time, commenting on the proceedings in no inaudible voice. . . . We all bathed in the afternoon, including J who has not done so for some days, as he has had a cold. In the afternoon he and Barfield read a book of [Wordworth's] *Excursion* while I continued my Temple.[133]

Wednesday 26th July.

In the evening J and I went in by car to Exeter [College] to dine, as the guests of Dyson and Tolkien jointly. Exeter is a delightful place, the chief feature being the garden—a quiet oblong of close shaven, walled and treed fringed grass, ending in a little paved court

132. Alexander Barfield, the adopted son of Owen and Maud Barfield.
133. A book of essays by Sir William Temple (1628-1699), essayist and statesman.

with a sunk pond where a small fountain plays on water lilies: this court is overlooked from a terrace or rampart which is approached by a flight of stone steps from the lawn. Duke Humphrey's library overlooks the garden on its non-Exeter side. Dyson and Tolkien were in most exuberant form, expecially the former. Anything less like the ordinary idea of a common room than that of Exeter, it would be hard to imagine: to begin with, there did not appear to be a man over forty in the room, and the noise was such as I have not heard at a meal since I last had a meal at the R.M.C. We were a party of nine, and dined, not in hall, but in the Common room, as is apparently the custom in all Colleges during the vac. I sat next to Tolkien. . . . I should like to have seen more of a man on the opposite side of the table, Coghill:[134] big, pleasant, good looking in a sort of musical comedy way, except for a vicious mouth. What I could overhear of his talk sounded good. We had an excellent dinner, just right for a really hot evening—cold soup, lobster salad, sweet-draft cider to drink. After dinner we went into another room where we were given sauterne instead of the usual after dinner wines—a very sensible idea—and then went out into the garden where we sat in deck chairs and had our coffee. Here I got into talk with the junior fellow, a man called Neill and the conversation fell on how to catalogue libraries. Apropos of libraries he told me that it would be quite a simple matter for me to become a reader of the Bodleian if I wanted to, and I spoke to J about it on the way home. He promises to look into the matter. After our coffee we went up on the terrace at the end of the garden, from where there is a most unusual view of Oxford: the terrace is perhaps fifteen feet above the square in which the Bodleian stands, and one thus gets on better terms with it than you are ever able to do from the road level: it looked wonderfully dignified, backed by St. Mary's and a pale yellow afterglow of sunset. After we had chatted there for some time the party broke up, Tolkien, Dyson, J, a little unobtrusive clergyman, and myself walking to Magdalen where we strolled in the grove, where the deer were flitting about in the twilight—Tolkien swept off his hat to them and remarked, "Hail fallow well met"—until ten o'c. T told a good story about one of the old guard, the head of a house, I think within his own lifetime, who,

---

134. Nevill Coghill (1899-   ), Fellow of Exeter College, Oxford until 1957, when he was elected Professor of English Literature. During his time at Oxford, he was the producer of numerous and widely acclaimed theatrical presentations. He was a close friend of Jack Lewis, and a member of the Inklings. See also, Humphrey Carpenter, *The Inklings;* and C. S. Lewis, *Surprised by Joy,* pp. 212-213.

greeting a newly elected fellow of his college, observed "now that we have elected you, Mr. _____, I hope you mean to come amongst us as a gentleman, and not take up with any of these new fangled ideas about TEACHING". Spooner being mentioned, J produced a very good one which was new to me—Locke's "Rape of the Pope". At ten o'c., judging that Benekhe would by then have vacated the common room, we adjourned there for drinks: there was a spirit case and syphons on a side table, all the decanters in the case being low, with the result that we had a most miscellaneous selection of drinks—some got whiskey, some brandy, and I myself gin. While we were drinking Dyson kept us in fits of laughter with an account of a visit he had recently paid—or states he has paid—to a bone setter. We broke up reluctantly at about twenty past ten after a thoroughly enjoyable evening, and so home by car. For the second evening running I skipped reading the lessons after I had gone to bed. I must not let myself degenerate into tropical slackness under the influence of this hot weather.

Friday 28th July.

J turned up in College this morning and carried me with him to the Bodleian, for which he had, to my great joy, got me a paper of application for membership. On arriving there I found that what I have always understood to be the Bodleian is really the Radcliffe Camera, a sort of annex: the Bodleian proper is on the corner of the Broad: you pass under an arch, cross a lovely little quad, go in at a door in the right hand corner of it, up an interminable series of flights of shallow stone steps, and there you are. As J said to me, "You will observe that the first essential for research work in Oxford is to be in thoroughly good physical training". Of the library itself I only got a vague impression of portraits, rows of reading desks, and exhibits in glass cases, before being introduced to a sort of malevolent, spectacled dwarf who was poring over a little brown leaved book of the shape of a cheque book, written in unintelligible characters. This was Gambier-Parry, the librarian on duty, whose main business, according to J, is to keep the place clear of undergraduates. He was civil, if not affable, asked me what I wanted to study, told me that I would be spending most of my time in the Camera (I won't), and sent me to sign the book. The page was headed with a declaration of things I would and would not do, and had to be signed by J and I jointly. The same ceremony had to be gone through in the Camera. I was warned by J to avoid attempting to sit in the part of the library called "Seldon end", as it is reserved for high dignitaries and readers of old standing.

I think this library is going to be a good deal of use to me: I tested it by getting J to turn me up the memoires of Marshal de Gramont,[135] a book of which I have never seen a copy, and with very little difficulty we found the appropriate catalogue and discovered that they had at least two, I think three copies of it. Actually getting the book you want is however, I understand, a lengthy process: this of course I didn't test, but came straight back to College and drank beer with J at the buttery. . . . This evening before going to sleep, I read more of the *Excursion:* I have always rated this higher than J has, but last week end he and Barfield read a couple of books of it together, and he has begun to think that there is more to it than he had remembered. But it must be admitted that it is in places, as bad as anything in English poetry.

On August 3, Warren and Jack left on their long-anticipated Clyde Shipping Company Tour cruise. They were first to travel by train to visit relatives in Scotland, and then to sail from Glasgow to London on the cruise.

Thursday 3rd August.

We had a comfortable dinner, during which we fell into talk about the modern tendency which may be summed up as the substitution of Scar Face Al Capone for Sir Galahad. I found that by an odd coincidence, J and I have had the same dream of how to utilize the enormous wealth—qualify as a solicitor and fight the battles of all the victims of capitalist tyranny, to the house of Lords, if necessary. We had an interesting chat on this theme.

Saturday 5th August.

As we neared Helensburgh I became very nervous: I wished myself almost anywhere else, and thought what an ass I was to reopen a relationship which had been very comfortably dormant for more than twenty years. None of this feeling was lessened by getting a glimpse of Helensburgh station of a sort of obscene caricature of what I remembered of Uncle Bill.[136] He has become enormously fat, and is now quite definitely an old man: I may as well go on to describe him here, tho' of course this is the result of forty eight hours observation.

---

135. Gramont, Mémoires du Maréchal de Gramont, 2 vols. (Paris: Petitot, 1826-1827).

136. William Lewis (1859-1946), the brother of Albert Lewis, moved (with another brother, Richard) to Scotland in 1883 to set up a business partnership. Though the business was centered in Glasgow, both brothers located their homes in Helensburgh, on the Clyde River, fifteen miles from Glasgow.

His resemblance to grandfather, as I remember him is startling: if he wore a white beard, short and sprouting from the corners of the lips, it would be the man—the same heavy lidded, pouchy eyes, the same size and sweep of forehead: but grandfathers is a better and less sensual face. He has become too, very like grandfather in his speech—not in the thing said, but in the manner of saying it—the slow, halting delivery, with half mumbled corrections, helped out with vague gestures, as if the modelling of a sentence had in it something analogous to the modelling of a piece of clay. Superimposed on the resemblance to grandpudaita is a perhaps even stronger echo of the pudaita. Here the likeness is of speech, both in manner and matter—sometimes uncannily so: his stories (tho' duller and much less well told) are helped out by exactly the gestures which P would have used in telling the same tale. . . . But if there are resemblances, there are also marked differences which are all in favour of P. . . . He remains, just as I remembered him, a thorough going snob. . . . [Aunt Minnie's][137] one contribution to family history was involuntary but very illuminating—she persistently addressed J as "Allie".[138] [There is] an unexpected and pleasant trait in Uncle Bills character which I had forgotten: he became a vegetarian for about a year because "he could not bear to see the dumb, patient brutes driven to the slaughter" and only gave the habit up, because he was a nuisance in the house. He has also a kindness for birds. . . . Uncle Dick[139] is an old man too, but an old man of a very different type. . . . He still has all his ancient fondness for a story, whether his own or anothers: I was lucky enough to please him with a couple of "wheezes", and he appeared to enjoy some fooling between J and myself as thoroughly as he would have done in his best days. I was far more sure of my welcome from him than in that I got from Uncle Bill. Uncle Dick is most obviously and unaffectedly pleased to see us again. Eileen says she can notice him failing, but the only real signs of age I saw in him were the slowness of his walk and the trembling of his fingers when he lights a cigarette. His laugh is as ready and genuine as it ever was. . . . I was a little surprised and very much pleased to find how that I was instantly at home in his company. Aunt Agnes I recognized as soon as

---

137. Wilhelmina ("Minnie") Lewis, wife of William Lewis; Uncle Bill and Aunt Minnie had three children—Norman, Claire, and William.

138. Family nickname for Albert Lewis, Jack and Warren's father.

139. Richard ("Dick") Lewis (1861-?), brother of William and Albert, who with his wife, Agnes, lived near to the William Lewises; they had two children—Eileen and Leonard.

she came into the room though she has grown very stout and walks with a stick: facially she hardly seems to have altered at all, and it was delightful to hear her soft Scotch accent, just as I remember it from my earliest days. I find that in her quiet way she has a great deal more genuine humour, as opposed to jocularity, than has Uncle Dick. To sum her up in J's words, "She's a dear". Eileen I could remember nothing of except that I had liked her when she was a flapper. She wears very well, for she must now be over forty, and is I think rather good looking. But this is all rather unimportant beside the fact that she is a remarkably nice girl, and an intelligent girl. We both took to her at once, and I think she liked us. She talks like an educated woman, and sees the family as it is: she understands the dangers of being a Lewis. Poor girl, I don't think she is too satisfied with life: she has had an art training, has taught in various schools, and now at forty has relapsed into housekeeping for her parents in the house in which she was born.

Sunday 6th August.

[Uncle Bill spoke of] Grandfather Hamilton . . . with the greatest respect and said he was "a fine old gentleman". He told me the following good story of him. Some little Belfast snob had seen him dozens of times without bothering to speak to him, although he knew perfectly well who he was: at length the snob found out that Grandfather was connected with the Ormond family—so when he next saw grandfather he greeted him effusively—"Oh, Mr. Hamilton, I hear you are connected with the Ormond people". "Dear me" replied Grandfather gravely, "I hope they haven't been boasting about it".

On August 7, Warren and Jack took a train from Helensburgh to Glasgow, where they boarded their ship, the Eddystone, *for the Clyde Shipping Company cruise. The first day's journey took the* Eddystone *down the Clyde River and across the Irish Sea to the port of Belfast, Northern Ireland.*

Tuesday 8th August.

We got to Belfast very early, about five I imagine, which woke me up, and I only dozed until half past six when I rang for some tea and got up. It was a pale grey sunny morning with eerie appearance of a hot day. . . . As soon as we had finished an excellent breakfast, we set out: it was odd, pleasant, and slightly painful to find oneself again on the dusty squaresets of Belfast. . . . J talked of what he would do if he were offered a job in Belfast. We discussed the pros. and cons. for some time. On the whole, I would be in favour of it if our joint incomes were sufficient to maintain The Kilns as a holiday retreat. To cross over to England at the end of every term would be a whimsical inversion of the time honored procedure. . . . I can now look at Leeborough quite unemotionally—or nearly so, perhaps. It is strangely unaltered from the road: a few trees have been planted on the front lawn, and the shrubs outside the study windows have been grubbed up: a sort of fringe curtain hangs along the upper part of the window of the little end room. Otherwise I noticed no change. . . . The walk from Little Lea to the Low Holywood Rd. is just as it was in 1905. I was very pleased to find that we were able to get into St. Marks by our own old door without the nuisance and waste of time entailed by a call at the Rectory for the keys. . . . our own window [in honor of Mammy and P] is the chef d'oeuvre of the church. I was delighted with its masses of rich colour and the suggestion of a Morris town at this base. J had warned me that I would find the lettering poor, but I did not think so: I liked it. I am profoundly pleased that we spent that money on what I think is a real addition to the stock of first class modern stained glass.

The Eddystone *sailed from Belfast early Tuesday afternoon, August 8, and docked at Waterford, Waterford County, Republic of Ireland, early Wednesday morning.*

Wednesday 9th August.
Having found out that our ship was sailing at 4 p.m., J and I set out in macs. to explore the countryside. We did about five miles, and I may say at once it was one of the hottest and most uncomfortable walks I have ever had. But not only physically uncomfortable. There is something wrong with this country—some sullen brooding presence over it, a vague sense of something mean and cruel and sinister: I have felt the same feeling in the hills behind Sierra Leone, and once in 1919 at Doagh in Co. Antrim. A beastly feeling. On the merely physical side, it was most depressing country. I have never seen any place so enclosed before: wherever you go, the grey road is flanked by old stone walls, and banks on the top of which grow thick hedges, the whole over hung by heavy motionless foliage on old trees and lidded with a grey brown sky. After a time the longing for any sort of escape from these everlasting tunnels became acute, and one almost fancied it to be accompanied by a sensation of choking from trying to breathe air from which the oxygen was exhausted. The natives were as depressing as their landscape: during the whole morning I did not see

anyone of any age or either sex who was not definitely ugly: even the children look more like goblins than earthborns. . . . I wonder can it be possible that a country which has an eight hundred year record of cruelty and misery has the power of emanating a nervous disquiet? Certainly I felt something of the sort, and would much dislike to see this place again. . . . [Later in the day, after leaving Waterford on our run down the Suir River, we passed Ballyhack, where there were some early Norman castles.] There was [also] a long succession of big houses, all very shut in and desolate, of which J remarked that Walter de la Mare[140] could write detestable stories: and we talked for some time about horror and its treatment in fiction.

After leaving the Republic of Ireland, the Eddystone *sailed around the southwest tip of England ("Land's End") and docked at Plymouth, Devon, off the English Channel, at noon on Thursday, August 10.*

Thursday 10th August.

[During dinner] J and I argued briskly about the country [around Plymouth that] we had walked through, J contending that not to like *any* sort of country argues a fault in oneself: which seems to me absurd. He also said that my description of what we had seen—"lacking in distinction", was "almost blasphemous". But I suspect that he was talking for victory.

Friday 11th August.

Slept profoundly. . . . When I got on deck it was a dull rainy morning. When J came on deck we discussed plans for the day, and ultimately decided to go by the 10.12 from Millbay to Liskeard in Cornwall. . . . Cornwall, though full of high hedged lanes, is a much pleasanter country than Devon. . . . There were some very pretty, heavily wooded gorges. As we went on, the day became darker and darker until it was the dim half light of the entrance to the under world, and the detail of the bottoms of the gorges were lost in vague hints of tree tops—very eerie and most impressive. . . . It was the sort of country in which one would hardly have been surprised to see Fafnir[141] on the sky line: "Fafnir banked down" amended J, and added a minute later "there he is", pointing to where a thin spurt of steam from a sunken lane showed very white in the gloom: and such was the

---

140. Walter de la Mare (1873-1956), poet and novelist.
141. Fafnir, a dragon in Norse mythology who guards a hoard of gold. (Later adapted into the character of Fafner, in Richard Wagner's opera cycle, *Der Ring Des Nibelungen* (1845).)

abnormality of the landscape that one could easily play with the idea of a dragon shuffling down the lane. Liskeard is a nice little town with steep ups and downs and narrow streets which, under modern conditions are not too safe. . . . They have odd names in these parts: I can remember "Globb", "Gubb", "Ouch" as examples. I was also tickled by one gentleman who is the manufacturer of the famous "Pudlo". What a magnificent name it would make for a firm of solicitors! "Globb, Gubb, Ouch, Globb, and Pudlo". [After having a drink at the pub] it was again raining heavily and thundering, so we dropped the idea of a walk and went to look at the parish church instead, and found it well worth the seeing. . . . In the porch was a record of a man who had left to certain categories in the parish "a penny loaf a day, for ever", and this sent us back to our inn for lunch discussing how far we are justified in misappropriating the money which is bequeathed in these sorts of ways. J thought that a man cannot attempt to dictate to posterity, even in money matters, but I am not so sure.

The Eddystone *sailed from Plymouth late Friday evening, and docked the following morning at Southhampton.*

Saturday 12th August.
[Once we arrived at Southampton, J and I set out to explore the town and do some shopping errands. When we had accomplished our tasks, we found that] it was now a pretty hot morning and we were glad to put into a very pleasant pub. called "The Dolphin" where we drank a pint of beer, and, apropos of de Sales, got on the subject of when Xtianity first became an aristocratic creed: J told me, which was new to me, that Judaism was fashionable amongst the women of the upper classes in Rome.

Sunday 13th August.
J and I left the ship shortly before half past nine to catch the 9.52 to Winchester from Southampton West. . . . Winchester as first seen from the environs of the railway station, is an enclosed, low lying town where Dissent flourishes, but this impression is soon altered. The Cathedral is one of the best I have seen: perhaps externally it is not as fine as Salisbury, but the interior is far better. . . . After service we went to a pub. outside the Close and drank a pint of bad beer while the Cathedral emptied, and discussed the sermon. . . . Winchester on the south side of the Cathedral is one of the most tranquil and lovely towns I have ever visited, and oh! the relief of such a place after

the "holiday" places we have been visiting! A week in Winchester would be a real holiday. J thinks that as civilization destroys more and more of the country, people will turn to the blind streets of cathedral towns for that which the country used to give. Perhaps he's right. Certainly one would be hard put to it to find anything in the country now as restful as the streets about Winchester Cathedral.

Monday 14th August.

[The next morning on board ship,] it suddenly occurred to me that it would be a good idea to revisit Romsey Abbey [just north of Southampton], which J had never seen. He agreed. . . . Of Romsey Abbey it is difficult to write, for its beauty is entirely satisfying. It is predominantly Norman, and the arrangement of the windows gives it externally some resemblance to Winchester. . . . It dates from 907, but the original building was destroyed by the Danes, and the present one is early Norman and Gothic. . . . Whatever the outside may be, the interior is perfection. We sat at the West end for perhaps half an hour and enjoyed the cool clean sweep of the nave and choir, which runs, unbroken by screen or projecting choir stalls, right up to the High Altar. . . . A great peace descended on me here. . . . The vicar of this church must be a good and zealous man, and also a man of real taste. The whole church had that unmistakeable feeling of "aliveness" which used to be so noticeably absent from St. Marks in the old days. . . . There was a very good selection of tracts etc. at the door, and of these we chose three, but not having sufficient change to pay for them, we went to a pub. just outside the precincts and had a pint of good beer, of the local brew I presume, and then went back to the Abbey. By this time the sun had come out strongly, and it was more beautiful than ever with great dusty drafts of light slanting down into the nave from the clerestory windows, so we had to sit down and have another look at it. . . . I should like to have stopped longer in this completely satisfying place, but we had to go off and see about some lunch. . . . Spent the afternoon [back on board ship] sitting on the after deck where I finished Chesterton's *Man Who Was Tuesday*,[142] a book which is in a class by itself, being what J describes as a "theological shocker".

On Tuesday morning, August 15, the Eddystone *docked just below Tower Bridge, London. From there, Warren and Jack taxied to Padding-*

---

142. Correctly titled *The Man Who Was Thursday* (1908), by Gilbert Keith Chesterton, essayist, novelist, and poet.

ton Station, where they took the afternoon train home to Oxford and the completion of their holiday.

Monday 21st August.

Maureen drove me in as far as Headington P.C. this morning, and while I was waiting there for a bus, a pleasant thing happened to me: a nice little girl about six or seven came up to me and said, "Please would you *send* me across the London road?" So I duly escorted her to the other pavement. I never heard this expression before.

Wednesday 23rd August.

Mintos brother Willie, Dean of Kilmore in Co. Cavan came to stop with us today, Maureen meeting him in the Singer at Reading at 9 a.m. J spent the morning in the college library, carrying me to the buttery at midday for beer. . . . I made my first acquaintance with the Dean at bathing time—a big, clean shaven, grey haired, rather good looking man, who talks incessantly in a strong Irish accent. . . . The Dean is a true Askins (or a true Irishman?) in his lack of manners: as an interrupter, he far outclasses Minto. In fact it must have been a quarter of a century since I had the same sort of meal as we had this evening—every attempt at general conversation was shouted down by the Dean and Minto, without the pretence of an apology or an open-ing: ultimately "the children" viz. J, Maureen and I carried on a sub-motif of talk, while M and her brother battled for the monologue: as far as I could see, the Dean won. M, J, and I went for a stroll down the lane after supper. There was a most lovely smooth russet and green sunset, very suggestive of about four o'clock on a frosty win-ter's evening. . . . I quite suddenly got very bored with M's conversa-tion tonight. She has lately developed a tiresome habit of becoming a mere compendium of Paxfords views: every conceivable topic is met with a reply beginning "Paxford[143] says. . .". I am resigned to being adressed by my new name of "Pax-Warnie", but if she is to become a mere conduit of the Paxford philosophy, it will be a very great bore. Further, it makes me angry with myself to find that the perfectly natural, and utterly unfair result is that I begin to dislike Paxford, no exercise of will convincing me that it is not the unfortunate P who is boring me with his views on everything under the sun.

---

143. Fred W. Paxford (1899-   ), gardener and general handyman, who served faithfully at The Kilns from shortly after its purchase until his retirement after Jack Lewis's death. See also, *C. S. Lewis: A Biography,* Roger Lancelyn Green and Walter Hooper, editors (New York: Harcourt Brace Jovanovich, 1974), pp. 122-123.

Friday 1st September.

[A]fter breakfast [J and I] bussed into College, where J had very decently offered to accompany me in order to do the honours to Parkins brother who had expressed a desire to see Magdalen. . . . I was very glad to get the chance of going round myself. . . . In the old library there is a good deal of theology: Father Parkin was ill advised enough to attempt a Latin unseen from one of the Fathers, and J told me afterwards that it was evident that he knew no Latin. This surprised me, but Onions,[144] whom we met at lunch, said that it was a mistake to imagine that the ordinary priest was a well educated man. . . . I think on the whole Parkin enjoyed his visit, though with a man of that stamp it is not easy to tell. He certainly brightened up considerably at hearing the suggestion of a pint of beer in the buttery, and became quite communicative whilst drinking it. He and his brother had been last night to see *King Kong* and he gave such an account of it that J and I decided that we would go to the 2 o'c. performance. We first had some excellent cold beef in the common room (Onions and Denham Young in) and then went on by bus. This is as good a film as I have ever seen. Behind a huge wall on a tropical island, built by no one knows whom, but kept in repair by a native tribe living on its hitherward side, lives *something*. The inevitable white girl is kidnapped and sacrificed to the something—which proves to be a gigantic ape perhaps thirty feet high. There were some astounding representations of the various prehistoric monsters which also lived on the island. How they were done I cannot imagine. . . . I enjoyed my afternoon much, though as usual it left me with that stale debauched feeling which is inseparable apparently from a visit to the cinema.

Wednesday 6th September.

As I was working this afternoon, J rang up to say that he was going in to have a bathe at Parson's Pleasure. Would I join him? Of course I said yes. The water seemed very clean after that of the pond, and I had forgotten the wonderful feeling of freedom which one gets when bathing without bathing things. I can't remember when I last bathed at P.P., but certainly not since before we left Hillsboro.

Warren, Jack, Maureen, and Mrs. Moore vacationed for one week at Milford on Sea, Hampshire, about 10 miles east of Bournemouth.

---

144. Charles Talbut Onions (1873-1965) began his work on the staff of the *Oxford English Dictionary* in 1919. A distinguished linguist and a Fellow of Magdalen College, he became a close friend and associate of Jack Lewis.

Sunday 10th September.

Up at week day time, and before I had my bath accomplished the difficult feat of packing what I will need for a week at Milford in a week end suit case. . . . Todays experiences leave me with no doubt about the truth of the stories Minto is so fond of telling about the agonizing discomfort of almost every journey she has ever undertaken. Given a serviceable car, a ninety mile run, a fine day, and half the day in front of one, I would not have imagined it possible to make any journey so uncomfortable as ours was. The car was of course overloaded, and Minto made it worse by bringing lunch with us on the ground that there was no place en route at which one could get that meal. Most of the way she disparaged the car, and every five miles or so we were told that Tykes was saying how much worse it was than the old car. Maureen, who was having a very nasty job in holding the car in a strong cross wind was assisted with that maddening form of Pudaita advice which is (a) absurd, or (b) comes a few moments after you have taken the action indicated. . . . At 3.30 Minto decided that we would stop for tea at four: at ten to four it was decided that we would stop where we were at the moment (the main road through a forest) and substitute for tea, thermos coffee. I was hot and thirsty, and of course the thick sweet Kilns coffee, tho' admirable after dinner, is useless in such cases: however, the atmosphere being rather electrical, I judged it prudent to drink half a cup of it. Ultimately, we arrived at the Hotel Victoria about five, I feeling that I wanted only two things, firstly, a large whisky with not too much soda, and secondly a taxi to the nearest railway station. I was however somewhat cheered by seeing the bedroom which J and I are sharing which has two windows looking out over the sea. . . . At about half past five we bathed. . . . It was glorious to find oneself in salt water again, and I not only did off the journey physically but emerged with all my irritation washed away. (But mem. next time we go for a holiday en famille, to remember to have some excuse ready which will make it essential for me to travel independently either before or after the main body.)

Tuesday 12th September.

I dreamt that I was in some sort of railway station, apparently the approach to a big industrial terminus, standing on the track, and train after train rumbled out, each slipping badly on a greasy track. I woke up in the first light of dawn to find that the slipping train was J snoring. . . . After breakfast I read *Precious Bane*[145] for an hour, a book of which I think better and better the further I go with it. Later on Minto and Maureen drove into the village to do some shopping and J and I took Mr. Papworth for a walk along the cliff, eastward in the direction of Hurst Point. Mr. P is getting too venturesome by half down here, and has developed a habit of walking on the extreme edge of the cliff: once this morning my heart was in my mouth, for he actually had one paw over the abyss. He also runs out on groins in the most nonchalant way. . . . At lunch time Minto suddenly announced that we would go to Beaulieu Abbey this afternoon, so I went up and changed into something warmer, got out the map and we set off. Unfortunately I was too busy map reading to see much of the country—but from the glimpses I got, it appeared beautiful—rich parkland and fine sober old houses, with some lovely timber. . . . Beaulieu Abbey is one of the very best places of the sort I have ever had the good fortune to see. The first glimpse of an old grey outbuilding, seen at the end of a narrow paved and walled court through a small Norman arch is one of those things which lingers long in the memory. One of those perfect moments like the first view of Minikoi, or the Great Buddha of Kamakura, or the headlands of Antrim seen from Island Magee. . . . I got here a clearer idea than any reading has given me, of what it must have meant to have been an Abbot in the palmy days of monasticism, and tho' I cursed the memory of Henry VIII, I also got an idea of the utter incompatibility of monasticism and despotism. . . . Minto was much more affected by it than I should have thought she would have been, and before we had finished our tour had worked herself up into quite a passion about the iniquities of Henry VIII. . . . In the field beyond the abbey is the ruin of what was I expect one of their tithe barns. I enjoyed my visit to Beaulieu greatly. . . . We got back to the hotel in time for tea. After tea J and I sat at the rickety table in our room, I at one end writing my diary and J at the other writing to Arthur Greeves, until half past six when I went out for a bathe with Maureen. . . . When I had changed, J and I had a whiskey and soda together in the porch and talked about Voltaire and Masefield and Mary Webb until dinner time.

Wednesday 13th September.

After breakfast I sat in the lounge and finished *Precious Bane*. A melancholy book in spite of its happy ending, but absolutely first rate work. Scenery and the atmosphere of landscape is better handled in it

---

145. *Precious Bane* (1924), by novelist Mary Webb.

than in any thing I have read for a long time. . . . at quarter to twelve J and I and Tykes went out for a walk, or rather a long stroll. One thing I notice here is that there cannot be any children in this country, for on the public roads the hedges are loaded with ripe blackberries—very different to home, where the only ripe blackberries I have seen have been in our own garden. [At] the village of Burley . . . we saw our first piece of real forest, stately and solemn: it reminded me of what I have not thought of for many years, the foret d'Argues near Dieppe, and oddly enough, when we stopped later on, J said that he was reminded of the same thing. . . . [We also visited] Upper Canterton Wood, one of the most impressive places it is possible to imagine. It is not very big, but the huge still beeches of which it is composed are so wide spaced and the place is so quiet that one loses the sense of its smallness. It is floored with yielding green moss, with few leaves lying about, and most of the trees tower up thirty feet or so without branching. It was a solemn place. Tykes, who is very sensitive to atmosphere, felt it immediately, and sat down. It is one of those places to see alone: I should like to stroll there for half an hour by myself on a summer morning.

Thursday 14th September.

[A]fter breakfast . . . J and I took Mr. Papworth for a stroll: the sea air or something is debauching his character rapidly. Today he broke away from us and ran back to the hotel in search of Minto, and he is becoming chronically slow at coming to heel. . . . After lunch we all went off in the car via Lyndhurst to Southampton. This is a lovely time of the year for driving: the colour of the woods is actually changing from day to day. . . . It's surprising how the forest ponies stray all over the place, including the main roads. In Lyndhurst itself we were amused to see two, apparently reading the notices on a churchyard gate. [At Southampton] Maureen was quite excited at the distant prospect of Southampton docks. Minto had some shopping to do, so we dropped her and J in Bargate St. and arranged to meet them at the "Dolphin" at half past four, and then drove down past the South Western hotel to the Docks Entrance. . . . Maureen was apparently genuinely interested in everything she saw, and asked most surprisingly intelligent questions. I enjoyed my trip amazingly, which was just as well, as it was the last enjoyment I was to have for some considerable time. We got to the Hotel first and Minto bustled in a few minutes later saying "Where's Jack? Where's Jack?" We said we didn't know, and she went off to wash—Maureen observing resignedly "I knew this would happen if Jack was fool enough to let her out of his sight". A few minutes later the tea appeared, followed by Minto who stood in the middle of the lounge saying, in a voice that drew everyones attention to us "Oh, where IS Jack? I know somethings happened to him! Where is he?" I then offered to go and look for him, and M insisted on accompanying me: of course it turned out that J had last been seen at the extreme opposite end of Bargate Street—so off we set, Minto pushing people right and left, and repeating time after time like some infernal repetition gramophone, the details of her last conversation with him—pausing only to assure me after about every fourth repetition that everything had been so concise and clearly understood, that the only possible explanation of his absence from the hotel was that he had met with a serious accident. She has the most diabolical power of generating and communicating panic of any person I have ever met, and long before I had got to the end of Bargate St. I was feeling quite sick with fright. Fright faded into relief and relief into anger when at long last I saw J standing on the edge of the pavement gazing vacantly across the street. He proved to be much angrier than I was, but quickly cooled down. . . . The resulting post mortem revealed what should of course have been obvious from the start, and would have been in ten minutes if J had shown any common sense, viz. that Minto had made a balls of the arrangements for remeeting J after they separated. As Maureen observed with satisfaction "I knew Mintins didn't know what she had said to Jack, because she got so muddled in trying to tell me". When Maureen left the room Minto observed pathetically that the result of this would be that Maureen would never let her out of her sight again when they went shopping together. If she hoped to get any sympathy from me she was disappointed, for I was still very angry with her for the abominable fright she had given me, so I told her that that was precisely what Maureen had already told me twice. . . . Poor Minto, who has been rather piano since the afternoons mares nest, was very depressed and depressing at dinner this evening on the subject of old age. And certainly old age must be a terrible thing to an atheist. Bad enough for the atheist of intellect and noble character, but there must be times when for a selfish and stupid old woman it must be sheer hell. And the pity of it is that there is nothing at all that one can do for her except pray that even yet she may somehow find out the truth.

Friday 15th September.

[A]t lunch time today I hit on an idea for a character for his Oxford satire which pleased J—the Tupper Professor of Proverbial Philosophy. . . . [On our afternoon walk, near the village of Hordle our] lane soon changed into a delightful foot path between high brambly hedges: as J very aptly remarked, it looked just like the sort of country one gets in the illustrations to the Beatrix Potter[146] books. . . . Over our nightcaps J and I had some very interesting conversation about how and when the upper classes first developed the taste for privacy. To bed shortly after eleven.

Saturday 16th September.

As soon as lunch was over, we set out for Lymington, to visit the Isle of Wight which Minto was very keen to see. . . . [Enroute,] I saw my first British Fascist. He looked so like one of the more cowardly sort of criminal that I suppose he must have been an honest man, in spite of his mean and untrustworthy appearance. He was dressed in a black flannel shirt and tie with a golden coloured pin representing the fasces and the axe, and a very dirty pair of light grey "Oxford bags" without a turn up, and was bare headed. If there are many like him, I would as soon trust myself to the Communists. . . . The twenty minutes cross [on the ferry] pleased all of us except Mr. Papworth who seemed to entertain dark suspicions that the whole thing was a complicated prelude to a compulsory bathe. [Upon our return from the Isle,] Maureen and I went down to the beach and had the very best bathe we have had since we came here, the inflowing tide having worked up quite a sea. I fear it will be my last bathe this year. The last little touch of satisfaction to a perfect day was added by my finishing *Guy Mannering*[147] just as the dinner gong sounded. How rarely does it fit in like that with a holiday book! After dinner I wrote till quarter past ten and then joined J in the billiard room for a nightcap. . . .

The kafuffle of the trip to Milford on the Sea convinced Warren of the advisibility of returning home to Oxford on his own by train; the other members of the household traveled to Oxford by car.

Sunday 17th September.

The others got home about a quarter of an hour before I did. They had stopped for tea at Winchester where Minto was both surprised and annoyed to find her sons name wrongly inscribed in the Rifle Brigade Roll of Honour in the Cathedral. . . . It is nice to be home again, even after one of the most enjoyable holidays I have ever had, excepting of course those which I have taken with J.

---

146. Beatrix Potter (1866-1943), author and illustrator of children's books.
147. *Guy Mannering* (1815), a novel by Sir Walter Scott.

Friday 20th October.

Earlier in the day Minto and Maureen had gone into Oxford and brought out two wireless sets on approval: Paxford was messing about with them when we went in to dinner, and asked me which I liked best: I decided at once. "Ah, but this one" said Paxford reproachfully, pointing to the one I liked least, "has a moving coil injector" (or some such remark), and to my further criticisms he merely continued to mumble "moving coil injector". Both sets were on the dining room table when we got home, and we tried them again: Maureen agreed with me, but Minto was of course firm for the other. I was especially tickled at the subsequent conversation, having in view the fact that the choice of a set had been deferred until today in order to have the benefit of Maureens advice: it went something like this:

Maureen: "Well, the A set certainly has the better tone". Minto: "Oh, no dear, Paxford says the B set has a lovely tone: he says the A set is tinny". Maureen: "Well, it blurs the sound: you can't hear the 'underneath of any of the music' ". Minto: "Paxford and I were saying it was so clear". Maureen: "Then its easier to find stations on the A set". Minto: "Paxford says the B set is easier: Paxford says he got 40 stations on it: he made it work beautifully". Maureen (trying the B set, which emits a series of syren like whoops and then a muffled jazz band). "It doesn't seem particularly easy to get ANY station on the B". Minto: "Ask Paxford dear: he'll show you how to work it in the morning". Myself (internally) "Bugger Paxford" (aloud) "Well, goodnight. I'm off to bed". Minto: "Goodnight PaxWarnie". "Paxford says ——" (I close the door and go to bed). Moral: If you want to get anyone disliked, see that you include his name in every sentence you frame.

Wednesday 1st November.

I wonder is it possible to adduce any evidence of the immortality of the soul from the satisfaction with which one regards the ending of a month and the beginning of another? Or is it merely the subconscious asserting "man never is, but always to be blessed"? In my army days there were good reasons for looking forward to the first of the month—it was pay day for one thing, and for another it brought me nearer to my next leave. But now it means nothing to me financially, and though I certainly prefer the vac. to the term, this hardly seems to account for it. Perhaps it's mere force of habit.

Tuesday 7th November.

FK[148] came to tea this afternoon and left a book for us—*A Wanderer's Way* by one Charles Raen, Canon of Liverpool. I read it between supper and bed time and enjoyed it greatly. It is a spiritual autobiography, beginning with his introduction to formal religion as a child, its withering at a Public School—this part very well done—his relapse into agnosticism and the beginnings of his formulation of a creed at Cambridge, and the final triumph of faith. A stimulating book, tho' alien to my way of thinking in many places. He has one difficulty which I gather from books is fairly common but which I have at all times been unable to understand. I will give it in his own words: he is speaking of a religious society at Cambridge, and talking at a time when he has ceased to be an agnostic: "It seemed incredible that anyone with sufficient education to pass the Little-go should still believe in the talking serpent, or Jonah's whale, or Balaam's ass, or Joshua's sun" . . . p. 49. Whether from an atheist or Christian point of view I can see nothing "incredible" about it: as an atheist I should have said, "Granting your premise that there is a Something Who can perform miracles, i.e. arrest or alter the whole natural order of things, these stories are just as credible as any others in the Bible". As a Christian, the mentality of the Believer who picks and chooses the miracles in which he will believe is to me at any rate baffling. If you believe that sundry dead people were brought to life in the same flesh which they were going to be buried in, why should not Balaam's ass have spoken, or the sun stood still for Joshua? . . . This is not to say that I am convinced of the literal truth of these stories myself: I have never succeeded in making up my mind whether (a) Such things actually happened in the words stated, or (b) whether God produced a conviction in the persons concerned that they had happened or (c) it was the most adequate language the people concerned could find to describe an overwhelming pressure exerted upon them to follow a certain course of action. But if (a) is the correct interpretation, I find no difficulty in believing it.

Wednesday 15th November.

The calm midday routine of The Kilns was interrupted today by an invasion of the local hunt. The first sign of them was a hound or two crossing the field to the north of our avenue, and a cavalcade coming down from the head of the lane as we drove up it from Ox-

---

148. Reverend Edward Foord-Kelcey (1859-1934), a retired priest, and neighbor and friend of Jack and Warren.

ford. Then while we were at lunch the bulk of the pack crossed the Low Countries, followed a little later by some stragglers who ran mute right up to the Hall door. So far the proceedings had been mildly interesting, but Act III was much less amusing, and took the form of a mob of people on the edge of the cliff: this seemed altogether too much of a good thing, so J and I went out to see what was to be done. By the time I got up there the bulk of the people had disappeared into the lower wood, and more and more were streaming down the path from the top and brushing past us—not insolently, or furtively, or defiantly but with an insouciance which I found maddening and which roused all the Forsyte in me. I asked one of these gentry sternly how he had got there: he told me, quite politely, and continued on his way. As there was obviously nothing to be done with the foot people, we plunged into the lower wood and shouldering our way through the crowd, came upon a young man in pink and a cap, smoking a cigarette, who was just about to give directions for the digging of some unfortunate animal from the bank near Las Pelotas. I must admit he was profuse in his apologies when J spoke to him (he claimed to be the Master), hoped J bore him no malice, insisted on shaking hands with him etc., and called hounds off at once. . . . By the way, I wonder what we would have done if this fellow had behaved differently. Supposing instead of apologizing and going, he had said "Get to hell out of this" and had proceeded to dig? This is the sort of problem I am ill fitted to deal with. The afternoon quiet of the garden was even more delicious than usual after all this kafuffle.

Friday 17th November.

A varied and interesting day. At about half past eleven when I was at work in the front room in College, in burst Dyson in his most exuberant mood—more "boisterously at ease in Zion" to quote Tweedlepippin,[149] than I had ever seen him. I was glad he didn't come earlier, because I got the maps of our next stage of the Wye valley walk today and during the 11 o'c. break was able to look at them with J and have ten minutes of that best of all kinds of chat which consists in making the preliminary arrangements for a jaunt together. These maps name the source of the Wye, which is so much farther to the East than I thought that we think it will be possible to accomplish the final stage of the walk this year instead of making two more bites of it. . . . It all looks most exciting on the map. But to return to Dyson: He began by saying that it was such a cold morning that he would

---

149. Jack Lewis's invented name for one of his University fellows.

have to adjourn almost immediately to get some brandy. I pointed out that if he was prepared to accept whiskey as an alternative, it was available in the room. Having sniffed it he observed "it would indeed be unpardonable rudeness to your brother to leave any of this" and emptied the remains of the decanter into the glass. After talking very loudly and amusingly for some quarter of an hour, he remarked airily "I suppose we can't be heard in the next room?" then having listened for a moment "oh, it's all right, it's the pupil talking—your brother won't want to listen to him anyway". . . . He next persuaded me to walk round to Blackwell's with him, and here he was the centre of attraction to a crowd of undergraduates. Walking up to the counter he said: "I want a second hand so and so's Shakespeare, have you got one?" The assistant: "Not a *second hand* one sir, I'm afraid". Dyson (impatiently) "Well, take a copy and rub it on the floor, and sell it to me as shop soiled: I have no objection, have you?" This ingenious suggestion not being agreed to, he turned his attention to a large table on which were arranged some fifteen or twenty leather bound volumes. Dyson: "What's all this?" A. "Exhibition of old bindings sir". D (taking up a XVI Cent. quarto—with intense satisfaction). "Good! Good! I see you've remembered to punch all the little holes in the cover: now what I always say—(picks up another, a Milton at £20: to me) "why *just* the thing you're looking for: put it in your pocket my boy, put it in your pocket". He was next attracted by a gorgeously got up octavo—an eighteenth century "boudoir" book. "I suppose you made a mess of binding it, and put all this business on to make it look less bad?" At this stage I said I had to go and catch a bus. When I left, he was telling the assistant that he looked pale and cautioning him against the dangers of overwork.

Thursday 23rd November.

Tolkien came to tea [today]. . . . In the evening I dined with J at Univ., having first changed in his rooms. They have a pleasant little common room, much smaller than Magdalen, lined with curiously carved panelling, including a bit of mildly bawdy. I was badly placed at dinner, both for seeing and for talking. . . . After dinner I fared better, sharing a table with Keir for my wine—a very pleasant man, who has done the same Clyde Shipping Co. tour as we have, which was something to set the conversation going. I was very interested when he began (before I had said any thing about it) to comment on the eerie atmosphere of the country round Waterford: I am glad to find that it was not merely my imagination. (Or am I? Would it not be a more reassuring business if it *was* merely my imagination?). As J was reading a paper to the "Martlets",[150] I came away early—about twenty to nine.

Friday 24th November.

Went this evening to the Playhouse to hear Gluck's *Iphigenia in Aulis,* which I had hoped J and I would be hearing together, but which has somehow got itself turned into a family party—and I must say I do object to going on any sort of jaunt with Minto. Everything turned out much as I expected: the show was at 8.15, and at 8.12 we were stepping out of the car several hundred yards from the theatre. (J had had the sense to go on from College on his own). Then when we got in, Minto kept her knees warm with the only available programme until at last J suggested that "perhaps Warnie might like to have a look at it?" And of course a minute after I got it into my hands the lights went out, and I was left in complete ignorance of what was to come. I had suggested bringing the little opera glasses, which J did, and would have liked to see how the people looked through them— but the nearest I got to doing so was a half hearted remark from Minto at the end of the second act that "I must have a look through them presently". . . . But enough of all this, which cannot in any circumstances come under the head of being in love and charity with my neighbours. And Minto has rheumatism which I suppose excuses her. I enjoyed the opera immensely, though it was not I think particularly well done. . . . I agree with what J said when we came out, that it is better worth while to hear a great opera indifferently done than an indifferent opera done by first class people.

Thursday 30th November.

J brought out with him today a copy of *The Oxford Magazine* for 9th Nov. which has in it a faery poem ["Errantry"] by Tolkien, excellent in itself and also very interesting as being in an entirely new metre. I think it a real discovery.

Monday 4th December.

Up at the same time as yesterday and had breakfast with Barfield at a quarter to eight, and into town by car. Much amused by Barfield

150. The Martlets Society was an Oxford Literary Club, which Jack joined in 1919; he remained a member until November 1940, when he presented his last paper to the Society. On this particular occasion (the evening of November 23, 1933), Jack Lewis read a paper titled, "Is Literature an Art." See also the essay, "To the Martlets," by Walter Hooper in Carolyn Keefe, *C. S. Lewis: Speaker and Teacher* (Grand Rapids, Michigan: Zondervan publishing House, 1971).

at breakfast who first borrowed 10/- from me and then said a few minutes later "I find I've no change: could you lend me a shilling?" . . . J turned up about half past ten and we came out to lunch together. When we were about to start out, I found that he was engaged to go for a walk with Tolkien this afternoon. Confound Tolkien! I seem to see less and less of J every day.

Thursday 7th December.

A pupil of J's, a very nice fellow called Pirie-Gordon, who is working for his B. Litt., came to tea today. He told us the following remarkable story: During the war his father served in the R.N.V.R. in the near East, and while out there formed a friendship with a certain Naval Officer, X. This X was after a time posted away, and it was not until sometime afterwards that they met again: when they did so, it was in the bar of the club at Malta. PG was especially glad to see him, for X's name had appeared in the casualty list as killed in the battle of Jutland some months earlier. He referred to this, and X said that mistakes were often made in these lists: they had a long talk, which included references to topics of mutual interest which they had discussed whilst serving together in the earlier part of the war. X drank a cocktail with him and they parted. Subsequently PG found out that it was beyond any possibility of mistake that X had been killed in the battle of Jutland, some months *before* the meeting in the Malta Club. I can attempt no explanation of this: I am assured that the nature of the conversation prevented it being explained by a mistaken identity. The drinking the cocktail was the part that stuck in my gizzard. I asked who paid for the drinks, but he could not tell me. A very odd business.

Monday 11th December.

Skating today for the first time this year. . . . FK [Foord-Kelcey] turned up and watched us for some time from the new path: he was particularly exasperating today at tea, defending the action of the magistrates who have sent two boys to prison for six months for being suspicious characters. FK is an example of how far English muddle headed tolerance can go: here is a man who for the best part of a long life has been allowed to hold a living in the Church of England—he disbelieves in the Virgin Birth, has doubts of the immortality of the soul (but believes in spiritualism), thinks drunkenness a greater sin than murder or incest, and is so far as I can make out, quite indifferent to human suffering or injustice. It's a queer world.

Thursday 21st December.

This day last year my retirement appeared in the Gazette, and the time has come to take stock of the great experiment so far as it has gone. How far has it proved above and how far below my expectations? Does it work? The answers to these questions involve two sets of actors—people and things. First as regards people: the more I see of Minto, the more I realize that the quality which we call Pudaitism was in the main not peculiar to P, but is a basic element in the upper middle class character of the latter half of the last century—like P, Minto regards good manners, not as an integral part of character, but as a form of behaviour which one adopts in dealing with those with whom one is not intimate—like him again, all real conversation is impossible in the same room with her—like him, she has no doubts, but with her dogmatism is carried to a point to which P never ventured: life to her is a very simple business—on any conceivable subject from the washing of a plate to the nature or existence of the Trinity, there are two opinions: the right one (i.e. the one held by her), and the wrong one (that held by everyone who does not agree with her). She is quite incapable of thought—at least as I understand it—and supplies its place with a bundle of prejudices, whose origin, when it can be traced at all, proves to be a point of personal selfishness. . . . The only instance in which she has broken away from this is in rejecting Christianity. . . . She nags J about having become a believer, in much the same way that P used to nag me in his latter years about my boyish fondness for dress, and with apparently just the same inability to grasp the fact that the development of the mind does not necessarily stop with that of the body. . . . Her selfishness is her most prominent characteristic. . . . It fills me with both admiration and irritation to see how completely the whole of J's life is subordinated to hers—financially, socially, recreationally: the pity of it is that on his selflessness her selfishness fattens. . . . All this that I have written, I see reads as if I myself disliked Minto, but this was not at all the impression which I intend to give: I have written captiously because this entry is in some sort the balancing of an account, and every good accountant depreciates his assets to the utmost before striking a balance. Per contra, there is much that I like about Minto: she has always been charitable, even in the days of her greatest poverty: her kindness to animals is unfailing and extravagant: she loves flowers and woods and sunsets and birds: and if she makes great demands on J, she is also obviously very fond of him and looks after him meticulously: and finally, she accepted my intrusion into the household without the least sign of protest, although from the very nature of things it cannot have been entirely agreeable to her. And lastly of all, without being in any way intimate, we are on very good terms with each other.

Looking back on the forecast which I made when I first resolved on this scheme, I find that Maureen is an item which must be "written up". I had thought of her as one of the snags of the scheme and find she has turned out one of the assets. This of course is largely owing to my having started to learn music, for it is in the music room that one sees the best and most intelligent side of Maureen. I now enjoy her society in the house and regret her departure, whereas in the old days it was exactly the reverse. . . . Of J's society I do not get nearly as much as I would like to have, but I get as much as I budgeted for, so here is no cause for complaint. So much for persons.

As regards things, I cannot at the moment think of a single crumpled rose leaf. For the first time in my life I find myself busy every day and all day at tasks of my own devising, at which I feel more and not less enthusiasm as time goes on. As I hoped would be the case when I first broached the scheme to myself, the days, so far from needing filling in, are too short—much too short—for all I want to do. On the purely aesthetic side, ten times my present income might not make me free of such a lovely place as this, and instead of seeing it in samples I am now free (a thing that never happened to me before) to watch spring, summer, autumn, and winter revolving over it. And perhaps best of all, this has come to me while I am still young, but yet of an age to know that I am mortal: and it is not until one has thoroughly grasped that fact, that the full pleasure can be got from every passing moment. So both as regards people and things, the answer is, most emphatically the experiment does work: when everything possible has been raked up against the household and the life, I can say with no reservations whatsoever, that the past twelve months has been incomparably the happiest of my life. I thank God every night for bringing me safely into such a harbour and ask Him to keep me there for the rest of my days.

My routine varies little, and I will here set it down, knowing from the family papers how soon one can forget. At 7.45 I have my tea, and get up at 8.10—shave, bath, dress, take Mr. Papworth for his morning stroll, breakfast, walk down to London Rd. and catch the 9.30 bus to Rose Lane. Then to work on the papers in College: if it is term time, I come out with J by car and have lunch at home: if it is the vac., I eat half a pork pie and drink a whiskey and soda in college and come out by bus. Then in the afternoon, usually "public works",[151] sometimes a walk, until tea time. If it is summer, I do not come out until three o'c., and then bathe instead of doing public works. After tea, piano practice until six: then J and I sit and read in the study until seven, with a bottle of beer about six thirty. At seven we have supper, after which we take the dogs down the lane and then water them. On coming in, J goes and sits with Minto in the common room and I return to the study where I read and write until eleven, when I make up the fires, make the dogs beds, and then go off to my room. Having said my prayers, I then read the two evening lessons in bed, and then read poetry until midnight—generally having about 20 minutes for this purpose. It is surprising the amount of poetry one can get through in this way: since I came home, I have read Milton (complete), Cowper (complete), Wordsworth's longer poems, and am in the middle of the last of the *Canterbury Tales*. (But on second thoughts, *is* it surprising? 20 minutes X 365 = 121-2/3 hours = five and a half days! This is a good example of the sort of silly thing one says without stopping to think it out). In summer, while my working hours in College are longer, my reading hours at home are shorter, for after supper Minto, J and I generally walk for an hour with the dogs. Music deserves more than the casual mention I have given it in speaking of Maureen. That I should learn the piano was something quite unforeseen when I adopted this manner of life, and has already become one of my most valued pleasures. Of course at my age there is little prospect of my ever becoming even a tolerable player, but the increased pleasure with which I can now listen to music surprises me. Then too, I spend hours playing at composing, with the greatest relish. The only grievance I have against it is that it crowds up a day which is already almost inconveniently full.

Yes! Once again I will give myself the pleasure of writing it down, the experiment has been a triumphant success.

Monday 1st January, 1934.

The first morning of our [third] annual walk, always one of the best events of the year: it was as little satisfactory today, for a variety of reasons, as it could be. I had been warned by Minto not to hang up my new calendar until today, and scoffed at it: however, the Little

---

151. In an unpublished letter to Clyde S. Kilby of December 29, 1966, Warren writes: "Jack and I made a path through the jungle country at The Kilns up to the crest of the hill, and every afternoon J indulged in what he described as 'Public Works'. It was quite a job, first hacking down the undergrowth, then levelling and laying the track with rubble, and adding a top dressing of sand. Happy days those were."

People were on the alert and got to work almost as soon as I was out of bed—item the first:—while shaving I gave myself the worst cut I have had for a very long time—an extraordinarily painful one too—and had to go about for the rest of the day with a great bloodstained wad of cotton wool on my face. When I got out with the dogs I found it a dim morning with the hedges and grass spangled with hoar frost —a trifle cold perhaps for going into "furrin parts" but by no means a bad holiday morning for all that. Maureen drove us into College at ten o'c. where when we arrived we found Hatton carrying out a spring cleaning, so we soon collected our sandwiches and walked down to the station, J stopping on the way at the Davenant to buy a book: I had with me Trollopes *Miss Mackenzie*[152] which I had brought from the house. After another stop to buy a pair of woolen gloves we got to the station where the Little People delivered Item No 2: the ticket collector received our proposition to travel by the 11.32 with incredulity, and pointed out that the 11.15 would have saved us two hours on the journey—to which the guard of the 11.32 added the comforting information that the connection at Worcester did not wait for his train. Item No 3 was luckily postponed until I had had a glass of sherry and got into the train, to wit, the breaking of one of the straps of my rucksack. This last disaster thank goodness exhausted the run of bad luck which that unfortunate calendar had to discharge on me, and the rest of the day was a great success. . . . We again this year made a miscalculation about the haversack ration: last time we found the Magdalen idea of "sandwiches for two" very Spartan, so today we had a ration for four, which proved too much. (Mem. Next time to order for *three*). At Hereford we set out to find a sadler to mend my broken rucksack, and had more difficulty in doing so than I would have expected in a "huntin" and farming town. . . . Ultimately a policeman found us one, who sewed up the strap for me while we waited. By the time it was finished there was nothing to be done but go back to the Station where we had tea and took the 4.7 for Three Cocks—the same train by which we travelled to Moorhampton last year. After Hereford you feel the change—you begin to get into the real country where the stations are lit by oil lamps, and that only on the platform at which the train comes in. It was dark when we got out on the curiously continental platform at Three Cocks and heard again the well remembered sound of rushing mountain water—next to that of the sea, the best sound there is: here to our great surprise, was a

---

152. *Miss Mackenzie* (1865) by novelist Anthony Trollope.

refreshment room, which suggested a pleasant way of filling in the half hour we had to wait—having gone in and discussed what we should have, it was a considerable jar when the woman announced that "they kept no intoxicants": but we consoled ourselves by walking up and down the platform and imagining to ourselves how P and Uncle Bill would have behaved in similar circumstances. We got to Builth at 6.12 and found our old stopping place The Greyhound, after a little difficulty.

Tuesday 2nd January.

We got off at 9.15 [and] . . . started out across the park which runs along the left bank of the Wye, and across the shaky suspension bridge. On the other side, we found ourselves part of a procession of cows, which we had some difficulty in outmarching. All this time it was still misty, and we saw everything in half tones, but having crossed a railway bridge, a stiff climb—the first of the day—took us up to 700 ft., and there we halted: the view looking back was an uncommon and remarkably beautiful one: the valley out of which we had climbed was full of pure white fog, the edge of which thinned and swirled so that objects showed momentarily clearer and dimmer, and wherever there was a cleft in the mountains, a river of white fog ran down to join that in the valley—and added to this, this was the first moment at which I felt the silence of the real country. A great moment, that of the first halt on the first day of a walking tour! Carrying on past a farm with the curious name of Goytre we came out on a common. We had been eager to see what we would find at this place, for which the Welsh name was Commin Coch (with nearby, Commin-y-garth). But although it was a common, J was not satisfied that *Commin* is the Welsh for "a common".[153] All the way along during the morning, we had the most glorious mist effects on the hills and in the valleys—sometimes whispey and sometimes opaque—with the solemn friendly hills all round us, and never out of the sound of rushing water. There is something more than mere fancy in the theory of an hereditary affection for a country. It by no means satisfies me to say that I like Wales because it is beautiful—I feel it draws me more deeply than mere beauty without associations could do. We halted for our morning whiskey and brook water at a spot where the road ran down sharply into a wood which was traversed by a brook, and there sat for some time on a log by the roadside, not entirely

---

153. The Welsh "comin" actually translates into "land" in English. Hence, Commins Coch is Red Land.

enjoying the "unanchored" feeling which comes to one when you first take off your pack and coat after a march. From there we went on and crossed the Wye by Bryn-wern Bridge, just above where it is joined by the river Ithon: this is where the Wye first changes its nature—above the junction, it definitely becomes not a river, but a very big stream. My so putting it led me into an argument with J who will not admit with me that stream, brook and river are terms of magnitude. I on the other hand contend that every watercourse begins as a spring, becomes a brook, then a stream, and when fully grown, a river. A short walk along the main road brought us to the Black Lion in the little town of Newbridge on Wye where we stopped for lunch—the same pub. at which J put up on his Easter walking tour last year, but rebuilt since then. After lunch we set out, again on the main road, for rather over a mile, until we came to a spot where a ford was marked on the map which we hoped would be a bridge, but it was not so—and worse, when we got down to the waters edge, there was nothing in the swift brown water to indicate that it was fordable on foot—so rather reluctantly we continued along the main road. As we were doing so, the sun came out and converted the hillside into a glory of golden fir trees, the effect after the dull morning of the slanting light being exquisitely beautiful, both there and on the abrupt slope of a lovely hill called Dol-y-fan on our right. Just under this hill we at last found a bridge—a very nasty one, and the nearer we got to it the less we liked the look of it. It consisted of a double width of thin planking suspended on wires, and of course swayed abominably—added to which the swift running water far beneath it produced the illusion that it was being swept sideways: however, we crossed without mishap and sat down with our backs against the level crossing gate on the Railway to enjoy the view, and very peaceful and satisfying it was. . . . I enjoyed the next three or four miles better than anything in the day—on the one side the "close up" of wild unspoiled country, and on the other, the wide prospect of a similar scene. Once we came up [on] a red squirrel who hopped on a low branch and sat upright, looking at us out of his little boot button eyes, holding his head first on one side and then on the other. . . . Near a quarry, we halted in a copse in the early twilight. . . . [Also] near here a man with a lorry stopped and offered us a lift, which was typical of the general niceness of the Welsh people as we have seen them so far. When we got under weigh again, it was twilight in good earnest: a rose coloured cloud rested over Corn Gaffalt Hill on the far bank of the river, and under the dark high mass, a little patch of river ran rose red—an exquisite bit, perhaps the very best we saw during the whole day. We crossed the river again by the railway bridge near the junction of the Wye and the Elan and reached Rhayader in the last of the daylight by a bye road. . . . On arrival at our pub, The Lion Royal, we had a hot bath of dark brown water and a late tea. When we had been there a little time, we were visited by the maid to know if "we would have dinner or a grill": we chose the latter, which proved to be chop and chips. (Query? Would it also have been chop and chips if we had chosen "the dinner"). By the time we had finished our dinner, the fire had burnt up and the room was much warmer, so, with the assistance of a large whiskey and soda, we finished our evening very tolerably.

Wednesday 3rd January.

Had a very comfortable night and slept very soundly. . . . When we at last got started, we found it a frosty morning, again with a mist. Rhayader is not an easy town to get out of in spite of its small-ness, and ultimately we had to ask the way. It was splendid once we were clear of the town to feel the thin frosty air, and to see that we had got so far in subduing the Wye, which could now be described (at a distance) as a mere stream. We had not gone very far before we came across two red squirrels, much tamer than the one we saw yes-terday: one of them let us come quite close to him and then hopped up on the branch of a big tree where he sat upright and inspected us with his little boot button eyes cocking his head first on one side and then on the other. The next one was even tamer and ran about on all fours in front of us for a long time. He moved very like a rabbit I thought. We did another couple of miles before crossing the river, this time thank goodness by a good strong cart bridge at the end of a track. Having got over, we found ourselves in the company of a num-ber of Welsh sheep—creatures with long tails, something the shape of a beaver's, but fat. The shepherds who were looking after them spoke in Welsh. . . . We had a nine mile stretch this morning, and by the time we had done between seven and eight, we were very glad to see the spire of Llangurig church ahead of us at the end of the valley. A good bye road brought us to it a few minutes before one, and after a little anxiety as we drew near, we saw the sign of a pub., the Black Lion. . . . When we had had our lunch, J suggested that as we had only another five miles to do, and the room was a comfortable one, we might as well stop for tea and finish the journey afterwards: which we did. . . . During the afternoon the weather changed for the worse, and when we set out in the dusk after tea, the sky was completely overcast: before we had gone very far, a thin rain began to fall, and the last of the daylight disappeared. Then J began to think his plan of stopping all afternoon at Llangurig was not so good as it had at first appeared, and I agreed with him. What I had not visualized was how *very* dark a remote countryside, with which you are not familiar, can be on a wet night: we almost had to feel our way. We stopped once and smoked cigarettes under the lee of a hedge and bank at the entrance to some sort of private road. After an uphill pull we reached Pant Mawr soon after six o'clock. . . . The parlour was a good deal warmer than our last nights sitting room, and after a supper of tongue and bread and butter, with a pot of strong tea, we spent a couple of hours there very comfortably.

Thursday 4th January.

Called at seven and got up by the light of one solitary candle, to the disquieting sound of the wind roaring in the eaves. As the daylight came, saw that in addition to the wind, a driving horizontal rain was coming out of a grey sky. However, we decided to face it, and were on the road soon after half past eight. About half a mile brought us to the point where our track left the main road, and although it was marked "Private", no one appeared to mind our using it: I suspect that the people of the farm to which it belonged were still in bed. In spite of the wind and the rain, I enjoyed the next stage of the walk: we had a good firm track under foot, with the Wye sprawling below us, now quite definitely a stream, and on either side bare hills, down the face of which little torrents showed white. A couple of miles of this sort of thing brought us to a grim ruin of the dark sort of stone used for building in Co. Down, with heaps of slag on the opposite side of the river—an abandoned lead mine. It was I think being used as a sheep slaughtering place—anyway it was one of the most disgustingly dirty spots I have ever seen, and dreary beyond expression in the steady driving rain and fog, which latter was now crowning all the hills. Here the map showed a bridge, but this has disappeared: so we had to prospect higher upstream. A little farther on we came upon a single plank stretched across the stream, and with some misgivings entrusted ourselves to it: J merely got his shoes wet, but it bent under my weight until the water ran over the tops of my trousers—but we were already so wet, that at the moment this seemed to produce little extra discomfort. We were now in really open country—nothing in front of us but a steep hill up which we began one of the most ex-

hausting climbs I have ever undertaken: the rain beat upon us incessantly, the soggy ground was full of waterholes and subterranean
rivulets, and worst of all, the higher we got, the thicker became the
fog. Ultimately, somewhere about the 1700 ft. contour mark, it
became obvious that in addition to being soaked through and pretty
well played out, we were running a serious risk of losing our bearings
in the mist, and, very reluctantly, we decided that there was nothing
for it but to abandon the attempt. When we had made the decision,
we turned our backs to the storm and had a mouthful of neat whiskey
each—I don't know when I last enjoyed a drink so much: I must have
needed it too, for I got no feeling of the sting of spirits as it went
down. We then turned in our tracks, meeting on the way down a
shepherd who had evidently crossed the river by the plank and then
walked up the hill, carrying a big load of hay on a fork. I got if
possible wetter still in crossing the plank again, and when we reached
the lead mine we took shelter in the ruins and made a light meal off
ammoniated quinine and whiskey. The whole scene reminded me
vividly of the sort of life which must have been led in the Highlands
by Alan Breck Stewart[154] and suchlike in the years immediately after
the forty five, and we talked of those days while we rested. . . . With
the exception of some experiences in the war, I don't remember ever
having had a more damnable walk: we were in the narrow valley of
the Afon Tarenig, through which valley the wind roared in our faces,
bringing a heavy rain with it, with such force that I had to walk bent
nearly double: we were soaked to the skin, and our clothes were so
heavy with water that every movement was an effort: and the road
went up hill steadily and apparently interminably. I wanted to turn
and make to Llangurig and stop there the night, catching a train from
Llanidloes the next day, but J wouldn't hear of it, and I felt I should
have lost my temper if I had tried to argue. Just when I had decided
that this would be my last walking tour, on the ground that no
possible enjoyment could compensate for such a degree of suffering,
an ever to be blessed man with a saloon car pulled up and offered us
a lift—may all prosperity attend him in this world and the next!
Thanks to his help we reached the George Borrow at Ponterwyd at
about half past twelve—in a deplorable plight certainly, but at least
under cover. Here we were lucky in falling into the hands of a really
kindly and intelligent landlady, who grasped the situation at

---

154. Alan Breck Stewart, a character in Robert Louis Stevenson's novel *Kidnapped*
(1886).

once—got us as hot a bath as the house could produce at that hour of the day, and gave us beds with hot water bottles in them, while all our clothes were taken down to the kitchen to dry. Half an hour later she came up to our rooms with dressing gowns and offered us the use of her sitting room to have lunch in in our pygamas—and though the lunch was stewed steak, I most heartily enjoyed it. J went back to bed after lunch, but I sat in the room where we had lunched and read Buchan's *Dancing Floor*[155] all afternoon, and also dozed a bit. After tea we got our clothes back, not only dried, but washed and ironed. I was very glad to get mine back again. It is surprising how helpless one feels without one's clothes. At this inn we made the acquaintance of a delightful dog, one Chloe, a young Labrador bitch of about eleven months, quite untrained, but who, we were told, is "going to school" shortly. She introduced herself by bringing in her bone and showing it to each of us in turn, and at meals she put her paws on the table to beg, which put her face on a level with mine—a proceeding generally ending in an affectionate lick! We decided that she would make a capital wife for Mr. Papworth—whether he would really enjoy having a young bride is another matter!

Friday 5th January.

Woke up after an excellent night's sleep to find that it was much the same sort of morning as yesterday—a truly dismal prospect! I then and there determined that whatever the day might bring forth, no persuasion would induce me to repeat yesterdays experiment of "facing it". At breakfast we discussed the possibilities of hiring a taxi, and at last consulted our hostess, who told us that there was a bus at quarter to ten for Aberystwyth. . . . We had scarcely left Ponterwyd when it came on to rain more violently than at any time yesterday—it drummed on the roof and danced in the gullies in a way that made me uncommonly thankful for the frowsty security of our bus. It was a pleasant, pretty run, and the weather cleared and the sun came out as we dropped down out of the mountains into Aberystwyth, which we reached about half past ten. Here we put up at the Lion Royal— apparently a popular name in Wales this—a very comfortable pub. suffering only from the almost universal disadvantage of not having a hot water supply, and possessing a desperately talkative bar maid. . . . The town, I was glad to find, is full of good book shops, one at least of which had not a single book in the window which was not in Welsh. Another had German and Italian daily papers—evidently this

---

155. *The Dancing Floor* (1926), by John Buchan.

is a really intelligent place. I went into one shop and bought *The Moonstone* by Wilkie Collins,[156] a book which I have a faint recollection of having read when I was a boy. . . . It is very pleasant to find so near home a country with a living language and culture of its own, just quietly going on *living,* after all this wearisome nonsense of pretending that Ye quainte olde Irishe is the language of a nation. There are the remains here of what must have been a very large Norman castle, but so ruined that it is now really little more than a few pieces of masonry scattered about a public recreation ground. . . . The biggest building in the town is the University of Wales, a place of which we have decided J must become Principal. . . . Having provided ourselves with books, we spent the afternoon, with the exception of the time taken for a short stroll, in the lounge, where amongst other things I found a pamphlet extolling the river Usk. . . . Afternoon tea is not very well understood in this hotel: one has to have it at a table in the dining room, and, though their enquiries were tactfully made, I gathered that the staff were in doubt if we would be requiring a further meal during the evening! . . . After tea J and I fell into talk on the subject of personal immortality, J maintaining that he would understand as such, the addition of new faculties of perception etc. to the "me", whereas I hold that "me" can only exist in the next life if it is quite recognisably the survival of me, stripped of course of all sensual tastes, but with a core of WHL. It was an interesting talk, and arose out of the subject of youthful genius. We decided tonight to pay one of our rare visits to the cinema, and set out for it after eating our mixed grill. Here they have a very dismal "palace", and the horrors of the earlier part of the programme were such as to confirm me in my opinion that the cinema is not for me. True, some of it was funny, viz. a local butchers advertisement in which we first saw flocks roaming the Welsh mountains, and finally the butcher himself standing in an attitude beside a Ford van from which carcasses of mutton were being unloaded. But this was soon replaced by a thing called a "silly symphony", a set of drawings something on the lines of Felix the cat, quite incredibly beastly: I should imagine that a particularly nasty minded man in delerium tremens must see something of this sort: but even worse was to follow—a real music hall "turn" of two men, one of whom played various sorts of banjo while the other had an enormous concertina, with a keyboard like a piano—even three or four fiddles, a piano and a drum were powerless

---

156. *The Moonstone* (1868), a classic detective story by William Wilkie Collins.

to drown this diabolical instrument. The main film was *Waltz Time* founded on Fledermaus, which I had seen in Oxford during the summer with Denny. I enjoyed it greatly, and so did J—a good example of what musical comedy ought to be. Unfortunately they had a very bad talkie apparatus, so I missed a good deal of the book. We got home in time to finish a whiskey and soda in the lounge just as a talkative fellow guest made his appearance, and so to bed after an excellent day, at about eleven o'c.—a very late hour judged by walking tour standards.

Saturday 6th January.

An excellent night. They have a curiously "tinny" town clock here, which, as it is placed in quite an imposing clock tower, sounds rather ridiculous. We had a good breakfast in a really warm room— no common luxury in a provincial hotel: on the wall was the well known poem "I shall not pass this way again etc." said to be from a sampler of A.D. 1450—but J doubts if it is as old as that. Somehow we got on the subject of food in the Middle Ages, a subject on which J had a good deal of interest to say. When we had done, we paid our bills, and leaving our haversacks behind us, went out into a warm windy morning to take the air on the front. Quite a sea had got up in the night, and at the north end of the promenade, the waves were breaking over the road. . . . From the promenade we made our way to the University, where J boldly asked to be directed to the library. This proved to be a fine big room, end on to the sea, lit by plate glass windows let direct into the stone without any frames. . . . It appeared so far as I could judge, to be a very fairly good collection. J inspected the philosophical section and found it more than adequate. On a low dais under the windows they had a show case in which the most interesting exhibit was a copy of Shakespeare used by Johnson in compiling the *Dictionary,* the words and letters underlined and marginally noted in his own hand—doubtless one of the very volumes of which Boswell says "The authorities were copied from the books themselves, in which he had marked the words with a black-lead pencil, the traces of which could easily be effaced. I have seen several of them in which that trouble had not been taken; so that they were just as when used by the copyists". Amongst other things we noticed, was a copy of a book by Barfield, and J found a paper by himself. . . . We then went and collected our traps, and so down to the station. . . . We left at one o'clock, and had one of the most gorgeous railway panoramas I have ever seen in my life for the next three hours: to describe it in any detail would be quite impossible. After getting a final glimpse of the sea at a place called Borth, we began to ascend the valley of the Dovey, which was the first of a succession of exquisite valleys, some of which we went through, and others of which we crossed over. My recollection of the journey is of brown rushing streams, glens of all shape and colour rising up interminably in front of us as the train laboured on. . . . (Note: two things I have forgotten to mention in their proper place, (1) in central Wales they burn turf, so we got once more the good smell of the Co. Down country side: (2) Just before Llangurig I saw that mythical creature the black sheep —a much finer animal than his common or garden brother). The Welsh are a desperately sociable people: we had two girls in our compartment who got in at Borth and seemed to know someone at every station we stopped at—which of course meant a long chat with their friend, with the door of the compartment open. Also they seemed to know everyone in the train, including the ticket collector. . . . We got to Shrewsbury about four o'clock, and after a long wait were backed on to a Liverpool train which had a tea car on it—much to our relief, for after my very light lunch I was beginning to feel peckish. . . . At Leamington we changed and had a drink under difficulties, in a very crowded refreshment room, and ultimately got to Oxford just before eight. . . . In college we found a good fire burning and a noble supper awaiting us—cold duck and salad, a tart and cheese, and a bottle of Burgundy. This put the finishing touch to a holiday which, in spite of the Ponterwyd day, I look back on as one of the very best I have ever had. Its only real fault is that it has given me aesthetic indigestion: I am not constituted to absorb beauty in such very large helpings. [A]fter supper J tried a ridiculous experiment of Barfield's—reading "Mariana"[157] aloud, but substituting the words "bottom upwards" for Mariana when ever it occurs—extremely amusing. Maureen came in with the car for us at nine o'clock. . . . It was very pleasant to go to bed in my own room once again.

Friday 19th January.
Poor Minto had a bad night, and to add to her misfortunes has managed to catch a cold. I am not at all easy about her, and look forward to Dr. Radford's report, who comes out to examine her to-morrow.

---

157. According to Owen Barfield, this reference was actually to Alfred Tennyson's poem "Eleänore" (not to his "Mariana"), and the phrase was "bottom upward".

Sunday 21st January.

A hard frost during the night. Minto had a good deal of pain early this morning, but I do not think she is any worse. . . . After supper I read Moffat's translation of Romans, and found it very difficult. After the very fine passage at the end of Ch. VII describing the struggle against sin, *before* receiving Christ, he goes on with Ch. VIII, apparently on the assumption that to become a Christian is to be relieved from all temptation to sin. What the whole epistle boils down to in fact is, that if to be a Christian means, as St. Paul apparently says, to be free from any and every sinful desire, it is to be doubted if many, even of the Saints, have been Christians. Then again there is the fearful stumbling block of predestination—does St. Paul in fact say that certain are predestined to salvation, and that it doesn't matter what they do? And if he says so, is he right? J has been reading this epistle with a commentary, but could get no help from it.

Saturday 27th January.

I wonder is dreaming a sign of increasing years? Does one in middle life and after, go back in this respect to childhood—move,

> out of a red flare of dreams
> Into a common light of common hours
> Until old age bring the red flare again.

Certainly until the last few weeks, I had not, barring a very occasional nightmare, dreamt for years. Now I seem to dream almost every night. . . . Today I bought the *Columbia History of Music Vol. I.,* and after supper Maureen, J and I formed a Committee on it. We were unanimous in thinking it a great success, especially the specimens of plainsong which are simply glorious. I have not played all the records yet, but have heard enough to be delighted with it. Apropos of music, my new tune was approved by Maureen and heard by the rest of the household, and in fact has obtained at least a succes d'estime!

Sunday 28th January.

J and I went to the eleven o'c. service when Thomas preached remarkably well on St. Matt. XX.16. In explaining the parable of the labourers in the vineyard, he put forward an idea which is quite new to me, viz. that while the same reward is offered to those who come early and who come late to God's work, it may be that the early comers will have a fuller joy in their service, while those who came late will regret their wasted years. But will there be any room in the future life for such a feeling as *regret,* if as we believe, it is a state of *bliss?* J raised this point on the way home, and I must say I don't see my way through the question. . . . On coming back from Church we got hold of Paxford and went up to view the site of the projected great viaduct. Much discussion as to (a) the number of pillars needed, (b) the material and (c) the site of the pillars. After my *fifth* unsuccessful effort to contribute to the discussion, I gave it up and set off for home, followed at a distance by J and Paxford, still talking loudly, continuously and simultaneously.

Monday 29th January.

This evening I finished RLS's letters[158] which I have been reading alternately with de Pontis. What a man! Always on the verge of death, hard up, for many years at least, and yet so bouyant and whimsical and full of fun—his is a life to make most of us ashamed of ourselves.

Friday 16th February.

A lovely morning, white frost on the ground and the sun diffused through a pale mist. While taking Mr. Papworth for his morning walk I went in to our neighbour the "Samarkand Weavers" and bought two hand woven ties which have been in the window for some time, and which I have been hovering over for the last three days. They are pretty and look as if they would wear well, and were much admired by Minto: I gave 5/- each for them. I did a very good morning's work in College, getting as far as J's first stay with M at Bristol. A strange business. One has to be always on ones guard against pandering to the dramatist in one, which picks on a trivial accident and says, "from this, almost unnoticed at the time, so and so arose" or "by not doing this, I was led into such and such a circumstance". But I do feel very strongly that here is as striking a small thing as ever lead to large results. The Quartermaster's clerk of the Cadet Bn. goes through his list—J and K are allotted one vacant room, and the next goes to L and M—Lewis and Moore: it might just as easily have been Lewis and Sergt. Muggins or Lewis and Lord Molineux, and the very fact would have been forgotten by now—but it was Lewis and Moore, and when the clerk filled in the names he permanently and almost immediately altered the whole course of five lives. Why should this have been so? As I said, a strange business.

---

158. *Vailima Letters* (1895), the letters written by late-nineteenth-century author Robert Louis Stevenson from his house, Vailima, in Samoa; he lived there from 1890 to 1894, when he died unexpectedly of a brain hemorrhage.

Monday 26th February.

This evening I read Stevenson's "Ordered South",[159] in some ways one of the most attractive of his essays. There is however one point which he might have made and doesn't—or rather I suppose I should say there is one experience which one would have expected him to have—and that is how *wasteful* we are of beauty in our youth. We enjoy it, pass on to something else, and forget it. To me at any rate, middle life has brought this positive gain—that ever since I first knew I was mortal, I have formed the habit of memorizing bits of scenery which take my fancy: I say quite deliberately "This I will remember" and proceed to fix it in my mind. And I find it works: all sorts of things which in the old days soon became a pleasant haze, now stand out sharply: nor does this process of deliberate memorization exclude in any way the pictures which come by chance. I wish I had started doing this at an earlier age, for in my work in College in the past week or so I have been startled to find how very little one does in fact remember: take for instance the shelling of Croix de Poperinghe where I was uncommonly nearly killed and which only happened seventeen years ago: I ought surely to remember that—yet I have only a vague recollection of a stubbly sloping field with trees on the sky line, near which were the water troughs—but *can* there have been water on top of the hill? And what was at the foot of the forward slope—dust and glitter, so presumably some one else's wagon lines. Not of course that one particularly wants to remember such a place or such an episode, but it serves as an illustration of what I mean.

Thursday 1st March.

No talk about servants at supper tonight, which leads me to hope that things are at last settling down in the kitchen, and that the new girl has been accepted. Apropos of servants, I wonder why girls of that class are so beastly to each other? . . . No decent man would tolerate such conduct on the part of a manservant—which leads me to think on second thoughts that perhaps this conduct is not a matter of class at all, but is merely *feminine*. The more one sees of women the more one realizes that they live in a world which is utterly different to, and largely repugnant to the male—which indeed is sufficiently obvious from the fact that if a woman does not attract a man sexually, his feeling towards her varies from detestation to a mild boredom. I generalize of course, and possibly other men may feel differently—I

159. "Ordered South," from a collection of essays by Robert Louis Stevenson.

don't know. But in my own case I can only think of three—possibly four—exceptions to this rule.

Tuesday 20th March.

This evening I finished G. K. Chesterton's *Everlasting Man*[160]— what a book! It is one continuous feast of pun, paradox, epigram faith, good humour and sound convincing argument. It begins with a trouncing of the Evolutionists which is really admirable—and so far as I can judge quite fair. Indeed a great deal of the book is made up of shrewd hard hitting at various self complacent people—viz. the man who complains of our empty churches—"how does *he* know that they are empty?" is GKC's pertinent query. The man who says he reveres the "Jesus of the Gospels in all His simple loving kindliness" but cannot stand the harsh Figure of the Churches is shown that it is precisely the other way round, etc. etc. In addition to every other good quality of this remarkable book, I recaptured from it a feeling I never expected to feel again—the thrill of fine writing for fine writing's sake.

Friday 23rd March.

The first unmistakably spring day. In the afternoon J and I did the railway walk with the dogs, and I enjoyed it very much: it was wind-less, with quite a hot sun, and long pale panoramas of countryside fading in every direction into the dim blue of our encircling hills— between us and Brill Hill a deep pool of shadow cast by one big cloud. We lay and basked in the sun for some time in the railway cutting and listened to a lark, high up, faint, and clear. It led us, via Kirk's[161] "mere expression of the cosmic emotion" to a discussion of pantheism, polytheism, and theosophy: J explained the latter to me, which I had never understood before.

Saturday 24th March.

J and I have been for some time intending to ask Tolkien to dinner with us at the Eastgate and to read the *Walkure*[162] in J's rooms after-wards. The subject came up again at tea today, and Minto said that from her point of view Tuesday would be the best day for us to do it. T was accordingly asked for Tuesday over the phone—couldn't come Tuesday, had to be with his wife—could come Monday, so Monday

---

160. *The Everlasting Man* (1925), a theological work by Gilbert Keith Chesterton.
161. W. T. Kirkpatrick (1848-1921), tutor to both Warren and Jack. See also C. S. Lewis, *Surprised by Joy*, pp. 131-148.
162. *Walküre* (or the Valkyrie), the second of the four operas in Richard Wagner's *Der Ring Des Nibelungen* (1845).

was fixed. Then Minto went off at full cry: "Perfectly ridiculous, any woman who had been decently brought up knew better than to come between a man and his men friends . . . a man should begin as he intends to go on: once you give way to a woman you have to keep on giving way to her . . . a woman should never interfere when men want to have a talk . . . to expect a man to hang about the house doing things for her is absurd . . . " etc. etc. Only Moliere could have done the scene justice.—and if there was a certain grimness mingled with my amusement, the latter was none the less genuine.

Palm Sunday.

To church in the morning where there was a distribution of palm crosses: Thomas came down to the steps at the top of the nave, accompanied by a server with a basket of palms, and we all went up and got one, except J. I too would have liked to avoid doing so, for I do not find that sort of thing is of any help to me from a devotional point of view: and I think there is a quite real risk that an imaginative child may get the impression that its bit of palm is in some way a magical charm: however, I hadn't the nerve not to go up for mine. I burnt it as soon as I got home. [This evening I went] with J to Evensong, where, oddly enough, the Bursar of Cuddesdon College preached on Prayer. We did not quite agree about the sermon: I thought it on the whole good, and J thought it on the whole bad—but we agreed that it was at any rate not dull. . . . [O]ne of his stories I was however glad to hear: how St. Theresa wrote to a friend that she never finished her prayers without saying to herself, "Well thank goodness that's over".

Monday 26th March.

Tolkien, J, and I met by appointment in College at four o'clock to read the *Valkyrie*: T looking tired and worn I thought, but in very good form. When we had had some tea we started on the play, I reading in English and T and J in German. I think our English version must be the acting version, for it fits the German syllable by syllable —as a result it was I found very easy to follow the others parts: I did not need prompting more than a couple times. Coming to it with the idea of an opera libretto in my mind, I got a very agreeable surprise. Even in this rather doggerel version it remains a fine play. We knocked off soon after six and T went home, meeting us again at the Eastgate where we had fried fish and a savoury omlette, with beer. We then returned to J's rooms and finished our play (and incidentally the best part of a decanter of very inferior whiskey). Arising out of the perplexities of Wotan we had a long and interesting discussion on religion which lasted until about half past eleven when the car called for us. A very enjoyable day.

Good Friday.

At half past ten I went to Church. The altar hangings and curtains had been removed, revealing it as a six legged oak table, on which stood a cross: the choir were in cassocks and Thomas in a plain surplice. With the exception of two hymns, we had no music, the Prophetic Psalm (XXII) and the Canticle being read, a verse by Thomas and a verse by the congregation alternately. The simple service was very impressive, and several times I managed to raise myself to—what shall I call it?—that level of realism?—what I mean is that conviction of the overwhelming reality of the Christian faith which unfortunately comes to one so infrequently, and never at demand. I see I have expressed this very badly: I do not of course mean that at times one disbelieves and at times believes: one's intellect assures one that the facts are beyond dispute, at all times. The nearest I can get to it is this mundane illustration: (a) I *know* that the first sight of England seen from a steamers deck after a long absence is a moving sight, but (b) this knowledge does not give me the catch in the throat which the actual experience does.

Sunday 3rd June.

Since I made the last entry in this book I have been laid up with flu: getting it unfortunately within 24 hours of J, so poor Minto had two patients on her hands for over a week. Whether it is increasing age, or that the flu germ is becoming more virulent, I don't know, but each year I find it harder to shake off these attacks. This one in particular has left me very limp and depressed, and has tailed off into a heavy cold which I show no signs of losing. Retirement brings with it one drawback, too trivial to be called a disadvantage, but worth noting here: in the old days, I *enjoyed* a mild illness—for so often, to lie in bed with a novel was preferable to the alternative occupation of a fit man: but now when my time is my own and every day is filled with interest, sickness is merely a nuisance. I have got through an enormous amount of fiction—indeed got up, sick of the sight of a novel, and started on making a general index of all my unindexed French books—a big job, which I have been shirking for years, and of which the end is not yet in sight. I had the pleasant thrill this year of taking to my bed in spring and re-emerging to find it summer. My first stroll with J (also convalescent) was a delight. We were particularly struck by the bit of the middle wood at the head of the "grand excalier"—in winter, one of the most open of our wild bits, and now transformed in a few days into a green roofed, sombre room. And to come out of the house and find the May out and the early bluebells, was delightful. Nothing has happened, in one sense, since I wrote last, and yet dozens of trivialities which go to make up the sum total of my life—the swans have had three cygnets, and show every sign of neglecting them as disgracefully as they did their last family: Jill has had five kittens: a heron has been a constant visitor to the pond (which by the way is swarming with tadpoles) but was ultimately frightened away by a hawk—J and I were out in the punt at the time and saw the whole episode—both birds screaming, and the hawk fluttering round, but afraid to attack: all the snakes seem to have disappeared from the middle wood: rabbits very numerous: "public works" have ended, and bathing has begun—tho' as regards the former, I have put up a single sleeper bridge on the concrete pylons, and whilst bathing the other day, we cleared "Stinkhaven" of dead wood etc. Indoors, I now write from time to time, a doggerel history of the reign of Louis XIV,[163] to my own intense amusement, and, being under no illusions as to its practical value, do not see any danger in so doing: my music is much behindhand, but I am catching up again.

Saturday 16th June.

My thirty ninth birthday—Ye Gods, 39! The same age as the Oldish was when I entered S.H. [School House at Malvern College]; the same age as P was when I was seven.

Tuesday 19th June.

In the evening J and I went to the Chequers at 7 p.m. to meet Parkin, as a preliminary to supping with him. . . . After supper [at the Georges] we adjourned to College, where it was deliciously cool and peaceful, and had a most enjoyable chat. Conversation drifted via primitive man, and Wells' *Outline of History* to anxiety as to the future —Parkin and I taking the view that such anxiety is cant, and J maintaining that the future was as interesting to us as the past.

Tuesday 26th June.

All day in College and made fairish headway. J was in too and was visited by a friend called Bullock, a lecturer at the Naval College at Greenwich, to whom I was introduced. We went to the buttery for a pint of beer at about half past twelve. When I joined them, Bullock

---

163. This was later adapted, expanded, and revised in 1942 into *The Splendid Century: Some Aspects of French Life in the Reign of Louis XIV* (though it was not published until 1953).

was talking most enthusiastically about Beecham's[164] merits as a conductor. It appears that Beecham is that rare thing, an educated man, *and* a musician, and Bullock claims that his education enables him to get that something more out of a musical composition, which makes all the difference. . . . He told us two capital stories of him: (1). At a rehearsal of Tristan and Isolde, the Tristan "died" before Isolde had time to come on the stage: Isolde (bustling on) "Oh Sir Thomas, the Tristan died too soon". Sir T "NO opera singer ever died too soon". (2). Beecham on conductors: "There are two sorts of conductor: the one has the score in his head, the other has his head in the score".

Monday 2nd July.

It is really amazing how like Minto can be to P in many ways. This morning I got a letter from Kelsie,[165] who is staying with George Harding at Boris in Ossory: in this house there is an irritating custom that all the mail is taken to M before being distributed: so of course she had had ample opportunity to scrutinize my mysterious letter before I got it at breakfast. She and I breakfasted alone, and the following dialogue ensued: M. "I see you've got a letter with the Irish stamp on it. It's not very often *you* get a letter from the Free State". S. "No". M. "Is Major Parkin in Ireland now?" S. "No". M. "Oh, I thought he might be, the handwriting's exactly like his, isn't it?" S. "There is a slight resemblance". M. "But it's not from him you say?" S. "No". and finishing my breakfast I got up and went into town in a state divided between amusement and irritation. The more I see of Minto, the odder I find the psychological problem of J's feelings towards her and those which he entertained for P.

Tuesday 10th July.

I had an argument with J on the ethics of social lying, he maintaining that a lie must not be told, even in indifferent matters, as a conversational counter in talking with a fool, I denying this strenuously.

On Saturday, July 7, Warren and Jack traveled to Belfast for a visit with their Uncle Augustus (Gussie) Hamilton and various other friends and relatives, and for a business meeting with J. W. A. Condlin (their father's former law clerk).

---

164. Sir Thomas Beecham (1879-1961), conductor.

165. Isabello Kelso ("Kelsie") Ewart (1886-1966), second cousin and Belfast neighbor to Warren and Jack. See also, C. S. Lewis, *Surprised by Joy,* pp. 43-45, for a personal view of the Ewart family and their home, "Montbracken" (actually Glenmachan).

On Tuesday, July 10, they sailed to Glasgow for a visit with their Lewis uncles (William and Richard) who had settled in Scotland. On Friday, July 13, Warren and Jack left Glasgow for a return voyage with the Clyde's Shipping Company Tour—though this cruise had a slightly altered schedule of port calls. On Tuesday, July 17, they arrived in London at the end of their cruise.

Tuesday 17th July.

[Today, in London, after] an excellent simple meal of bread and butter and cheese and glass mugs of beer. . . . J and I sat on for a little while, discussing how we should spend the afternoon. Ultimately we decided on going to St. Paul's, which J had never seen, and accordingly took the underground to Blackfriars. This left us with a desperately hot walk to the Cathedral, and indeed, not being sure of the way, I was on the point of suggesting the abandonment of the attempt, when it loomed into view. I have never really admired St. Pauls, and found no reason to alter my view on this, the most detailed inspection I have yet made of it. But I admired its perfect proportions: it is not until one notices the tiny figures walking in the gallery under the dome that one begins to realize the vast size of this building. And, if you like florid magnificence, it is here done to perfection. . . . From the profane point of view, the real interest of St. Pauls is that it is a sublimated Mme. Toussaud's. Here are grouped together the effigies of more famous people (mainly admirals) than one normally sees in a twelve month. I have a hazy general impresion of winged victories, mourning Brittanias, cannon, and strong, complacent eighteenth century faces. The Nelson memorial struck me as being among the poorest. That which interested me most was the Johnson, and as I looked into his eyes, I really got something of the feeling which must have been roused by meeting [him] face to face.

Wednesday 18th July.

I shall here try to digest the various bits of family history which I collected during our tour [to Belfast and Glasgow]. Most important and most disconcerting is the flood of new light which I got on Grandfather Lewis's character: as Aunt Mary and Aunt Agnes[166] corroborate each other in this account, I fear it must be substantially correct. It obliterates entirely the picture of the simple, humble old man which I had formed on half memories of childhood and the

---

166. Aunt Mary Taggert Lewis (wife of Albert's brother, Joseph) lived in Belfast, while Aunt Agnes Young Lewis (wife of Albert's brother, Richard) was one of the Glasgow Lewises.

evidence of his writings. But if it is in one way disconcerting to find out the sort of man he really was, it is in another way a great relief, for it extinguishes the feeling of shame I always had at the recollection of the brusquerie with which he was treated by P. Apparently "Stop your nonsense, Pa"! was entirely the right sort of remark to address to him. Aunts Mary and Agnes both agree that he was a fearful snob: so does Eileen.[167] He was also arrogant and very offensive. . . . Both the Aunts told me that he expected to be served first at table, even if there were guests present, and if this was not done, he would stare reproachfully at the server. He was troublesome about his food and Aunt Agnes told me that at Aunt Mary's he would upbraid Aunt Mary for not letting him decide what guests should be asked to meals. May[168] remembers him at table, "ordering" his helping, and pointing with his knife—"I'll have that potato—no not that one, *that* one". If pieces of food did not please him, he would throw them on to his neighbour's plate! Aunt Agnes told me that he admired nothing but wealth, and despised nothing so much as poverty.

Sunday 29th July.

J in bed today with a temperature, having apparently caught a chill—just when at last, after incredible kafuffle, everything has been settled for our departure for Kilkeel on the 1st.

Warren, Jack, Maureen, and Mrs. Moore vacationed at the seaside resort of Kilkeel, County Down, Northern Ireland, near the Mourne Mountains and about forty miles south of Belfast. Warren continued in his resolve not to travel long distances with Mrs. Moore (a resolution made on the last family holiday in September 1933). Consequently, Warren made the journey alone by train, while the others traveled by car to Liverpool, where the entire household boarded a ship for Belfast.

Tuesday 31st July.

To our great relief J was pronounced fit to travel today: I wanted him to change places with me and go by train, but he would not. He, M, and Maureen set out in the car sometime during the morning for Tarporley in Cheshire, where they proposed to spend the night, en route for Heysham. I went into town as usual and did my mornings work, and came home in due course to the delicious quiet of an empty

---

167. Eileen Lewis, cousin of Jack and Warren, and daughter of Agnes and Richard Lewis.

168. May Lewis, cousin of Jack and Warren, and daughter of Mary and Joseph Lewis.

house. . . . Supper all by my self, and a very pleasant evening, not reading much except Rose Macaulay's eulogy of being idle and alone and the difficulty of compassing these two delightful things.

Wednesday 1st August.

I was down early to the "Ulster Express" as they call it now a days, and lucky that I was, for nearly all the corner seats had been reserved in advance. . . . I was much interested by the quartet at the other table in my section—three public school bloods and the young prep. school brother of one of them. . . . My heart warmed to the way in which they were enjoying their cigarettes and their cider. I would have loved to have spoken to them, but remembered in time that while I knew accurately and vividly what they were feeling like, I to them could be nothing more than an intrusive old man, who must long ago have lost all interest in everything which makes life worth living.

Thursday 2nd August.

Ultimately it was decided that Minto and Maureen should go on by car [from Kilkeel to Belfast], and that J and I should travel on the 4.45. We then separated, J going out to spend the morning with Arthur Greeves (who had 'phoned up the ship before we left it), and I taking tram up to the Cemetery. . . . I walked up to P's grave, or rather to our family colony of graves in a dim, misty atmosphere of dripping cypress trees not inappropriate to the occasion. Everything was alright. It struck me while standing there that there is an uncommon difference between the platitudinous and the trite: the former is always base metal, while the latter may at any moment become vested with tremendous significance, i.e., the platitudinous is generally false, but the trite is true. All this came to me as I reflected what a tremendous thing it is to look at a plot of grass and say, "In a very few years now, I (or the shell of me) will be lying under that identical plot". And yet how trite! One would groan if one found a man in a novel indulging in such reflections.

Tuesday 7th August [in Kilkeel].

I am worried about J who has taken to his bed again with a low temperature: he is well enough to come down to meals, but returns to bed immediately after. I don't like his not being able to shake off this fever: he however seems to be pretty cheerful. . . . After midday dinner Minto, Maureen, Tykes and I went for the best drive I have had since I have been here: it in fact would have been perfection had it not been for Minto who was snappish and irritable and continued so for the rest of the day. However, I brushed the rust off my anti-Pudaita armour, or in other words withdrew into my own secret world, and enjoyed myself very well. . . . The last stretch I found rather tedious, mainly because Minto's comments were increasing in acidity to a point where it was becoming increasingly difficult to ignore them: in fact I thought that point had been reached when, on my making a remark to Maureen who was sitting beside me, she rasped "What is he so politely and cleverly saying now?" . . . Still I was very glad when we got home. Maureen's conduct throughout excited my warmest admiration. After tea—an unpleasant meal, atmosphere very tense, and even J angry with M—Maureen and I escaped in the car to Cranfield beach where we found a high tide and had a delicious bathe.

Sunday 12th August.

I today finished *The Well at the World's End*[169] and have enjoyed its dreamy sensuous beauty immensely: I have not read it, I suppose for ten years, and I had partly forgotten how extraordinarily rich is its texture. I have now started a book of J's on the influence of Christ in the ancient world, which promises very well.

On Monday, August 13, Arthur Greeves drove down from Belfast to spend the day with Jack.

Monday 13th August.

Arthur is thinner than he used to be, and that, coupled with the fact that he is now completely bald, except for a fringe, makes him look taller than ever. I enjoyed meeting him again. He talked a little of Spain, where he has been, but he has not the faculty of describing what he has seen. He told us of some cave dwellers who still exist in the vicinity of San Sebastian. He had seen Loyola's monastery, of which the architecture is supposed to be very fine, but he was not impressed with it. He has been in the Basque country and says the language is quite unlike that of any other part of Europe. He went soon after tea.

Wednesday 15th August.

We got back to dinner about quarter past one, and it was arranged that we should leave for the bathing beach at three: at seven minutes to three Minto announced (a) that she would come with us, and (b)

---

169. *The Well at the World's End* (1896), a fantasy novel by late-nineteenth-century author William Morris.

that she and Dotty[170] would first walk up town and do some shopping: they left the house at five minutes past three. Tomorrow I shall be driving all day, so will miss my bathe two days running. I hope and think I gave no sign of my feelings, but I then and there registered a determination that no pressure short of the certainty of an open rupture with J will ever induce me to go on any expedition of which Minto is a member in the future. Certainly on no holiday.

Thursday 16th August.

I haven't spent such a beastly day since my drive to Milford last summer—and it was at any rate much shorter: I drove and drove through detestable country until I began to feel that I had never been doing anything else: J of course sat in the back with Minto. . . . Somewhere in this interminable nightmare we stopped for sandwiches and I sought a little sympathy from J: but my very guarded criticism of Minto sent him stumping away in a temper. So off we went again, my head aching worse than ever. As the long long day wore slowly on, I became too tired even to feel angry.

Tuesday 21st August.

Still blowing hard, with sudden squally showers at infrequent intervals. Although it looked very unpromising, Maureen and I set off for the beach at ten thirty. It is nice to have her back again,[171] especially for the bathing, for no day can daunt her, and she has a real gust for the sea. Tho' it rained hard while we were in. I enjoyed this more than any bathe I have had so far. The sea was, for such a place, very rough and I floated up hills of water and swooped down the other side of them until I felt, as Swinburne says somewhere, that I myself was a part of the sea. The rain and spray beat on my face, and I lay for a long time in the shallows letting the waves break over my shoulders and head. A good bathe comes very near to being the summit of physical happiness. . . . I got back to the village about twelve o'clock and, leaving Maureen to take the car home, went to the Kilmorey Arms: just as I was going in, I saw J in the distance and whistled to him. I wonder why it is that whenever you shout or whistle at anyone in the street, that person is the *only* one who does not turn round? However, I got hold of him and we went in to our alcove and had a drink and I discussed my seaside cottage—J raising the topic of what I would do if he were to predecease me: a subject which does not bear

---

170. Dotty, a friend of Mrs. Moore, who was invited to spend some of the Kilkeel holiday with The Kilns household.

171. Maureen had visited Vera Henry at Annagassin for several days.

thinking about, for I dare not contemplate a life which does not centre round J. I however pointed out that if such a thing were to happen, I would probably be less lonely in a cottage in Ulster than anywhere else in the world.

Thursday 23rd August.

A pleasant and busy day. . . . We went first to a bathing beach near the Slieve Donard Hotel, which was empty, tho' a recognized bathing place with boxes, and Maureen and I proceeded to change: about half way through this operation I glanced out of the peephole in my box, and saw, with stupefaction, that there were at least 150 people on the beach! We emerged and pushed our way through the crowd to the water. This was not one of our successful bathes—very stony and the water intensely cold: but it was worth doing for the glorious view of Slieve Donard which one got from the water line: I can't imagine why water line views of an object are always the best, unless it is that there is no foreground to distract one's attention. We came out, dressed, and emerged from our boxes—to find the beach quite empty again! This has certainly been the most successful mass mobilization of the Little People which I have ever come across. J explained with much laughter how it had come about: as soon as we had started to undress, five charabancs had arrived and disgorged a "tour": after ten minutes on the beach a whistle was blown by the "tourmaster" and they all packed into their charabancs and drove off again—"See the whole of Beautiful Ulster in twenty four hours for 10/-" or something of that kind.

Friday 24th August.

[J]ust as I was entering the town, a poor old "shawly" asked me for a penny with which to buy some tea: I gave her 6d.: whereupon she thanked me profusely and added "may you soon be a bright angel in heaven"—as ambiguous a compliment as I have ever had paid to me!

Sunday 26th August.

We got to Joey's[172] about four. . . . After tea we all strolled out across the golf links (a club by the by, Joey tells me, which has never recovered from the fact that the Prince of Wales once played a couple of rounds there). We walked along sand dunes for a mile or so and then turned home again. Joey had offered to run us home in his car,

---

172. Dr. Joseph Lewis, cousin to Warren and Jack, who lived in Belfast.

so the bugbear of catching a nine o'c. bus had vanished. We got back to his house about twenty past six and I moved an adjournment to Kilkeel. The two children sat in the back with J and he had a lot of talk with them. The eldest is a girl after my own heart—likes history, has an imaginary country called Toyland, and finds the day much too short for all she has to do. I had forgotten this intense *busyness* of young childhood. I heard little of the laws and polity of Toyland except that it is now ruled by King Brownears the 100th—a dynasty Chinese in its tenacity apparently! . . .

Monday 27th August.
Looked through Saturday's *Times* which contains the very interesting news that the only known MS of Malory's *Morte d'Arthur* has just been discovered in the library of Winchester College.

Thursday 30th August.
When I had seen J off [on the train to Belfast] I drove back to Kilkeel, storing up in my brain all the beauties of the way: I realized one thing as I drove along—namely that while it may be my fate to spend all the rest of my days in England, I shall never be at home there: Co. Down is my home, and, as J wrote to me in a poem once, the rest

      Will be raw rough colonial country till we die.

Friday 31st August.
I got home [to The Kilns] about seven, and as soon as I had had supper I unpacked for J and myself and stowed everything away in our respective rooms: and so to bed, thoroughly tired, at eleven o'-clock. As I dozed off, I reflected that there has been more that I liked than the reverse about this holiday, but still, the credit balance is not sufficiently large to tempt me to repeat the experiment. See the motto on the title page of this volume![173]

Sunday 2nd September.
Poor Minto sadly out of order today, so much so that she was unable to attend our Sunday recital.[174]

---

173. "Better is an handful with quietness, than both the hands full with travail and vexation of spirit" (Ecc. 4.6).

174. The Sunday evening gramophone recital of phonograph records selected by Warren.

Wednesday 5th September.

It was a lovely evening on top of Shotover [Hill, behind The Kilns], with perfect light and shade effects, and Eileen[175] said that she appreciated the richness of our Southern landscape after Scotland: talking of her own mountains, and while fully admitting their beauty, she said that after a time she "wanted to tear them apart" (making a gesture with her hands as of pulling back window curtains: I can quite understand this feeling). She took to the animals and had a great success with Troddles[176] in particular, who never growled at her once.

Tuesday 11th September.

I spent most of the afternoon picking blackberries for this year's wine vintage. I had thought that it would amount to almost the same thing as an afternoon's loafing, but I was soon undeceived: it proved to be quite hard work, and I sweated considerably. I got 5 lbs., Maureen four, and Kathleen[177] three. There is this pleasant about work, that it embodies one, tho' only in a trifling degree, in the agriculturalists calendar. I have at least reminded myself that it is harvest time.

Monday 17th September.

In town all day and did fifteen sheets of the family papers. In the evening, while J and I were sitting in the study, the rest of the family entered, escorting Anna[178] who carried a small hedgehog on a sheet of newspaper. He (or she) lay curled up, breathing deeply: a saucer of milk was sent for: we all watched in great silence. He took no interest in the milk, but started on a slow ramble round the room. Finally we took him out and put him where he was found, viz. on the grass in front of the pergola. I hope he will turn out to be no casual visitor, but the first of a family of hedge pigs which is taking up residence here.

Saturday 22nd September.

Heavy rain for about two hours this morning, and a very welcome and lovely sight it was. While I was watching it from our windows in College, I was struck by a curious thought, viz. that there must be now precisely the same quantity of water in the world as there was at the time of its creation: for water does not grow, nor, so far as I know

---

175. Eileen Lewis, cousin of Jack and Warren, lived in Helensburgh, Scotland with her parents. She was visiting The Kilns at the Lewis brothers's invitation.

176. Troddles was the second of The Kilns dogs.

177. Kathleen Whitty, a friend of Mrs. Moore and Maureen, from Bristol.

178. Anna , an Irish maid at The Kilns.

has it any natural way of forming itself—tho' it can of course be created artificially in a laboratory: nor is there any source outside the planet from which we can draw fresh supplies. So that all that happens is that there is this quantity, X, of water, which is always constant, but the quantities (a) held in the earth as in a sponge, (b) in the sea, wells, rivers etc., and the clouds, and (c) in living organisms, varies from day to day. I discussed this idea with J when we were out for our walk, but we both found ourselves too grossly ignorant of physics to get beyond the bare hypothesis.

Wednesday 26th September.

Today comes very bad news of Maureen's friend Joan H. Of the unfortunate families we know, their plight is as bad as any: the family consists of Mr. and Mrs., three brothers, and Joan. Mr. is slowly dying of the same complaint as Randolph Muir: Mrs. is too poor to keep a servant and suffers from heart disease: two of the brothers are married and in poverty: the third is a curate in a slum parish. I gather that the only money which comes into the parents house is that which Joan earns as a music teacher. Now Joan has had a fall coming downstairs and has fractured her skull. She had just secured three new jobs: the father has recently had an expensive operation. I find my Christianity powerless to prevent me asking why such things should be. Minto, who shows up at her best in such circumstances, immediately moved us over our breakfast into a Relief Committee with herself in the chair. It was ultimately decided that she should go up and see Mrs. H tomorrow, and take with her a cheque book and also a hamper of eggs, vegetables etc. I offered £5 towards the fund: and now see how promptly one is sometimes rewarded in this world for doing one's duty! A completely unexpected cheque for £16 odd dropped in from Condlin shortly afterwards, to be divided between myself and J.

Sunday 30th September.

Up shortly before seven this morning and to early Communion with J. . . . In church I managed to concentrate fairly well, and I hope with some useful results. At eleven o'c. service Thomas preached an excellent sermon on angels, clear, sensible, and with a touch or two of quiet humour. He began with the tepidity, or even absence of our belief in the angels, attributing it to the fact that many people confused them with the faeries in which they definitely disbelieved: mentioned in parenthesis that *winged* angels are only twice mentioned in the Bible: pointed out that the existence of angels was an integral part of the Bible story: pleaded for a livelier interest in an element of religion, without which it would be duller and more common place ("and we too, if we were not so already"): and wound up with a rather beautiful suggestion of the hint which the winds give of angels going about the world on man's behalf. I enjoyed it thoroughly. I had some interesting talk with J on this subject when we got back to the study—the angels according to St. Denys, the different Gospel accounts of their appearance, angels in Art etc. J had always as a child thought of the angels as women—I had always thought of them as men, in chain armour with shield and sword—Maureen had thought of them as "men and women but that there were far more women angels than men ones". Which J said "was not only erroneous but impudent".

Monday 1st October.

In the evening by appointment to the King's Arms to meet Parkin, who returned from leave yesterday. . . . Dinner at Georges. Here Parkin developed the original and ingenious theory that the supremacy of the European rests not on what he has got in his head, but what he has got on his feet—viz. boots: He pointed out that no slippered or bare footed peoples have ever secured an exploitable victory over booted ones, and touched on the feeling of inferiority felt by oneself in one's socks. It was most amusing. Home about 10.30 after a most enjoyable evening.

Saturday 6th October.

Barfield, who had first been expected for the week end, but now was here for "a few hours", turned up about twelve o'c. . . . I worked steadily and with great enjoyment until four, when I went across to the Eastgate and had tea, and then came back and continued till 5.30 and so home. Found Barfield with J in the study, and drank a bottle of beer with them, and talked about Browning, whose *Ring and the Book*[179] I am now reading. I said that, except for some tremendous lines, I got the impression of some such work of art as an almost finished bit of statuary, which you can see is going to be magnificent when the artist has put the final touches to it. I also said that I objected to Browning's habit of digging one in the ribs. Barfield agreed with me, but J said that Barfield had always underrated Browning. They both tried to explain the metre of [Robert Bridges's] *Testament of Beauty* to me, but I could not make much of it. . . . I did a little

---

179. *The Ring and the Book* (1868-1869), a book-length poem by Robert Browning.

practise after supper, and, going down to the study about nine, found that Barfield had now decided to stay the night: so took my book and pipe to the dining room. I was annoyed to find to what an extent I am becoming the slave of habit—Johnson's "complete scoundrel". Tho' the dining room is quite comfortable, I could not get rid of the feeling that I was "camping out", simply because I was not sitting in my own arm chair.

Monday 8th October.

In the afternoon . . . I took the dogs for a walk. I did so with quite an unusually vivid enjoyment of the country, going round the shoulder of the hill and home by Cowley and the churchyard. It was hot and sunny and intensely still, with occasional bird music very loud and sweet and clear. Tho' very bright and hot, I had the glorious knowledge that what I saw was the mere facade of summer—that I was looking at what J and I used to call a "thin" scene, and that behind it the scene shifters were busy getting on the sets for "Act. III.—Autumn".

Monday 15th October.

A really cold day at last and I was very glad of a coat when driving in to College. Paxford and Len turned up about half past eleven with our new bookcase and installed it: I considered it a great success. He brought with him the news that FK [Foord-Kelcey] died in the Acland [Nursing Home] at five o'clock last night, unconscious to the last. Poor old boy! Here should be no cause for tears, for he was, I believe 77: but one feels for him as one would do for a much younger man, because he had such an intense gust for life. . . . He was very fond of J and Minto. He is to be cremated, but there will be a funeral service at 12 on Thursday at Old Headington. I went for a blustering sunny walk in the afternoon, and could not get him out of my mind: I was full of those thoughts of death which look so trite when reduced to writing, but which are so tremendous when their real significance strikes one afresh—the amazing insecurity of life, and the thought that no single one of us has even a second's guarantee of tenure, and so on. I did not enjoy my walk much and was glad to be home again.

Thursday 18th October.

Up, made my own bed etc., and dressed in my best for FK's funeral, to which Paxford drove me at half past eleven. We had with us a cross and a wreath which Paxford laid at the entrance to the choir, in which stood a plain unvarnished coffin on a trestle draped in purpose, round which were burning candles. When I got there, there were about a dozen people in the church and our numbers gradually swelled to seventy four—mainly women, of the poorest classes. The service was as unimpressive as any well could be. . . . I could only find one detail in which the service agreed with that laid down in the Prayer Book—one of the prayers. The priest who took the service (I presume the Vicar), was only partially audible and fumbled for his words as if he were about to say "No, don't tell me: it's on the tip of my tongue". We had neither the proper lesson nor the proper psalms, and the hymns were a couple of 18th century ones, commonplace as to word and melody, and breathing a vaguely pious optimism. . . . I came away chilled, and dispirited at the meanness of the whole ceremony, and walked home from Headington cross roads. Walked round the foot of Shotover in the afternoon with the dogs: autumn has really come at last, and the tints are beginning to acquire some beauty. Near St. Ebba's we were overtaken by a rascalt of boys, who began to shout "Heel! Tykes"—so apparently J's stentorian performances have not escaped the notice of the neighborhood! I came home to two hours of the worst boredom which I have endured this year—an interminable visit from Helen R.'s mother, and Wendy[180] of all people, whom I don't think I have met since I stopped at Hillsboro in 1922. The former is a shrill voiced, vulgar, stupid sort of woman: the latter has improved in appearance since the old days—less red in the face, not so fat, and now looks like a retired musical comedy actress. We assembled in the dining room about 4.30, and there sat till 6.25, enduring a vociferous torrent of words—I cannot call it conversation—of which not one single word was of the faintest interest. I reached the stage of boredom where I began to allow imbecile speculation to become more and more insistent in me—"What" I said to myself "would happen if I seized this woman by the nape of her neck, pressed her face into her plate, and shampooed her with the tea pot?"

Sunday 11th November.
To church quarter of an hour earlier than usual this morning to attend the 10.45 Armistice service in the churchyard. . . . We assembled round the War Memorial, a good congregation, and the best showing of the corporate life of the parish that I have yet seen: Foresters, Ex-Service Men, Women's Union, Y.M.C.A., and Scouts and Guides, most, I think all of whom placed wreaths at the foot of the

---

180. Friends of Mrs. Moore.

cross. It gave me a sudden vision of what the world might be like if ever Christianity became the controlling force in it. . . . Walk with Maureen, and J in the afternoon. In the evening we had our usual gramophone recital, the piece de resistance being Mozarts clarinet quintet—a failure, to my very great surprise, for it has all the obvious, broad second rate merits of Beethoven's Fifth Symphony. Minto described it as being "whiney" and J as being "dull". Minto's criticism left me uninterested, but J's worried me for the rest of the evening: what is the unknown "x", in a man who is full of enthusiasm about the Fifth and finds this dull? I finally come to the conclusion that it must be the *comic* strain in the Fifth (an element which, as distinct from *humour,* is lacking in Mozart) which makes the difference with J. I feel wickedly tempted to give them some more Mozart next week and put it down on the programme as Beethoven! I wonder what would happen?

Monday 12th November.

Up early. Dull autumnal weather. Most unpleasant moment at breakfast when J snapped at Maureen—who took it very well. I spent all day in College and got through a great deal of work. It was very interesting to re-read the reviews of *Dymer:*[181] from them I gathered clearly why the book was not a public success—it is philosophy disguised as poetry. A thing, which the public, quite rightly, will not stand. While I was eating my bread and cheese I speculated on what might have happened if J had never got mixed up with the Greats School—but very quickly realised that this was only the old Kirkian absurdity of "if I were you": being what he is, the study of philosophy was to him as inevitable as death will be. I finished my lunch feeling that if I were Emperor of the World, I would start a pogrom against philosophers. From what I have seen of the subject in J's diaries, it seems to be an elaborate means of making a man think that his own personality is the only important thing in the world: a device for persuading a man that he is of a caste apart.

Thursday 15th November.

Maureen has recently expressed a desire to learn chess, and yesterday we had looked out the old Leeborough box of men and the board: this we set up, and started a game during our lunch. I had forgotten what good fun it is, and Lord! how it carried me back. It must I

---

181. *Dymer,* Jack Lewis's second published work, a book-length poem (London: J. M. Dent, 1926).

suppose be fifteen years any way since J and I sat down to a game together. We could not of course finish it, for Minto and Maureen called for us with the car at ten to two and took us round to the Sheldonian for the concert which we were all attending at 2.30. . . . This concert was I think the very best one I have ever attended, and J said the same thing afterwards. Beecham is a very great man: I thought I knew the Fifth Symphony inside out, but in his hands it became almost a new work—or rather it was the difference between listening to a set of old fashioned acoustic records and the same work on the new electrical records. What he got out of his orchestra amazed me. Beecham not only does not use a score, but he had not even a music stand in front of him—and this for three major works, and a Debussy suite. The latter by the way was delicious: I liked it better than any Debussy I have heard before. . . . *Tapiola* was magnificent in its grey grim Northern atmosphere, but seemed to me to lack unity and cohesion. As J and I said of it afterwards, it really seemed to be incidental music from an unwritten opera about these Northern gods: as such it would have been beyond praise.

Saturday 17th November.

J's friend and former pupil Pirie Gordon came to tea this afternoon: he is just back from Germany, and talked interestingly about his experiences there. He told us—on the authority of the *Times* correspondent—that in a concentration camp near Munich (?) 40 persons have died by torture since the camp opened, and 150 of "natural" causes. He notices a distinct falling off in the Nazi enthusiasm, as contrasted with his previous visit in the summer, but admits that in the summer he mixed chiefly with students, and this time with the middle aged. The Term still continues, and people are constantly being arrested and vanishing. He doubts if Hitler is fully aware of the cruelties which are being practised in his name. A Herr Himmler is head of the Ogpu or whatever it is called, and is the most sinister figure in Germany. There appear to be rumours that Hitler is mentally deranged: it is common knowledge that Goering was in a private lunatic asylum at the time of the Nazi coup—his insanity being caused by excessive drug taking.

Wednesday 21st November.

After going to bed I finished *The Ring and the Book*—a very wonderful poem, which I have enjoyed enormously. The Canto where Guido is waiting to be led out to execution is one of the most tremendous pieces of horror and terror in the whole of English literature, and his breakdown at the last is almost intolerably painful. Nothing shows the consummate artistry of Browning better than this Canto—we feel the dreadfulness of this trapped beast awaiting death, listen patiently as the Pope, to all that can be urged on his behalf, and yet feel that a reprieve would be an outrage. . . . It is the greatest discovery I have made since I found Masefield's "Dauber":[182] not of course that I mean by this in any way to compare the two poems.

Saturday 24th November.

A still foggy November day, such as I love. Barfield came out for the week end at lunch time, having spent last night with J in College. I had a longish solitary walk through the dim and silent countryside over towards Cowley in the afternoon: mentioned because of the extraordinary keenness with which I enjoyed the privacy of the fog, which seems to me to combine the pleasures of walking and being in a room alone. A great wave of happiness suddenly swept over me, and I realized, I hope with gratitude, how very good life is.

Friday 30th November.

Many flutterings of the English dovecot these days. Percy Tweedlepoppin is shortly retiring from the Goldsmith Readership: I had hoped that J might get this—a very nice thing, £600 a year I understand. But this cannot be, because he will not stand in the way of Brett Smith who needs the job more than he does. . . . Today at lunch J told us that de Selincourt, Professor of English at Birmingham, is resigning, and modestly gave us to understand that if he applied for the job, he would at least be a strong candidate: upon this interesting piece of news the family went into debate over the lunch table. . . . Minto of course was very much opposed to any plan which involved giving up The Kilns. I was very anxious that for once J should, in a matter which affected his whole future life, make his own decision independently of extraneous considerations: so was Maureen who showed great balance and good sense throughout the discussion. . . . At last J said that if he had only himself to consider, he would not care to live in Birmingham. So that's that.

Saturday 1st December.

Letter this morning from Major Scott, our churchwarden, appealing for subscriptions to pay off the deficit of £15 on the repairs recently carried out to the heating apparatus. On hearing of this Maureen remarked "I call it jolly cheek of them asking for money for the church,

---

182. *Dauber* (1913) by poet John Edward Masefield, O.M.

considering how little Mr. Thomas visits". I don't recollect ever hearing in so few words such a complete and many faceted misconception of the whole place of Christianity in the scheme of things—unless indeed it be Maureen's other remark which J told me when we were out for our walk, viz. "that she thought religion quite a good thing provided you didn't let yourself take it up too seriously". . . . Minto is the same, or indeed worse, for her conception of a Priest implies as a sine qua non that he be a "gentleman", as well as insisting that his primary duty is visiting in the parish. To me it appears perfectly plain that the paramount duty of a Priest is the administration of the Sacraments, the second duty to instruct his flock, and the third and least important, to visit and act as the social cement of the parish. . . . I discussed the subject with J on our walk but found that he did not attach the same importance to the Priest as the administrator of the Sacraments as I do: this he held to tend towards the Romish error of the magical efficacy of a Sacrament; and he thought parish visiting of great importance, quoting "feed my flock": to which I objected that visiting, as understood in Ireland, was in no sense feeding the flock, except possibly in the purely literal sense. We had an interesting discussion on this.

Monday 3rd December.

I make an entry in my journal today only in order to record such a fact as would have delighted P: I am evidently my father's son after all! Well, here goes: at nine o'c. this evening I was comfortable, strolling hatless and coatless in the lane, and when I went to bed at eleven, the thermometer by the open window in my room stood at 56°.

Tuesday 4th December.

Another dark hot day. J and I had lunch together in College, after which he caught the 2.20 to Birmingham, where he spends the night as the guest of Dods and gives a lecture. I came home and found the family getting ready to set out for a sale of work at Blenheim [Palace, near Oxford]. . . . When I met the others at dinner they were very full of the glories of Blenheim, where they had been shown the state rooms. Maureen told me that the rooms were finer than those of Buckingham Palace (which she hasn't seen), and Minto told me that Blenheim was the largest house in England. "Is it?" said I, with memories of Arundel,[183] "how did you find that out?" "Paxford says so" she replied in a tone of finality. I wondered gloomily if the breach

---

183. Arundel Castle, a massive stone and flint castle built soon after the Norman Conquest (1066). The Castle, in the county of West Sussex, has been improved and enlarged by successive dukes.

with J would have been irreparable had I given this observation the retort which first occurred to me, viz. to rise from the table, twitch the cloth and its load smartly to the floor, clap my hat on my head and stump off to the Chequers. I thought we were over the period of Paxolatry, but I fear me not.

Wednesday 5th December.

J returned from Birmingham about 10.45 and I had a few minutes talk with him before he began a tutorial at eleven o'c. He appears to have disliked Birmingham in general and the University in particular, and not to have been much impressed with the Dons. His host was Dods, the Irish-conscientious objector-Sinn Fiener[184] who was up at Univ. with him, and whom J says "is a man he doesn't much take to"—which, from J, is saying a good deal. . . . The attractions of the Birmingham Professorship were put before J, and he was given to understand that if he applied for it he would receive strong backing. He said he would not stand, and tried to interest them in Dyson. The other guest at dinner was the retiring English Professor, de Selincourt, who is a brother of the man who does the *Sunday Observer* reviews. He told J the following astounding story. His brother recently wrote an unfavourable review on some work of Ezra Pound's: since then he has received from EP not one, but several long letters consisting solely of the lowest barrack room personal abuse. . . . As J said, it is like finding a man who cries in public. I didn't think anything was able to lower my opinion of Pound, until I heard this story. . . . Maureen had a couple of pleasant boys up to play trios with her this afternoon—one an organ scholar of Wadham, and the other an organ scholar of New. I mention them for an amusing episode which Maureen tells me happened in the music room when they returned there after tea. She mentioned to them that she was teaching "one of her brothers" the piano, and they, much interested inquired "Which one?" "The fat one" replied Maureen: "Yes, but *which of them do you call the fat one?"* Needless to say, I lost no time in passing this story on to J!

Saturday 8th December.

I had an interrupted morning, but as the interrupter was Dyson, I really couldn't regret it. He was in—even for him—vivacious spirits and we had a longish chat while J, the indefatigable, celebrated the last

---

184. Sinn Féin, nationalist political party in the Republic of Ireland, committed to the unification of Ireland.

hour of term by taking a pupil. By an odd coincidence, almost the first thing he did was to ask me if I knew anything about Molinism, as he was taking pupils through *The Ring and the Book*—in answer, I handed him J's copy of Browning, to which I the other day added a typewritten note on the Molinists. We discussed Ezra Pound and his reaction to reviewers, and what action, if any, should be taken by the recipient of such letters as he wrote to de Selincourt. I said that dignified silence was the only possible attitude but Dyson—how like him—was in favour of replying by a Post Card containing merely two words—"Yes, quite": which, if such filth is to be answered at all, seems to me a reply which could hardly be bettered. J, who now joined us, asked Dyson if he were thinking of putting himself forward as a candidate for the Birmingham job, to which he replied very emphatically that he was not: which struck me as odd, as Birmingham is £1000 and I don't suppose he can be getting more than £400 at Reading. But as J said to me later in the day, the axiom under which we were brought up which states that any man will go anywhere and do any thing which will raise his income is entirely false: and indeed I need not look further than my own case, for there are hardly any circumstances which would persuade me to take a job in the unlikely event of anyone offering me one. I was sorry not to see more of Dyson, but he was lunching with someone and had to go off at ten to one. J went off at the same time to eat his weekly apple tart in Univ. and I lunched alone in his rooms. . . . Both Maureen and Jack very tired tonight, the former indeed worn out. Thank goodness another term over.

Sunday 9th December.

I have just finished reading through the last volume of my diary with a good deal of enjoyment, and think it is the most interesting that I have so far written. But I was concerned to find how much of it is made up of abuse of other people. What seem at the time to be occasional comments—amply justified—on the exasperations to which one is subjected, turn out in reading through to be anything but occasional, and to give a carping tone to the whole: and God knows my own position is pregnable enough; I must be at least as exasperating to others as they are to me. So I think I could hardly have come more apropos upon a more suitable quotation to make the motto of this volume than that which I have just put on the flyleaf.[185] I must try to live up to it.

---

185. "Let all bitterness, and wrath, and anger, and clamour, and evil speaking, be put away from you, with all malice" (Eph. 4.31).

Christmas Day.

My alarm clock failed to waken me, but I woke up with the sound of the church bell for the 7 o.c. service in my ears. Upstairs and wished J a happy Christmas at 7.15, and both of us out at ten to eight, finding quite a little procession going churchwards down the lane. (I suppose we must soon, alas, give up calling it the lane!). It was a grey, thin morning, but warmer than it became later in the day. There was a very good congregation, but not so big as last Easter. These major festivals are nearly always to me something of a disappointment, and this morning I found it particularly hard to concentrate: the very knowledge of the greatness of the occasion produces a determination to "live up to it" which is foredoomed to failure, and then, so easily distracted am I, that the mere presence of such an unaccustomed number of people increases my difficulties. But I hope I didn't communicate entirely unprofitably. . . . After church played J a game of chess, and checkmated him, thus getting my revenge for the defeat he inflicted on me on Sunday. We had an impromptu concert after dinner, I having at last got Vol. I of the Delius Society's records. (N.B. discovered the parcel, quite by accident, when I was going to bed last night, tucked under my wardrobe!)

On January 3 through 5, 1935, Warren and Jack took their fourth annual walking tour—this year walking in the Chiltern Hills near Oxford.

Thursday 17th January, 1935.

[Today] I tried the experiment of having beefsteak and kidney pie, which so far as I can remember I have not tasted since the last time I was at Leeborough: rather to my surprise I really enjoyed it. (Horrible thought which just occurs to me as I write—am I turning into a Pudaita? Does *every* Lewis begin to turn into a Pudaita when he gets to the age of forty? But as E. M. Delafield says in the *Provincial Lady*,[186] "subject too depressing to pursue any further".)

Monday 21st January.

[Today, on our return to Oxford, from our holiday at Southsea, Parkin and I passed through Reading,] where we stopped to thaw ourselves out over some tea, followed by a short walk. Whilst walking, we came upon rather a good toy shop, and Parkin, who is as much of a child in these things as I am, instantly decided that it would be politic to buy his General's son a box of model gradient posts for

---

186. *The Diary of a Provincial Lady* (1931) by novelist E. M. Delafield (Edmée Elizabeth Monica de la Pasture).

his railway which we saw in the window amongst a crowd of other fascinating things. So we went in and spent a very pleasant half hour strolling about. Lord! what couldn't J and I have done in the old days with the resources open to the modern child! You can now get model civilians of all sorts, model villages, fields, fences, trees, gardens, animals, railway stations (really like), and all well within the means of a thrifty boy. It is interesting to speculate on how far Boxonian history would differ from what it is, had all these things been available for us.

Thursday 7th February.

Today I adopted Rose Macauley's slogan and "lived life to the full".... worked until a few minutes to twelve when J carried me with him to the Schools to hear Nichol Smith[187] lecture on Swift. I was introduced to him outside the lecture room, but did no more than shake hands, for it was already late. I was very agreeably surprised at the schools—we went into a large, not unhandsome room, hung with oil portraits, and excellently warmed, where we sat on chairs, each at a small table.... The lecturer *sat* throughout his discourse, which struck me as odd, and, unlike the sort of lectures to which I am accustomed, no questions were asked at the end. He struck me as being an uncommonly good man, and I like both his manner and his matter, tho', as regards the former, he might have spoken a little more loudly. I do not know enough of Swift to say how far his portrait is to be trusted, but it certainly gave me a more favourable impression of him than I had before—tho' I could not understand why he was at such pains to prove that the ferocity of Swift's satire was not the fruit of a disappointed old age but had always been part of the man.... It was very interesting to see the type of notes which undergraduates take at a lecture: hardly any of them failed to write down every *fact*, though of course this is precisely the sort of information which it is not at all necessary to come to a lecture for. We got out a few minutes after one and went to College where we had a light lunch—bread and butter and sausage—in J's rooms and afterwards walked up to the town Hall for the subscription concert.... Maureen, who normally comes with me to these Thursday shows, was playing in the orchestra today. I enjoyed this as much as any concert I have been to recently. The Beethoven I thought dull, and it was played rather lifelessly, so presumably the orchestra thought it dull too. The Vaughan Williams was simply

---

187. David Nichol Smith, Professor of English Literature at Merton College, Oxford.

magnificent—indeed J went so far as to say that it was as good a symphony as he had ever heard. . . . I enjoyed *[The Planets]* very nearly as much as the London Symphony and that is saying a great deal. J thought Mars and Saturn the best, I thought Mars and Jupiter: but we both thought Mars was the best of the three—"the finest piece of anti-war propaganda I have struck" said J. The description of it on the programme gives its effect very well: the wild savagery of the outside instruments held in check by the disciplined rhythm of the marching time pattern gives as good a picture of war (realistically treated) as probably any music ever will do.

Friday 22nd February.

Went with Minto, Maureen, and a Mrs. Thomas this evening to see the O.U.D.S. do *Hamlet* at the New Theatre—a party which had started by J urging me to come with *him* and M to *Hamlet*. Long after the tickets were bought, he discovered that Barfield was coming to stop with him tonight, and he couldn't go, so I was badly let in: I considered backing out myself but felt it would be rude, and determined to go, but "in a spirit of no satisfaction". . . . As for *Hamlet*—my goodness! Coghill was the producer, and had I thought done his work well, though some of the critics didn't appear to think so: the costumes I liked. There is one admirable character in this play, Pollonius, (very well acted I thought), and whenever he was on the stage I enjoyed myself: his scene where he explains to the King and Queen what he thinks is wrong with Hamlet is capital fun: but alas, all too soon he was killed, and from that point onwards I was desperately bored. As for *Hamlet* I have rarely conceived such a sudden antipathy to any character, and there was an intolerable deal of him: every few minutes all the characters would hard heartedly sneak off and leave us at the mercy of this snivelling, attitudinizing, platitudinizing arch bore for hundreds of lines at a stretch, and I could have screamed. In fact if I had not been fortified by a double whiskey and soda half way through, I would not have stuck it to the end. . . . What dramatic merit the play had, seemed to have been supplied by Coghill and not by Shakespeare. The murders in the last ten minutes would have disgraced a Punch and Judy show.

Sunday 10th March.

Went to evensong where there was a fairish congregation, and a service that I enjoyed much. . . . I was much struck by an incidental remark in [the] sermon. He said that natural beauty leads the mind to thoughts of God, and ugliness has the opposite—"this fact is of course known to certain people, and hence the deliberate destruction of beauty which is going on all over the country". Does he mean I wonder that the Devil is instigating people to destroy beauty without any clear consciousness of why they are doing it, or does he mean to suggest that there are conscious forces at work (i.e. human forces) which want to prevent mens minds from being turned to thoughts of God? A startling thought this latter.

Wednesday 13th March.

Last night I finished the first of my Lent books, and the very best religious book which I ever read in my life—Latham's *Pastor Pastorum:* first published in 1890, and since reprinted *seventeen* times. . . . Throughout the book he keeps on hammering in that had our Lord shown "A Sign" i.e. a miracle so stupendous as to *force* belief, it would have been tantamount to destroying humanity and putting another order of beings in its place—for if you are *made* to believe in God by an act of God, how then are you a man? One of those points so obvious (when someone else has thought of it for you), that one wonders why one didn't start thinking *from* that point oneself: he points out how all through our Lord's life on earth, there is always left some fairly plausible loophole for the sceptic to refuse to believe. It is of course for the same reason that Our Lord did not show Himself to, say, Pilate, after the Resurrection—had He done so, *belief* in the Resurrection would have become meaningless. . . . He clears up too the point which has often puzzled me—why did Christ not found a Church, thus avoiding all the weary story of heresy etc.? Because a Church must be *alive,* and had he founded one, it would have been fixed for all time—man would have had nothing to do or think about.

Monday 18th March.

Much exercised by reflections arising out of a conversation yesterday at lunch, in which Minto appeared very shocked at the idea of servants being allowed to use the telephone—not on the ground of expense, but on the ground that it is "A Good Thing" that they should not be allowed to do so. Which raises the question, when did the Mintonian, or late Victorian attitude towards the domestic section of "the lower orders" arise? Presumably when employers ceased to be certain of their own position: but when was that? Or I should rather have said "ceased *subconsciously* to be certain etc.", because they thought themselves certain enough of their own position. I asked J, who could throw no light on the subject. . . . I must confess that Minto's social concepts always leave me with a feeling of uncomfortable indignation—a sort of shame, as if I myself entertained or expressed the same ideas: but then again, these glimpses of the pit from which she has emerged are good in this way, that they show how far she has advanced—the really remarkable thing is that she should be so likeable, so tolerant, so broadminded.

From March 18, 1935 until January 13, 1936, no entries were made in the diary of Warren Lewis. His interest in his diary was revived with the advent of his fifth annual walking tour with Jack. This holiday, taken later in the month of January than usual (13 through 16), was in the county of Derbyshire, north of Oxford.

Tuesday 14th January, 1936.

[Today, at Taddington, we turned] aside to see the village church, a beautiful old building of the local stone. . . . In a little side chapel the Sacrament was reserved, and a notice asked you to enter with "special reverence" on that account; this led me later in the morning into an argument with J on that subject: I said that there was room only for a clear cut division of opinion—if one is a Catholic, the aumbry contains Our Lord, and of course even prostration is hardly reverence enough: but if one is Church of England, it contains but wafer and a little wine, and why in front of that should one show any greater reverence than in any other part of the church? J was not satisfied, and seemed to think that there was a middle view between the two.

Thursday 16th January.

I called J's attention to the lovely snow clad trees and remarked that in spite of the cliche "a veritable fairy land", fairies are not generally associated with snow. J's idea is that the reference is to the transformation scene in a pantomime, and I think he is right.

Saturday 18th January.

Kipling died at ten minutes past twelve this morning, age 70.

Monday 20th January.

The news of the King's health[188] was ominous this morning, and at half past nine this evening when I was sitting in the study, Minto came down to tell me that an announcement had just come through that all further broadcasts were suspended and that an announcement would be made at ten o'c. I went up to listen to it, and as soon as Big Ben had tolled ten it came—a bulletin from the doctors at

---

188. King George V (1865-1936, reigned 1910-1936), the second son of Edward VII.

Sandringham: "The King's life is moving peacefully towards its close". Rather beautiful words, and very impressive. I must say the B.B.C. showed great dignity and feeling in the matter: as soon as this had been given out there was a short and (to me at any rate) very moving service, including a prayer for the King's soul in its passing.

Tuesday 21st January.

The King died at 11.55 last night: when I got into college J, who had been to the early Communion, had already heard the prayer for our gracious Lord, Edward the Eighth. Poor George V! What a reign of it he had; Lords Reform, the Ulster crisis, the war, the years of unrest, and unemployment. And how well he did! He who was looked upon as the weakling of them all in 1914—Wells once described him as "the husk of a King"—was the only one to weather the storm. Emperor, Kaiser, Tsar, Ferdinand of Bulgaria, Constantine of Greece all swept away, and he came out of it with enhanced prestige. He touched my life at three points: the weeks holiday, spent with Blodo Hilton[189] at Lambourn, in honour of his accession: then three years later, the inspection at the R.M.C. when he made us a little homily on giving us commissions "in my army": and my presentation at St. James', the latter the only time I saw him in state.

Thursday 30th January.

Took Minto and Maureen this evening to the Electra to see the King's funeral, which, even in that not very satisfactory medium, seemed to me full of beauty and pathos: most of the music seems to have been provided by the pipes of the Scots Guards. The King[190] cut a very poor figure—dead tired, looking from side to side, and trudging along with little attempt at marching, in the uniform of an Admiral of the fleet.

Saturday 1st February.

News today that Tolkien, playing squash and stretching for a high ball, said sharply to his partner "Don't do that again: it hurts"—thinking that the partner had playfully kicked him on the leg. He was then taken off to a doctor and it was found that he had broken a

---

189. Edward G. ("Blodo") Hilton, a friend from Malvern College, who had accompanied Warren on a four-day holiday (granted to all schools in honor of the coronation of George V).

190. King Edward VIII (later the Duke of Windsor).

ligament in his leg and will be in bed for the next ten weeks. J went in to see him after tea, but found Madame there, so could not have much conversation with him. Of all the men I have ever met, poor Tolkien is the most unfortunate.

Sunday 16th February.

Poor old Papworth's long life is ended at last; he has been with us since 1922—and thus, with a very short interval two dogs, Tim[191] and Tykes, have been an essential part of the background of my life since 1907—twenty nine out of my forty one years. Tykes carried his years wonderfully well until last autumn when Heather knocked him off walks: I don't know whether post hoc was propter hoc, but certainly retirement suited him no better than it does some humans: within a few weeks he was a very old dog: then came blindness and perpetual ailments, though he kept his appetite almost up to the last. The last three or four days of his life he was barely able to stand, and was kept going with whisky. He was alive in his basket at ten thirty last night, and died sometime during the night. I miss him, and even the nuisance of him, and the after dinner walk. Paxford buried him this afternoon on the edge of the cliff near our eastern fence.

Tuesday 25th February.

Went over to Reading on the 4.30 to meet Parkin who is down south for a few days, and en route enjoyed the lovely sight of the Cornish Riviera express overhauling us at about seventy five m.p.h., in charge of "King George V", with its gleaming golden bell: there is nothing in myself which pleases me more than the fact that at my age a famous ship or train can still move me almost to tears just as it did twenty five years ago.

Thursday 27th February.

This evening went to a sparsely attended but very enjoyable concert in Exeter, where Maureen was one of a quintet led by Coghill which played an admirable Schumann which I have never heard before—I think too the only Schumann that I have ever liked. This was a very intimate concert, in the dim lit hall, with two blazing fires throwing a flicker on the barely discernable portraits, and the physical comfort in which we sat induced an unusually receptive mood. There was some delightful unaccompanied polyphonic singing by an octette which sat round a table in the old Elizabethan way—but it would be easy to have too much of this sort of music.

---

191. A family pet from Warren's and Jack's childhood at Little Lea.

1936

After the entry of February 29, 1936, there is a large break in the diary. One probable reason for this gap was Warren's acquisition during 1936 of a twenty-foot motor boat, the Bosphorus. *A small, two-berth cabin cruiser that Warren had specially built, the* Bosphorus *was based at Salter's Boatyard at Folly Bridge on the Thames.*

In an unpublished letter of April 4, 1966 to Mrs. Betty Jones, an American correspondent and friend, Warren was later to write: "My boating days were spent as what is over here called a 'Ditch crawler'. That is to say that I did inland cruising only, on our various canals and rivers, and great fun it was. I couldn't go to sea because, as my boat was designed to go almost anywhere inland, she only drew 1 ft. 10 ins., aft when fully loaded. The real beauty of having a boat you can live in is that in the cruising season no one ever knows where you are, and you have no mail (tho' of course there is the day of reckoning when you get back to your home port). Ditch crawling would suit you because of course you can tie up and go for a walk—generally in quite unspoilt country—just whenever you feel like it."

During his time on the Bosphorus, *Warren faithfully kept a log (unfortunately, no longer in existence), which no doubt served an equivalent purpose to his previous diary record.*

The vast majority of Warren's time on the Bosphorus *was spent alone, though not infrequently a friend from the Army would join him for a brief holiday cruise. These were happy times for Warren, for the* Bosphorus *afforded him both a freedom and a privacy which he found increasingly lacking in his home situation at The Kilns. Though still genuinely fond of Mrs. Moore, Warren began to resist her interest in his daily activities—much as he had resisted the overtures of his father, Albert, in earlier days. Thus the* Bosphorus *provided Warren with an escape from household tensions he was incapable of resolving.*

Based as he was on the Thames, Warren continued to spend as much time as possible with Jack, though there is no indication as to how frequently (if at all) Jack was able to accompany Warren on holiday cruises. It should be noted, however, that the name of Bosphorus *found its origin in the brothers' shared world of* Boxen; *for in* Boxen: Volume I *written by Jack in 1912, Captain Macgoullah serves as the honest skipper of the small schooner,* Bosphorus.

After the break in entries, Warren's diary resumes, as it had in 1936, with his annual walking tour with Jack. January 5 through 9, 1937, records the sixth of these yearly holidays—this one in Dulverton, Somerset.

Following this, Warren's pattern of silence extends once again to January 10, 1938, and the beginning of the Lewis brothers' seventh annual walking tour, a walk of 51-1/2 miles in the county of Wiltshire.

Tuesday 11th January, 1938.

As we progressed, the morning improved, and gradually the rain stopped. Far below us on our right was a ring of firs, with a clump of the same tree in the centre—like an enormous faerie ring as I said: J reproved me for calling the Little People by a name that they so much dislike and threatened all sorts of catastrophe—"Why can't you keep a civil tongue in your head?" he asked. However, they apparently decided to overlook my rudeness, for the improvement in the day held.

Warren's and Jack's 1938 walking tour ended on January 14. Once again, Warren's diary is silent until the beginning of the 1939 holiday, January 2. This eighth and final annual walking tour, January 2 to 6, was a walk of 42 miles in the Welsh Marshes; a visit to Malvern was also included in this holiday.

Thursday 5th January, 1939.

A lovely morning—of the sort. After a good breakfast and a small bill—rare combination—we went off in a perfectly lovely morning to catch the 9.47. Though I am sick of snow and it has spoilt our walking tour, I was conquered by its exquisite beauty. . . . I don't remember anything for a long time which has given me quite the thrill of the low morning sunlight falling in shafts through the woods flanking the road we came in by last night: and the uplands which had seemed so dreary as we came in last night were wonderful this morning. Certainly if one must have snowscape, one could not have it more perfect than we have seen it today. [At Great Malvern, we booked] tickets tonight for *Snow White and the Seven Dwarfs*. Every time I visit Malvern I like it better, not only for old sentimental relations, but for its peace and quiet, and the way it preserves so much of the atmosphere of a vanished age: J too feels the same and that we might do worse than spend our declining years there. Today it was looking particularly lovely, with the Priory tower standing up gaunt and grey against the snow sprinkled hills. . . . Snow White, a few touches of abominable vulgarity apart, is first rate; especially all the scenes in which the animals figure. It was worth going to if only for the scene of the spring cleaning of the dwarf's house. We came out into a lovely night:

the effect of the quiet town, in the moonlight, with the snowclad hills behind is one that I shan't soon forget.

In the margin of the diary entry for January 6, 1939, Warren later pencilled the following simple notation: "The end of our last walk together."

PART III
1939·1973

The year 1939 was significant for Warren Lewis, but it also marked another year of silence in his diary. Certainly chief amongst all concerns at this time was the tension mounting in aggressive and hungry Germany. Inevitably, as events in Europe rapidly surged towards the outbreak of World War II, Warren was notified of his impending return to service. Official recall to active service came on September 4, and a stricken Warren was posted to Catterick, Yorkshire.

At age forty-four, Warren Lewis felt understandably uncertain of his ability to withstand the horrors of still another war on the battlefields of France. The service he had given almost cheerfully in his early twenties now seemed to require a strength that he feared he no longer possessed. Confused, frightened, and yet desirous of serving his country with honor, Warren was assigned to the No. 3 Base Supply Depot, Havre, France, in October.

Struggling as he was with the fears of his inadequacies, Warren attempted to serve with such distinction as he was able. This was rewarded on January 27, 1940, when he was granted the temporary rank of Major. Shortly thereafter, in February, Warren was hospitalized with fever (his second such illness since October), and remained in hospital until the middle of March. Then, in May, Warren was evacuated with his unit from Dunkirk to Wenvoe Camp, Cardiff, Wales.

Finally, on August 16, Warren (along with numerous other retired officers who had been recalled to active service) was transferred to the Reserve of Officers, and sent home to Oxford. His relief at his return home to Oxford was matched by his resolve to continue to serve for the duration of the war—now, however, as a private soldier with the 6th Oxford City Home Guard Battalion. During the summer months, Warren was also to serve as part of the "floating" Home Guard from the Bosphorus.

During Warren's painful time of duty, Jack agonized with his brother

[177]

by letter, and he was equally relieved when Warren was finally posted to Reserve Officer. Jack himself was serving as a volunteer religious lecturer for the R.A.F., and with the Oxford Home Guard.

Little detailed record of Warren's and Jack's lives during these early troubled war years exists. Warren's diary does not resume until his entry of February 22, 1943.

Monday 22nd February, 1943.

As I look over these pages, I wonder whether J and I are ever to have another walking tour:[192] probably not, in the regimented hungry world which is all we can look to after this war is over. However, here is at least a jaunt together, a little oasis in the dreariness, and the first holiday we have shared since our last walk: for one can hardly count the weekend he came down to Cardiff in 1940 when I was at Wenvoe. The world's fate, to say nothing of our own, seemed too grim then for there to be any pleasure in that memory. This trip we owe to the fact that J had to give the Riddell lectures[193] at Durham University—actually delivered though in Newcastle—on three successive evenings. I began the day badly by discovering that my faithful old Bulford and round the world suitcase is so battered as to be unfit to travel: so had it brought into College in the car and there transferred its contents to the formidable "Brady" case, built to the highest Pudaita specification: which I was to regret before the holiday was over.

Tuesday 23rd February.

York, where we took in a big influx of passengers, has been badly bombed, apparently right on the station and permanent way, which is pretty shooting. The Cathedral and town however appeared to be untouched, and this I heard later is the case. At Darlington I had the exquisite pleasure of hearing the sad harsh voice of the girl at the loudspeaker directing the unfortunate troops to the "next train for Catterick", and thanked God for His mercies to me since that September evening in 1939 when I got out of the London express at Darlington with my world in ruins round me. The next landmark

---

192. Though Warren and Jack were never again to have another of their beloved walking tours, they were to have numerous short holidays in the years to come—and even an occasional brief, day-long walk. Nonetheless, for Warren, no matter how happy any future jaunt might be, none would ever quite be as enjoyable as the much anticipated, now greatly remembered and treasured, eight annual walking tours taken with Jack.

193. The Riddell Memorial Lectures given by Jack Lewis were later published in book form as *The Abolition of Man* (London: Oxford University Press, 1943).

was Durham, which, in its unexpectedness as well as its intrinsic beauty, delighted us. But I will keep Durham until later.

Wednesday 24th February.

[A]rrived at Durham at 9.51 in the still early morning sunlight of a lovely day and set out on foot, down so steep a decline that we saw our own train trundling off many hundreds of feet over our heads. I had always thought vaguely of Durham as a colliering cum manufacturing town with a minor university and some sort of cathedral tucked away grimly in it, and so had J. In consequence, its exquisite beauty came upon us with an impact I shall long remember. Crossing a high stone bridge over the Wear, which here runs in a wide steep timbered bed, we walked along under the wall which encloses castle, cathedral, university and Bishops Palace. Each and all lovely, but especially the Cathedral which is one of the most splendid Norman buildings I have ever had the good fortune to see, built of an almost honey coloured stone, with twin towers at the west end, and a great central tower.

Thursday 28th September, 1944.

Benecke[194] died in the Acland, sometime in the early morning of Monday, 25th of this month, "Malvern" Thompson[195] having spent the night with him. His last words on worldly matters were to ask Thompson to convey to the Fellows his thanks for their unvarying kindness to him. At 2.30 I went today to his funeral in the College chapel, where there were many people representing the various facets of his very full life—University, Collegiate, Diocesan, and Musical. Thompson read the lesson magnificently, and there was a Mendelssohn anthem. . . . With him passes an epoch: he had lived in Magdalen for fifty eight years, and had been a Fellow since 1891. The absolutely best man I have ever known in my life. . . . As J says of Benecke, "one has no difficulty in thinking of him as being in Heaven". My difficulty is in thinking of him *dead;* it is incredible that, as I look out into the quad, there is no chance of seeing him cross it at five miles an hour, coatless and bareheaded, his hands clasped behind him, and his body bent slightly forward: and that never again will I

---

194. Paul V. M. Benecke (1868-1944), a Fellow of Magdalen College and tutor in Ancient History. In his autobiography, *Surprised by Joy* (1955), Jack Lewis describes him as one of the five great Magdalen College men who enlarged his image of what the scholarly life should be.

195. The Reverend Patrick John Thompson, Dean of Divinity and Fellow of Magdalen College.

see his beautiful face in the front row at a Subscription Concert: nor sit beside him in Common Room listening to his long stories of earlier days in the musical world. To have known him is a pleasure and a privilege.

Tuesday 19th December.

In the humdrum of the sixth year of war an outing of any kind with J becomes an event: even so trivial and uncomfortable a one as this. It arose through Minto's seeing a chance to make some money out of J's operation, by claiming on the Ministry of Pensions for his operation this summer, on the grounds that it was a war injury. In due course he was provided with a 3rd Class Warrant to Reading, and bid present himself there to a medical board at 2.45. . . . It was close on 11 a.m. when we took "a train" for Reading. . . . I have rarely, even in war time, had an unpleasanter journey. There was of course no question of seats, but there was even insufficient standing room. . . . I was *very* glad when ultimately we got out at Reading. J fared better, and during the journey his voice could be heard booming over the rumble of the train in conversation with a stranger on Chas. Williams novels. . . . We found ourselves in a flat and dismal park, admirably signposted, and containing a number of one storied, flat roofed brick offices. J dived into one of them, and left me to my meditations. Fog has always a curious attraction for me: and for J, who is indeed the only other person I have ever met who likes it. And I spent the best part of an hour strolling not uncontently in its opalescent wetness among the ghosts of rare trees. . . . Ultimately J emerged: his board had consisted of one Doctor, so colourless that it was impossible to talk of either liking him or disliking him, and so ill trained that he had been unable to decide which were the scars of the 26 year old wound in the wrist, and which were those of last summer's operation.

Tuesday 2nd January, 1945.

Our dear, delightful June Flewett[196] leaves us tomorrow, after

---

196. Jill ("June") Flewett Freud, one of the numerous children evacuated from London during the Blitz. She came to stay at The Kilns in the summer of 1943. During her time there, June (as she was nicknamed by Warren and Jack) assisted a frail and ailing Mrs. Moore with the household chores. In September 1950, June married Clement Freud—author, Member of Parliament, and grandson of Sigmund Freud. Her kindness to the Lewis brothers continued even after she moved out of The Kilns. In later years, she frequently offered Warren the use of her vacation home in Walberswick, on the west coast of Suffolk. Warren's deep affection for June remained constant throughout his life.

nearly two years, for London and the Dramatic School where she is to be taught to be an actress. She is not yet eighteen, but I have met no one of any age further advanced in the Christian way of life. From seven in the morning till nine at night, shut off from people of her own age, almost grudged the time for her religious duties, she has slaved at The Kilns, for a fraction 2d. an hour; I have never seen her other than gay, eager to anticipate exigent demands, never complaining, always self accusing in the frequent crises of that dreary house. Her reaction to the meanest ingratitude was to seek its cause in her own faults. She is one of those rare people to whom one can venture to apply the word "saintly". . . . From a personal selfish point of view I shall feel the loss of June very keenly: for in addition to her other virtues, she is a clever girl, and with her gone, it means that when J is away, there is no one to talk to in the house.

Wednesday 3rd January.

I said goodbye sadly to June this morning when I came back with Bruce,[197] and left that horrid house with a depression of spirits which surprised me and is most unusual at what is generally the most cheerful moment of my day. But for the child's own sake, it is high time she was gone. Travelled in on the bus with the Lance Corporal storeman H.G., a man well versed in Quarry history, from whom I learnt that the constant theft of our timber is a little bit of English social and economic history. Until about a hundred years ago, our garden was the villagers common, where all had a right to cut their fuel wood, and what is now our reservoir was the village spring. One fine morning Quarry woke up to find its common being enclosed for shooting land—stolen from them without compensation in fact. The story of the theft has been handed down from generation to generation, and the injustice is resented to this day. Taking our wood is the assertion of a right to whose relinquishment they never assented, and the cutting of our wire is a parish duty; there is an old man in the village who keeps a pair of wire cutters for that special purpose!

Tuesday 8th January, 1945.

Maureen gave birth to a son [Richard Francis] in the Radcliffe at 5 p.m. today.[198]

---

197. Bruce, a successor to the previous Kilns dogs (Papworth and Troddles), and a great favorite of Mrs. Moore.

198. On August 27, 1940, Maureen had married Leonard J. Blake, Director of Music at Worksop College (later music-master at Malvern College).

On May 9, 1945, the war in Europe came to an official close.

Tuesday 15th May.

At 12.50 this morning I had just stopped work on the details of the Boisleve family,[199] when the telephone rang, and a woman's voice asked if I would take a message for J—"Mr. Charles Williams[200] died in the Acland this morning". One often reads of people being "stunned" by bad news, and reflects idly on the absurdity of the expression; but there is more than a little truth in it. I felt just as if I had slipped and come down on my head on the pavement. J had told me when I came into College that Charles was ill, and it would mean a serious operation: and then went off to see him: I haven't seen him since. I felt dazed and restless, and went out to get a drink: choosing unfortunately the King's Arms, where during the winter Charles and I more than once drank a pint after leaving Tollers at the Mitre, with much glee at "clearing one throats of varnish with good honest beer": as Charles used to say. There will be no more pints with Charles: no more "Bird and Baby":[201] the blackout has fallen, and the Inklings[202] can never be the same again. I knew him better than any of the others,

---

199. With the Lewis Papers long since complete (the final volume was bound in 1935), Warren had turned his talent for research to his early interest in French history. He had in fact written the basic text of his first book, *The Splendid Century: Some Aspects of French Life in the Reign of Louis XIV,* in 1942, though this volume was not published until 1953. At this time, however, Warren's concern was not with publication, but rather with personal enjoyment.

200. Charles Walter Stansby Williams (1886-1945), editor of the Oxford University Press, author of numerous and varied books, and member of the Inklings. Jack Lewis first met Charles Williams after they had exchanged letters of admiration for their respective works, *Allegory of Love* (1936) and *The Place of the Lion* (1931). When Oxford University Press relocated from London to Oxford during the Blitz, Jack invited Charles Williams to become a member of the Inklings. See also, the Preface to *Essays presented to Charles Williams,* C. S. Lewis, ed. (Grand Rapids, Michigan: William B. Eerdmans Publishing Company, 1966).

201. An Oxford pub, *The Eagle and the Child,* nicknamed by the Inklings "the Bird and the Baby." The Inklings met regularly on Tuesday mornings at the Bird and the Baby—so regularly in fact, that Edmund Crispin in his detective novel *Swan Song* (1947), has one of his characters (seated in the Bird and the Baby) remark: "There goes C. S. Lewis . . . it must be Tuesday."

202. The Inklings was a group of male friends gathered around Jack Lewis because of their mutual enjoyment of good conversation and friendship. Because of the shared literary interests of those who attended this informal group, members frequently alternated in reading aloud their current work. Criticism was freely offered, and it was to the audience of the Inklings that J. R. R. Tolkien's *The Lord of the Rings* (1954, 1955), Charles Williams's *All Hallows' Eve* (1945), and Jack Lewis's *Perelandra* (1943) were first read.

Though it is not possible exactly to determine the beginning of the Inklings, the probable date is 1933. It also appears likely that regular (i.e., weekly) Thursday meet-by virtue of his being the most constant attendant. I hear his voice as I write, and can see his thin form in his blue suit, opening his cigarette box with trembling hands. These rooms will always hold his ghost for me. There is something horrible, something *unfair* about death, which no religious conviction can overcome. "Well, goodbye, see you on Tuesday Charles" one says—and you have in fact though you don't know it, said goodbye for ever. He passes up the lamplit street, and passes out of your life for ever. There is a good deal of stuff talked about the horrors of a lonely old age; I'm not sure that the wise man—the wise materialist at any rate—isn't the man who has no friends. And so vanishes one of the best and nicest men it has ever been my good fortune to meet. May God receive him into His everlasting happiness.

Monday 17th September.

Bleiben[203] recently mentioned to me that he had spent his convalescence at the "Bull" at Fairford, and had been very comfortable there; so I determined to go over and investigate its possibilities as an occasional place of refuge. I had the all too rare good fortune of finding J ready to spend a night out of Oxford. . . . We got to the delightful little terminus at Fairford about 10.30, and immediately set out in brisk pursuit of a paratrooper who appeared to know a short cut to the town. . . . A pleasant lane, liberally sprinkled with crab apples brought us to our first glimpse of Fairford, and we both exclaimed at the beauty of the old stone house in a paddock on our right. I may as well record here as later that Fairford is one of the loveliest small towns I have ever seen; my prevailing impression is that Georgian and Queen Anne dominates it, and every house is a gem.

---

ings of the Inklings did not begin until April 1940. Though members of the Inklings often met at various times throughout the week, the regularity of Tuesday mornings at the Bird and the Baby, and Thursday evenings (after dinner) in Jack's rooms at Magdalen College were constant. Regular members of the Inklings included Owen Barfield, J. A. W. Bennett, Lord David Cecil, Nevill Coghill, Commander Jim Dundas-Grant, Hugo Dyson, Adam Fox, Colin Hardie, R. E. ("Humphrey") Havard, Jack Lewis, Warren Lewis, Gervase Mathew, R. B. McCallum, C. E. ("Tom") Stevens, Christopher Tolkien, J. R. R. ("Tollers") Tolkien, John Wain, Charles Williams, and Charles Wrenn. It should be noted, however, that attendence by most of the Inklings was erratic, and that intermittent invited guests were not uncommon. For further information, see Humphrey Carpenter's *Inklings* (1979).

203. The Reverend Thomas Eric Bleiben (1903-1947), parish priest at Holy Trinity Church in Headington Quarry.

Tuesday 18th September.

Was much amused at J who last night fell asleep almost at once, woke about an hour later and got up, asserting indignantly that he had not been asleep for a minute! . . . It was a bright sunny day, and after a fruitless effort to pay our bills, we set off without macs. to do a map walk in the district to the S.E. of Fairford. . . . [Before long,] it began to rain heavily; as J remarked, the Little People had obviously objected to the idea of that walk from the outset. Here we had such a piece of luck as does not happen once in a hundred times, J finding that on the other side of the hedge was a deserted R.A.F. barrack hut, with the back door broken open, and the bedsteads in situ. Here we spent a considerable time, how long I don't know, as we were both watchless, talking of this and that—Scott's novels and Spanish grammar amongst other things. There was a touch of the eerie in that loud speaker somewhere in this area of silence and decay kept on giving instructions to the members of N. Squadron. At last the rain released us—or we thought it had—but we were soon forced to shelter under a tree. As J remarked what is wanted in this country is not fewer, but *more* deserted camps. But in end the storm did really roll on eastward, and we walked briskly back to Fairford, getting into our pub almost quite dry in ample time for a drink before lunch.

Saturday 15th December.

I got back yesterday afternoon from a three days holiday at Fairford, more impressed with the place than ever. The party was to have been the "Victory Inklings", but in fact degenerated into J, Tolkien and myself. Tollers and I went out by the 9.35 on Tuesday morning and spent a pleasant day together; he spoke with much more frankness about his domestic life than he has ever used to me before, and did me good in making me realize how trivial after all are the things which I have to complain of at Kilns. . . . The "Bull" under winter conditions is remarkably comfortable: well warmed, good food, excellent beds, and was not too full. . . . We were very cosy in our own lounge in the evening where I read Lewis Carroll's *Life* by Collingwood,[204] and Tollers my Dr. J. Brown's *Letters*.[205] J arrived, without Barfield who was ill, by 9.35 on Wednesday, and Humphrey turned up to lunch by car; after which we had one of the best winter walks I

---

204. The *Life and Letters* of author Lewis Carroll (Charles L. Dodgson) edited in 1898 by Stuart Dodgson Collingwood (a nephew).

205. Dr. John Brown (1810-1882), Scottish physician and essayist. His letters were edited by his son and D. W. Forrest in 1907.

ever took: round by Quenington. I don't remember ever seeing more exquisite winter colouring, both of sky and landscape, of the subdued type. On Thursday morning we saw the Church. . . . In the afternoon we walked through Horcott and Whelford and home by the main road.

Whelford, a mere hamlet, has a simple little Church where we all felt that God dwells; nothing to "see" in it. There, to my surprise and pleasure, Tollers said a prayer. Down on the river was a perfect mill house where we amused ourselves by dreaming of it as a home for the Inklings, contrasting it with yesterday's choice, the manor at Quenington. Friday morning was again fine (we had wonderful luck with our weather) and we walked to Coln St. Aldwyn, a dream village, spoilt only by a small war factory, luckily of a temporary type; here we drank beer at the "Pig and Whistle", which opened at 10 a.m.— the first time in my life I have ever met a pub. of that name . . . and so home to lunch, and an unpleasantly hurried departure to catch the 2.12. As if our holiday had been intended to end then, the sky clouded over and the world became dim: the curtain had fallen most dramatically on our jaunt. In the evening Christopher Tolkien[206] dined with J and I at the Royal Oxford, after which we taxied to The Kilns. I got in with the usual drop in spirits, and lay long shivering in my hard damp bed before I could drop asleep, though I was tired. J, with his usual generosity, paid my hotel bill, so it was a cheap excursion for me.

Monday 24th December.

Uncle Gussie died at Holywood this morning in his 79th year. I always liked, indeed loved him, mainly I think because from my earliest years he always talked to me sensibly; I can never remember a time when I did not sharply differentiate between him and the other Hamilton and Lewis "grown ups". He was selfish, egotistical, and very thrifty; and with these qualities had a charm of manner which sunk them into laughable eccentricities. He was excellent company always, and brightened many a dreary evening in the study at Little Lea. As I grew to manhood myself, I defined him as being "much more like an ordinary person" than anyone else in the clan; in my 'teens it never occurred to me to "make conversation" with him as

---

206. Christopher Tolkien (1924-   ), the third son of J. R. R. Tolkien, and "official" member of the Inklings since 1945. He served as a pilot in the R.A.F., later resuming his studies at Oxford after World War II. He resigned his Fellowship at New College in 1975 to work exclusively on the editing of his father's unpublished writings.

one did with the other uncles. Up to the last he retained a good deal of the insouciance of a school boy. I shall miss him greatly.

Monday 18th March, 1946.

Woke with that lightening of the heart which always comes with the realization that I am going to spend even one night away from this horrid house, and this time I have got the best part of the week! . . . We waited long in the Royal Oxford lounge for Hugo, talking of mediaeval ships and exchanging greeting with a very gentlemanly Labrador, and ultimately went in to lunch by ourselves, and had a piping hot curry. Hugo turned up about half way through, in great spirits, having been delayed by a College meeting. At the station we lost him (this happened more than once). . . . The Run to Bletchley on the 2.40 was the best part of the journey, and Hugo and I behaved over engines like a couple of school boys. He had brought nothing to read with him, but this we sternly corrected at a later period. From Bletchley to Rugby we had a crowded corridor train, and reached the latter in time for a cup of tea: here once more we lost Hugo, who, as J said, should always have a collar and lead when one travels with him. . . . Hugo, who admires the shires—what we call the L.N.W. corridor—was a mine of information whilst the daylight lasted, and behaved heroically after dark, singing and telling stories: "if I stopped I should become hysterical" he said . . . it was 8.50 before we at last detrained. . . . Here we did the best we could on watercress sandwiches and beer—the sandwiches clean and fresh for a marvel—and then took a taxi through grim familiar old Liverpool down to the ferry. Tired and disgruntled though I was, the sight of the river brought the old familiar thrill which is associated with some of the happiest memories of my life. The first glimpse of the Woodside Hotel is disconcerting, for the reception office is also used as the bar, and consequently the hall was full of people drinking—all looking extraordinarily sinister, as northern manufacturers do when one is fresh from long residence in the south. Hugo immediately announced that we had blundered into a meeting of the Liverpool sabotage gang, and we all went into a rather crowded lounge, which smelt strongly of paint, (as indeed the whole hotel did), and there had three large whiskeys and sodas each. I can't remember when I last tasted whiskey, and certainly I haven't enjoyed it so much since I arrived in Liverpool under somewhat similar circumstances a year ago. To bed in a much more equable frame of mind than had at one time appeared likely, and slept very well.

Tuesday 19th March.

One of the most satisfying things that has happened to me for a
long time was to draw my curtains this morning and find myself
looking out on a big ship in a graving dock not five hundred yards
away, and to see the men hurrying in to work; one difference which
Hugo put his finger on later in the day is that in the north the working
man looks like a working man, whereas in Oxford he looks as if he
was intended to be something else. . . . J had breakfasted earlier, and
later in the morning we all three crossed to Liverpool under a typical
grey sky. At the parish church we were nobbled by the Vicar, who
showed us his tin church standing in the roofless shell of a much
larger Georgian building, burnt out in the blitz. He tells me that
preliminary investigation for rebuilding discloses the foundations of
four churches here, one on top of the other. [This afternoon, after] tea
. . . we crossed once more to see the Cathedral, and frankly this was
the one real failure of the trip. We should have gone by tram, or
better still, by taxi, but were deceived into a long tiring and desolat-
ingly dreary walk through very badly bombed slums: one of those
walks in which at the end of each dirty street, your objective seems
the same distance away as it was ten minutes earlier. At last we
reached it, only to find it shut. But the main entrance is magnificent,
and the huge mass glowing rose red in the level rays of the setting sun
was worth coming for. . . . This infernal walk took such a time that
we had to hurry straight home to dinner and the very moderate solace
of half pints of beer. However, the dinner was by no means bad, and
afterwards we had the lounge to ourselves, Hugo with *Marius the
Epicurean,* J with *Ecce Homo,*[207] and I with Haydon's autobiography,[208]
which I finished with renewed enjoyment during the trip. But we
read only for a little, and then talked. I was the unhappy and
inadvertent cause of launching an argument on the distinction
between Art and Philosophy; towards the end of the first hour J and
Hugo discovered that they were talking about different subjects. Each
side then restated its war aims, and they set to again. When or how
the argument ended I don't know, for it was still going strong when
I went to bed at eleven.

Wednesday 20th March.

Called at 7.30 after a good night, and found it a warm, sunny
altogether delightful morning. Hugo has developed a passion for ferry

207. *Ecce Homo* (1865), a theological work published anonymously by late-
nineteenth-century historian and essayist Sir John Robert Seeley.
208. Benjamin Robert Haydon, artist, and friend of poet John Keats.

voyaging, which is indeed the best diversion this place affords, so nothing loathe we all sallied out after breakfast to Liverpool and from there took the other ferry to Wallesey. . . . For some time we strolled on the prom. and then adjourned to the Ferry Hotel, which might have been in Belfast—a huge mirror bearing an ornately lettered whiskey advertisement, bare boarded floor, and frosted stars in the window glass. Here we drank bottled beer until it was time to cross again, and had an interesting return voyage. . . . I have forgotten to say that at the landing stage was *Georgic* full of Italian prisoners. . . . [Then] poor J went off to his task, and we crossed to lunch. After lunch Hugo, who has become a ferry addict, went for another voyage, and I, after a siesta, went for a more extended stroll in Birkenhead than I have yet had; it is exactly Hell as described by J in the opening chapter of *Grand Divorce*. How can any government expect content from the inhabitants of such a place? . . . I came in depressed and was glad to join the others at early dinner, which we all took together and then crossed, J to his brains trust, and Hugo and I to see Liverpool. . . . On the way down to Pier Head, we saw a still blacked out pub called the "Angel", which proved to be comfortable and nearly empty, and there we rapidly revived under the stimulus of bottled Guinness, and had much talk about army life. For the first time since the war ended we were approached by an alleged ex-soldier, asking us to invest in highly scented sachets of the authentic leaping house smell; we were glad enough to give him something, but he insisted on our taking the sachets: and as he went to the bar to spend the proceeds of the sale, we dare not leave them behind us. So out into the street full of laughter and smelling like a couple of chorus girls. . . . We found J in the lounge when we got home, and a conversation started on the wit of the 17th Century. Hugo quoted an epigram of Suckling's on the birth of Nell Gwynn which was the most disgusting thing of the sort I have ever heard.

Thursday 28th March.

A good meeting of the Inklings, though scantily attended. Present, J and I, Christopher, Humphrey, Colin Hardie, Gervase Mathew.[209] Interesting discussion on the possibility of dogs having souls.

---

209. *Robert E. ("Humphrey") Havard* (1901-   ), a doctor who practiced medicine in the Oxford suburb of Headington. He was the close friend and physician to both Warren and Jack Lewis, and was a member of the Inklings. *Colin Hardie*

Sunday 31st March.

To Evensong in our own Church, where J preached an excellent sermon, illuminating for me an old difficulty of my own. He began by speaking of the doubts which some of us feel about the wording of the Book of Common Prayer: e.g. the confession before Communion, when we say of our sins, "The burden of them is *intolerable*". Not having this feeling, I always leave this sentence out; but J's theory is that the matter of *feeling* does not arise—the sense of the phrase is that, whether we are aware of it emotionally or not, we are carrying a load of sin which unless we get rid of it, will ultimately break us as an excessive load will break a bridge: and in this sense our sin *is* "intolerable".

Tuesday 2nd April.

An exquisite spring morning, J poor devil, in Manchester. To the Bird and Baby where I was joined by Humphrey, Tollers, and Chris. Tollers looking wonderfully improved by his restcure at Stonyhurst, and in great spirits (having packed his wife off to Brighton for ten days). He has shut up his house, and he and Chris are living at the Bear at Woodstock, whither we all repaired in Humphrey's new car for lunch. Fine old house, a shade too fashionable, where over an excellent lunch we argued of the morality of the Nuremburg trials. Afterwards out into the gleaming grey Cotswold country, low toned even in the sunlight, until we came to the valley of the Evenlode, where we stopped the car and sat for a long time on the bank of the river in a rank neglected piece of meadow, backed by neglected wood. Humphrey dropped me at College about five. I did not enjoy myself as much as I should have done, having for the last few days been suffering from that restless melancholy discontent which fine spring weather always produces in me; it is one of my oldest feelings; I can remember feeling it in the days when I looked *up* into the delicious fragrant mass of a flowering currant at the old house. For years I thought it a materialist phenomenon—that the discontent would be instantly cured by a change of station, more money, more leave etc. But I begin to suspect that it is spiritual, a subconscious longing for another world.

(1906-   ), Fellow and Classical Tutor at Magdalen College from 1936 until his retirement in 1973, was a member of the Inklings. *Gervase Mathew* (1905-1976), a member of the Catholic Order of Dominicans, ordained a priest in 1934. He lived at Blackfriars in Oxford, and was a general lecturer in Modern History, Theology, and English at the University. He was also a member of the Inklings.

Wednesday 26th June.

Today J, with his usual generosity, carried me with him at his charges on a jaunt to which I have long been looking forward: his investment with a D.D. at St. Andrews. . . . [Tonight] After dinner [in London] we strolled out into the area of rather drab squares, quiet under a pink cloud sunset, which lie south of the Euston Rd. This area has been badly bombed, and J remarked on the good fortune of the children who have grown up in these unintended play grounds. Of the local church nothing remains but a fine Norman doorway. The northland trains were packed tonight, and the station hot and airless . . . but we each had a single berth room, elaborately fitted with lights, fans etc. Odd to find oneself again in a cabin with the fan running, and it brought back many memories.

Thursday 27th June.

Sleeping in a sleeper (I don't remember when I last did it) is an acquired habit. I had one of those nights on which one imagines one has been sleepless, though in fact one has actually slept pretty well. . . . Breakfast showed us the difference it makes to get out of miserable hungry England [into Scotland]—real porridge, of which I had almost forgotten the taste, plenty of butter, edible sausages, toast, marmalade, coffee! The scenery was to us very lovely—trim little stone towns by a calm sea, backed by swelling country like Salisbury plain, coppices enclosed in grey stone walls, distant hills—all that "northerness" which was my first love and will be my last.

Friday 28th June.

It was a fine breezy morning when after a good breakfast we set out to walk to the station with our suitcases, liking the town more and more as time went on. Having left these and decided on catching the 5.20 train, we strolled past our pub and into St. Mary's College. . . . J now noticed with concern the academic town was waking up, and that all the bustling figures were wearing white ties; so we went across the road to one Fudyce, a draper, who to our relief let him buy a white collar and tie on a promise to post the coupons to him. As we sat smoking a final cigarette in the hotel lounge, J, now correctly clad, remarked that this graduation business was the only regrettable feature in the holiday: and I agreed with him. We already found quite a crowd at the Younger Hall, where the graduation ceremony was to take place, the undergraduates looking very well in their red gowns with fur trimmings. . . . When at last the dignitaries arrived, the girls struck up "The animals came in two by two . . . ", and among the "animals" was J, now clad in a black cassock with scarlet buttons, and with him twelve others in similar get up, the only one of whom I recognized being [pianist Dame] Myra Hess. The actual ceremony was pretty, but tedious: difficult indeed to see how it could help being so, though some of the girl graduands were very pretty. . . . There were perhaps 70 or 80 degrees conferred, and then came the honoraries, of whom J was the last. Each honorary recipient was the subject of a poorish eulogy, delivered not as at Oxford by the Public Orator, but by the Dean of the Faculty concerned. . . . Each recipient was handed a sort of tubular case containing his degree, and a great nuisance J was to find his on the journey until he could get it stowed in his suitcase. I slipped out just at the moment when the Vice-Chancellor's announcement that he was going to cut out more of his speech was being given a hearty round of applause. . . . At 4.55 I picked up a taxi by arrangement and went round with it to St. Mary's where I found the Vice-Chancellor just showing J out from tea; he asked to be introduced to me, and chid me for not inviting myself to the meal, which I thought was uncommonly civil of him. We had, very stupidly, thought of a quiet train journey . . . but of course the train was packed with graduates etc. "going down": but still, we had corner seats from which to get a last view of this town, for which I have conceived a very lively liking. . . . At Dundee we had a good deal of trouble in tracking down the pragmatical station master from whom we had to get our sleeping berths, but we ultimately did it, and having left our bags with the ticket collector at whose barrier we had emerged, we set out to hunt for a dinner. . . . Here we struck another Royal Hotel, and began operations by drinking beer in a comfortable bar: after which we had the very best dinner I have eaten since before the war. . . . I was sorry when the time came to make a move back to the Station, where we found the inferior London express already crammed; I expressed indignation that people should be expected to stand in the corridor all the way to London, but J with his usual common sense, pointed out that when one rails at "they", one is only seeking a cheap release from one's own discontent.

Saturday 13th July.

That very rare thing an English summer day: so warm that I find myself comfortable in white ducks. J and I went by invitation to hear Gervase Mathew lecture on Byzantine civilization at St. Hugh's. . . . The garden of St. Hughs (in which I have not been since I heard

"Comus" there) is considerably spoilt, several gloomy one story hospital wards having been built in it during the war; but we found a pleasant seat, on which we smoked a cigarette and watched a woodpecker at work within five feet of us. How does he keep up that battering without injuring himself? . . . The audience at the lecture was mixed and elderly—a university extension crowd I gathered. We were both glad we had come. Gervase was excellent, and had got a capital collection of slides for his discourse. Byzantine painting grows on one; at first their portraits seem primitive, then they "focus" with extraordinary rapidity. . . . The most interesting thing Gervase said was that Charles, to whom the results of modern Byzantine research were unknown, had managed to give a much truer account of Byzantium in *Taliessin*[210] than that given by Gibbon, his sole authority.

Thursday 25th July.

By appointment with J to dine with the Hugo Dysons in their new house, 12 Holywell—very reluctantly, for with all my army experience I am still as shy of women as a hobbledehoy: and also it would otherwise have been an Inkling night. We had a glass of sherry in the smoking room and then set out across the grove, where the senior rabbit, "Grandma Biscuit" came up to us and sniffed our fingers. Neither of us had a watch, but in spite of this we I think hit it off alright: at any rate we were warmly welcomed and given an excellent dinner—fish salad, sweet, savoury, and hock to wash it down. Mrs. Hugo looking very pretty and attractive, and some pleasant talk. No. 12 I thought a delightful house: so compact, so defensible after our slatternly straggling Kilns. And the beautiful clean silver and table linen, forming such a contrast with our own thoroughother menage, with its air of being a perpetual *picnic*. I have now endured The Kilns for over fifteen years, and it is no more "home" now than it was when I first entered it: I still have the feeling that it is a billet which I have marched into late in the evening and will be leaving for ever after an early breakfast. The Hugos did not seem to me sufficiently appreciative of their good luck in having such a place. J and I both agreed afterwards that their bedroom would make a beautiful study. There is too a nice little walled garden. After dinner two she-tutors and Gervase Mathew turned up, and we sat about—drinking whiskey and soda no less!—until 10.30 when J and I cleared off.

---

210. Charles Williams's Arthurian poem, *Talliessin Through Logres* (London: Oxford University Press, 1938).

Thursday 8th August.

This evening Hugo carried me to dine with him in Merton, the first time for many years that I have dined in any College other than Magdalen. He was in high spirits when I met him, and his spirits rose steadily for the rest of the evening. I was more than ever struck with his amazing knowledge of Shakespeare; I don't suppose there is a man in Oxford—with the possible exception of Onions—who can quote so happily, e.g. tonight, apropos of J: "O cursed spite that gave thee to the Moor": poor SPB's whole catastrophe epitomized in nine words! . . . I saw tonight why Hugo rarely gets to an Inkling; every one he meets after dinner he engages in earnest conversation, and tonight, even with steady pressure from me, it took him 40 minutes to get from Hall to the gate. . . . [Finally] we went on to Magdalen, where there was a well attended Inklings—Stanley Bennett[211] of Cambridge, who had been dining with J, Humphrey, Ronald [Tolkien], Gervase. But not the sort of evening I much enjoy, mere noise and buffoonery: though Hugo as improvisatore was very funny at times. Humphrey left early, taking me to the end of the Green Road in the car.

Thursday 15th August.

The horrid undertaking of having my hair cut this morning; for some time we had the shop to ourselves, and poor Victor unburdened himself to me. Amongst other things he spoke of the great spiritual comfort the hymns bring him in Church on Sundays, quoting couplets which made me almost blush they seemed so banal. But it was a valuable experience, showing how rash it is to dogmatize about what "everyone" feels about this or that part of the service. I should like no hymns at all: Victor would, if I had my thoughtless way, be deprived of his nourishment for the week, or at least of a good part of it. Dined with J in the evening, sitting next Hope at dinner and between Dixon and Griffiths in Common Room, a very pleasant break in my somewhat monotonous evenings. A small Inklings afterwards, only Ronald [Tolkien], Humphrey, ourselves, and J's new lieutenant, brought in by Ronald from Queens, where he had been dining. I hear with dismay that Ronald has since talked of "bringing him in occasionally": with dismay for two reasons, firstly that he is a dull dog, and secondly that he is an R.C. I don't mind his being one in the least, but Hugo, who has puzzlingly strong views on the matter, has several times lately threatened that if any more Papists join the Inklings, he will resign. . . . During the evening I made the always cheering dis-

211. Henry Stanley Bennett, Life Fellow at Emmanuel College, Cambridge.

covery that what I had assumed to be an individual mental anfractuosity, is shared by J, i.e. that we can both only imagine what comes
into our heads, but cannot direct our imaginations. For instance, said
I, when I picture the country house I would have if I were a rich man,
I can *say* that my study window opens on a level park full of old
timber: but I *see* undulating ground with a fir topped knoll. I can of
course fix my mind on the level park, but when I turn to the window
again after arranging my books, there is the knoll once more. J says it
is the same with him when he is writing a novel: he *must* use the knoll
and can't force himself to use the level park.

Thursday 22nd August.

Was shocked and sorry to see in the *Times* this morning that
Davenport of Quarry House died yesterday; I did not even know that
he was ill. He was one of the pillars of our little community, a member of the P.C.C., and has been Vicar's Warden since I was called up
in 1939. . . . I shall miss him, and am uncomfortably reminded that I
am 52: odd to reflect that I am now six years older than Mammy ever
was. In the evening I went to dine at Merton with Tollers: a grey
evening of thin steady rain. . . . A good dinner, and a glass of better
port than Magdalen gives one. Then coffee. . . . and so across to
Magdalen with Chris, whom we picked up in his father's room.
J and I much concerned this evening by the gate crashing of B; Tollers, the ass, brought him here last Thursday, and he has apparently
now elected himself an Inkling. Not very clear what one can do about
it. J read a fine new poem on Paracelsus' view of gnomes, and Tollers
a magnificent myth which is to knit up and concludes his Papers of
the Notions Club. I walked out to The Kilns and got there at midnight.

Friday 23rd August.

J and I bussed out to Margaret Rd. at 1.30 for Davenport's funeral
in our own church. . . . I can't say I am ever quite happy about the
funeral service: the "hearty thanks" for the "deliverance of our brother out of this sinful world" seems to me to have about it a perilous
touch of something not far removed from humbug. To all, Christians
or not, death is terrible, and why ignore the fact? Which of us *wants*
deliverance out of this sinful world? I at any rate was very conscious
of the sweetness of the wind in my face as I went down the path under
the rustling trees to get the bus back into town, and I cannot feel that
there was anything sinful in my feelings.

Thursday 5th September.

Dined with Christopher at the Angel. As we came out afterwards the High was a picture of exquisite beauty. . . . We sat long in the Bird waiting for Humphrey to pick us up, and to the Inklings after nine. Present, J and I, Humphrey, Christopher, Wrenn[212] and Gervase. The talk turned on communications with the dead, and I read them St. Simon's account of the Blacksmith of Salon, which was new to them. Gervase remarked that it was a double to the Joan of Arc story. Just as we were warming up there came a call for Humphrey, and I had to go early.

Tuesday 10th September.

Second and, thank God, last day of St. Giles's Fair,[213] so the Bird and Baby out of bounds. Humphrey called at Magdalen at 12.10 and carried J, Christopher and I out to the Trout at Godstow which was looking perfectly lovely under a cool bright light. We sat in the garden and discussed Dr. Johnson's probable views on contemporary literature and the nature of women. The pub closed at one, and we had to climb out over the road bridge.

Thursday 19th September.

In the evening I took Humphrey and Christopher to dinner at Georges—a bad and expensive meal, but I enjoyed it—after which we drank a pint at the Bird, and so round to the Inklings. Present, J and Tollers, and we three. We talked of Hugo's figityness which Tollers attributes to his harness galling; at Reading, having practically no work to do, he could live by whim, but here he has to work and doesn't like it. We also talked of the moral aspect of atomic bombing and total war in general. Got home in Humphrey's car, at 12.50. A very good day.

Thursday 10th October.

Dined with J in College, after which an Inklings at which Tollers continued to read his new Hobbit [i.e., *The Lord of the Rings*]: so sui generis, so alive with the peculiar charm of his "magical" writing, that it is indescribable—and merely worth recording here for an odd proof of how near he is to real magic. Yesterday J gave a mixed lunch party in the New Room, at which I found myself sitting next Ruth Pitter,[214] the poetess; inter alia she told me of how in her youth she

---

212. Charles Wrenn (1895-1969), Professor of Anglo-Saxon, Oxford.
213. St. Giles's Fair, medieval in origin, is still held every September in Oxford.
214. Ruth Pitter (1897-   ), poet, was a friend and correspondent of Jack Lewis.

had known AE[215] in Galway, and he had tried to introduce her into the circle of the adepts by means of a golden ring. "Think very hard of a gold ring" he used to say, "and you will find it expanding in front of you, and through it you will see all your heart's desire". An evil man apparently.

Wednesday 14th October.

I am getting frightened about Minto. It is an appalling thing to say, but she seems to me to be going mad through trying to live on hate instead of love: tho' goodness knows my own efforts to live on love are feeble enough. Still, I *do* see love as an ideal to work towards, whereas her ideal seem to be hate. I feel that she has been dying for years, and all is white ash now except the flame of greed and hate which is burning even more brightly than it did ten or fifteen years ago. The immediate cause of my fright happened at dinner, when she suddenly snatched the conversation to . . . [say] that she went in bodily fear of Vera, who, a night or two ago, she thought was going to attack her in bed. She then [said] . . . that some time ago Vera attempted to murder a woman in Oxford by throwing her out of an upper story window: and that the victim's struggles were so successful that she escaped with a broken rib: and that the matter had been hushed up with great difficulty. . . . One often uses the phase, "not believing one's ears".

Thursday 24th October.

Spent all day in College, the King and Queen being here to open the new Bodleian, and went to Evensong in the College Chapel, where the music is definitely better than at the Cathedral: but I missed the comfort of the "two or three gathered together" which makes Thursday evening at Christ Church so pleasant. At the Inklings Christopher told me that, having hazarded a flippant remark at Trinity about the Royal visit, he was "nearly lynched" by indignant Royalists. A surprising and comforting sign of the times. What an irony it would be if now when the whole Empire is collapsing fast, Royalism should become the fashionable sentiment! Gervase Mathew looked in for a short time, looking like a sparrow that had inadvertently settled on the same branch with a cat, and told an immensely long and complicated story about the net of jealousy and intrigue in which Mrs. Charles Williams is entangled. When he had gone, Tollers read us a couple of exquisite chapters from the "new Hobbit." Nothing has

---

215. George William ("AE") Russell, 1867-1935, Irish poet and mystic.

come my way for a long time which has given me such enjoyment and excitment; as J says, it is more than good, it is great. Humphrey took me home as far as Sandfield Rd., from where I walked in an icy east wind. The first really cold night we have had, with the authentic bite of winter in it.

Thursday 28th November.

A pretty full meeting of the Inklings to meet Roy Campbell,[216] now with the B.B.C., whom I was very glad to see again; he is fatter and tamer than he used to be I think. He read us nothing of his own, except translations of a couple of Spanish poems—none of us understood either of them. Wain[217] won an outstanding bet by reading a chapter of *Irene Iddesleigh*[218] without a smile. Humphrey carried me home early, but the others I heard did not break up until one.

Sunday 7th December.

To Mattins at 10.30 of a bitterly cold wet day, and had the Litany: an extreme rarity at our Church. I kept my mind with difficulty off the recollections which it stirred up: recollections which no one now lives to share with me, for they are pre-J—Memories of St. Mark's, the reflection of the organist in his mirror (even of a time when I thought they were two men!), dust floating down the sunbeams: endless boredom: P repeating at intervals for hours at a stretch what I understood to be "We beseech Thee *do* hear us, Good Lord": his whisperings to me to keep quiet "and there would be some more music in a little while": Peacocke's voice like the plopping of stones falling down a well: then the walk home, holding P's hand, at a pace which meant a trot for me (obviously in case we should meet anyone!). The whole problem of child education in Christianity seems to me insoluble; what good can this sort of thing do? But perhaps it is no very cynical asperity to suppose that the main idea on Mammy's part was to get us both out of the house while she did her chores!

Sometime during 1947, probably due to the rising cost of maintenance, Warren Lewis was forced to sell his beloved boat, Bosphorus.

---

216. Roy Campbell (1902-1957), poet and Inklings visitor. See also C. S. Lewis, *Poems* (New York: Harcourt, Brace & World, 1965), pp. 66-67, for the poem, "To Roy Campbell."

217. John Wain (1925-   ), former pupil of Jack Lewis, author, Professor of English at Reading University until 1955, and later Professor of Poetry at Oxford. He was a member of the Inklings.

218. *Irene Iddesleigh* (1897) by Irish novelist, Amanda M'Kittrick Ros (Belfast: W. G. Baird).

Sunday 25th January, 1947.

The bitter cold continues. Went to early service through an iron hard world, powdered with snow, across which blew a slow, searing wind. Naturally there was a small congregation, a state of affairs which I'm ashamed to say induces a more devotional state of mind in me than when the church is well filled. Walked to Oxford via Cuckoo Lane after breakfast, in great discomfort, and fell into a melancholy train of thought at my ill fortune in being trapped in the closing scenes of a dying civilization: nothing to look forward to but poverty, perhaps actual want, even a cruel death: and so meditating turned into St. Clements for mattins, where I found the Psalm for the day, "why art thou so heavy, O my soul: and why art thou so disquieted within me? O put thy trust in God . . . ". And so on my way to College with a lighter heart.

Thursday 6th February.

The bitter cold continues without a break, and each day the same dirty yellow sky covers a world of frozen snow. . . . Inklings after dinner, present ourselves, the Tolkiens, Colin, Wain, and Gervase. Colin read an interminable paper on an unintelligible point about Virgil: of which Wain remarked afterwards, "To say I didn't understand it is a gross understatement". Chris then gave us an admirable chapter of the "[new] Hobbit", beautifully read. I didn't get to bed until 1.30, but had a better walk home than I anticipated.

Monday 17th March.

Since I opened this book last Minto has been within measurable distance of death—threatenings of pneumonia. It gave me pleasure and gratitude to find that I am not as wicked a man as I thought I was: I found myself sorry for her plight and was able to pray sincerely for her recovery. But alas my feelings reverted to normal when she was out of danger: not I think entirely my fault, for I was shocked at her behaviour. Here is a woman, who has been, if not at Death's door, at least at his front gate: and the very minute returning strength enables her to do so, she is hard at work building up again the flame of her envy, hatred and malice. . . . Maureen came up from Malvern for a couple of nights after the crisis was past, and, to my astonishment, proved herself to be a diplomatist of the first order. Like everyone else, she is chronically indignant at the slavery in which M keeps J, and had determined that J *must* have a holiday: which she accomplished by getting Dr. Radford and Nurse Figett to make M believe that proprio motu she herself had come to this decision. And this is true, for M gravely announced to me on Saturday that "she thought J was looking very tired etc. etc." Well done Maureen! The plan is that she is to come to The Kilns from 4th to 15th April while Leonard is at Rossall, and J and I are to occupy 4, The Lees [home of Leonard and Maureen Blake], at Malvern. As poor J said to me, it will be the longest holiday we have ever had together—if it comes off. But I strongly suspect that M will repent her of the good she has done before we get to the 4th.

Thursday 17th April.

But we did get our holiday after all! On 4th, Good Friday morning, J and I attended mattins at 8 a.m., we being the only people in church, and soon after breakfast left in Sweetland's car for Malvern: a grey cold day, both of us glad of heavy coats and scarves. But oh! the relief to be leaving The Kilns behind us at 50 miles an hour. We got to 4, The Lees in time for a late lunch, and in a remarkably short time found ourselves on the easiest of terms with Maureens French factotum, Bernard Le Varlet. He is a French Christian, aged 23, from Dordogne, and a man of considerable ability; indeed if his English had been better, I think J would have found him no mean adversary in theological controversy. . . . I don't propose to write a full account of our holiday, for I took no notes and left this book at home. For the first part of our stay the weather was cold and windy, and we did little except discover the "Unicorn" opposite the Foley Arms—a pub after our own heart, with a perfect nest of bars and some odd characters in it, to say nothing of excellent cider. . . . On Easter Sunday we made our Communion in the beautiful Priory, where the wafer was placed in a chalice, a thing I never saw done before. After Easter spring came at last, and the rest of our stay is a blur of exquisite impressions, already fading alas! . . . What shall I say of the hills? No words can describe the combined peace and exhilaration that they gave me, the sound of the lambs, the clean air, the vast landscape, the springy turf on which we flung ourselves for a smoke; looking west I forgot thirty five years. . . . Hugo arrived by the 1.28 on Saturday, and we met him with a taxi at the station, having, before his train came in, much reminiscent talk about the old days. He was in excellent spirits, and I think enjoyed his visit. . . . On the Monday Hugo, greatly to my surprise, blossomed out as a walker; taking a haversack ration, we did the Camp walk, including the ascent of the camp. The soak on the hot short turf of one of the great trenches at the top rests in my mind as one of those rare perfect moments. . . . We again dined at the County on Monday, on which occasion we had a couple of bottles of Algerian wine, under the influence of which Hugo's spirits, already high, rose to a prodigious extent, especially after a couple of gins in the rather nasty bar of the Foley Arms. To my horror in College Road he burst into the "Red Flag", and when we got back to the Lees I began to be seriously alarmed, for he treated the place as a rather unusually noisy Inklings. What Bernard made of the spectacle of a grey haired "professeur" roaring out "Ta-ra-ra-boom-dy-ay" with appropriate high kicks I don't suppose we shall ever know. Even when he and J got quieter, the noise could be heard at the raquets courts, and I was very glad when we all got to bed without the intervention of the neighbours. Most evenings however passed most soberly, J and Bernard reading French and English poetry together and correcting each others accents. . . . On our last day we sauntered up North Hill in a hot sun and cool breeze, I a prey to such despondency as surprised me at the thought of being back in that horrid house this evening. I often wonder whether it is a gain or a loss to have a temperament like mine—aesthetically I mean, for morally there can be no doubt. It is true, I have lost The Kilns: for though I can still force myself to see that it is beautiful objectively, I loathe every stick and stone and sound of it: my Christian dream is to live to see it vanish into a road identical with Netherwoods. This is very bad: but if I was any other sort of person, could I feel as if I could kiss every pebble on the High Holywood Road [near Little Lea, Belfast]? . . . By 6 p.m. it was all over, and I was hearing how the dog had been sick, the shopping left over for my benefit etc. etc. But for a bit "Fate cannot touch me": I have heard, still hear, the lambs on the Malvern Hills.

Thursday 24th April.

Dined with Chris at the Angel, after which we went to the Bird and Baby. . . . A well attended Inkling this evening—both the Tolkiens, J and I, Humphrey, Gervase, Hugo; the latter came in just as we were starting on the "[new] Hobbit", and as he now exercises a veto on it—most unfairly I think—we had to stop. Tollers, to everyone's annoyance, brought a stranger with him, one Gwynne Jones, professor of English at Aberystwyth. But he turned out to be capital value; he read a Welsh tale of his own writing, a bawdy humorous thing told in a rich polished style which impressed me more than any new work I have come across for a long time.

Wednesday 11th June.

The incredible has happened. I am off on my Irish adventure, which since the beginning of the year has seemed the merest day-dream—without Parkin of course, who characteristically refused to move in the matter until too late. I went in by taxi at 9.15, feeling very guilty at leaving poor J alone with that horrid old woman in that abominable house, though if I had stopped there I would not have been allowed to do anything to ease his burden.

Monday 30th June.

I have been in very deep waters since [June 12th]. It all began with the feng shui of the cottage, which was more, and more immediately wrong than that of almost any place I have ever struck in these latitudes, and though I told myself it was all nonsense, great waves of depression began to overwhelm me from the very first: added to which the practical difficulties were almost insuperable—an inefficient oil stove, and water had to be fetched from a farm well over a mile away. But it was the eerie greyness that killed me, or rather drove me to the drink that did in actual fact very nearly [kill] me: for the artless Irishman spins out his exiguous supply of gin by mixing it with *methylated spirit,* and it was to this I turned unwittingly for consolation. On Friday 20th I realized I was a very sick man, and for once in a way showed some sense; I got hold of the local doctor, who got me into the Convent Hospital of Our Lady of Lourdes in Drogheda, where I arrived in the evening by taxi. The first night I shared a ward with three other men, but on Saturday was given a private room; on this day I was so ill that I thought "is this death?" But God in His great mercy spared me. The doctor too (a nice man called Costello) took such a serious view of my case that in spite of my expostulations he insisted in wiring for J. On Sunday I was quite obviously better, and wired J not to come. On Monday I no longer had a night nurse at my own disposal. J arrived, anxious and travel stained, on Monday morning, and the sight of him did me more good than any medicine: for I still hadn't recovered from the fright of the possibility of dying without seeing him. From this moment I began to mend rapidly, and though I am still weak and shaky, I am obviously cured—thanks to God and the Sisters of the Medical Missionaries of Mary. Once convalescent, I began to take a great interest in my surroundings. To the Protestant—or at any rate to me—there has always been something sinister, a little repulsive, almost ogreish, about the practice of the R.C. religion. So far as I had any idea of a convent, it was of some-

thing grey and secret, with sad faced women gliding about noiseless-
ly; rarely speaking and never smiling, spying and spied upon. There
could be nothing more preposterously unlike the truth: the first thing
that strikes you is the radiant happiness of these holy and very loveable women, from Mother Mary Martin [founder of the Medical Missionaries of Mary at Drogheda, Ireland] their superior down to the
youngest novice: whatever else it is, it is a life of *joy,* and a place of
laughter. As I got to know them better and gave them my precon-
ceived ideas of conventual life, they exploded into delicious mirth.
This order is only ten years old and exists for staffing mission hospi-
tals in tropical Africa: aims ultimately at having its own nun doctors.
Revd. Mother, to whom I took a great liking, is that not uncommon
type, a saintly religious, and a born leader and organizer, though frail
and often in ill health. The amount of work she gets through is amazing, and yet, like her nuns, she is never too busy for a gossip. I cannot
describe the wonderful spiritual refreshment of a week in a community where everyone takes it for granted that the Christian way of life
is the only possible one; I had not realized before how much one
stands on the defensive in England—"Yes, I *am* a Christian, and why
shouldn't I be?" sort of thing. It was lovely to have a sister saying as
she saw I was alright for the night, "God be with you": and in the
morning "It's a fine day, thanks be to God". Once I said in the English way, "But I'm afraid it will cloud over later": "and is that any
reason for not thanking God for what we've got now" was the reply.
One day after I was up, I was, to my great surprise, shown over the
whole convent—exquisitely clean, beautifully furnished, full of light
and peace, and obviously happy novices reading and praying. I shall
not soon or easily forget this little fortress of happy, valiant Christianity. The only bore was Father Quin, the chaplain, who *would* come to
my room and try to convert me in a set piece oration: moreover, he
was a Co. Tyrone man, and I could not explain to him that had he the
tongue of men and angels, it would be ludicrously impossible for me
to be converted by anyone talking with an Ulster accent! Finding J
having tea with me one afternoon, he tackled him but here of course
he caught a Tartar; his main point, if I understood him, seems to me
to be absurd—the honour of "our Lady" as the mother of *God.* To
support which he kept on quoting from the feast at Cana "and the
mother of Jesus was there". However, doubtless he was but doing his
duty as he understood it. On Wednesday I was let get up, and found
that my illness had taken a good deal more out of me than I thought,
and I was not at all sorry when the time came to go back to bed. J,

who was installed at the "White Horse" in the town visited me twice daily, growing each day more enthusiastic about Drogheda and its environs—reporting with delight that the hotel boots was called "Meekul"; and when all anxiety was over, we rejoiced in the chance which had given him this unforeseen holiday. On Thursday I was up and out, taking what was for a convalescent quite a considerable walk out into the quiet green countryside. On Friday morning J went off by taxi to Dunany and packed up all my belongings in the ill fated cottage and brought them back to the hospital: for I have decided to abandon my holiday, or rather to finish it at the pub. in Drogheda: and on Saturday, having said goodbye with very genuine regret to my nuns, I moved by taxi with J in a downpour to the White Horse, arriving in time for a bottle of Guiness before a most substantial mid-day dinner. I saw at once that it is my sort of pub—shabby, comfortable, easy going. There is something of the old unreformed "White Hart" at Blackwater about it. In the evening we had a stroll along the banks of the Boyne, a dark fast flowing river with a big tidal rise and fall; this was the second turn we had had together, for I forgot to mention one on Friday evening, amusing for seeing an ass returning home on his own and solemnly turning into his stable as if to get in out of the rain which was just then beginning. [Today] I said goodbye to [J] with much depression at quarter to five; there are times when in retrospect my life seems to have consisted in saying goodbye to J. . . . I got back to my room before going to bed had my solitary glass of sherry; whilst drinking it I was struck with the haunting fear that is so often with me—suppose J were to die before I did? And a sheer wave of animal panic spread over me at the prospect of the empty years; but I pulled myself together, said my prayers, and tumbled into bed. I did not, though very tired, get to sleep so soon as usual, but when I did I slept well.

Wednesday 2nd July.

A most kind and sympathetic letter from Tollers this morning, saying that he had invoked the aid of "that child of Grace who is nearest his heart", St. Bernadette, to assist his own feeble prayers for my recovery. I wrote him as good an answer as I could manage after my siesta. To the convent chapel at 10.15 for the ceremony of taking of the veil by five novices. A long but beautiful service, which included High Mass, conducted by the Bishop of Armagh and two other priests. . . . Throughout the proceedings I managed not to disgrace myself by getting up or down at the wrong times, but it in-

volved keeping a very alert eye on the people in the pews in front. . . .
I had a word afterwards with Sister Ruth who expressed herself as
delighted with J's article,[219] which is to be published in a special
number.

Friday 4th July.

After dinner I read about half of the batch of [the new] Hobbit
which Tollers sent me: how does he keep it up? The crossing of the
marshes by Frodo, Sam and Gollum in particular is magnificent. . . .
After tea another walk. . . . While I was hesitating in the wet grey
twilight, a corncrake started up in a field of young wheat, and no
nightingale could have ravished me as did its harsh song. . . . As I
plodded home in the rain, under weather conditions themselves extraordinarily reminiscent of old days, my mind was full of pictures
evoked by the corncrake: particularly of smoking cigarettes with J on
the top of the bow of the study window, reached by climbing out of
our bedroom window. But while my thoughts are tender, I could not
summon a single regret; at 52 I may be nearing the end of the race,
but how infinitely preferable it is to be 52 rather than 16! It is astonishing to me that practically the whole weight of literature takes it as
axiomatic that nothing can make up for the loss of youth; at least
Lamb and Stevenson are the only two men I can think of at the moment who have anything to say on the other side. Meditating as I
walked, I came to the conclusion that discontent and envy made the
permanent background of my youth—envy, hopeless permanent envy
of those who were good at games: of those with attractive manners:
of those who got their clothes made in town and owned motor bykes:
even of those who were good looking: and all coupled with that self
consciousness which at 15 or 16 can be a perfect torment. . . . No,
give me the level road of the 'fifties, and anyone who likes may sigh
for the ecstasies of youth. Ecstasies there are to be sure: I remember as
if it were last week the first time I walked up Coll. with a double first:
but then so do I remember the time when I was senior enough to
suffer agonies at being snubbed by the head of the House.

Saturday 5th July.

This evening I started [Wordsworth's] *The Prelude:* which satisfies
my test of a poem of the first rank, i.e. that when you reread, you say
"This is better than I remembered it to be".

---

219. C. S. Lewis, "Some Thoughts," *The First Decade: Ten Years' Work of the
Medical Missionaries of Mary* (Dublin: At the Sign of the Three Candles, 1948), pp.
91-94.

Wednesday 9th July.

Two letters by the English mail: a long, interesting one from Tollers, mainly theological, and one from Minto containing an unexpected expression of affection which touched me greatly.

Friday 11th July.

Was surprised by a pleasant and sympathetic note from Little Pig Robinson[220] this morning, to which I replied before lunch. . . . Spent most of the afternoon in answering Toller's theological letter—a difficult task. As part of my general objection to the R.C. attitude to the B.V.M. [Blessed Virgin Mary] I quoted (what I had learnt at the veiling service), the theory of the Immaculate Conception, which states that the Virgin was endowed with full reason *from the moment of her birth:* suggesting that it was a *pointless* miracle. For how did her coming high destiny in any way make it necessary? And why should this be done for her when her Son *"grew* in stature and in *wisdom"?* I put it however a little less bluntly than this: and was able to finish by heartily endorsing his contention that most of the talk about conventual corruption was nonsense.

Sunday 13th July.

[O]ut to early Communion. A congregation of 18. I was at my poor best, and got much joy and comfort from the service. Strolling home, I tried without much success, to sort out a hazy idea that came into my mind that there is some *physical* magnetic attraction between God and a *mass* of Christians, independent of the relationship between God and the individual human soul. How otherwise account for the fact that in Drogheda, which is a Christian "power station", one is lifted to a devotional level totally unattainable in say a garrison church? This general "magnetic attraction" would I'm sure be even stronger than it is if only R.C.s could be got to think that our common faith is vastly more important than our technical differences; and I doubt if even Inklings really believe that this is the case. It may be, probably is, heretical, but to me it doesn't seem of very great importance whether Christ *is* the bread and wine, or whether He is present with the bread and wine; that He *is* present in a special and mysterious way, we both agree. . . . But there it is, it's no use even opening such topics to even the most broad minded R.C. . . . After lunch I retired

---

220. Edward Robinson, friend of "Humphrey" Havard and occasional Inklings visitor. Jack Lewis nicknamed him "Little Pig Robinson" in honor of Beatrix Potter's *The Tale of Little Pig Robinson* (1930).

to my room and before tea finished one of my new Penguins, *The Turn of the Screw* by Henry James: golly, what a yarn!

Friday 18th July.

After supper I began [William Morris's] the *Glittering Plain;* it is really unfair to both to compare Tollers and Morris, as the Inklings so often do. The resemblance is quite superficial: Morris has his feet much more firmly planted on the earth than Tollers: Morris's world is an agricultural and trading one, Toller's is one in which (except for a little gardening), the soil is not the source of life, it is scenery: then again, Tollers is an inland animal, whereas you can't wander far in Morris without hearing green waves crashing on yellow sand. On the other hand there are whole chapters of the new Hobbit in which Morris is beaten on his own ground—especially the journeys: and indeed the whole concept of that world is far beyond Morris's powers.

Sunday 20th July.

See in the paper today that the cure for all our ills is, not more food and production, but more planning and regimentation. The trouble with these people is that they suffer from arrested mental development. Every elder brother remembers his irritation in the nursery when his younger brother ceases to be a copy of himself and develops a will of his own—wants to read when he wants to play and so on. Well these people seem to me to be just at the nursery stage: I believe they are honestly hurt and perplexed that when they say "We'll do so and so today", forty five million eager voices don't shout "Oh yes, *do* lets".

Thursday 24th July.

The older I grow the more I come to think that "scenery" is the champagne of the eye—delicious, but for special occasions. I should not like to live in a famous beauty spot, any more than one would want to marry a famous beauty. A countryside such as this gives me all I require for my aesthetic daily bread.

Friday 25th July.

As I sat in the embrasure on the canal bridge at the gates of the great house in a silence broken only by the sound of rushing water, I began to wonder sadly if I would ever sit there again: but remembered one of the lessons I had learnt from the good nuns at the hospital. One morning when the nun on duty drew my curtains she said "It's a fine day, thanks be to God". I replied in my English way that it was, but looked the sort of day that would turn to rain later—"and is that any reason" she said "for not thanking God for the pleasure He's giving you *now?*" So I, a little ashamed of myself, proceeded to thank God for the pleasure of the moment, and felt all the better for so doing.

Saturday 26th July.

Alas! the last day. What a merciful dispensation it is that when the last day of all comes, we shall not know it for what it is. . . . Thence to the Convent to say goodbye to Mother Mary Martin. She was as kind and charming as usual, and I really think was glad to see me; our chat lasted longer than I had expected, for coffee and cakes were ordered for me as soon as she appeared. This holiday has been worth while if only for meeting her. . . .

Warren Lewis arrived home at The Kilns from his Irish holiday on July 28. Just a few weeks later, he embarked again on a brief vacation (August 4 through 18)—this one to Malvern with Jack and Tolkien.

Tuesday 19th August.

I took this book to Malvern with me, intending to keep a full record of what may easily prove to have been my last holiday, but found the pace too strenuous for diary writing; what with long days in the open, plus cooking and catering for three, I had no energy left for anything else. I must now try to jot down a few impressions. On Monday 4th J and I slept in College, where Tollers was to have joined us for supper in J's rooms, but couldn't get away: not entirely to our sorrow, for we had a real pre-war supper as a result. . . . Next day, a bright sunny morning, we all three went down on the 11.28, travelling 1st on 3rd tickets without being called upon to pay excess: sandwiches in the train, and up to No. 4, the Lees, soon after 2 p.m. Tollers looked a little blank at the idea of sleeping on the divan, but we soon had him fixed up by taking Maureen's bed out of her room and setting it up in the nursery. Tollers fitted easily into our routine, and I think he enjoyed himself. His one fault turned out to be that he wouldn't trot at our pace in harness; he will keep going all day on a walk, but to him, with his botanical and entomological interests, a walk, no matter what its length, is what we would call an extended stroll, while he calls us "ruthless walkers". However, we managed two good days with him including one to the top of the Camp, where I was more than ever impressed with the beauty of the northward view. On this day we had the company of George Sayer,[221] an old pupil of J's, now an English master at the Coll: an R.C., a most likeable fellow, and very good company. Our nice bar lady has left the camp, and been replaced by a sulky Glaswegian with a patch of plaster in his forehead, who was truculent at our disapproval of his abominable beer: as Tollers said after the encounter, it was easy to see how he came by his patch! . . . From time to time I contrasted this holiday with the Hugo one, and was struck with the diversity of taste and interest we have in the Inklings: particularly when Tollers stopped one day and gave us a talk on the formation of the Spanish chestnut at the identical spot which prompted Hugo to tell us the scandalous circumstances under which the late Earl Beauchamp was ordered out of England by George V. Tollers left us on Saturday 9th by the morning train, and I was sorry to see him go, although it made my work lighter. He had dined with us, both at the Foley and the County (we all were agreed that the latter is much the better), and had drunk with us at the excellent pub. the Unicorn: of which he heartily approved: and his visit added a private piece of nomenclature to Malvern—the christening of the mysterious and ornate little green and silver doors in the wall of the old cab rank in Pring Rd. as "Sackville-Baggins's".[222] . . . I enjoyed my house work, which I had not expected to do; and one abiding impression is of the exhilarating freshness of the early mornings from the back door when I came down to begin my day. . . . On *Wednesday 13th* we had a grand day; Sayer called for us in his car, and, equipped with sandwiches, we set out southward for a whole day's pleasuring. Our first stop was at the old Monastery church at Little Malvern. . . . Sayer has the supreme car driving virtue that he is always ready to *stop:* and stop we frequently did to drink in the beauty and peace of it all. About 11 we found ourselves in an open lane, where to the North West across Hollybed Common, was a magnificent view of the hills: utter silence, not a house in sight, far or near. As J said, such a view of those hills as the dinosaurs must have had.

---

221. George Sayer (1914-   ), head of the English Department at Malvern College, and later Librarian at the school. A former pupil of Jack Lewis, he and his wife, Moira, became close friends of both Jack and Warren—frequently having either brother as a houseguest in their home at Malvern. Sayer was an occasional Inklings visitor.

222. The name of a family of hobbits, who were related to Bilbo Baggins and his heir, Frodo, the Ring-bearers in J. R. R. Tolkien's *The Hobbit* and *The Lord of the Rings*. These characters were chiefly distinguished by their materialistic greed.

Tuesday 26th August.

When I dream, which is rarely, the outlines are vague and confused; but last night I had one of startling clearness, which de la Mare could turn into a crackerjack of a story. It was twilight, and I was sitting at a bare table in a ground floor room with a man. The dream opened at the point where I had realized that the only course to adopt was to strangle that man, and this I proceeded to do. Just as I finished a terrific knocking broke out on the front door: I had to push the corpse out of sight: the uproar continued: it was too early to pretend I had had to get out of bed: so gulping some neat whisky and tousling my hair, I pretended to be roused from a drunken stupor, and staggered to the front door. There was no one there, and I knew then that there hadn't been. I returned to the sitting room to consider the question of disposing of the body, and had hardly sat down when the terrific knocking broke out again, this time on the sitting room door. Nothing would have induced me to open that door: instead, I pulled the corpse into a bedroom, furnished only with a bedstead and mattress and locked the door: immediately and more menacing than ever, the knocking broke out on the bedroom door. Then I woke up.

Thursday 25th September.

J had Sayer up from Malvern to spend the night, and we went round to Magdalen shortly after nine. Present, J, Sayer, Colin Hardie, Christopher, Hugo and myself. J produced a bottle of Cyprian wine, very sweet and smooth, from which we got a glass and a rabiot apiece. Some enjoyable talk arising out of T. S. Eliot, one of whose poems J read superbly, but broke off in the middle, declaring it to be bilge: Hugo defended it, J and Sayer attacked. I thought that though unintelligible, it did convey a feeling of frustration and despair. J thought he had nothing to say worth saying in any case. Christopher, in an interlude with me in the privy, was captious about quarreling with Eliot for not being Masefield, Auden, or any of the other poets whose names had come up. When we got back the conversation had drifted to whether poets create or reflect the mood of their time; I was inclined to think they helped at least to create it, but I was in a minority. Later in the evening we got on to the subject of sleep, and Christopher, in the face of a chorus of incredulity, maintained that the sensation of falling asleep was a horrible one, as indeed was the idea of sleep itself. . . . We broke up at midnight. An exquisite starry night, the tower black against a moon lightly veiled in thin silver cloud. I thoroughly enjoyed my walk home.

Saturday 4th October.

About 11.30 this morning as I was battering my way through the Bournonville family, Tollers and Hugo arrived, with the inevitable result; which means that I have been out drinking every morning this week, except (I think) Monday. . . . We went to the Bird and Baby via Mansfield, Hugo in excellent and steadily improving spirits, which reached a climax in the Bird, where I thought he was going to have hysterics. We could not have chosen a better day for our frolic, for there was no beer, and consequently the place was nearly empty. Eureka! I've at last found a man who has *invented* a story: at least Blagrove[223] claims to have done so, and I think he's truthful. It was at the time short skirts came in, and here it is: Q. "Do you think short skirts made girls look taller?" A. "They certainly make men look longer". He thought of it in a bar and presented it to a pair of cross talk comedians who were there, and who used it with great success. Tollers was very interesting on the early history of Sweden, and Hugo amusing on various College gossip. . . . I told T that J agrees to his plan of establishing cellarettes in Merton and Magdalen for the Inklings. Looked through the new *Atlantic Monthly* over my tea; it's astonishing how naif and behind the times America is in some respects—long, serious review of a book by some philosophic-scientific fellow who at this time of day is allowed to get away with the old stuff about "mankind being a minority of life on an inferior planet in an insignificant constellation": and of course *therefore* mankind is unimportant.

Sunday 5th October.

J had a poor night, and is still in pain, but insisted on getting up to do the washing, in spite of my attempts to do it for him.

Tuesday 7th October.

Fell into a heavy unfreshing sleep after lunch, from which I woke, more tired than before, at 3.15, and started on J's mail, which was—of course—an exceptionally heavy and dull one: eighteen letters in all.[224]

---

223. Charles Blagrove (?-1948), landlord of the Bird and the Baby.

224. Warren had begun serving as full-time secretary to his brother as early as 1943 (see letter of June 1, 1943 from Jack to Arthur Greeves in *They Stand Together,* p. 496), typing approximately twelve thousand letters for Jack in the twenty years he served in this role. Warren later explained that, while acting as Jack's secretary, he "read all his mail before passing it on to him after answering the routine stuff on his behalf" (unpublished letter to Clyde S. Kilby, February 17, 1967). Occasionally, too, Jack would scribble a brief note on the margin of a letter, returning it to Warren for composition. Or, as Warren elaborated to still another correspondent: "[Though the

Thursday 9th October.

A very good day's work on my DNB, 25 pages. Chris and I dined at the Angel in the evening. . . . We went to the Bird after dinner, where Blagrove gave evidence for the incredible vulgarity of the Bullingdon Club: at the Bullingdon dinner nothing was ever used a second time, and the table was not cleared—crockery, silver, broken meats etc. when finished with were flung out of the window! A pleasant Inklings in Merton, tho' less interesting than some: present, two Tolkiens, J and I, Colin, David Cecil[225] and John Wain from Reading. (The Tolkiens rather too obviously annoyed by the arrival of the two latter in the middle of a chapter of [the new] Hobbit). . . . David read a chapter of his forthcoming book on Grey: very good indeed I thought, though he is perhaps the worst reader of his own works in Oxford.

Tuesday 14th October.

To the Bird and Baby in the morning where Dundas-Grant,[226] himself a Highlander, gave an interesting illustration of second sight. Before his holiday he was on the top of a London bus, behind a lorry loaded with trusses of hay: the load slipped, and several of the trusses fell off. He mentioned the incident to his wife, who, shortly after they arrived in Scotland for their holidays, had a vivid dream that she was in a car following a lorry loaded with big rolls of paper, which began to fall off. She told the dream to some friends who had driven over to visit them. The friends on their way back came up with a lorry load of tree trunks, and were about to overtake it, when the woman said "No, remember Mr. D-G's dream". So they pulled up and had a smoke. When they got going again, they found the road a little way ahead blocked by the lorry and its load, which had slipped off into the road, and would have fallen on their car if they had tried to pass. I was sitting next Colin, who is a believer in second sight. Troubled to hear

---

letter] is unsigned I can say positively that my brother drafted it and not me. I know the style too well; for some reason or other he would often draft a letter himself and then get me to type it, instead of signing and sending off the draft" (unpublished letter to Belle Allen, August 1, 1967).

225. Lord David Cecil (1902-   ), Goldsmiths's Professor of English at Oxford from 1948 until 1969, and Fellow at New College, 1939-1969. He is a well-known biographer and literary critic, and was a member of the Inklings.

226. Commander Jim ("D-G") Dundas-Grant, Commander of the Oxford University Naval Division in World War II, and resident during this time at Magdalen College. After the war, he and his wife supervised a residence for Catholic students in Oxford. He was a member of the Inklings.

from Tollers today that he has an alarming internal pain, and has to be X-rayed. I do hope it is nothing serious.

Thursday 23rd October.

Today I have been what Rose Macaulay would call "living life to the full". The "living" began with the arrival of Hugo in College at 11 a.m., who carried me to Baker's to help him to buy some beer mugs: which we did. . . . After some pleasant desultory talk, back to Magdalen where I finished off J's mail. . . . To Merton to dine with Tollers in the evening. . . . Thence to Tollers' very restful room for the Inklings, where we drank green tea: seemed to me to be the same as one gets in Chinese eating houses. The smallest Inkling we have had for a long time, only Tollers, Humphrey, J and I. J read a new poem, "Donkey's Delight",[227] which I think the best thing he has done since he took the craze for playing about with metre. Tollers then gave us a chapter of [the new] Hobbit: but I think we all missed Christopher's reading. We buzzed a bottle of commanderia at 3/6 a man. J suggested that Stevens[228] should be invited to become an Inkling, and all those present were in favour. I should like to see him join us.

Thursday 30th October.

Dined with J in Magdalen in the evening. An excellent dinner, lobster salad, partridge and peche Melba. . . . A very small Inkling afterwards, only Tollers, Humphrey, and us two. A long argument about the ethics of cannibalism, how arising I forget: Tollers very firm, though in a minority of one, that no circumstances—death or consent of the victim included—can justify it. J instanced the Communion rite without shaking him. This led to a discussion on the possible confusion which exists in our minds between aesthetic distaste and hatred of sin, e.g. in sodomy, do we really hate the *sin* as we should do, or have we a mere disgust at the thought of the act? Tollers then read us the last chapter of the [new] Hobbit, that is to say the last he has written: so I fear this toothsome standing dish will be off for some time to come. There is some fatality over the wine at Magdalen Inklings: never have we yet had a bottle since the new rule came into force. Tonight each man had counted down his siller and I had

227. The poem "Donkey's Delight" was first published by Jack Lewis under the pseudonym Nat Whilk (N.W.) in *Punch,* Vol. CCXIII (November 5, 1947), p. 442; a revised version is published in C. S. Lewis, *Poems,* ed. Walter Hooper (New York: Harcourt, Brace & World, 1965).

228. Courtnay E. ("Tom") Stevens (1905-1976), Fellow and Ancient History Tutor at Magdalen College from 1934, was a member of the Inklings.

Jack, on vacation from his studies at Oxford, with his father, Albert Lewis, in the garden of Little Lea, July 1919. Photograph was taken by Warren Lewis while home on leave from Belgium.

Leeborough ("Little Lea"), the Lewis family home in Belfast, Northern Ireland, July 1919. This photograph was taken by Warren Lewis while home on leave from Belgium.

Jack Lewis in the "little end room" at Little Lea, Belfast, Northern Ireland, December 1919. This photograph was taken by Warren while home on leave from England.

Captain Warren Lewis and fellow officers from the No. 2 Junior Officers' Course at Aldershot, England. This photograph was taken outside the blacksmith shop classroom during the three-month summer supply and barrack course, June 1920. Warren is second from the right in the first row.

Jack Lewis seated on one of the stones at Stonehenge, Wiltshire, England, April 8, 1925. This photograph was taken by Warren when the two brothers were on a short Daudelspiel through Wiltshire.

Jack Lewis with Maureen and her mother, Janie King Moore, on holiday at a teashop at St. Agnes Cove, Cornwall, England, August 1927. The family dog, Baron Papworth ("Tykes"), is in the foreground. This photograph was mailed by Jack in a letter of September 3, 1927, to his brother, Warren, who was stationed in Kowloon, China.

Albert Lewis (father) standing outside a vacation cottage in Bangor, County Down, Northern Ireland, 1928. This is probably the last photograph taken of Albert before his death in September 1929.

Warren Lewis with fellow R.A.S.C. officers in Shanghai, China, 1929. Captain Lewis is third from the right.

The Kilns and grounds, ca. 1930. Note especially the two brick kilns visible to the right of the house, and the pond in the foreground. This photograph was taken by Warren Lewis from the top of Shotover Hill (where the Lewis brothers often walked).

The Kilns, ca. 1930. This photograph, also by Warren Lewis, may have been taken shortly after Jack and the Moores moved into The Kilns in October 1930.

The pond behind The Kilns, with a punt drawn up along the bank, ca. 1930. Photo: Warren Hamilton Lewis.

Warren Lewis seated in a lawn chair (possibly in Ireland while on vacation), ca. 1945.

Jack Lewis seated in Magdalen College sitting room, ca. 1948.

Jack and Warren Lewis on vacation at Vera Henry's bungalow, Golden Arrow, Annagassin, Republic of Ireland, ca. 1952.

Mollie and Len Miller with Warren Lewis along a Cotswolds roadway, July 1969. Photo: Clyde S. Kilby.

HORSA HOLDINGS LTD

Please Reply to:- 119. Gt. Ancoats St.
Manchester 4.

$76/63

Date: 20/11/63

Shall I tell
him your communica-
tive acumen is a minus
quantity? W.

yes. Answered 22/11/63 W.

Dear Dr Lewis,

I apologise for the delay in writing to thankyou for your kindness to my wife & I when we called to see you last Wednesday. What a wonderful recollection Judith has been left with!

A page (119) from Warren Lewis's diary, volume 21, which shows the last letter Warren answered as Jack's secretary. Photo: Robert Mead.

the corkscrew in my hand, when J, who had been indulging in continuous spasms of yawning for half an hour, announced that he had a bilious attack and the idea of wine filled him with horror: so back the bottle had to go into its cupboard. Humphrey drove me home, very pessimistic about the state of the world.

Wednesday 5th November.

The perfection of an early September day. . . . Crossing the Parks is the nearest thing to being in the country that has happened to me since I left Malvern, and I enjoyed it, indeed did much more. . . . Seeing a birch tree with its russet leaves in the bright sunlight, I got that feeling—or rather *vision* that comes like a flash of lightening, and leaves a confused feeling that this is only a pale shadow of some unimaginable beauty which either one used to know, or which is just round some invisible corner. I accept it with deep thankfulness whenever it comes as a promise of immortality. And am rather strengthened by the fact that it never bears analysis: even as I write, the feeling is fainter than when I opened this book.

Sunday 9th November.

Walked into town after breakfast, and to 11 a.m. service at St. Peters-in-the-East. The old, improbably named Vicar, Mr. Wooster, has disappeared and been replaced by one Dyson, who has noticeably increased what Dorothy Sayers calls the "candle power" of the Church. Congregation of fifteen.

Monday 10th November.

A staggering blow in the papers this morning: potatoes are put "on rations" on a scale of 3 lbs. per week for the bourgeois. And so the last "filler" food disappears from the diet, and the days of real hunger come upon us.[229] It's extraordinary how one is conditioned by a secure past: even now I can't grasp the fact that this means that I, WHL, will go to bed hungry and get up hungry; these, I say, are things that happen to nations one reads about in the papers, not to me. . . . If only one could learn from St. Paul the secret of being content in whatever state one is! I am increasingly worried by how badly I am facing life these days—or rather I am not facing it at all: my futile rage over trifles, the perpetual despondency and fear of the

---

229. Shortages in post-war England continued to be acute—assuaged somewhat for The Kilns household, however, through the generosity of Jack Lewis's American admirers who sent parcels of scarce and rationed food items. These "luxuries" were frequently shared with members of the Inklings.

future, the mixture of hate and envy with which one regards the tombstones of the Victorian dead in a churchyard, the constant brooding on the past. Even if there is no comfort in the material future, surely one should as a Christian be able to draw some brightness from the other worldly future? And yet how rarely even prayer brings that comfort!

Tuesday 11th November.

A warm boisterous morning, up early, and got through the shopping with less annoyance than usual. To the Bird and Baby at 11.30 where there was a thin meeting—Tollers, J and I, Colin, Humphrey and Dundas-Grant. J and I had some time together before the others arrived and fell to discussing the Charles Williams essays which are out at last:[230] a very handsome volume, though outrageously priced at 12/6. J's preface first rate, also his essay on "Stories". I objected to his dictum that *The Three Musqueteers* has neither scenery or weather: to which he retorted that he had adopted this view from me! When Tollers arrived I congratulated him on his excellent paper on Fairy Stories: he sat down opposite me and we fell into general talk. . . . In the evening after a snack in College, sweetened with a pint of beer supplied by J, I went to the Men's Musical. . . . Nevill Coghill spoke to me before the show. How I envy that man his apparently effortless ease in always speaking en honnete homme! To me tonight he said "I always like to see you at a concert because then I know it's going to be a good one". Of course it means nothing, but the fact remains that we all like butter, and rightly so, for it *is* a lubricant. We had a composer tonight whose work is new to me, and whom I liked, Samuel Barber: I must watch for him in future.

Thursday 13th November.

Inklings at Merton in the evening, only the two Tolkiens, Colin, who left early, J and I. Colin, the lucky bargee, goes to Ireland next summer to examine at Dublin, Cork, Galway, and Mayerooth. Spent a pleasant unexacting evening. Tollers read a rich melancholy poem

---

230. *Essays Presented to Charles Williams*, C. S. Lewis, ed. with a preface (London: Oxford University Press, 1947). This festschrift volume, published posthumously due to Williams's unexpected death, contained five essays by members of the Inklings (J. R. R. Tolkien, C. S. Lewis, Owen Barfield, Gervase Mathew, and W. H. Lewis), as well as one by Dorothy L. Sayers. (Sayers (1893-1957), author of detective stories and religious essays and dramas, shared Williams's passionate love for Dante's *The Divine Comedy*. It was, in fact, Williams's *Figure of Beatrice: A Study in Dante* (1943) that launched Sayers's own vast contribution to Dante scholarship—culminating in her translation of *The Divine Comedy*.)

on autumn, which J very aptly described as "Matthew Arnold strayed into the world of Hobbit". He also showed us his very beautiful £55 edition of the Canterbury Pilgrims in facsimile from the earliest MS. Somehow the talk drifted to public schools, Christopher (of course) reporting conditions at the Oratory in his time to have been "incredible". Thence to the psalms, I complaining that a great many were violently unChristian in sentiment: I was in a minority of one, but remained unconvinced. J showed that old reluctance to the opening of a bottle of wine which he has ever shown since the arrangement came into force, though he agreed enthusiastically when it was proposed. He says it alters the character of the club. I left for home at eleven, and was in bed soon after 12.

Thursday 18th November.

The snow, the cursed snow, is back again. Even, knowing myself, I'm surprised at my feelings about it. Last winter gave me such a "scunner" of it, that all through the long hot summer I retained the feeling that the snow was "just over": so now I feel as if this winter and last are one, with a short break of fine weather in the middle of it. . . . A jolly meeting at the Bird and Baby, this morning. Present, Father John,[231] Tollers, D-Grant, Colin, Humphrey, J and I. Father tells me that in his slum parish in Coventry the people voted Conservative in the municipal elections: also that a govt. taipan recently came down to "see what the trouble was" in Coventry, i.e. why the electorate was swinging right. . . . The conversation drifted to a second sight and John told a very interesting story: when he was training for the priesthood, one of his instructors was a Hungarian Jesuit. A few days before the Sarajevo murder in 1914, the Jesuit had a vivid dream, in which he saw an important person murdered at a street corner, which corner he recognized. Then came to real Sarajevo, which murder was committed in quite a different part of the town. It then fell to the Jesuit to confess the convicted assassin, and he learned from him that the murder had been planned to take place at the corner which he saw in his dream, but, owing to the police having changed the Archduke's route, the murderers had had to recast their place. This very remarkable story is subtly different from second sight, and very much more mysterious—not a dream of the future at all in fact, but a dream of what would take place in another man's mind.

---

231. The Reverend John Francis Reuel Tolkien (1917-   ), eldest son of J. R. R. Tolkien, Roman Catholic parish priest at Coventry. He was an occasional Inklings visitor.

Sunday 23rd November.

I was unusually dissatisfied with myself in church: no wicked, or even worldly thoughts, but a downright lackadaisical inattention. "Can ye not watch with Me one hour?"—alas, not one half hour, God forgive me.

Thursday 27th November.

Stevens made his debut as an Inkling tonight in Tollers' rooms. A very pleasant meeting: Tollers, J, self, Stevens and Humphrey. We talked of Bp. Barnes, of the extraordinary difficulty of interesting the uneducated indifferent in religion: savage and primitive man and the common confusion between them: how far pagan mythology was a substitute for theology: bravery and panache. Stevens said that Vauban's fortresses killed the old style panache: and told me a very interesting thing viz. that our stand in the actual forts built by Vauban at Calais enabled the bulk of the B.E.F. [British Expeditionary Force] to escape through Dunkirk in 1940. J announced roundly this evening that the system of our clubbing for wine must be given up: as we were in process of consuming a bottle of Toller's port and half a bottle of his rum, it was perhaps not the happiest moment at which to come to such a decision!

Sunday 21st December.

Whilst at Malvern I picked up and read A. L. Rowse's [autobiographical] *Cornish Childhood:* well written, interesting, and intolerable, it might except for less covenances have as its sub-title, "Self Portrait of a Shit". It is the best bit of self revelation that has come my way since Pepys, and, gosh, what a man it reveals! The only excuse for the fellow is the terrible loneliness which is the price he paid for emerging from the working class into academic Oxford, and which has left him brutal, arrogant, and intensely conceited—modesty, he says, is a vice, not a virtue. . . . Whilst on the subject of books, I have started to read Shakespeare's tragedies for the first time, making it my evening "poetry book". *Othello,* the first I tackled, in spite of the absurd figure of Othello and his idiotic suspicions: *when* was Desdemona unfaithful to him? And the ridiculous overheard conversation! But what a man, this Shakespeare! In spite of all this nonsense, he faces the "willing suspension of belief".

Monday 29th December.

Got back today from yet another visit to Malvern, this time with J: a little holiday we owe to the great kindness of Maureen, who offered to do duty at The Kilns over Christmas in order to let J get away. The more I study Maureen, the more I realize what a very delightful man the mythical Mr. Moore must have been! I went down on 23rd and was pretty busy on that day and 24th, when Maureen left for The Kilns on the same evening Edna went on leave, and I became the cook whilst Leonard took over charge of Richard, a loveable and excellently behaved little boy. J was due to arrive on 24th but was unable to get into the train at Oxford, and came down on the afternoon of Xmas day—travelling in great comfort on the 12.10, with a full Xmas dinner enroute! I went to the 7 a.m. celebration on Xmas morning at the Priory, not entirely without profit, though I always find great festivals a difficulty. Dawn was breaking as I emerged, the line of the hills sharp, black, and cold, and an entrancing chorus of bird music. . . . In the evening we had our Xmas dinner, cooked by me, which was a great success—soup, turkey, boiled potatoes and sprouts, pudding. Leonard, most surprisingly, produced a half bottle of gin: I bought one of vermouth: and J contributed two botts. of burgundy and one of Commanderia—so we had quite a feast. Leonard was this time much more "forthcoming" than I have ever known him before, and on one evening was really interesting on the correspondence of colour and sound.

Thursday 1st January, 1948.

[Tonight] we had a drouthy though pleasant Inklings in Tollers' room: present, both the Tolkiens, Stevens, Humphrey, J, and myself. An interesting talk on the various versions of the Bible, and the Collects: which drifted somehow to Houseman and the ferocity of his prefaces: and thence to the *Chanson de Roland*.

Thursday 22nd January.

Saw a remarkable display of canine sagacity this evening by the poodle of the "Kings Arms". The middle bar there is "men only", and there were perhaps a dozen of us there when in came a woman in slacks. The poodle shot out of the office—I had almost said "his" office—and fairly barked her out into the passage. . . . I had a snack "in chambers", followed by a very pleasant little Inklings, present Colin, Tom Stevens, Christopher, J and I. We drank wine and finished a noble "old Kentucky style brandied cake" which someone had sent J from America. Much talk of Mauritius, public schools, and Sherlock Holmes stories.

Monday 26th January.

I'm afraid Parkin really means business about Mauritius.[232] I had another letter from him today in which he speaks of it as a settled thing, and regrets that I can't join him. J, Parkin, and the Inklings, in that order, form the capital on which I had hoped to live out my life, and I feel very keenly the loss of such a large portion of it. But who's to blame him? If he stops here, what has he to look forward to except increasing discomfort in increasingly second rate boarding houses until, as he recently put it to me, he "dies like an unwanted dog in some Cottage Hospital". I can now only hope for his sake that there is no flaw in his calculations.

Thursday 26th February.

Well attended Inkling in the evening, with McCallum,[233] whom we all thought had tacitly resigned. Tollers and Chris there, both looking the better for their trip to Brighton. . . .

Thursday 4th March.

A very poor Inklings in Merton this evening. When I arrived Hugo's voice was booming through the fog in the Quad, inviting a party of undergraduates up to his rooms, he really can be very irritating at times. Present, the Tolkiens, J and myself. J was worn out with examining, Tollers had a bad cold, Chris was moody: and the talk was slack and halting. We talked of philology, various ways of saying "farewell", and of the inexplicable problem of why some children are allowed to die in infancy. Home by midnight.

Thursday 11th March.

A red letter Inkling this evening. J's old benefactor, Firor[234] of Baltimore, recently sent him a ham, and round it was raised a capital dinner in the New Room, which I enjoyed as much as anything of the sort I have ever attended. The staff did the thing in style: beautifully decorated table, and excellent service. J put up sherry, and the

---

232. On January 21, Warren had received a letter from Major Parkin detailing his proposed plan of retirement to Mauritius (an island in the Indian Ocean and dominion of the British Commonwealth). Though Parkin's description of a land of "lovely climate, good bathing, *no* Income Tax, and rum so cheap they use it in their cars instead of petrol!" was a temptation to Warren, he also realized that he "would not for an instant contemplate a life of voluntary severance from J. . . [though] I'm upset at the thought of losing Parkin" (diary entry for January 21, 1948).

233. Ronald B. McCallum (1898-1973), Fellow of Pembroke College until 1955, when he was elected Master of Pembroke, was a member of the Inklings.

234. Dr. Warfield M. Firor of Baltimore, Maryland, one of Jack Lewis's American admirers and correspondents.

dinner—soup, fillet of sole, the ham, and an excellent pate savoury: Tollers and Hugo each contributed 2 bottles of a most delicious Burgundy from Merton: and David sent in two bottles of port. We sat down eight to dinner, all in the highest spirits: J and Colin at top and bottom respectively, Tollers, Humphrey and Christopher one side, Hugo, David, and I the other. Colin covered himself with glory in the ungrateful role of carver. There was just the right amount of everything, including drink. I don't remember much of the talk, except the curious discovery that David's mother and P shared a common anfractuosity, viz. an utter inability ever to get hold of a name accurately, or pronounce it correctly if known. After dinner we went over to J's rooms where preceedings opened with the great Tuxedo raffle—or an American dinner jacket suit, won by Colin, whom it didn't fit, and who with great generosity waived his claim in favour of Christopher, who looked admirable in it. I think, everyone was glad when he got it.

Tuesday 16th March.

[We went] to the Bird and Baby where we spent a pleasant morning, in spite of there being no cider. Tollers with amazing tactlessness, insisted on talking reminiscently and joyously of the Inklings dinner across Dundas-Grant, who of course had not been asked. As J said subsequently, he is in that respect very like a woman: whatever is uppermost in this mind must come out.

Thursday 18th March.

A pleasant Inklings, attended by Humphrey, Tom Stevens, the Tolkiens, Colin, Hugo, J and I: to say nothing of McFarlane's Siamese cat, Stubbs. I never knew before that this type of cat has eyes that shine *red* in the dark. Some good talk, largely philological, and about obscene words, arising out of my not understanding the meaning of "stool" as used in a verse of the psalms we had at evensong in the cathedral.

Thursday 25th March.

Being Maundy Thursday, no Inklings this evening, but I and J dined in College together, where there was a small attendance. After coffee we walked home under a rising moon through the Fellows garden and Cuckoo Lane: much talk of old days, apropos of J's autobiography,[235] which promises to be first rate—though of course there

---

235. Jack's autobiography, *Surprised by Joy: The Shape of My Early Life,* was not actually published until 1955.

could hardly be anyone less competent to criticise the early chapters of such a work than I am. We talked of games, and our dullness in continuing them long after the toys had become the merest symbols—not being for some reason able to see that "a game" could have been carried on with equal satisfaction and infinitely less trouble in a conversation, or story. We called in at the Mason's Arms for a pint of Burton, where we watched some very skillful bar billiards, and so to bed.

Saturday 17th April.

While I was at work on J's mail today, in comes Hugo, and carries me off with him to the K.A. [Kings Arms Pub]: by no means unwillingly for my part. Under the influence of his second pint, Hugo's spirits rose prodigiously: then Tollers turned up and *volunteered* a round: whereupon Hugo became the Hugo of twenty years ago. Councillor Brewer arrived and put his vast bulk in the chair facing Hugo across the table: it was plain that Hugo had never spoken to him before, but he leant forward and addressed him with an almost servile deference—"you will pardon the liberty, Sir; I trust you don't think I presume: but I shall call you Fred. You look the sort of man who ought to be called Fred". This the Councillor took well, and conversation became general: but a minute later, Hugo, gazing intently at his huge pale face, broke in again—"You'll excuse me sir, but am I looking at your full face or your profile?" The Councillor, still smiling determinedly, turned to his friend and began a reminiscence of their having rowed together in the Teddy Hall boat the year Teddy Hall was bottom of the river: but we never heard the story—"Bottom? Bottoms" said Hugo, "admirable things if ample enough: but you Sir of course have no difficulty about that, Ha! Ha! Ha!" An idiotic but amusing morning.

Monday 24th May.

I was sitting in the study this evening when Paxford came in with a very sad piece of news: Charles Blagrove, landlord of the "Bird and Baby" died very suddenly on Sunday. He was I think about 63, and had been complaining of shortness of breath for some time, but I had no idea that there was anything seriously wrong. With him I lose not only a publican, but a friend, and an irreplaceable one, for he had endless stories of an Oxford which is as dead as Dr. Johnson's: the past Oxford of the turn of the century. Through his father, also a publican, his tales went back to an Oxford in which it was not uncommon for undergrads. to *fight* a landlord for a pint of beer: both would strip to the waist, have a mill in the backyard, and then the battered undergrad. would throw down a sovereign and depart. Many stories he had too of his father—literally—throwing people out of his pub. Charles himself was a big, clean shaven, burly, smartly dressed fellow, with "horsey man" written all over him; he had begun in life as a cab driver, and from that graduated to a handsom. And was never tired of repeating that any man who had 18/- a week before 1914 was far better off than his son is today. His was the Oxford of undergraduates who made nothing of giving a couple of new suits to cab drivers because the fit was not exact: of leisurely country drives to Godstone and such places. Of lavish tips for taking what he used to call "fancy goods" to secluded spots: of people who would hire his cab and ask to be taken "somewhere where they could find a fight: of the Bullingdon Club, of rags, dinners, that general reckless extravagance and panache which prevailed when the security of the upper classes was still absolute, and England ruled the world. . . . The loss to ourselves will be severe; even if the new land-lord tolerates Tuesday mornings, things can never be the same again. Poor dear Blagrove, he had long dreamed of retiring to a little coun-try pub. somewhere, and I like to think that perhaps in some form he has his wish; for is there not wine in the next world? God rest his soul.

Monday 26th July.
I finished *Lost Horizon*[236]. . . and have enjoyed it though I think it might have been better done: but as J said subsequently, that is a comment which one refrains with difficulty from applying to some of the Creator's handiwork!

Friday 13th August.
J and I paid one of our very rare visits to the cinema this afternoon to see Walt Disney's *Bambi,* the story of a deer, in which there were no human beings. Some beautiful autumnal colouring in the woods, and strokes of real genius here and there. Notably the prince of the deer, who, without caricature, was given a more than brutish dignity and majesty. Some good fooling, and some moments of great tender-ness and terror. Before seeing this we had to sit through a lunatic performance on board an American trooper, which didn't "end": it just stopped.

---

236. *Lost Horizon* (1933) by novelist James Hilton.

Saturday 14th August.

Read a good article by J at tea in *Time and Tide*[237] on the admission of women to the priesthood. . . . Before going to bed I finished [Homer's] *Odyssey* for the second time. What a yarn it is! Though not faultless. Odysseus' journey to Hades is distinctly tedious, and I feel that what follows after the slaying of the Wooers is an anticlimax: though one would be sorry not to have the meeting of Laertes and his son. J tells me that the explanation is that to the ancients, the ending of the feud, not the bedding of Odysseus and Penelope, is the real climax of the story.

> *As they had done on several previous occasions, Jack and Warren "traded" households with Maureen—she to care for her mother at The Kilns and the Lewis brothers to vacation at the Blakes's home in Malvern. On this particular holiday, August 16 through 31, though Leonard remained at home, Warren's duties included some cooking and the part-time care of Richard, Maureen and Leonard's three-year-old son.*

Thursday 19th August.

Called by alarum and had to get up instantly, the clock being on the mantelpiece. . . . Made the tea, washed and shaved, cooked breakfast, ate it, and was very thankful to J who did the washing up while I strolled on the Senior. . . . Having found out from Edna that I should be back at twelve for the vegetables, I read . . . for a bit, then J and I walked up to the Unicorn, where we found that the cider had come in: and drank a couple of pints each with much satisfaction. Then back to the Lees and dealt with the dinner problem, though in fact most of the work had already been done by Edna. . . . J, after he had washed up, went off for the rest of the afternoon; I could not go with him as Leonard was going out to tea. . . . Richard is a model youth, and my charge of him while Leonard was out proved a sinecure: he playing perfectly happily by himself out on the Common. . . . For supper I gave my flock scrambled eggs and mushrooms, preceded by soup, and followed by stewed fruit. . . . The real trouble about domestic work is its habit of producing a tiredness which brings with it none of the satisfaction which follows on a hard day in the open air.

---

237. "Notes on the Way," *Time and Tide*, Volume XXIX (August 14, 1948), pp. 830-831. This article was reprinted in C. S. Lewis, *God in the Dock*, edited by Walter Hooper (Grand Rapids, Michigan: William B. Eerdmans, 1970), as "Priestesses in the Church?" pp. 234-239.

Wednesday 25th August.

[Tonight after] a pint of beer . . . [at the pub, we] emerged into a grim and threatening night, with curiously frightening cloud effects to the north, and the lights of Worcester twinkling to the N.E. J remarked that as only stars twinkle and planets shine steadily, the natural assumption would be that the former are lit by gas and the latter by electricity.

Thursday 26th August.

J went out alone for the afternoon, and I read some very poor scientifiction in the study; extraordinary how these fellows think that a battle can be made exciting by locating it in the galaxy, not realizing that if you can *write,* a battle between villages will be just as exciting. It is on a level with their other naive assumption that if you call a man Put-Tut instead of Smith, he automatically becomes mysterious and sinister.

Friday 27th August.

During [dinner at the Beauchamp, J, Leonard and I] had an interesting talk on hymns and their tunes, with enough difference of opinion to keep the ball rolling. When we got home, Leonard played us a couple of his own hymns—very good I thought, and illustrated our earlier talk by playing the three settings of "For All the Saints"—the traditional, V. Williams', and the little known Stanford's. J preferred the latter, I the V. Williams. There was also some discussion about "opacity" and "transparency" in their technical musical sense. To bed at 10.30.

Sunday 29th August.

[W]hile breakfast was getting ready, I read a new (to me) Beatrix Potter, *The Town Mouse,* which pleases me greatly. . . .

Wednesday 27th October.

I am amused to detect in myself an interesting instance of heredity. Several times lately I have found myself going back to J's room after I have left for the day, to make sure I haven't left the stove on, or a lighted cigarette end smouldering. What is this but P's exaggerated nightly precautions against a leak of gas in another form?

Sunday 31st October.

Walked into town after breakfast through Mesopotamia, and attended the ante-Communion service at St. Cross. Whilst waiting for it to begin, I had one of those blinding flashes of exquisite happiness which come and go like lightening. Always a mysterious thing, and must I think be a direct individual intimation of heavenly bliss—and a strong hint to strive for it. I suppose this was Shelley's "spirit of delight".

Tuesday 23rd November.

Dull and foggy. A good Bird and Baby in the morning, and the rest of the day as usual. To The Kilns in the evening, where I found a very angry Vera, who tackled me over the cocktail about Minto's meanness. . . . I . . . cut the thing short, for I saw I was going to be asked the question I am so tired of, and to which I shall never find the answer, viz. how anyone so nice as J ever came to make himself the slave of such a detestable woman? It's a very odd thing how impossible it is to be believed when you are telling the truth. I have been asked this question by all the Inklings, by Parkin, by many of our "lady helps" and servants: and when I reply, perfectly truthfully, that I don't know, and that J and I never discuss this side of his life, I always see that I am suspected of an honorable reticence.

Thursday 27th January, 1949.

Dined in College with J. The first fruits of Tom Stevens' Vice-Presidency is the return of the spirit decanter, so we had gin and French; odd to reflect on the many years of my life which a gin and French before dinner was no more to be remarked upon than the evening bath! . . . A good Inklings afterwards: present, J, McCallum, Gervase, Tom Stevens, John Wain, and myself. We started on the *Lays of Ancient Rome*[238] and thence to poetry in general, on which Wain talked an astonishing amount of nonsense—even going so far as to illustrate his point by reciting a song of Harry Champian's, which he claimed was as good as Macaulay. If I got him aright, his point is that poetry whose meaning can be apprehended at a first reading, is not poetry at all: I should for my part say that exactly the reverse is true. The sense of the House was strongly against him. He recited a pretty good poem of his own composing . . . and then read us the first two chapters of his book on Arnold Bennet: absolutely first class, and I enjoyed them greatly.

Friday 28th January.

Brought home my reconstructed Chad Walsh[239] suit this evening,

---

238. *The Lays of Ancient Rome* (1842), a collection of poems by Thomas Babington Macaulay, nineteenth-century historian, essayist, and statesman.

239. Chad Walsh, an American correspondent and friend of both Jack and Warren

which Vera pronounces to be a great success; and it certainly *feels* satisfactory. Found Lee in greater indignation at a ukase which Minto has issued forbidding J to sit in the study in the afternoon: dining room fire to be lit *instead* of the study fire in the afternoon "to save fuel". "But where," I said, "is the saving of fuel?" "There isn't any" said Vera "but she can worry the unfortunate man easier if he's in the dining room": which on reflection seems the probable explanation. How long, oh Lord, how long?

Thursday 4th February.

An enjoyable Inklings in the evening. Present, J, McCallum, Colin, Hugo and myself. Was glad to hear that Kein, late of Univ. now of Queen's Belfast, has been elected Master of Balliol—"one of the most important beings in the Universe": but apparently by no means nem. con.[240] This set talking of red brick universities from the job hunting point of view; from where the talk drifted, by channels which I have forgotten, to torture, Tertullian . . . the contractual theory in mediaeval kingship, odd surnames and place names. McCallum very good on kingship; he much improves as time goes on, and if one gets the impression in listening to him that you are having a tutorial, well I suppose a history don cannot very well talk history in any other way. We broke up early, I getting home on foot at midnight. A pleasant walk in the silent stinging night. Temperature in my room 31° when I went to bed.

Friday 4th March.

I emerged from the Acland yesterday morning, where I had been as a finale to the wearisome cycle of insomnia—drugs—depression—spirits—illness. The saddest feature of the thing is that I can see that J, mine own familiar friend doesn't believe this to be the cycle, but assumes it to be spirits—insomnia—drugs—depression—spirits—illness. But his kindness remains unabated, and what more can I want?. The contrast between the warm cosy Acland and this cold dreary house was disastrous; went in to make my bow to Minto and was given a lecture on the extreme coal shortage, the iniquities of Betty, and an enquiry as to how long I proposed to stay cured this time? Went down to the refrigerated study feeling that I was indeed "home"

Lewis. He is the author of *C. S. Lewis: Apostle to the Skeptics* (New York: Macmillan Company, 1949); and, more recently, *The Literary Legacy of C. S. Lewis* (New York: Harcourt Brace Jovanovich, 1979).

240. *Nemine contradicente*—"unanimously."

again. Whether from cold, temper, depression, or all three, I had a shocking night, and when I tried to pray I found the line "dead".

Monday 13th June.

Got back here today after a pleasant weekend with the Sayers to find disaster; I had a premonition of it when on going into College I found that J had not been in. Went out to the house and found an ambulance at the door waiting to take him in to the Acland, with a high temperature, violent headache, and a sore throat and glands. I went in with him.

Tuesday 14th June.

A very anxious day indeed. J was light headed during the night, and obviously a very sick man when I went in to see him; he is having injections of penicillin every three hours. I could get little out of Humphrey except that it is "a serious illness for a man of fifty". Pray God it is going to be alright. . . . Humphrey explained to me that J's real complaint is exhaustion, and that he would certainly have been knocked over by the first germ that came along, whatever it was. To my joy, he added that when he got him on his legs again, he would insist that he accepted no responsibility for J's health unless he took a good holiday away from The Kilns. I got home sick with fright and savage with anger, and let her ladyship have a blunt statement of the facts: stressing the exhaustion motif and its causes. I ultimately frightened her into agreeing to grant J a month's leave.

Wednesday 15th June.

Thank God, SPB out of danger! And not only out of danger, but quite cheerful, though still in considerable pain. On Humphrey's advice I did not tell him of my triumph in getting him leave, as he thought that it might excite him too much. (M by the way now seems convinced that it is *her* thoughtfulness which suggested the idea of J taking a holiday! But just as well). A most remarkable interview with Miss Griggs, usually so shy, just before I left the house. It appears that M has at last worn out even that good woman's charity; Miss G really *angry,* stamped her feet and waved her clenched fists during a tirade on M's selfishness: told me with such pride that on entering M's room she had forestalled any possible Mintonic opening with the words, "No, I don't want to hear anything about Bruce's health, I want to hear about Dr. Lewis's health"! A novel experience to be buttonholed by Miss G like this. A busy day, but a happy one, dealing with J's mail. Now that the anxiety is over, I have come reluctantly to the conclusion that I must cancel my own holiday: a hard decision to make, and indeed I am ashamed of how much I feel it. But it would never do if M died while we were both in Ireland; it would be the supreme irony of J's career if the disastrous relations between him and M were to end in a Coroner passing a censure on his "heartless and callous neglect of a helpless old woman" etc.!

Thursday 16th June.

A lovely summer morning, and when I got to the Acland was overjoyed to find SPB quite definitely better: so much so that I had no hesitation in breaking the news of his holiday to him. To my immense relief (I had expected an argument), he agreed almost at once, and his delight did me good. Poor man, it will be the first holiday he has had for at least fifteen years.

Friday 17th June.

On getting to the Acland I was rejoiced to find that SPB is beyond all question better: out of the wood, God be thanked. He talked with his usual critical animation about Masefield's *Captain Margaret*,[241] which he is reading for the first time, and of his coming holiday. . . . An invitation for J today to a Buckingham Palace garden party: here's a nice problem in etiquette! How does one answer such a thing? . . . A busy and troublesome day, largely school business,[242] which becomes more burdensome all the time: I wish I could get rid of that job.

An absence of entries in Warren's diary from June 17 until August 14 allows only speculation as to the reason for Jack's foregoing of his promised holiday in deference to Warren's long-anticipated Irish vacation. Nevertheless, Jack did remain at home with Mrs. Moore while Warren, with great thanksgiving, was able to holiday in his beloved Drogheda until September 26.

Sunday 14th August.

The Little People celebrate the first of my long anticipated holiday with a burst of "glorious weather": which makes it difficult to know how to dress. . . . Lunched in the refreshment room at Euston, and spent a long, tedious afternoon strolling and reading: but consoled by the thought of being away from The Kilns for a long spell: but feelings tempered by thoughts of poor J, about whom my conscience is still very raw. . . . I didn't sleep for more than a few minutes in the

241. *Captain Margaret* (1908), a novel by John Edward Masefield, O.M., Poet Laureate.

242. Not only did Warren assist Jack with his correspondence, he also carried out all of the details for University business that were Jack's responsibility.

train, and was pretty tired when soon after three I got on board the new 5,000 ton *Columbia* built by Harland's. However, a steak and a pot of tea, followed by "getting up" for the day, viz. a good wash and a shave, worked wonders. After that I took deliberately the risk of going to the bar and drinking a large Power and soda, and very thankful I am that I did so: for it looks as if my prayers were to be granted and that, with a constant vigilance, I may learn to use alcohol and not to abuse it. I enjoyed my drink immensely, and felt no temptation to go on drinking—and that under the most unfavourable circumstances: tired, no bed, beginning a holiday, a pocket full of money, and a well stocked bar which didn't close until six a.m. Thank God for this minor success which I pray may be the prelude to a complete victory.

Thursday 25th August.

To *Karamazov*[243] after lunch, which I find very much better than on first reading; but it convinces me of the impossibility of collaboration with any conceivable Russian government. The more one reads of them the more alien and remote they seem. . . . More *Karamazov* in the evening. Johnson's famous critique of Richardson applies to some degree to Dostoevsky, but I find the long religious digressions very profitable reading: am especially struck by his doctrine of collective responsibility.

Sunday 28th August.

During the day I finished *Karamazov*. I had forgotten how unsatisfactory the conclusion is: in fact there is in the artistic sense, no conclusion at all. The story just stops. We are worked up to a great pitch of excitement about Dmitri and Grushenka, Ivan and Katya, and then comes the last chapter—a beautifully told, but quite irrelevant story of the last illness and death of a minor character. What happened to the stars we shall never know. But a book well worth reading a third time. J, I see, has read it twice, and even equipped it with a skeleton index. I must confess however that after supper I turned with considerable relief to Pickwick.[244]

Sunday 18th September.

The big news in the paper today is that the £ is to be devalued. . . . What exactly devaluation means is not at all easy to discover: in fact the

---

243. *The Brothers Karamazov* (1879-1880), by nineteenth-century Russian novelist Fyodor Dostoevsky.
244. The *Pickwick Papers* (1836-1837), by novelist Charles Dickens.

only intelligible comments I found were (a), that "it would increase the burden of misery in England" and (b) would—of course—fall heaviest on "those with pensions and investment income". Why one should be a social outlaw, almost a criminal, for having many years ago entered a pensionable profession is difficult to understand: I can see the case against investment income, but not against pensions. Indeed this government itself has vastly increased the pensionable jobs. . . . To St. Peter's for 11.30 service, and took a stroll in the sunny churchyard before going in. . . . I was in a rarely humble and thankful mood this morning, and don't remember when I last spent an hour so profitably: and, it being five weeks today since my curious experience of ceasing to find any temptation to drink in other than strict moderation, I even ventured to make a personal song of Psalm 116.

Wednesday 21st September.
The news of the devaluation continues increasingly depressing, and I was glad to finish breakfast and get out on the road. . . . sitting on a well, I found myself looking at a stone posted gate into a field, with some dim stirring in my mind of having looked at a very similar gate when I was a small boy at some seaside place, and enjoying its unfamiliarity. It suddenly occurred to me that the warning, "unless ye are like little children" etc., may not refer to one's *moral* state at all, but may mean that heaven is only for those who retain something of, or at worse the remembrance of a child's infinite delight in ordinary things in the days when the whole world was a magical place. I can imagine for instance that wallflowers and flowering currants, as they were when I first became conscious of them—when the former grew knee high, and the latter was a large tree—may very well be part of the furniture of heaven and produce the same indescribable delight.

Sunday 25th September.
After lunch I changed and went out for a walk, by no means rejoiced to find that high summer has returned. I did the reservoir walk under a windless baking sky. . . . None the less it was delicious to get out of the noisy town on to the comparative quiet of the main road, and then into the real silence of the deserted country lanes. The reservoir has fallen considerably, even since I was there last, and while I smoked a cigarette on the fringe of the fir trees, I fell to thinking what a panic there would be in the water if the fish were rational beings: to their men of science the evidence that the end of the world is near would seem irrefutable—for it is demonstrable, that their world, the reservoir, has shrunk by two thirds since this time last

year, and is still shrinking. I might make a story with a moral out of it.

Warren returned to Oxford from his Irish vacation on September 27.

Wednesday 5th October.

J has bought a pair of alleged hand sewn brown shoes for 20- and bids me make a note of the fact to see how long they last. . . . The best Inkling story of my absence is of Humphrey's instructing young Mark in the elements of Christianity. "God" said Humphrey "has no body". "Do you mean Daddy that His legs join straight on to His head?" Though I have now been back a week, I have not got Ireland out of my system yet, and am still regretting Drogheda.

Thursday October 20.

A couple of Hugo stories, too good to be "lost in memory's flow". (1) At a ham supper in J's rooms, H bellows uninterruptedly for about three minutes, and as he shows no signs of stopping, two guests at the bottom of the table begin a conversation: which being observed by Hugo, he raises his hand and shouts reproachfully— "Friends, friends, I feel it would be better if we kept the conversation *general*". (2) He is to lecture this term on Henry V, and the other day in Merton was bombarding the History Tutor with questions about the period, finishing up with—"What I want is not facts, but ideas". Gared, intervening with his lisping drawl: —"An admirable summary of your disabilities, Dyson".

Thursday 27th October.

Dined with J at College. . . . No one turned up after dinner, which was just as well, as J has a bad cold and wanted to go to bed early. . . . We have in Morrell's park Bertran Mills' Circus at present, and as I passed in the moon light, I saw a noble spectacle; six elephants, in their enormous stable rugs, padding in single file down the road! On the neck of the first sat a man with a hurrican buttie, and the others seemed to be loose. Presently they stopped at a gate, which, not being immediately opened, the leading elephant began to show signs of temper, stamping a huge forefoot, and squealing; an elephant is ill advised to give way to such a display, for his squeal is exactly like that of a pig, and when he indulges in it, he is sadly shorn of his dignity!

Tuesday 1st November.

Milton Waldman of Collins, the publishers, last time he visited J asked to see my "Duc du Maine",[245] and this morning comes his verdict on it. Much what I feel about it myself, viz. that the material or a biography is insufficient, and interesting material is wasted by being used as padding. He finishes by suggesting an interview, and holds out hopes of business materializing.

Thursday 10th November.

No Inklings tonight, so dined at "home".[246]

Saturday 12th November.

I have just finished in MS. Tollers' sequel to *The Hobbit, Lord of the Rings*. Golly, what a book! The inexhaustible fertility of the man's imagination amazes me. It is a long book, consisting very largely in journeys: yet these never flag for an instant, each is as fresh as the one before, new colours available in profusion, whether the journey be beautiful or terrible. Some of the scenes of horror are unsurpassed, and there is wonderful skill in the way in which the ultimate horror— the Dark Lord of Mordor—is ever present in one's mind, though we never meet him, and know next to nothing about him. The beauty of Lothlorien, and the slightly sinister charm of Fangorn are unforgettable. Frodo's squire, Sam Gamgee and the dwarf Gimli are I think the two best characters. What is rare in a story of this type, is that there is real pathos in it; the relationship between Sam and Frodo in the final stages of their journey moved me greatly. How the public will take the book I can't imagine; I should think T will be wise to prepare himself for a good deal of misunderstanding, and many crits. on the lines that "this political satire would gain greatly by compression and the excision of such irrelevant episodes as the journey to Lothlorien". Indeed by accident, a great deal of it can be read topically—the Shire standing for England, Rohan for France, Gondor the Germany of the future, Sauron for Stalin: and Saruman in the "Scouring of the Shire" for our egregious Mr. Silkin, the town planner (and destroyer)! But a great book of its kind, and in my opinion ahead of anything Eddison[247] did.

---

245. Eventually published in 1955, by Eyre & Spottiswoode (London) as *The Sunset of the Splendid Century: The Life and Times of Louis Auguste de Bourbon, Duc de Maine, 1670-1736.*

246. The last Thursday night meeting of the Inklings recorded in Warren's diary was October 20 (Tuesday mornings at the Bird and the Baby continued).

247. E. R. Eddison (1882-1945), fantasy novelist and author of such works as *The Worm Ouroboros* (1922).

Wednesday 16th November.

Maureen gave birth to a daughter today, and the report is that both are doing well. Thank God.

On January 10, 1950, Jack Lewis received his first letter from an American correspondent, Joy Davidman Gresham.

Tuesday 17th January 1950.

Met J in the Cloister who gave me the joyful news, "Bruce is dead and buried": and so walked out of town in the twilight, happy in the thought that the penultimate gate of poor J's prison is down at last. Maureen, who was here last night, says that it is fifteen years we have put up with this nuisance, which has made poor J's life a perfect burden to him. Latterly things have been intolerable: as Minto's brain began to give way, his "little walks" became an obsession with her. I have known him taken out three times in an hour. Things would have been even worse but for the amazing kindness of Miss Griggs who came down daily to take him out. . . . My thoughts turn to the death of poor old Tykes, but with very different feelings. This dog [Bruce] I never liked since the heartless treatment meted out to poor Troddles on its account which destroyed any illusions I had left about M's much trumpeted "fondness for animals".

Saturday 4th April.

Tollers rang up this morning and asked me to meet him at the Bird and Baby, he being in those parts to be fitted with a set of false teeth. He had a remarkable story, told him by his dentist, Mr. Pegler, which I can account for only by supposing Charles [Williams]'s theory of Substitution to be fact and not fantasy. A girl child, after a night of great pain, was brought to Pegler, who found on investigation that it would be necessary to cut into the inflamed flesh round a bad tooth without administering an anaesthetic. The child was warned that the treatment would be extremely painful: but unavoidable, and she must be very brave. As Pegler cut into the diseased tissue, a pang of such severity shot through his own jaw that he dropped his lancet and stomped up and down his surgery. When the agony had worn off a little, he returned to his patient—sitting in the chair with a slash in her jaw—and asked her if she was in much pain? The child laughed and replied that she had felt nothing at all!

Saturday 29th April.

Got home in the evening to find that last night, or rather this morning, M fell out of bed at 1 a.m., 3 a.m., and 5 a.m. And has since been removed to Restholme, where she will, apparently spend the rest of her life. . . . Apropos, J in discussing the matter with Vera and I, mentioned, greatly to my surprise, that "when he first knew her, she didn't get on any too well with her son". I mention it because of my own ingenuousness, and to show the power of propaganda. All this Paddy-worship business had gone on so long, that I had come to believe—with a liberal discount of course—in the legend of the perfect son and the perfect mother united in the perfect relationship. . . . The first news from Restholme is that Sister Haydon is already commenting unfavourably on "her very strong language": and M wants to know how soon she will be able to escape from this hell on earth in which she is imprisoned. On the whole the outlook is as black as it well can be.

Friday 16th June.

A sunny, windy morning and my 55th birthday; as I lay in bed I made efforts to determine that this, my personal New Year's day, should be very different to that of the calendar. So far I have passed a despicable year, and who knows how many more chances I shall be offered of amending my ways? And, alas, how often have I tried to turn over a new leaf. But with the help of God I am about to make another effort. After finishing the mail I bussed up to Restholme, where I had a very nasty fright: found M in tears, who handed me a letter from Maureen, sobbing out with difficulty "Very bad news: killed". I tore the letter open and found nothing but a half sheet of the usual feminine *petits riens*. Astonishing how even in a state of semi-imbecility, Minto retains the power of importing a hideous plausibility to her wildest mare's nests! . . . Hugo, whom I have not seen for some time, dropped in during the afternoon, and he and I strolled back to Merton through the Physic Garden: a delicious spot, and I don't know why I do not visit it more frequently. Tea and a walk home as usual.

Wednesday 21st June.

Went over to Reading on the 10 a.m. to spend the inside of a day with Parkin—the only sort of meeting we can afford in these pinching times. A considerable number of cruisers under way on the river, and they set me thinking how igenuously God tempers the wind to the shorn lamb; ever since I had that pain in my side a couple of years ago, Humphrey has forbidden me to lift weights or take any sudden muscular strain, e.g. crank a petrol engine. So that even if 1939 conditions had continued and even had I been a rich man, I should have had to give up ditch crawling. The result is that I can now look on a cabin cruiser without the pang of envy I'm sure I would feel if I was still completely sound.

Monday 4th September.

One of the few hot days we have had this summer—it would be! Up in my best clothes and in to town where I caught the 10.15 fast for Paddington to represent The Kilns at our dear June Flewett's wedding. . . . J, who has been poorly for the past few days, wisely stopped at home; I was glad he did so, but greatly missed his moral support on what promised to be a grim day. . . . Town was always a dreary place in which to be alone, but since the war, it is intolerable; I know few more depressing places than the Hyde Park residential area as it is today—dingy, bomb spattered, empty shells of the rather vulgar opulence of the days of Edward the Bookmaker. . . . St. James's Church proved to be a huge sham-monastic building, but the obvious fact that struck me about it was that it was *cool:* and by this time I was very hot. I sank gratefully into a chair at the back, and watched a large and rather fashionable crowd arrive—even including one man in complete Ascot rig, grey topper etc. At last June came sailing up the aisle on her father's arm, all in white of course, and looking perfectly lovely. I experienced, as I suppose all bachelors do on these occasions, that absurd sense of *injury* that June should have been getting married at all, and particularly that she should have been marrying Clement Freud. It is I suppose an atavism is it? "We are very little changed from the semi-apes who ranged India's prehistoric clay". . . . The crush and heat at the reception were appalling. Was welcomed at the door by Mrs. Flewett, who said all manner of nice things to me and then passed on to where Clement and June were receiving their guests: kissed the latter by special command, which was the only enjoyable part of the function.

Sunday 10th September.

Grace Havard[248] died of cancer at eight o'clock this morning—without pain. It appears that the lay belief that this disease is horribly painful is wrong: it is not *cancer* which is painful, but a cancer pressing on a nerve. This does much to dissipate the nightmare that the subject is wrapped in. Poor Humphrey! This will be a crushing blow to him I fear, for they were very fond of each other: nor is it only a wife he

---

248. Grace Havard (?-1950), wife of "Humphrey" Havard, was actually descended from the House of Plantaganet.

has lost, for she was also his secretary. I did not often see Mrs. Havard, but I shall miss her: a very gracious lady, and the last of the House of Plantaganet. God be merciful to both of them.

Monday 11th September.

Out of town as soon as I had finished lunch, and got down to a hard afternoon's work, which however I have been looking forwards to with a childish impatience with which only Pepys could have sympathized: no less an undertaking than taking possession of what used to be Maureen's room. At last, after *eighteen years,* I have got my uniform cases unpacked! To say nothing of escaping from a nasty little room, bitterly cold in winter, mosquito infested in summer. . . . By seven o'c. I had finished my job, very tired and very satisfied: even Maureen's pictures had been replaced by my own when I knocked off. I found it difficult to leave my new room: am like a child with a new toy.

Monday 18th September.

Humphrey dropped in after supper, and I was very thankful to see that he is determined to pull himself together; both J and I warned him of the disaster of P's withdrawing into solitude after Mammy's death. Before he went, we had persuaded him to take the plunge by coming to the Firor ham feast tomorrow night.

Tuesday 19th September.

Bird and Baby morning. I looked into Blackwell's on my way up, and was lucky enough to get copies of C. Doyle's *Study in Scarlet,* and Hugh Walpole's *Jeremy at Crale:* neither of which I have ever read. At the Bird, Tollers, Colin, DG, J, and I. Tollers very confidential and "in the know" about the details of the Communist plot. A good and quite unintentional *gaffe* by J: the question was propounded whether Tollers' voice production or Hugo's hand writing gave more trouble to their friends. J "Well, there's this to be said for Hugo's writing, there's less of it". Home late to lunch, and worked hard at my concordance until after six. J had by appointment that indefatigable talker Marjorie M , at 5 p.m. She had come to "consult" him, but supplied at least 90% of the conversation. This is the woman of whom Owen Barfield remarked in his dry way: "She's a good creature when all's said and done: especially when all's said and done". Ham supper in J's rooms at 7.30, same party as this morning, plus Tom Stevens. Humphrey I'm sorry to say didn't turn up: hope it is owing to work, and not to funk. Walked home early, and to bed at 11.15.

Friday 22nd September.

George Sayer left on the 2.10 for Malvern, having been here since before dinner last night: a very pleasant interlude. This morning he has been visiting his old undergraduate friend Hourani, now a research fellow: and found him very unhappy, and much regretting that he had come to Magdalen. Hourani complains of the isolation in which each don lives. . . . J and I decided that we must try to draw him out of his shell.

Wednesday 27th September.

J's ignorance in some directions amazes me as much as his knowledge in others. Last night at dinner I mentioned Tito's volte fact in Yugoslavia, where there is a state fostered return to Christianity. I thought J very stupid about the whole affair, and we had talked for a minute or two before I found out that he was under the impression that Tito was the King of Greece!

Wednesday 17th January, 1951.

Minto died of influenza at Restholme about 5 o'c. on the evening of Friday 12th, and was buried in the Churchyard at 2.30 on Monday: I escaping the funeral owing to having 'flu myself. And so ends the mysterious self imposed slavery in which J has lived for at least thirty years. How it began, I suppose I shall never know but the dramatic suddenness of the "when", I shall never forget. When I sailed for West Africa in 1921, we were on the terms on which we had always been: during my absence we exchanged letters in which he appeared as eager as I was for a long holiday together when, for the first time, I was to have a long leave and plenty of money: and when I came home, I found the situation established which ended on Friday. The long holiday boiled down to J agreeing—with extreme reluctance—to spend ten days with me at Leeborough, and it was made quite clear to me that in future I must be content with, to quote Carlyle, "such adminicles and parings" of his time as could be spared from Hillsboro: and these were very scanty, for M early adopted the convenient theory that "holidays never agreed with him"—except in her company, when merely the scene of his daily labours was changed. It is quite idle, but none the less fascinating to muse of what his life might have been if he had never had the crushing misfortune to meet her: when one thinks of what he has accomplished even under that immense handicap. It would be Macaulayesque to say that he took a First in the intervals of washing her dishes, hunting for her spectacles, taking the dog for a run, and performing the unending futile drudgery of a house which was an excruciating mixture of those of Mrs. Price and Mrs. Jellaby;[249] but it is true to say that he did all these things in the intervals of working for a First. Did them too with unfailing good temper (towards her) at any rate. . . . Most infuriating to the onlooker was the fact that Minto never gave the faintest hint of gratitude: indeed she regarded herself as J's benefactor: presumably on the grounds that she had rescued him from the twin evils of bachelordom and matrimony at one fell swoop! Another handicap of this unnatural life was to keep J miserably poor at a time of life when his creative faculties should have been at full blast, which they could not be under the strain of money worry; for his allowance of £210 was quite insufficient to keep Minto and Maureen as well as himself in any sort of comfort. . . . But even this must have seemed to him a trifle compared with the ruthless selfishness with which his work was interrupted; in the last fifteen years of her reign, I don't think I ever saw J work more than half an hour without the cry of "Baw-boys"!—"COMING, Dear"!, down would go the pen, and he would be away perhaps five minutes, perhaps half an hour: possibly to do nothing more important than stand by the kitchen range as scullery maid. Then another spell of work, then the same thing all over again: and these were the conditions under which *Screwtape,* and indeed all his books were produced. What I think limited J more even than this, was the impossibility of knowing to within an hour and a half, when any meal would be on the table; for his presence was always required in the kitchen throughout the process of preparation. I wonder how much of his time she did waste? It was some years before her breakdown that I calculated that merely in taking her dogs for unneeded "little walks", she had had *five months* of my life. I don't think J ever felt as much as I did, the weariness of the house's unrestfulness so long as she managed it; even after ten or more years of it, The Kilns always seemed to me to be a billet which I had marched into, late at night, and would be leaving early the following morning. Apart from the major disaster of the rape of J's life, the next worst result of his complete submission to her whims, was the steady deterioration which it worked in her own character. It had never been an attractive one, and latterly it became frankly intolerable: an intense selfishness, an egotism, which excluded any pretence of interest in any subject but herself, and an arrogant and ignorant dogmatism on every topic however abstruse, made her company intolerably tedious. . . .

---

249. Characters from Charles Dickens's *Nicholas Nickleby* (1838-1839).

Great though her influence over J was, it was not absolute; for she never succeeded in making him quarrel with me. And indeed to do her justice, she put up with my debaucheries in a way in which many a better woman would not have done. In fact the only real grievance I have against her is due rather to an absurd defect in my own character rather than to anything she did, namely my curious habit of building up strong associations between people and places. By taking me on that Kilkeel holiday in the 'thirties, and there behaving in a manner uniquely unpleasant by her own standards, she robbed me of a good half of my own Co. Down. I never want to see any of it south of the Ards peninsula again. Well, God rest her soul, the chapter is closed at last, and I have naturally thought and prayed for the future—if indeed "future" has any meaning in the case of an immortal, which I don't think it has. . . . But there seem to me to be two saving clauses: firstly J tells me that it is very obvious that she has never come in contact with anything approaching Xtianity: secondly, if her curiously insincere character, which seemed to me rather a casual collection of random prejudices than a character, was sincere in anything, it was in her absolute conviction of her own perfection. Which raises the question, how far can anyone be said to *sin,* who, so far from having even a suspicion of sinful conduct, is certain that she is without spot or blemish? . . . . A sinful fool, no doubt: but surely an innocent sinner? It seems to me, having little theology and less moral sense, that if God punishes her (as opposed of course to reforming her) He—salve reverentia—reduces Himself to the moral level of the crew of a windjammer who in the doldrums used to catch and torture sharks—or the sin of being sharks. But these are deep waters, and one can but hope and pray. I add a biographical note, for the benefit of the yet unborn author of J's biography, who has my full permission to use it as "thickening". Jenny King Askins was born, I think at Clonmore, in Co. Louth in 1872, eldest child, and eldest daughter of the three girls and four boys of the Revd. Askins, rector of that parish. Her mother died when she was a schoolgirl at Lincoln, and the next few years she spent in "bringing up" her brothers and sisters, and fighting their battles against a tyrannical and oppressive father. . . . About 1897 she married a gentleman, a relation of Ld. Drogheda's family, a Charles II peerage . . . they separated. . . . After the separation she moved to Bristol, presumably to be near her brother Rob, and her Sister Edie, and to her son Paddy as a dayboy to Clifton. And there she remained until he was called up for a cadet unit at Keble: where he shared a room with J. And the rest of the tale, is it not written in J's and my diaries? And I am back where I started, reflecting on the tale of the wasted years.

Saturday 27th January.

A good remark of old Brightman's which I never heard before: "I can't stand Cambridge undergraduates; they talk to you as if they thought you were listening to them".

Sunday 28th January.

To the ladies Musical at Miss Dencke's in the afternoon, and before the concert was introduced to J's rival for the Chair of Poetry, C. Day Lewis. An impressive looking man in rather an obvious sort of way: rather like an ageing old time musical comedy star off the stage, same soigne appearance, and same ravaged grey face.

Tuesday 30th January.

Bitterly cold day, Bird and Baby morning. Present, Hugo Dyson, Colin Hardie, DG, Humphrey Havard, David Cecil, J and I. Hugo, who has been canvassing for J for the poetry chair, was at his most effervescent: ("If they offer you sherry, you're done, they won't vote for you: I had lots of sherry".)

Thursday 8th February.

While we were waiting to dine at the Royal Oxford—Barfield, Humphrey, David, Jaw Bennet,[250] J and I—came the bad news that J had been defeated by C. Day Lewis for the Poetry Chair, by 194 votes to 173. J took it astonishingly well, much better than his backers. The experts have I understand feared this verdict ever since Blunden withdrew from the poll; had it been a three cornered fight, B and CDL would have divided the votes of the group which wanted a poet rather than a critic. B's withdrawal gave C. Day probably the whole of that vote, plus those he was sure of anyway—the Atheist-Communist bloc. The only remark J has made is that he thinks votes were cast on the political issue on both sides. J's backers console themselves with the reflection that J had for him all the best people, whilst C. Day's were not only unknown in the University, but were evidently "Pentacostal sweepings" bearing all sorts of Slav and Balkan names: but this strikes me as slender ground for self-congratulation. I confess I'm astonished at the virulence of the anti-Xtian feeling shown here; Hugo told me that one elector whom

250. J. A. W. Bennett (1911-   ), Fellow and Tutor at Magdalen College, Oxford, until 1964 when he succeeded Jack Lewis as Professor of Medieval and Renaissance Literature at Cambridge. He was a member of the Inklings.

he canvassed announced his intention of voting for CDL *on the ground that* J had written *Screwtape!* In spite of our defeat, we had a merry dinner. Home at midnight.

Friday 1st June.

A warm sunny day, but with the northeaster still blowing. J and I lunched with Gervase at Blackfriars. Shades of Grandfather Hamilton, that I should find myself a guest in a Benedictine monastery! Large number of guests, forty or fifty of us altogether I should guess, including the monks. We assembled in a low and beautiful upper room, full of cool grey light, as was the whole interior: a room which had once been Walter Pater's study. The monk's robes are not white, as I had thought, but the colour of Shantung silk . . . we were led to a ground floor corridor, where we were lined up against the walls in two rows facing each other; a grace was said and then we filed into the refectory—a room with something of the atmosphere of a XVIIth Century Dutch interior—cool, light austere, floored with big black and white tiles. The tables were set in alcoves round the room, each seating four, side by side, and facing outwards. In the centre of the room was a small table at which sat a monk who read a short passage in Latin. . . . As soon as we had sat down, the Prior rang a bell and said that in honour of the visitors, he dispensed us from keeping silence. We had an excellent lunch—cream soup, fried fish with vegetables, a sweet, Gorgonzola, biscuits and butter, bottled beer. I sat between Gervase and Nevill Coghill, talking mainly to the latter who was, as always, very interesting. He explained to me that *Measure for Measure* has an esoteric meaning: The Duke standing for God, Isabella for the soul, drawn from an earthly convent to enter a heavenly one etc: Lucio the Devil. (*Did* Shakespeare really mean all this?) We then got on to the Russian torturers, and their claim to be able to remake a man and turn him out as obedient and totally different person. What in that case, said Nevill, had become of his *soul?* Where was it? He was thinking, he told me, of writing a play about a man who had been thus tortured; he would always be on the stage with a double, one the real or original man, the other the man manufactured by the N.V.D.K. or whatever it is. The other players would of course see only one man. A most remarkable fellow is Nevill, I wish I saw more of him. Lunch over, we lined up in front of our tables, and the Prior read some prayers from a book held up in front of him by a monk, and then came some beautiful plainsong graces; after which we returned to the upper room for coffee. Here the Prior had a word or two with me, and I took an instant liking to him. Then Gervase showed us over the house. The architect who built it knew his business. Peace, light, simplicity were the dominating tones; the beauty of austerity everywhere, nothing of that tinselly effect which R.C. interiors are so apt to have. . . . Gervase also took us to what he called "my chapel", a really lovely little building built in an arch not I should think bigger than Hartford's "Bridge of sighs". Here, he told me, Charles [Williams], not long before his death, had Gervase say a Mass for all those whom he loved, and acted as server at it. A beautiful thought, typical of dear Charles, though I don't quite understand the part either played in such a ceremony. Altogether, a most enjoyable couple of hours.

Monday 4th June.

I have been reading with considerable interest, Bp. Walter Carey's autobiography. *Goodbye to my Generation.* . . . There is a sentence in Carey's book which particularly struck me: "The beauty in nature only comes in its fullness to those who are innocent, or to those, like myself, who are not innocent yet have had their innocence restored through Christ". . . . Here is the explanation of the magical beauty of the garden at Dundela Villas in summer; after all these years I can still remember my joy in the wallflowers outside the drawing room window, and the flowering currant in the jungle on the peninsula between the drive and the entrance to the stables. I have never had any sensation at all like it since: which shows, alas, how I have failed in life, and how Carey has succeeded.

In September 1952, Jack Lewis met his American correspondent, Joy Davidman Gresham, at a luncheon party he hosted in Magdalen College. This event was not recorded in Warren's diary.

In 1953, Warren Lewis's first volume of French history, The Splendid Century: Some Aspects of French Life in the Reign of Louis XIV, *was issued by a London publisher, Eyre and Spottiswoode. Warren had begun work on this volume as early as 1942.*

Friday 17th April, 1953.

A sad day. Letter from Eileen Filgate this morning to say that our poor dear Vera died very suddenly. . . . She was up to the limit of and perhaps beyond her means, one of the most generous people I have ever met, and no trouble was too much for her to take to make us comfortable. The holidays which she gave us at her bungalow at Annagussan will be a happy memory. She was an admirable aunt, and never enjoyed herself so much as when telling stories of her nephews and nieces; her enjoyment of their cleverness and beauty was so unselfish and ingenuous that it would have been a bad hearted man who tried to shirk listening to her on this subject. . . . Dear Vera, I miss her now, and I shall miss her more as time goes on. R.I.P. "Lord so teach us to number our days—". Something tells me that my own time is getting short. This year, or rather this winter, I have begun to feel really *old;* vitality is ebbing out of me. I am many years older than I was this time last year. Even ships, and the XVIIth century are losing something of their glamour. Nothing seems any longer to be worth the trouble.

Monday 4th May.

Humphrey called for us by appointment at the house at 7.20, and drove us over to Studley for dinner, where we had a meal not unworthy of the golden age—potato soup, cold duck and salad, ice with chocolate sauce, and an asparagus savoury: eaten in the table at the west window on a perfect spring evening, with a slow sunset across the valley. At such moments, I feel with Johnson that a tavern is the height of human felicity. We had our coffee in the bar, where Bawtry the manager showed us a dead sparrow hawk which broke its neck this morning against a window whilst trying to pull out of a dive. Home in the dusk to Humphrey's house where we found Tollers. There had been some talk of listening to [Chesterton's] *The Man Who Was Thursday* on the wireless, but this was vetoed, to my very great relief. Here we had two bottles of Burgundy between the four of us, and some good talk: much of it on translation in general, and on Ronnie Knox's bible in particular, which was torn in pieces by Tolkien. Ronnie, he said, had written so much parody and pastiche that he had lost what little ear for prose he had ever had. Humphrey defended Ronnie.

In December 1953, Joy David Gresham (a divorce now pending from her American husband, William Lindsay Gresham) returned to England with her two sons, David (age nine) and Douglas (age seven). The Greshams spent an enjoyable four-day visit with Jack and Warren at The Kilns.

Friday 3rd December, 1954.

J finished his last tutorial at ten minutes to one today: after twenty nine years of it.

Thursday 9th December.

English Faculty gave an informal farewell dinner[251] to J in Merton; present, besides J and myself, Tollers and Chris., Hugo, David Cecil, Bryson, F. P. Wilson, Nevill Coghill, Browning,[252] Jaw Bennett, Humphrey, and an unfortunate young man with a face like a fish, who never so far as I saw, made a remark all evening. Excellent dinner, including turtle soup which I have never tasted before, and some delicious hock. Nevill told a good story of his daughter's adventures in America; a wealthy bograt[253] Irish man proposed to her and was rejected. The bograt pleaded for her reconsideration of his offer, but finding her adamant, finally said, "Well, if you won't marry me, will you at least sleep with me?"

Friday 10th December.

I began my third book, which is to be a "life and times" of the Gramonts between 1604 and 1678. "Began" this is in the sense that I began writing, for I have spent the last month in Bodder [Bodleian Library] collecting materials.

In 1955, Warren Lewis published The Sunset of the Splendid Century: The Life and Times of Louis Auguste de Bourbon, Duc de Maine, 1670-1736 (London: Eyre and Spottiswoode).

This year also saw the publication of Joy Davidman Gresham's Smoke on the Mountain (London: Hodder and Stoughton), *with a foreword written by Jack.*

In the summer of 1955, Joy, David, and Douglas Gresham rented No. 10 Old High Street, Headington—a house one mile from The Kilns. On April 23, 1956, Jack and Joy were married in a civil ceremony at the Oxford Registry Office.

Monday 5th November, 1956.

And today, nearly two years later, this book, *Assault on Olympus* was despatched to the agents. Nothing that I have yet written has given me so much trouble; the first version, 120,000 words, was finished in July 1955, was rejected out of hand both by Eyre and Spottis-

---

251. After thirty-seven years at Oxford (both as a student and as a don), Jack Lewis left the University to accept the Chair of Medieval and Renaissance English, Magdalene College, Cambridge.

252. John N. *Bryson,* Fellow and Tutor at Balliol College, Oxford; Frank Percy *Wilson,* Merton Professor of English Literature, and former tutor of Jack Lewis; and Irvine R. *Browning,* currently a scholar under Jack Lewis at Magdalen College, later a Fellow and Tutor in English at Pembroke College, Oxford.

253. Protestant Irish slang for Catholic.

woode and by Sloane of New York, and then sent to J's agent, Curtis Brown. I had long written it off as a stillborn, and in fact begun to use it as a quarry for my new effort, Louis XIV, when out of a blue sky CB placed it with Andre Deutsch in London and Harcourt Brace in New York: subject to its being cut to 100,000. This I did, and retyped the whole thing. Then the day before we left for Ireland came an airy letter saying that both publishers were of opinion that after all 90,000 would be a better length. . . . I made the second cut and typed the damned thing for the *third* time—doing the 90,000 in ten days, and incidentally driving myself into Restholme thereby. Much has happened to us since I last wrote anything in this book. Already it is hard to remember the days when I went into Magdalen immediately after breakfast and spent the day there. To sit down to work in the study is the normal routine, to be in Oxford at all, and especially before lunch, is a surprising break of it. But I still regret Magdalen, and even now am not habituated to hearing Paxford bellowing about the place all day. Still, J is undoubtedly happier and healthier, and that is the main thing. From all he tells me of Cambridge, it is evident that he took the wrong turning away back in 1917; on coming up to Waterloo from Bookham, he should have driven to Liverpool St., not Paddington. It is not Cambridge, but Oxford which is the hardboiled materialistic, scientific university. At Cambridge the majority of dons and undergrads. are *Christians*. Altogether a much more pleasant and humane atmosphere. And Magdalene common room is apparently much more to J's liking than that of Magdalen, which we now always call "The Impenitant". Domestically, we are in the midst of the tragedy of Joy Gresham, one of those fantastic things which does happen to J—as fantastic as the Minto business, though from every other aspect than fantasy, very different. Until 10th January 1950 neither of us had ever heard of her; then she appeared in the mail as just another American fan, Mrs. W. L. Gresham from the neighbourhood of New York. With however the difference that she stood out from the ruck by her amusing and well-written letters, and soon J and she had become "pen-friends". In the winter of 1952 she visited Oxford. I was some little time in making up my mind about her; she proved to be a Jewess, or rather a Christian convert of Jewish race, medium height, good figure, horn rimmed specs., quite extraordinarily uninhibited. Our first meeting was at a lunch in Magdalen, where she turned to me in the presence of three or four men, and asked in the most natural tone in the world, "Is there anywhere in this monastic establishment where a lady can relieve herself?" But her visit was a great success, and a rapid friendship developed; she liked walking, and she liked beer, and we had many merry days together; and when she left for home in January 1953, it was with common regrets, and a sincere hope that we would meet again. This was to be soon realized, for when she got home she found her drunken wastrel of a husband living with her cousin, whom Joy had installed to keep house whilst she was in England; and when Bill attacked her, she decided that she had had enough, and returned to this country in the winter with her two schoolboy sons, settling in London. Bill subsequently divorced her for desertion. In the summer of 1955 she hired a house in Headington, No 10, Old High St., and she and J began to see each other every day. It was now obvious what was going to happen, and sometime this year there was a secret marriage at the local registry office; the gap between the end of the Ancien Regime and the Restoration had lasted for less than four years. J assured me that Joy would continue to occupy her own house as "Mrs. Gresham", and that the marriage was a pure formality designed to give Joy the right to go on living in England: and I saw the uselessness of disabusing him. Joy, whose intentions were obvious from the outset, soon began to press for her rights, pointing out with perfect truth that her reputation was suffering from J's being in her house every day, often stopping until eleven at night; and all arrangements had been made for the installation of the family at The Kilns, when disaster overtook us. Joy had been complaining for some time of acute rheumatism in the hip, which gradually grew worse until she had to go into the Wingfield with it; and there it was found that the poor dear's trouble was really cancer. The chances of her recovery are put at evens. I never have loved her more than since she was struck down; her pluck and cheerfulness are beyond praise, and she talks of her disease and its fluctuations as if she was describing the experiences of a friend of hers. God grant that she may recover.[254]

Thursday 21st March, 1957.
One of the most painful days of my life. Sentence of death has been passed on Joy, and the end is only a matter of time. But today she had one little gleam of happiness; it has worried her all along that her's and J's marriage was only a registry office one, because the Bp. of Oxford objected to a religious ceremony. But this J's old friend and

---

254. For additional background information on Joy Davidman Gresham Lewis, see Humphrey Carpenter's *The Inklings,* and *C. S. Lewis: A Biography,* Roger Lancelyn Green and Walter Hooper (New York: Harcourt, Brace & Jovanovich, 1974).

pupil Peter Bide consented to perform—a notable act of charity, for he is not of this Diocese, and had no right to do so without the Bp's authority. However, at 11 a.m. we all gathered in Joy's room at the Wingfield—Bide, J, sister, and myself, communicated, and the marriage was celebrated. I found it heartrending, and especially Joy's eagerness for the pitiable consolation of dying under the same roof as J; though to feel pity for any one so magnificently brave as Joy is almost an insult. She is to be moved here next week, and will sleep in the common-room, with a resident hospital nurse installed in Vera's room. There seems little left to hope but that there may be no pain at the end. How glibly one talks of "resignation", and how difficult it is to practise; *why,* one asks, should J have had the life which has been his—the best 32 years of it eaten out by Minto, and then the prospect of "peace at eventide" so cruelly snatched away. How rapid the whole thing has been too; seven years ago we didn't know that such a person as Joy existed.

> *By September of 1957, Joy's health was improving, and early December marked her regained ability to walk. In June 1958, Joy's cancer was diagnosed as arrested, allowing Jack and Joy to take a July vacation in Ireland. Also in 1958, Warren published his third book,* Assault on Olympus: The Rise of the House of Gramont between 1604 and 1678 *(London: Andre Deutsch).*

Thursday 13th November, 1958.

The last entry makes curious reading now when Joy is busy in the kitchen cooking our dinner. A recovery which was in the truest sense a miracle—admitted to be such by the doctors. But it was not to add an appendix to the account of the marriage that I opened this book once more. When I got back from the Bodder [Bodleian Library] this afternoon I found a letter from a firm of Solicitors beginning "Lt. Col. Herbert Denis Parkin deceased"; and read no further for a full minute or more. He was a friend of almost thirty years standing, and one whose place no one can fill; though indeed in a sense he has been "dead" since he had his stroke in the spring of last year, for tho' I wrote to him I never got any answer. But we shared a stock of memories which were very precious to both of us, and he had a humour which was entirely his own. . . . At my age I shall miss him to the end—the only real friend I ever made in the army. The reason I have had this letter is that I am his Exor., and to my astonishment there is something to "execute"—a matter of £500, of which he leaves me £150. I can hear him now on the evening when he said, "Let's have a sporting bet on which of us passes upwards last". And we did, I, in view of the fact that I was nine years younger, having to leave him £300 against his £150. God rest his soul.

Thursday 12th February.

An odd sequal to [the death of John Wynyard Capron ("Wyn"), son of "Oldy"] comes this morning in the form of a letter from Dr. Watts, ex-Wynyard usher, written about *Surprised by Joy*. . . . I remember Watts better than most of the ushers, for he was there when I descended into the pit in May 1905. In general he confirms our impression of Oldy, and indeed makes him a bigger brute than we had thought him. . . . (Since I wrote this J has got into touch with Dot. . . . "My dear brother" was apparently "much hurt" by the Wynyard section of the autobiography and had thought of writing to J about it—who says "I wish he had").

In 1959, Warren's Louis XIV: An Informal Portrait (London: Andre Deutsch) was published.

Monday 30th March (Easter Monday), 1959.

Another Lent over, and I make a note of my doings; not as a Pharisee, but that if I am spared until Lent 1960, I may do better. (1). I was a teetoller, drank tea for breakfast, and had only bread and butter on Friday mornings. (2). I attended evensong on Sundays, in addition to my usual services. (3). I read Philipps *Letters to Young Churches,* Mauriac's *Life of Jesus,* Chesterton's *Everlasting Man,* Robertson's *Sermons,* and Latham's *Pastor Pastorum.* And when set down, how trifling it all seems!

In October of 1959, X-rays showed the return of Joy's cancer.

Tuesday 1st December.

This afternoon I sent my Regent book to Curtis Brown. I think it's rather good.

Wednesday 16th March, 1960.

Joy away fetching Douglas, and J spent the evening with me in the study. With the exception of the 15 minute walk back from St. Mary's twice a month, this has been the only time I have spent with him since the end of March 1957—just three years ago.

Sunday 20th March.

[L]ast week (i) I got a letter from the Ministry "sanctioning" my Old Age Pension from 20th June 1960, and (ii) A lorry driver stopped me in Kiln Lane with "Hey, Pop! Where's Carter's yard?" And in spite of these warnings I cannot succeed in feeling old!

In April 1960, Jack and Joy, together with their friends Roger Lancelyn Green and his wife, June, vacationed for eleven days in Greece. This trip to Greece was one of Joy's last remaining desires.

Tuesday 21st June.

Joy is dying in the Acland. Of course ever since the cancer reappeared last autumn she has been under sentence of death, but her courage and vitality were such that one was able to forget the grim fact for hours and even days at a time. I can see now that the beginning of the end was when she had her right breast removed on Friday 20th May; though she emerged from the ordeal radiant, and the surgeon spoke enthusiastically of her condition. She was home just a fortnight later, apparently with health much improved, and in great spirits. On Saturday 11th the Millers[255] took her out in their car after supper, and she came back about 10 p.m., having enjoyed herself, and not at all tired. On the following Tuesday which was a glorious day, I pushed her to the library, and afterwards up as far as the pond, with stops for her to inspect her favourite flower bed; and from there we went to the green house where she got out and looked at her plants. This was to be her last outing. She had been complaining for a day or two of indigestion, and it got worse, accompanied by constant retching and vomiting; diagnosed by her doctor as gastric infection, of which there is a lot in the town. She did not feel up to making the usual end of term visit to Cambridge on Saturday last, and that and the taxi for Studley Priory on Sunday were cancelled. The last time I spoke to Joy (or I suppose ever will), was at about 10.15 on Sunday night, the 19th, when she seemed much better and said she would shout for me if she needed help during the night. When I got downstairs on Monday morning J told me that he had been up with her all night, and, poor thing, she had been vomiting, or at least trying to vomit all the time. About 10 a.m. she said to Hibbie, "Nurse, this is the end, I know now I'm dying. Telegraph for Doug". But even then the old courage was still there; almost the last thing she said before falling into a drug induced coma was, "I've got enough

---

255. Maud Emily "Mollie" (1901-1976) and her husband, Leonard "Len" (1901-   ) Miller. Mollie, housekeeper at The Kilns since 1952, was at this time only looking after the Lewis household during the days. Later, after the death of Jack and as Warren's health gradually worsened, she and Len lived in The Kilns as companions to Warren.

cancers now to form a Trades Union of the darned things". And to the doctor she said, "Finish me off quick, I won't have another operation". Not that any would be possible, for the last trouble is supposed to be in the gall bladder or the liver. There is nothing now left to pray for but that she may die without recovering consciousness. Jack of course went in with the ambulance at 4 p.m., and to me fell the task of breaking the news to the boys. I met David at the bottom of the drive and broke the position to him as gently as I could. . . . Poor Doug, arrived in tears, having heard the news from his Headmaster who, with really wonderful kindness, had motored him down all the way from central Wales; and he has been very miserable ever since, though the resilience of his age protects him from the worst of the shock. Telephone ringing with kindly, futile enquiries most of the afternoon. Forgot to say that dear Joy was still well enough and thoughtful enough to make me a present of a doz. handkerchiefs on my 65th birthday, last Thursday 16th.

Friday 8th July.

Once again Joy has made fools of the doctors and nurses, having returned to us on Monday 27th June, looking, and saying that she feels, better than she has done for a long time passed. And in the middle of the previous week the night nurse, when going off duty, said to her relief, "I don't think I'll find Mrs. Lewis alive when I come on tonight". I suppose we must thank God for His mercies, and I am overjoyed to have her home again; but all the time there is the grim knowledge that it cannot be more than a reprieve.

Sunday 10th July.

I just finished *Little Lord Fauntleroy*[256] and cannot understand why it is never mentioned except for the purpose of being laughed at. Admittedly it is sentimental, here and there stilted, and the attempts at English vernacular are dreadful. But Mrs. Burnett seems to me to have more than a little of Charlotte M. Yonge's power of drawing a perfectly good child who is neither a prig nor a bore. J thinks much of the ridicule of the book is due to the illustrations; and certainly if one judged the unfortunate Fauntleroy by them alone, one would want to kick him. Anyway, I've enjoyed the book and will probably read it again.

Wednesday 13th July.

Dear Joy's condition has been giving us much anxiety for some days past, though until just recently I at least felt a tempered opti-

---

256. *Little Lord Fauntleroy* (1886), by Frances Hodgson Burnett.

mism. As late as Sunday 3rd she and J were over at Studley [Priory hotel for dinner] as usual, and on the following day she went for a drive into the Cotswolds with Hibbie. But this has been a bad week. Last night however when I took in hers and J's tea I found her looking remarkably better, and she herself said she felt much more comfortable. But at quarter past six this morning she began screaming which was a hideous shock to me, for when I left her she was playing Scrabble with J; and before I dropped off to sleep they sounded as if they were reading a play together. I ran down and found her in agonies with pain in her stomach (really in the spine J told me later) and called J, who rang up the doctor. He was here before seven and doped her, but even now she has tremendous resistance, and this and subsequent dopings did not more than make her drowsy. Hibbie thank God was here, and her presence was invaluable. After a nightmare morning of planning, improvisation, and errands, J at last persuaded Till, the surgeon, to give her a bed in his private ward at the Radcliffe. Even then the crisis was not at an end, for the ambulance—a very unusual occurrence—was an hour too early. However she was got into it in a wheeled chair, so far as I could see without too much pain. All that is left to do now is to pray God to take her speedily. When I was in my bath about 11.40 I heard J come into the house and went out to meet him. Self: "What news?" J: "She died about twenty minutes ago". She was, he tells me, conscious up to the last, just before Till called J out of the room to say she was dying rapidly. J went back and told Joy, who agreed with him that it was the best news they could now get. During the afternoon and evening she dozed from time to time, but was fully sensible whenever she was awake. She asked during these final hours that she should be cremated, left her fur coat as a parting gift to K. Farrer,[257] and was able to receive Absolution from Austen, whom she asked to read the funeral service over her at the crematorium. Once during the afternoon she said to J, "Don't get me a posh coffin; posh coffins are all rot". God rest her soul, I miss her to a degree which I would not have imagined possible.

Monday 18th July.

A sunny, blustering day, with big white clouds. We left the house in two taxis at 11.15, J, the boys, and myself in the first, the Millers, Hibbie and the Wilk in the other. At the roundabout—by chance, not

---

257. Katherine (1911-1972) and Austin (1904-1968) Farrer were friends of Jack and Joy Lewis. Katherine, in particular, was a close friend of Joy. Austin served as Chaplain and Fellow of Trinity College, and Warden of Keble College, Oxford.

design—we fell in behind the hearse, and for the last time poor dear Joy drove out along the road to Studley. Except the Farrers, none of J's friends bothered to put in appearance at the service, which was poorly read by Austen (under great emotional strain), in a nice, simple, sunlit chapel, with thank God, no music. At the end, the coffin was withdrawn and curtains, pulled invisibly, hid it from us for ever. There is no doubt that cremation is the most dignified ending; Joy really has become dust, returned to dust in clean sunlight, and one does not have the customary nightmare thoughts of a mass of worm eaten putrescence in a graveyard. At times during the morning I felt Joy very close to me.

Tuesday 22nd November.
I sent the corrected proof copy of *Scandalous Regent,*[258] together with an Index, to Andre Deutsch by this mornings post.

Friday 13th January, 1961.
I began to re-read *Arvieux* and make notes on what I read, with an eye to manufacturing a book out of him. . . . I see I last read *Arvieux* in 1930; how little I then imagined that I would ever live to be the author of five books on my pet subject!

Monday 22nd May (Whit Monday).
Began today to write a new book based on d'Arvieux' memoirs, and record the fact because as I'm an Old Age Pensioner I suppose I'll have to keep some sort of a Work-Sheet—being not allowed to earn more than £3 a week.

Wednesday 9th August.
I finished the Arvieux book which I began on 13th January, i.e. began the collection of material, but see entry of 22nd May.

Tuesday 5th September.
Completed typing and correcting of d'Arvieux book which will be sent off to Curtis Brown tomorrow. Whether it is any good or not I can't say, but I'm rather proud that it should have been done at all. The bulk of it was written while constant anxiety about J, overworked, in pain with a strained Tendon Achilles, and bitterly disappointed at the loss of my summer holiday, twelve days before I was due to go.

---

258. *The Scandalous Regent: A Life of Philippe, Duc d'Orleans, 1674-1723, and of his family* was published by Andre Deutsch (London) in 1961.

Friday 20th October.

During the year which ended today I have been a teetotaller for 355 days.

In 1962, Warren published his sixth volume of French history, Levantine Adventurer: The Travels and Missions of the Chevalier d' Arvieux, 1653-1697 (London: Andre Deutsch).

Sunday 4th March, 1962.

George Sayer came to tea today and told us an interesting thing; boys, even senior boys, at a public school now *cry* openly and una-shamedly. Stiff upperlipping is a thing of the past. Furthermore A will come to George and implore him not to criticize B's work harsh-ly "because he is so dreadfully sensitive".

Monday 1st October.

I began to write a 28,000 word 'teenage Louis XIV for *Horizon* of New York.

Wednesday 24th October.

I wish I'd never heard of *Horizon,* having just had a bland (and ignorant) letter from them asking me to re-write Chap. I and Synop-sis in accordance with their Literary Editor's "suggestions". I see no end to the business.

Tuesday 4th December.

I finished and posted the draft of my book for *Horizon.* But alas, with small hopes of acceptance.

Wednesday 19th December.

On the opposite page is a cutting from todays *Telegraph;* and what memories it brings up of Malvern days, the gramophone at Leebo-rough—! Not that Lily Elsie ever made any records so far as I can remember, but how SH [School House dormitory] loved her! And as J said to me last night, "there was a time when you would have given all you had to see her"; which is quite true. Thinking over my child-hood and 'teenage days before I dropped asleep last night, I concluded that even today I resent more even than the inertia of imagination which kept me at that hellhole Wynyard, the bitter poverty of Malv-ern days. In 1912, when I was the age Doug is now, I still had, as at 14, a shilling a week in term time and only an occasional tip in the holidays. I will never forget, nor has anything ever made up to me for the penniless days at the Coll., surrounded by, and trying to live with boys whose parents treated them with some understanding of the feelings of adolescence in a conformist society. The theory I believe was that poverty strengthened character. I fancy it would merely embitter him. As for the average boy it is as bad if not worse for him to be condemned to live with those three to five times as rich as himself as it is for an adult. At least the adult can try to increase his income. But the P'daitabird always had a relish for vicarious poverty. He positively *enjoyed* the thought of curates and bank clerks "keeping a stiff upper lip on £90 a year", though during the years I knew him he never denied himself anything.

In 1963, Maureen Moore Blake acquired the title Lady Dunbar of Hempriggs.

Wednesday 2nd January, 1963.

I entered this year having been a teetotaller for 15 days. From then until 21st June, a period of 172 days, my consumption of alcohol was one pint of beer, drunk whilst lunching with George Sayer at the Mitre on 29th April. I drank from 22nd June until 27th August while I was in Ireland, then was again a teetotaller from 28th August to 31st December, 126 days. So out of 365 days I was T.T. for 298 days. A poor performance compared with 1961.

Friday 15th February.

Now, 3.20 p.m., I am just back from posting the Nth version of my book to my Old Man of the Sea in New York.

On June 15, 1963, while Warren was on his annual vacation in Ireland, Jack Lewis was admitted to Acland Nursing Home with a heart attack, where he stayed until August. Unable to face the reality of Jack's failing health, Warren remained in Ireland until September, when he returned to The Kilns.

Then, for a brief time, things were as in the earliest and the best days (at least in Warren's estimation)—the two brothers together in quiet friendship.

Thursday 31st October.

J told me today perhaps the most astonishing incident I have ever heard. One of his ex-pupils was happily married and on the death of his wife, inconsolable. It had been a perfectly normal marriage as far as the sexual union was concerned, but this man, though no pervert, had always been tormented by a longing to be a woman. Now the incredible has happened. He *has* turned into a woman and a complete one. I don't envy SPB his first meeting with her; to have been friends for years with Mr. X, and to be confronted with him transformed into Miss X will be, to say the least of it, embarrassing. One sees immense complication in Miss X's future life. To begin with, she has to conceal the change of sex in order to hold on to her job. By no stretch of imagination can I visualize what must be the feelings of one who has been of the two sexes.

However, the quiet happiness of the two brothers was not to last. Swiftly and tragically, the most devastating experience of Warren's life came on November 22, when his beloved brother Jack died quietly at home in The Kilns. Four days later, Jack's funeral was held at the Headington Quarry Parish Church—an event not attended by the grieving Warren.

Tuesday 19th May, 1964.
Tonight I slept for the first time in my new home, 51 Ringwood Rd. I had feared that when I made this break with Kilns[259] I might leave the SPB behind me there. But thank God I still feel his presence with me, though the loneliness is perhaps thereby increased rather than decreased.

Sunday 23rd August.
[I learned this evening] that while I was in Ireland last summer J said, "Warnie is my dearest and closest friend, and I can never be sufficiently thankful for the way in which he accepted my marriage". I had always hoped it was like this, but did not *know;* for this is the sort of thing neither of us could have said to the other. It made me very happy—happier I suppose than I shall ever be again.

Tuesday 1st September.
My life continues very desolate, and I seem to miss my dear SPB more rather than less as time goes on. I have no one to *chat* with. . . . Whilst the perpetual ache of J's absence is the chief cause of my depression it is not the only one. He will soon have left me ten months ago, and still I haven't the smallest idea of the amount of my income or the extent of my liabilities. The thing is becoming a nightmare and is rarely out of my thoughts for an hour together. I've always been a poor man, but one in blessed state of knowing to within a fiver how I stood. Will I ever escape from this constant anxiety into that happy position again?

---

259. For a short time after the death of his brother, Warren rented a smaller Oxford house on Ringwood Road, while also renting out The Kilns to tenants.

Monday 22nd February, 1965.

One aspect of a solitary old age which I had not envisaged is its boredom. My mental powers seem to be failing, and I forget quite important names in French history even. More and more do I come to feel what poor P's closing years must have been like; I take up a book, read a couple of pages, throw it aside and pick up another—stare absently out of the window thinking as often as not of nothing—go for strolls—sit in pubs; and all the time there is the nagging pain of my terrible loss. Oddly enough as time goes on the vision of J as he was in his later years grows fainter, that of him in earlier days more and more vivid. It is the J of the attic and the little end room, the J of Daudelspiels and walks and jaunts, the J of the early and middle years whom I miss so cruelly. An absurd feeling, for even had he lived that Jack had already died. Perhaps it has been sharpened by the fact that I am reliving something of the middle years by going through our old walking tours in my diaries, and I can see him almost as if he was visible, on a path in front of me, striding along with stick and pack in his shapeless old fisherman's hat. I am glad to remember that J himself re-read these chronicles only a few weeks before his death and got a great deal of pleasure from them. Tho' he went over them without the maps, a thing I could not do. Another (minor) worry of my dreary life is my health. I've got a slipped disc, for which I have to wear corsets (very difficult to put on then take off) and an apparently permanently painful left shoulder. Nor am I sleeping well.

Eheu fagaces! Oh for the days when one fell asleep in five minutes and remained unconscious until the arrival of the morning cup of tea! Not that I idealize those days for they too had their hard times; but then they were bad times shared with J and that made all the difference.

On one of the pages of his diary recording his entry for February 22, 1965, Warren Lewis carefully taped a portion of a letter which he inscribed in pencil as "The last job I did as SPB's Secy. On the day of his death."

Later this year, Warren Lewis suffered a minor stroke that resulted in slight paralysis to his right hand and a temporary speech impairment.

Saturday 1st January, 1966.

So begins a new year, and it is hard to imagine that it can be more miserable than 1965. I am, and have been confined for weeks in that Hell-hole the Warneford—on the Cat and Mouse basis—whispers of impending release one day, long faces the next. My only comfort is that I get home from 8.30 to 7.45, and sometimes am allowed to sleep at home on Saturdays and Sundays. But the hospital atmosphere is killing me, and I am seriously worried at my mental decay. I often find myself wishing that God would send me another stroke which would carry me off painlessly in my sleep. God help me!

Friday 8th April (Good Friday).

Today I finished going through these diaries and indexing the good times I had with the SPB—good times extending from 27th Dec. 1918 to 3rd Dec. 1954. It has been a labour shot with pain but at the same time there has been a melancholy pleasure in doing it, for thank God nothing except my own death can rob me of my memories; and these have been vividly recalled whilst reading. Unfortunately my materials prove to be pitifully scanty. Oh if only I could have known in time that he was to die first, how I would have Boswellised him! But on second thought how horrible it would have been—a long long holiday with the known final parting drawing nearer and nearer every day. By far the longest and most reminiscently satisfying part of these fragmentary recollections are the eight walking tours which we took together.

Saturday 16th April.

Jock Gibb has sent me an advance copy of J's letters,[260] which I've read with very mixed feelings. To begin with, I think, I should have been sent proofs for me to give the book a last nihil obstat instead of being confronted with a fait accompli. Definitely it is no longer my book at all, for this busybody Derrick[261] has performed the most ruthless surgery on it; and some of it inexplicable. Why on earth has he cut out the dedication? Then all the early years have vanished, and J comes on the stage within a few weeks of his sixteenth birthday!

---

260. *The Letters of C. S. Lewis,* edited by W. H. Lewis, were published by Geoffrey Bles (London) in 1966. This was Warren's eighth and final book. (His seventh book of French history, *Memoirs of the Duc de Saint-Simon* [London: B. T. Batsford] was published in 1964, after Jack's death.)

261. Christopher Derrick had been engaged by Jock Gibb (Jack's longtime publisher) to adapt Warren's original biographical volume into a book of letters. Warren's initial volume attempted to portray his brother's life through excerpted letters and intermittent transitions — a style very similar to the *Lewis Papers.* This approach was deemed unacceptable by the publisher, and the manuscript radically altered. In an unpublished letter to Clyde S. Kilby of April 17, 1968, Warren Lewis wrote of his original biography: "Would you care to have the typescript of my biography of Jack, a book cancelled by Bles in favour of the Letters of C.S.L. which I substituted for it?" The typescript of this unpublished volume, *C. S. Lewis: A Biography,* by W. H. Lewis, is now a part of the Marion E. Wade Collection, Wheaton College, Wheaton, Illinois.

This in spite of fact well known that in a work of this sort nearly everyone finds the earlier portion the most interesting. But this isn't D's worst outrage. I had deliberately refrained from asking contributions from Barfield because I suspected they would be philosophical, or in other words unintelligible to the ordinary reader. This busy fool has obtained them, and sprinkled them generously throughout my material, and they prove to be exactly as I feared— unintelligible. This is bound to choke off the casual book buyer. Imagine myself for instance going into Blackwell's for something to read, and the book, to paraphrase Lamb, instead of opening on some pleasant walking tour, landing me bolt on some withering discourse on the nothingness of the utterness or some similar topic! I should do as many potential buyers no doubt will do—close the book with a shudder and move on in search of more palatable fare. But this not to say that I think it a bad book; I regret the omissions (and inclusions) but what has been retained seems readable. I wrote to Jock giving my criticisms much to this effect, but in milder terms than I have permitted myself here.

Monday 25th April.

Looking through my diaries I see that in the past I have generally given a description of how I spend my days in the altered circumstances. This, probably the last record of the kind, will I fear make dull reading even for myself, for behind all I do is the constant awareness of my irretrievable loss. The pain is perhaps not so acute, but it will be with me until the end, tho' I try to dull it by a steady routine. I sleep I suppose as well as I can expect at my time of life, generally waking up about 1.30, and again about ten to four. Up at 7 a.m., wash, shave, dress, make my breakfast, wash up, prayers and Bible reading, then out for an hours walk which I can manage comfortably and usually enjoy. Home and to my mail, then coffee with Mrs. M at eleven. More reading or letter writing until the Millers and I sit down to lunch together at one. They leave about two, unless they take me for a drive; if they don't, I sleep in my chair for about an hour. Then a cup of tea and a biscuit, and a lighter book until it is time for my 6 p.m. evening meal, which I get for myself, and wash it up when I've finished. Just before seven I get to the Millers, 15 Kiln Lane, and then I watch television until nine; then home to my empty house, another spell of reading, a cup of Ovaltine, and into bed as the study clock strikes eleven.

Saturday 30th April.

A perfect spring morning at last, and while out for my walk, I sat for a while in Bury Knowle and smoked a cigarette with as much happiness as I suppose I shall ever feel again. I am now sitting at J's writing desk[262] looking out on my modest display of apple blossom, tulip, wallflower, daffodil, and cherry; indeed the only bare branches in sight are those of the laburnum, but I'm told this blooms late. Before going to bed last night I finished *Our Village,* a book I thought I had read before, but I think I must have confused it with *Cranford.*[263] It reminds me of Cowper's letters, tho' in fact very different both in style and content; but, like Cowper who has the rare ability of making an interesting story out of nothing. What happens? A spinster, forty-ish, living on a small income in a Berkshire village, describes her daily walks, what flowers she picked, what village people she met, with some detail of their lives, and a good deal about the village arrivals; out of which she produces a book which keeps you interested for 340 Everyman pages. She writes in diary form, always mentioning the weather, and these entries are one more nail in the coffin of the idea of the wonderful weather England had in the past. Take for instance her August 15th—"Cold, cloudy, windy, wet. Here we are . . . clustering merrily round the warm hearth". Tho' as J would have done, she prefers it to the "strange dreaminess" of the previous August, "Too hot to work, too hot to read, too hot to write, too hot even to talk". And he would have endorsed with enthusiasm her claim that autumn is "the most gorgeous of the seasons". She was a woman after our own heart—"I hate all innovation, whether for better or for worse".

Saturday 7th May.

Today finished Homer's *Iliad* in the Everyman translation. What it may be in Greek I of course don't know, but in English it is tedious and perplexing. Tedious, because all early battle pieces tend to be so, but specially is this the case in Homer where an endless succession of fights is described, not only similarly, as they must be, but often in verbatim repetition of the preceding combat. Perplexing, because, if

---

262. This desk (originally from Ireland) was used by Jack Lewis at Magdalen College, Oxford, and later at The Kilns. It was purchased in December 1973, and is now a part of the Marion E. Wade Collection, Wheaton College, Wheaton, Illinois.

263. *Our Village* (1832) by novelist Mary Russell Mitford; and *Cranford* (1853) by novelist Elizabeth Cleghorn ("Mrs.") Gaskell. See the diary entry for August 31, 1930 for what was at least Warren's second reading of *Our Village.*

you know no mythology and every character has at least two, perhaps three names, you soon become completely fogged. What keeps one reading on to the end are the similies, all good, and the too rare glimpses of daily life and custom, all very interesting. Of one thing I'm convinced, namely that if Homer was blind he became so in later life; what man born blind could describe the chariot horses coming out of battle, "Their bellies cak'd with dust": or children building sand castles on the beach: and disturbing wasps in their nests? Or could have done other than *see* the flies feeding on the dead? . . . Here and there one comes across good lines and phrases. . . . But all in all, the dullest long poem I've yet read, and I doubt if its widely parted oases will tempt me ever to read it again.

Friday 27th May.

We—Mollie and Len Miller and myself—got back yesterday afternoon from a capital holiday in June [Flewett Freud]'s seaside "cottage" at Walberswick over in Suffolk, she with her unfailing kindness having lent it to me for a fortnight. . . . Suffolk is in fact a gently undulating country of gorse and broom-clad heath, with wonderful tree clad roads inland and here and there pretty large woods. . . . One peculiarity of the Suffolk sand and shingle beaches is that on them one sees no shells, and practically no seaweed. Apropos of beaches I'm not sure that the best part of the holiday wasn't hearing once more the music of breaking waves, a sound which was I think the first one in nature to captivate me. It brought memories joyous and sad and often the ache for days that are gone; a dozen times a day I saw something to which J and I would have called each other's attention, and which we would have shared with delight. One day Len and I paddled, but there I made the melancholy discovery that my bathing days are over; the racing waves made me giddy, and I would not have been safe in the water. On our last night at Walberswick I took a turn on the dim lit lawn before going to bed and there found a pair of hedgehogs flirting. I had forgotten how fast they can move. With a sharp pang I remembered a night long ago when J and I found one in the barn at The Kilns and persuaded it to come into the house and accept a saucer of milk.

Sunday 5th June (Trinity Sunday).

I must confess to a reprehensible feeling of relief when Trinity Sunday is over; J shared my feelings, and used to speak of the "Aah!" one had to try to suppress at what he called "the close of the ecclesiastical "Season". But I once heard the matter put in its proper perspective by a preacher who opened his sermon with the words, "Today we enter on one long pilgrimage to Advent".

Wednesday 15th June.

Yesterday afternoon I concluded the *Aeniad,* and it is a much better poem than the *Iliad.* (Having written this, I see what an absurd remark it is. What I should have said is that I have got more pleasure out of Virgil than from Homer.) True, one misses in the former Homer's vivid lapses into the ordinary everyday prose of life, but this is more than compensated for by Virgil's—what shall I call it?—stateliness, a sort of great work carved out of marble.

Thursday 16th June.

My seventy-first birthday, which Len and Mollie celebrated by carrying me to Whipsnade, a place I have not seen since I took J here in the Daudel in 1931 on what proved to be the most important day of his life. The run over was pleasant without being spectacular. . . . Of Whipsnade itself I found that I remembered practically nothing, but then, owing to the weather breaking, we really saw very little. I had even forgotten the Lion cut on the chalk hill overlooking the Zoo. One thing I did remember very clearly was the wolves' wood; also the road train which takes passengers round the grounds. The whole place is a masterpiece of planning and cleanliness, and unlike too many places of entertainment you are never out of comfortable reach of a privy. The first animals you see on driving in are the elephants, noble beasts, but to our astonishment, a reddish colour. . . . So ends another birthday and, thank God, how different from my last! In 1965 I was a helpless, almost hopeless prisoner serving what appeared to be an indefinite prisoner in the Hellhole, and on 16th June a warder took me in an ambulance, there to be told after a long wait that the paralysis in my right hand was incurable.

Thursday 23rd June.

At my age one tends to think a good deal about death and this no doubt accounts for a curiously unpleasant dream I had last night. I was in the place, or at any rate a place of the dead, though I think I was myself alive. It was a flat reddish plain, sprinkled with flints, under a leaden sky, on which a great multitude of people was strolling aimlessly about, all of them with listless movements and expressions of unutterable boredom. Presently I saw J slouching towards me and I ran with joy to meet him; but he looked at me without any sign of recognition, and when I tried to put my arms round him I grasped emptiness. In the distance P crossed my line of vision, but I was too depressed to challenge him. Oddly enough what gave me the acutest melancholy was not my failure to contact J but the sudden realization that the endless level space on which I was walking was the Belsen playground, hugely expanded. I could not see the house in front of me, the Black Shed on my left, or the fence and line of trees on my right; but I knew they were all there at some immeasurable distance below the horizon.

Sunday 26th June.

Late yesterday afternoon there was a knock at the door and I found myself confronted with a stranger who proved to be Clyde Kilby,[264] an old pen friend of J's. I took to him tho' he is a teetotaller and a non-smoker, being a Baptist to whom both these things are forbidden. He is one of that nice type of American about whom there is a faint suggestion of childishness, something of the dog which with wagging tail appeals to you to like him. We had some interesting talk. He told me that last year Tollers' *Ring* sold over quarter of a million copies in the U.S. I felt a swift and unworthy pang of envy that his success should have so far exceeded anything that ever came J's way. Kilby is over here to assist Tollers in some continuation of the *Rings* on which he is now engaged, but what form the assistance is to take I did not gather.[265] He thinks Tollers himself quails at the magnitude of the task, whatever it is. I saw Kilby to the bus stop and then found I had locked myself out of the house—in the rain of course—and had to go round Kiln Lane to borrow the spare key. I think I'm going to like Kilby, and am looking forward to seeing more of him during his stay in Oxford. He sits at seven guineas a week in Pusey House.

Tuesday 5th July.

Another Whipsnade day, this time at the request of Kilby who was very anxious to see the place. The trip was a great success, tho' we once more had heavy rain in the afternoon; but I think we all enjoyed ourselves. For me the great event was the discovery of the Marmots—brown, furry animals about the size of big rabbits, but otherwise squirrel-like except that they are burrow dwellers. Like squirrels they have hands instead of fore-paws and sit up on their rumps holding their food in both hands. They seemed very tame, and

---

264. Clyde S. Kilby (1902-   ), then Professor of English at Wheaton College, Wheaton, Illinois, now Professor Emeritus, and Founder and Curator Emeritus of the Marion E. Wade Collection, Wheaton College.

265. The account of this summer's work was later published as *Tolkien and the Silmarillion* by Clyde S. Kilby (Wheaton, Illinois: Harold Shaw Publishers, 1976).

the one nearest the wire amused us greatly. The burrows—there were a great many of them—run up a hill and this chap sat in the front door of his, arms akimbo, staring at us with an air ridiculously like a British householder. Once more we failed to find the Wallabies but did see most of the great cats and also the bears. I'm sure this isn't the bear pit where J and I saw Bultitude, nor could I be certain that the largest of the bears was of Bultitude's breed; he seemed to me much lighter in colour than I remember B to have been. Much talk with Kilby both going and coming back. He had much of interest to tell us, but like so many Americans (and nearly all Scots) he is a man with whom you cannot *chat;* ask him the most casual question, or make some indifferent remark, and after a short pause he will take it as the text for an intelligent and well put together leaderette which cannot be responded to except by more effort than I was in the mood to take. But he confirmed all our impressions that he is a really nice man.

Wednesday 13th July.

In the evening I ended my classical education by finishing the *Odyssey,* which in my opinion is far the best of the three great poems, and indeed as excellent, fast moving romance as anything else I can think of. How critics rank the three I don't know, but my grading would be 1st by several lengths the *Odyssey,* 2nd the *Aeniad,* and the *Iliad* a bad third. One of the chief reasons for which I rate the *Odyssey* so high is that in it we have no battles (unless one calls the massacre of the suitors a battle), and a second one is that here one gets more of the fascinating domestic and social life of those very ancient times. What nonsense to think of those people as barbarians as no doubt the 18th Century did! After meals tables were washed with sponges (p. 3) a polished spear rack formed part of the equipment of a well furnished hall (4), and clothes washing was an important, and apparently delightful domestic chore (71 sg). . . . This is indeed a very great poem and I hope I may live to re-read it. I don't know whether I will continue these jottings or not. What I make such an entry as this, there floods over me a painful longing to discuss it with J, to have one of our good talks again; in brief, an intense desire to recover an irrecoverable past. Eheu!

Sunday 17th July.

I had just made my four o'clock cup of tea when there was a rat-tat on the front door, and on opening it found what at first sight appeared to be some sort of deputation. However, it sorted itself out into Kilby, a brother Professor of Kilby's, a school marm daughter of the same, and her school boy brother. I took them in and offered them chairs—they preferred to stand. Tea?—no thanks. A cigarette?—polite negative. So we all stood for not above five minutes making idle talk and then Kilby hustled them out after they had had a good look at me as if I was something in a Zoo. Certainly Americans are a perpetual puzzle; imagine coming all the way out from Oxford by bus in the middle of a Sunday afternoon so as to be able to say that you had shaken hands with the *brother* of a famous author! It's rather as if in the early XIXth Century one had made a pilgrimage from York to London to have a five minute gawp at John Lamb.

Wednesday 27th July.

I've been re-reading Wilkie Collins's *Armadale*,[266] a good yarn but by no means his best. The fact would not be worth mentioning but for one thing. The plot demands some very involved relationships, and when J read the book he made out genealogical trees on the end paper—which of course I frequently consulted. Whilst doing so I had at intervals a very odd feeling that he was reading over my shoulder and explaining the complexities of the interrelation of the various families involved to me. After I had gone to bed I found myself wondering whether his apparent presence might not have been in some sense a fact; we know so little of the situation of the dead—what one might perhaps call their life. We are told that we shall all be changed in the twinkling of an eye in one place, elsewhere that we shall sleep until the day of Judgment. Not that this apparent difference has ever worried me. Whether the dead sleep until the Last Day or are at once translated to a new life must feel exactly the same to them; just as in our earthly life after a sound night's sleep, you may either regard day as having come in the twinkling of an eye or after seven hours death.

Saturday 30th July.

A long, interesting letter from Ruth [Hamilton Parker] who has just finished my CSL *Letters,* parts of which are worth preserving. (Alas, for whom). However I copy them here. "I think Pappy enjoyed teasing Uncle Allie—what they call over here 'having him on'—arguments as to the correct pronounciations of place names, a favourite being 'Magdalen College' and Mary 'Magdalen'. Pappy was very fond of your father but was also very much amused by him. Then Mother and Pappy were very much distressed by Uncle A's refusal to

---

266. *Armadale* (1866), by nineteenth-century novelist William Wilkie Collins.

go to see Jacks in hosp. . . . Mother did not like to go for fear of 'showing Allie up'. If she had gone she might have been able to give him the necessary feminine love and so saved his turning to Mrs. Moore for it. But then Mrs. Moore was there on the spot—and Mother's would only have been a fleeting visit, and I gather Jacks had made some kind of pact with her son to take on Mrs. M should the son be killed. Dear me, how they talked and talked, Mother, Pappy, and Uncle A. Uncle A wanted to know if Jacks had been killed would *he* have been adopted by the Moore boy? But Mrs. M seems to have had no hezitation in throwing herself on Jacks. And making him do the housework. . . . Mother resented her taking Aunt Flora's place, and she didn't like her going through Aunt F's things when Uncle A died. Mother was very fond of Aunt F." In quite a different vein I'm glad too to have heard the following—"Do you remember the Boyds who lived in Strandtown? Four girls, Molly, Dot, Eileen, and Sheila? Molly is unmarried and lives about 5 mins. down the road from here, and Dot who is recently widowed is staying with her. . . . One summer day the B girls were marking their tennis lawn. When you arrived with Jacks with a message from your mother . . . poor Jacks was dressed in a black velvet suit. The sight was too much for the girls and they promptly dabbed him with whitening, whereupon Jacks cried and said "Warnie take me home". The suit was ruined and Mollie, being the eldest, was sent along to Aunt Flora to apologize". I'm very glad indeed to have this story because I can still remember our emerging on the Newtonards Rd. from the Boyds in a disorderly retreat, but neither could remember ever since (or now) what had led up to the moment when we found ourselves on the safe neutral territory of the road. I have answered Ruth at length.

Monday 15th August.

Mainly bright sunshine, cool, with little cloud and by the use of a little imagination it was possible to tell oneself that it was a summer day. At any rate we thought it good enough to show Kilby something more of the country, and picked him up outside Blackfriars at Twenty past seven. I think he enjoyed himself and certainly I did. We ran over Witney way through that sort of scenery which pleases continually yet makes no clamourous demands on one's attention; the sort that J used to like so much and which he used to call "just country". . . . It was too cold to sit outside, but we found a pleasant little bar facing into a very beautiful sunset and a stretch of smooth river, its surface broken only by the occasional passage of a duck or a moorhen. In the middle distance, moored, was the largest cruiser I've ever seen so high up the river. The whole mis en scene filled me with nostalgia—thoughts of Parkin here, with Victor and the *Bosphorus,* and idle, pleasant chat by the riverside. Twilight crept over us on our way home, and with it white mist began to smoke up from the river putting me in mind of a melancholy last evening on board my boat in September with the thoughts of next day's return to all the horrors of The Kilns—the spite, envy, hatred, malice and all uncharitableness, the thousandth repetition of the pointless story, the pervading discomfort. And yet how I would leap at the chance to return to those bad days for the bright patches which made them tolerable—public works, or a walk with Tykes, Inklings, Bird and Baby mornings, and even at the end of the boating season, the distant prospect of the winter walking tour.

Tuesday 16th August.

The photo of J on the opposite page was taken when? I don't know, nor by whom, but almost certainly by an American, and I should guess by the date to be in the middle 1950s. It cannot have been taken after 1960 for J is wearing a coloured tie, a thing he never did after Joy's death. Apart from the fact that it is an excellent likeness, this snap is dear to me for the very clear background, which is that of his front sitting room—"our" sitting room in Magdalen—where I have spent so many happy hours. Those books recall them very poignantly. Here also I put on record a scrap of a letter which I did not use in my collected edition of J's letters, but which is illuminating. On 18th April 1951 he wrote to Mrs. van Densen, who had said that she envied him his life; Minto had been dead three months at the time: "I have lived most of it (my private life) in a house which was hardly ever at peace for 24 hours, amid senseless wranglings, lyings, backbitings, follies, and *scares.* I never went home without a feeling of terror as to what appalling situation might have developed in my absence. Only now that it is over do I begin to realize quite how bad it was".

Friday 19th August.

Another summer day, and in the afternoon we took Kilby for a drive. Not as interesting as the last one, for K is determined that he must photograph Warninghall, being the scene of Tollers's Farmer Giles.[267] But unfortunately a dull, drab hamlet which I fancy Tollers

---

267. J. R. R. Tolkien, *Farmer Giles of Ham* (London: George Allen & Unwin Ltd., 1949).

must have chosen for the dragonish *name*. . . . We were all pleased that Kilby so obviously enjoyed himself. The more one sees of him the more one realizes that there is a charming modesty and naivete at the root of his character—well summed up by Mollie, who said we had been "three grown ups taking a child for a treat". His College has one of those "projects" on hand of the kind so dear to the Americans, namely to make the definitive collection of all material bearing on J, Tollers, and Charles Williams. I undertook to insert a Codicil in my Will leaving Wheaton College the MSS. of J's Boxonian stories. (Mem. To re-read them to make sure that no excisions are needed before I part with them).[268]

Thursday 1st September.

A sad letter from Gundred [Ewart] this morning. Here is what she says: "A sad bit of news for you—about Arthur Greeves who . . . was found dead in his bed this morning (Monday 29th August), apparently having died in his sleep and what better death could we have wished for him than to go like that . . . he had a great regard for you both. . . . He did love talking and I may say that 50% of the time the talk was about 'you-ones' chiefly and the days that are getting farther away. . . ". This would have been a sore blow to J if it had happened in his lifetime, for I do not suppose that with the exception of myself he ever had a more loved friend. Indeed I can hardly except myself, for there was much of his imaginative life which only Arthur could share with him, all that "Northernness" as they called it, to which I could not respond. Thus inevitably to me Arthur was rather "Jack's friend" than any very prominent figure in my own life; indeed my most enduring recollection of him was of the early days at Leeborough when to both of us he was simply that most exasperating boy across the road who loafed in at unseasonable hours to interrupt us in our games, drawings, writings, the wholy busy world of Boxen in fact—and would not take the most brutal of schoolboy hints to go away. But of course all that phase was forgotten years ago and afterwards I cannot remember a time when I did not meet him with plea-

---

268. Aware of his future audience, Warren Lewis carefully reviewed all such material, including his diaries, which he willed to the Marion E. Wade Collection. Excisions in his diary, however, appear to consist of only one leaf — possibly concerned with his struggle with alcoholism while in Ireland on vacation. In this context, it might be of interest to note Warren's attitude on the preservation of diaries. When informed of the destruction of a Hamilton ancestor's diary, he indignantly exploded that the guilty individual "ought to be well flogged for a crime like that" (diary entry for February 20, 1921).

sure; and even if I had never grown to like him his going would still remain one of those parted strands of my own past which bring a sharp pang at my age. Of the old life of Strandtown there is now no one left but Gundred and myself, and soon all that unforgotten period will have no one to whom it will be even a memory. It is a queer coincidence that on the previous page I should have inserted the [postcard] photo of Crawfordsburn, the village in which Arthur spent the last years of his life and in which he died. A homely place such as he loved and I am glad his last vision of this world was of his own—*our* own—Co. Down which was so dear to all three of us. God rest his soul.

Sunday Christmas day.

A perfect winter morning, bright, windless, with frost on all the puddles. But to me, and I suppose to most people of my age, a sad day, for I could not recall the many Christmas mornings, in all kinds of weather, when J and I trudged off together from The Kilns for the eight o'c. service. . . . I've just finished re-reading Charles's *All Hallows Eve*.[269] It is so plausible that I found myself wondering if it could possibly have been written under inspiration; why should not death be the gradual process which he imagines it to be? Anyway, golly what a book!

Tuesday 27th December.

The Blue Tit is the only bird known to me which is passionately addicted to cream. One has discovered that a bottle of milk often stands at our front door and this morning I was shown his handiwork. He had done nothing so crude as to punch a hole in the foil cap with his beak, but had clipped all round the disc of the cap as neatly as a human could have done with a pair of scissors, then made a hearty cream breakfast—which I did not grudge him.

Thursday 5th January, 1967.

I wish I had kept a record of the number of times I've read Boswell. I've just finished him again, with as much pleasure as ever. This time I took in the whole corpus chronologically i.e. accompanied Johnson into Scotland in 1773, then laid the *Life* aside and read Boswell's *Hebrides*. What is described as a *Journal of a Tour to Wales* in 1774 I do not think was worth publishing for it is merely the kind of

---

269. *All Hallow's Eve* (London: Faber and Faber, 1945) is one of seven novels written by Charles Williams.

jottings which I used to make on walking tours with J when we got to our resting place in the evening, and used as aides memories in writing up the jaunt when I got home. . . . One Mr. Moorman whom I remember as an occasional correspondent of J's has sent me his book, *The Precincts of Felicity*,[270] a critique of the works of Charles Williams, CSL and Tollers. It is not a stupid book, nor a dull one, but I think a silly one. To begin with he dubs the Inklings "The Oxford Christians" which strikes a wrong note at the outset by suggesting an organized group for the propagation of Christianity, whilst in fact the title is justified only in the most literal sense, i.e. that we nearly all lived in Oxford and were all believers. His thesis is that in the Inklings a kind of group mind was at work which influenced the writing of every Inkling, and this he supports by assertions which seem to me very shaky. What he chiefly harps on is their common belief that there is a transitional state between death and our resurrection. Thus J "borrowed" the framework of his *Great Divorce* from Charles's *All Hallow's Eve* and so on. Just as if this speculation about a transitional state must not have occurred to hundreds of Christians who didn't even know of each other's existence. I smiled at the thought of Tollers being under the influence of Moorman's group mind, and think of sending him the book. He is frankly absurd when in his last chapter he brings in T. S. Eliot and Dorothy Sayers, neither of whom ever attended an Inklings in their lives; tho' to do him justice he tries to soften his absurdity on the first page of Ch. VI—"we have arrived at in a sense the periphery of that circle which had its center at Oxford. The influences here are thus more tenuous, more difficult to trace. . . ". You bet they are! Yes, on the whole a *silly* book.

Tuesday 10th January.

Last night my neighbour's Television was on full blast, and to my amazement I heard a song which took me back well over half a century. It was

> China town, my Chin-a town
> When the lights are low . . .

If I remember right it was sung by Shirley Kellog in a Hippodrome review and selections from the show made up the first "Album" we ever bought for the gramophone. So I suppose the show would have been in 1913. A wave of nostalgia came over me at the

---

270. Charles Moorman, *The Precincts of Felicity: The Augustinian City of the Oxford Christians* (Gainesville, Florida: University of Florida, 1966).

vivid picture the music conjured up—a fine summer morning, P safely off to town, J and I with two chairs in the shrubbery and the gramophone, each smoking a cigar, or if lucky, a cigarette, two hours before we must think of dressing to go up to Glenmachan for lunch. Eheu!

Thursday 19th January.

Last night I had a very unpleasant dream. J and I had apparently died at the same instant and found ourselves walking hand in hand in twilight over an immense featureless plain very like the latest wireless photos of the moon's surface. After a time some soft pressure, an irresistible one, began to draw us apart. I held tight to J but could not hold him. He withdrew steadily, backwards across the plain, holding out both hands to me until the last when he was absorbed into white light which gave out no radiance.

Saturday 4th February.

A perfect winter morning, cold, cloudless, and at breakfast the pot of crocus in the dining room window glowed golden in the early sun. . . . I'm at present re-reading these diaries, and came upon this, written at Drogheda in June 1947, nearly twenty years ago:

I was struck with the haunting fear that is so often with me— suppose J were to die before I did? And a sheer wave of animal panic spread over me at the prospect of the empty years.

But little did I realize how empty they were to be.

Monday 6th February.

Last night I finished re-reading my Diaries, or rather Vols. XI to XX, that is to say from 14th August 1922 to 15th September 1949. . . . In spite of huge lacunae I find these notebooks do amount to something of a biography in which I see myself much as I have lived, and often with pangs of remorse for my own selfishness and ill-living. On the other hand with much vividly recalled happiness. I find too that memory has played me no tricks about the good and the bad times. Aldershot and Sierra Leone, both bad, are behind me when Vol. VI opens at Hillsboro with me on leave from the latter and soon to enter on the happiest three years of my Army life, those spent at Colchester. . . . Incidentally one thing that stands out from these books is that the great pleasures of my life have been J's society, books and scenery, in that order. I do not include bathing for except at Colchester, that has always been a rare delight. 1932-51 is on the whole a sombre picture, with overhanging it all, the steady deterioration in Minto and the consequent increasing discomfort of The Kilns.

But a period shot with much happiness—"public works", walks and jaunts with J, long, busy, contented days in College. The walking tours I could hardly bear to re-read, so happy were they. I am, as so often, struck with the oddness of the snapshots which memory elects to preserve. Why, out of innumerable conversations with J, should I remember as vividly as if it had happened yesterday how one afternoon on Shotover we played with the idea of buying the two empty lodges, one each, as retreats for our old age? Or our standing in the twilight in mid-Wales looking down a steep tree covered slope at water gleaming in the early starlight? Or water rushing off the roofs of a train in Liskeard Station during a thunderstorm? The last three or four years of Minto's life were obviously very nearly unbearable owing to her hate, and malice. . . . Looking back over this miserable period I feel that the charitable, probably the true explanation of her horrible behaviour was that for some years before her death her brain was slowly giving way. One thing I now bitterly regret about these diaries is that I preserved hardly any of my innumerable conversations with J. If only I had known that he was to leave me to end my life in loneliness, with what jealous care I would have Boswellised him. As it is I have, beyond my memories, nothing of him but a stray remark here and there. A thing which struck me was our extreme good fortune in being walkers in the days before that rascal Beeching sabotaged the railway system. After he had done his worst, all the best of these walks would have been impossible except at the prohibitive cost of hiring a car for fifty to seventy miles. The Welsh railway system for instance has now vanished completely. . . . I doubt if anywhere in the island today one could find one of those little branch line trains chuffing through oil-lit wooden stations in which we so delighted.

Sunday 12th February.

A perfect winter's day of the sort of which we have been blessed with many this year—ground frost, brilliant sun, windless, bird music loud and sweet. . . . Buds coming out everywhere. Then to Church where we began with variations on the Communion Service. . . . The whole question of the Church of England these days is a bother to me. Personally what I want is not a Spike ritual or a C. of E. [Church of England] one, or a Low one with any of the urgency with which I desire a *uniform* one. In the old days the question did not arise; you got the service appointed for the day, and that was that. But under the new dispensation I find things very difficult. How can one join in Prayers one has never heard before? One's whole attention is concen-

trated on hearing what the words are. Here the further point arises—
to what extent, if any, should the Incumbent provide the service
which the majority of his flock desire?

Saturday 18th February.

I am curious to meet the proposed visitor who is Toller's grandson
Michael II, in his middle 'twenties and son of Michael I, the schoolmaster. But Lord how old it makes all to think of Tollers with a
grandson of twenty-five!

Tuesday 7th March.

I got back at lunch time yesterday from spending the weekend
with George and Moira at Malvern. Len drove Mollie and myself
down on Friday, a most enjoyable run, it being a bright early spring
day. We stopped for coffee at Broadway which I found little changed
from the village I remember in 1920 when J and I passed through it on
our first Daudelspiel. Pretty, very pretty, but too self-consciously so,
and I remember J passing the same comment on it 47 years ago. We
had expected to find spring in full beauty in Worcestershire, but to
our great surprise they are much behind our own county down in
those parts. I enjoyed all the old thrill of the first sight of the Malvern
Hills once more; some of my roots are still very deep there. And so
on to Hamewith where I parted with the Millers and was welcomed
by George and Moira whom I was very glad to see again. . . . Hamewith is a house in which one always feels at home, and by the time I
went to bed I felt as if I had been established there for weeks. . . . One
thing I do enjoy about Hamewith is its freedom. Unlike only too
many houses here you may go for a solitary stroll whenever the mood
takes you, and in the evening you are expected to settle down with a
book and a pipe; in short, you are not "entertained". I have a very
comfortable bed and slept better than I have done for a long time.
Before dropping off I relished that absolute silence which is so rare
these days anywhere. *Saturday 4th* was a lovely day and before breakfast I strolled in Alexander Road, enjoying wonderful light and shade
effects on the hills—and regretting that the quarrying vandals had not
been compelled earlier to stop their mischievous activities. In the
morning George drove me to the Camp Hotel car park, along the
pretty road running down the west side of the hills. There we left the
car and walked up past the Camp, nearly to the top and George with
his cine-camera took me as I laboured upwards. But tho' not tired, I
realized here that I am now an old man, and this kind of thing is not
for me any longer. As I looked at that beautiful bit above the reservoir

I came over quite giddy and had to keep my eyes on the path until we got back to level ground again—and this, tho' I told myself at the time that even if I slipped, the worst that could happen to me would be a tumble down a few yards of a long, rather steep grass slope. . . . On *Monday 6th* the same lovely weather continued, and we set out about ten thirty. Where we went I couldn't say, for my collection of maps is now of purely sentimental, indeed antiquarian interest. For the first time in my life I saw Bredon Hill, for so many years a distant landmark, from its base, and a delightfull hill it is, alternating grass and woodland, gleaming in the sun. J and George once walked up it, arguing fiercely about the admissibility of the "white lie". Thence onwards onto the Western slope of the Cotswolds. . . . On our way, George told a story which gave me a nasty stab, his informant being Humphrey. The latter said that J killed himself by not going sick before that fatal term at Cambridge—a term which, though ill, he undertook for the characteristic reason that if he had backed out, someone else would have had to undertake his examining. The result was that all day sittings drove his bladder complaint into poisoning his kidneys, and this affected his heart. By the time he eventually reported sick the disease was incurable, but had it been taken in time there was no reason why he should not have lived another ten or even twenty years. I wish George hadn't told me this, for it will remain with me until the end as the most poignant "If only—" of a lifetime.

Tuesday 21st March.

The flowering currant is now out in several places, and this is always one of the high lights of my year. Enjoyment of it and the wallflower are the earliest aesthetic experiences of my life—dating back to long before we left Dundela Villas. I can still remember the thrill of joy with which I used to greet the arrival of both, a thrill which one never experiences once childhood is past, and which is perhaps the purest one ever receives. Is it I wonder wildly fanciful to think that this thrill is a dim recollection of having just *come* from a better world?

Friday 24th March.

(*Good Friday*). . . . In the evening I finished [King] Lear, which is something to boast myself of, for sorrier stuff I haven't read for a long time. I wonder what it is in Shakespeare that most other people find to admire and I cannot see at all? From Lear's wildly improbable treat-ment of Cordelia at the start, right onwards, I could get nothing out of it except old blind Whatsisname's soliloquy on Dover cliffs, Johnson's "inspirsated gloom", which is good. The real trouble of this play is that there are no *characters* in it, just a set of ranting dummies; the villains are so villainous that they become ridiculous, whilst the good people are just plain bores, and one doesn't care what happens to either class. Shakespeare might have borrowed from a later playwright and called this work "The Three Loonies". Lear to be sure had some reason for being mad. I certainly would have been had I been compelled to listen to the conversation of A Fool *plus* Edgar disguised as A Fool. I lost count of the number of deaths and could not be bothered at the end to count them up, but retain an impression that by the end of the last scene the stage is pretty well littered with corpses. I wonder how they manage this when the play is acted? But the Fates preserve me from ever *seeing* Lear!

Monday 27th March.

Here is another Lent over, and one which gives me all too little ground for self-congratulations. I did indeed keep it as a teetotaller, doubled my offeratory money, and read selected literature for an hour every day. But that is mighty little when compared with what I might have done. As regards books, I read J's *Christian Reflections,* Law's uncomfortable but purgative *Holy Life,* Lathams excellent and helpful *Pastor Pastorum,* [Chesterton's] *The Everlasting Man,* [J's] *Letters to Malcolm,* and [J's] *Reflections on the Psalms.* My only failure was [J's] *Xtian Reflections* which was far above my head and which I think might more fairly have been called Philosophical Rs. In addition to these, I read, with the Bible alongside me, Neill's *Commentary* from which I got much benefit.

Tuesday 18th April.

Here I am, where I little thought ever to be again, sitting at my desk in the study at The Kilns (the house of course still in a hideous mess). Slept here for the first time last night, and have taken over Joy's room, the only one in the house which I haven't used before. It is strange that being there brings only faint memories of Joy. . . . The Millers have moved with me and now (6.30 p.m.) both our old houses stand empty. Only time can show whether I have been wise or foolish to set up this new schema vitae; socially speaking I've little doubts of its success, but I rather dread the financial aspect of the matter. If J's Royalties fall off heavily, will I be able to hang on? Grand though it is to be back here, it is not entirely without regret at having said goodbye to 51 Ringwood Rd.—a comfortable house in which I have been as happy as I suppose I can ever hope to be again.

But the loneliness at nights was becoming dangerous for a man of my age.

Wednesday 26th April.

The back-breaking job of settling up my books, which left me done all over, is now complete. But this still leaves me with the task of making a more selective arrangment of them so that down here I may have old favourites to hand. This morning I've collected all my poetry, and am surprised by how much of it there is. If not complete, at least well represented, are Homer, Vergil, Chaucer, Spenser, Milton, Dryden, Pope, Cowper, Thompson, Wordsworth, Scott, Arnold, Browning, Morris, Dobson, Kipling, Newbolt, Synge, Chesterton, Rupert Brooke, Flecker, Moira O'Neill, Benet, Sackville-West, and of course J, also Sister Madeleva.

Wednesday 3rd May.

Got up at 6.45 to find it a bright, bitter cold morning with a hard white frost, indoor temperature 47°; and so to my prayers in a very moderate temper, there to be rebuked by Geo. Macdonald who on some bygone 3rd May must also have resented the weather conditions before correcting himself:

> Another day of gloom and slanting rain!
> Of closed skies, cold winds, and blight and bane!
> Such not the weather, Lord, which thou art fain
> To give thy chosen, sweet to heart and brain!—
> Until we mourn, thou keep'st the merry tune;
> Thy hand unloved its pleasure must restrain,
> Nor spoil both gift and child by lavishing too soon.[271]

I'm re-reading Trollope's autobiography[272] and last night came upon this—"When we hear that memory has gone as age has come on, we should understand that the capacity for interest in the matter concerned has perished". Now in my own case I don't find that this is the case; my memory is unfortunately not what it used to be; I can no longer carry in my head details of my own period which once I remembered without any mental effort, but my interest in the 17th Century is I think just as keen as it used to be twenty years ago.

---

271. Passage taken from the May 3 entry of George MacDonald's *Diary of An Old Soul,* originally printed as *A Book of Strife in the form of the Diary of an Old Soul* (London: Unwin Brothers, 1880).

272. *Autobiography* (1883) of Victorian novelist Anthony Trollope.

Sunday 14th May.

(Whitsunday), but tomorrow is not Whitmonday, "They" having ordered that in future Whitmonday shall be the last Monday in May. . . . In the evening Len drove me in to keep a long standing engagement to hear Sister Penelope[273] preach in Wadham Chapel, and I had a word or two with her before going in—a woman I took an immediate liking to, and with whom I should have enjoyed a talk. Wadham has not one of the great Chapels, but nevertheless a pleasing one, with glass which to my uneducated eye looked like 17th cent. Dutch. It is a long time since I've enjoyed a service so much—just a plain straightforward C. of E. [Church of England] Evensong, few hymns, and what there were, with real music, most of it unknown to me. One each of us had our candle in a glass chimney on front of the pew, and the effect of the double row of points of light was very fine. I had been placed where I found it difficult to hear Sister Penelope, which I regretted, for from what I did hear, she was very good; subject, the creation of the world interpreted in terms of modern knowledge. I had hoped for a word or two with her after the service, but found the ante-chapel crowded.

Sunday 2nd July.

Owen Barfield arrived on the 6.55 to spend the night. . . . I was however genuinely pleased to see Owen again, and looking pretty well for our time of life; though he tells me, which I was sorry to hear, that he is threatened with diabetes. Still, no one dies of this in the Insulin era. We spent a pleasant, relaxed evening talking of books and of old days after dining tete a tete in the dining room—the first time I've used it since my return to The Kilns.

Tuesday 4th July.

Temperature 56, and fires a comfort. Today I've read *Much Ado about Nothing;* not one of Shakespeare's best, but still it's enjoyable reading. . . . I've also (I'm afraid the only word is "waded") half through J's *Studies in Words* but have had to abandon it—far too abstruse for me. I often wonder at the mystery of heredity. He and I, born of the same parents, he so brilliant, I so much the reverse. How and why?

---

273. Sister Penelope (1890-19 ?) of the Community of St. Mary the Virgin at Wantage, and a friend and correspondent of Jack Lewis. He dedicated his second volume in his space trilogy, *Perelandra* (London: John Lane the Bodley Head, 1943), to Sister Penelope and her fellow Anglican nuns: "To Some Ladies at Wantage."

Sunday 9th July.

On Television last night I saw the opening installment of J's *Lion, Witch and Wardrobe* by which I was agreeably surprised. Lucy is good, and looks the part, and Tumnus comes off. We got only so far as Lucy's return from her first visit to Narnia so one cannot yet form any opinion of the whole thing, but so far it's very promising and I think J would have been pleased with it—no hint so far of what he feared, a touch of Disneyland. Up to date the other three children have had practically nothing to do, and have left no impression. The scenery was first rate, and there really was something of magic about the transition from the wardrobe to the dim lit snow covered Narnia. How I wish J was here to talk it over with me!

Wednesday 12th July.

I dreamt last night that J came to me and asked for the return of his Prayer Book.[274] I went to the cupboard where I keep it, and while I was looking at it he vanished and I woke.

Friday 21st July.

This morning comes a little In Memorium for J composed by Clifford Morris, now retired, who used to be our hire-car man and drove J regularly to and from Cambridge every week in term-time. He now has what sounds like a pleasant job, as Custodian of a 15th Century Chapel at Rycote near Thame, the property of the Ministry of Works. What they do with it is not clear; I should have thought that if it was of historic interest the National Trust would have got it. Here is his elegy on J:

In Memory of Clive Staples Lewis.

My friend is dead,
And I have never missed
A dear friend more. I miss
Him in the town, and in
The countryside. I miss
His face, his voice, his smile, his
Presence by my side . . .

My teacher, too, has gone:
The man whose counsel and
Whose words I valued
Highly above all

---

274. Jack Lewis's Book of Common Prayer was given by Warren Lewis at his death to Len and Mollie Miller. They in turn presented the book to the Marion E. Wade Collection, Wheaton College.

The teachers I had known
Before. And now
I do not wait outside
His door . . .

Professor C. S. Lewis was but
Just a name to some, but he
To me was *Jack,* my
Concillor,
Companion, and my
Friend. He never
Failed me once. He never
Let me down.
He met my need: gallant
Christian warrior indeed.

The simplicity and obvious sincerity of these artless verses I find very comforting, and I wrote this morning to tell Morris how much pleasure he had given me.

Tuesday 1st August.

CSL's home, complete with the great man's brother, is [now a] show piece for any American who happens to visit Oxford. . . . And what is the worst of it is that this situation is going to continue for the rest of my life. . . . I suppose that on my death bed—or at any rate the day before—I shall have some verbose American standing over me and lecturing on some little observed significance of J's work. Oh damn, damn, DAMN!

Thursday 10th August.

David [Gresham] left for Cambridge this morning, having been here since Tuesday afternoon. . . . He is now a polite and undemanding guest, spending most of his time, as he always did, reading in his own room, and when out of it interesting and good company. I asked him to come and stop again, and meant the invitation to be accepted. A short time ago an American publisher—I don't know why—sent me a new verse translation of *Sir Gawain and the Green Knight,*[275] a poem which I have often heard Tolkien praise in the old days. I'd never read it, and indeed could not have done so, for it is written in obsolete English. According to the translator the unknown author lived in Staffordshire and was a contemporary of Chaucer's, to whom however he seems to me to have little or no resemblance. . . . He is

---

275. *Sir Gawain and the Green Knight,* translated by Marie Borroff (Professor of English at Yale University) (New York: W. W. Norton Company, Inc., 1967).

not a finer nature poet than Wordsworth, though in flashes I think him his equal. And he is easier to read than William, in whom at any moment you are apt to trip up on a slab of maundering philosophy mercifully absent in Anon. *Sir Gawain* is a wonderful poem, a fine story grandly told, by a man whose power of presenting close observation in telling flashes puts him absolutely in the front rank. I'm very grateful to that American publisher for sending this book to me, and *[Sir Gawain]* will certainly have a permanent place in my poetry shelf.

Sunday 20th August.

After tea I began to re-read *The Ulsterman*[276] and found it as good as ever—a burning, bitter, but lifelike picture of the Ulster of 1914. The most interesting thing is to find that the dominance, the ceaseless cross-examination, the unawareness that J and I were *individuals* which we thought was Lewisianism was in fact Ulsterism. True, we were never treated so badly as the Alexander family but in what follows there is enough our own adolescent grievances to give more than a hint of Leeborough conditions. The speaker is the younger son, now in his middle 'twenties, living at home on a pittance earned in his father's linen mill:

You know the relative position of father and son in Ulster. . . . The son is in a worse position than the errand boy. You know the way we have to give an account of ourselves wherever we may go. If I go as far as Belfast for a day, I'm cross-examined as to how I spent every hour. If I get asked out anywhere here I have to ask leave to go. I'm not supposed to make an acquaintance without father's leave. I daren't smoke even now except behind his back. Well, is it any wonder when we're treated like this, we sons turn out liars and hypocrites? Is it any wonder what we try to get the better of our fathers and show them that we have souls of our own?

Another and nastier feature of Leeborough life which we assumed to be a family anfractuosity turns out to be not family but native to the province:

The true humour of the Ulsterman . . . consists in the probing of an unhealed wound—the touching of a raw place with the broad top of a finger fresh from the pot of red pepper. In the writhings of the victims are to be found the elements of the finest humour, if the tormentor knows anything of what humour really is.

True, and to me only too familiar. I wonder how many hundred times P has said to me, "You used to say you would starve in order

---

276. *The Ulsterman: A Story of Today,* by Frank Frankfort Moore (London: Hutchinson and Co., 1914).

to be well-dressed". A nuisance for which I had only myself to blame, for once instead of holding my tongue I replied that although he might find it difficult to believe, many people altered their opinions between sixteen and twenty six. This was fatal. He had as he no doubt said to himself, "ketched me on the raw", and he continued to jab at the sore place for the rest of our joint lives. But worst of all was the fact that from the end of the war until the last time I visited him I doubt if he ever let 48 consecutive hours pass without some offensive sneer at my profession. Well, it is all over long ago, forty years ago in fact, but the recollection of these "humorous" sallies of his still has at times the power of irritating me.

Thursday 7th September.

I've now "done" [Shakespeare's] Comedies and am playing with the idea of reading the Histories—not for their value as dramatic literature but in the hope of correcting my ignorance of English history. It is ridiculous that I should go to my grave in utter ignorance of anything which happened in my own country except between the years 1642 and 1714!

Saturday 9th September.

While I was doing my mail this morning the typewriter broke down. Len took it to Hunts where the verdict was that as the pattern had long been obsolete, no spare parts for it existed and therefore nothing could be done. I shall have to get a new machine. There are few of my personal belongings which I say farewell to with deeper regret, for it has been my companion for thirty five years, almost half my lifetime. On it were produced *The Lewis Papers,*[277] my Biographies, and all my own books. Also on a rough computation at least twelve thousand of J's letters. I shall I'm afraid feel very lost on a new machine.

Sunday 10th September.

This evening we had the final Television instalment of *The Lion, the Witch, and the Wardrobe.* I hope the listener response will be large enough to encourage ATV to do some of the others, for this production has been admirable both as regards acting and production, not a

---

277. Ten unpublished volumes of biographical and genealogical studies of famous French families from the seventeenth and eighteenth centuries. These volumes were compiled by Warren for his personal research use and pleasure, and were sold at auction at his death.

jarring note in either from start to finish. How I wish J could have seen it!

Sunday 24th September.

In the evening Len and Mollie carried me to the Congregational Church in Collinwood Rd. for their harvest festival and what I saw and heard made me ashamed of the Parish Church. Five minutes before service began there was not an empty seat in the building, and Len told me afterwards that there was an overflow congregation in the gallery. The whole thing was quite unmistakeably alive, the whole congregation sung with fervour, and, in the famous words of Grandfather H "there was nothing in which I could not join". They do not kneel for prayers, but sit forward with bent heads. . . . I put the congregation at about five times the muster we get at the Parish Church.

Tuesday 26th September.

Continuing my Shakespearian pilgrimage I today read *Richard II,* a rather clumsily put together play containing some magnificent poetry. . . . Len went into Oxford this morning and inter alia made a fruitless search for some pen nibs for me. Apparently these, like pen holders, are an obsolete article. . . . Probably I'd better whilst there is time, lay in a stock of ink. As J used to say, it is melancholy to have been reserved for such times!

Tuesday 3rd October.

A bitter cold, bright morning with cloud and some rain after lunch. We started off at 10 a.m. on our long projected visit to Coventry. . . . Coventry is an exasperating place in which you are very conscious of municipal control, and it proved to be absurdly difficult to find the Cathedral which, at any rate from our angle of approach, seemed badly sited. . . . Seen from the East end, or rather the south corner of the east walk, it is a squat, shapeless pile of pale red brick, on the south corner of which is a thing like a gigantic jam jar containing either a Cross or Crucifix, I couldn't make out which. . . . The internal proportions, which are noble, struck me as the best feature of the building. Light is admitted in a curious way: the best description of the walls I can give is that they are vertical Venetian blinds with slats made of this pale red brick and the gaps between these "slats" are filled with narrow, high stained glass windows. . . . My impression of the Cathedral as a whole was that no reverence had gone into its design, and that the architect's sole ambition had been to produce something that should bear no resemblance to any of the other English Cathedrals—for example in one place I noticed that his pillars had not capitals to support their loads, but little round peg-like columns. . . . On the whole I was very disappointed. . . . It is not a place worth a visit unless one should happen to be in Coventry for some other purpose and find yourself with an hour to fill in before your train goes. What is really fine however is what is left of the old Cathedral.[278] The walls of the Sanctuary are still of some height, and in there, stands an Altar on which is a Cross made of two charred fragments of the original timbers. At the foot of the Altar is an appeal to pray for those who brought about the destruction of the building. Communion is celebrated on this Altar twice every year.

Monday 13th October.

The *Times [Literary Supplement]* seems to get duller every week, and the issue of yesterday, so far as I'm concerned, touches rock bottom. I don't see in it a single book reviewed, fiction or otherwise, which I should feel tempted to open if by accident I had it with me at a railway station where I had to spend an hour and where there was no bookstall. . . . The only thing of interest for me in the whole issue is that John Lawlor has published *Patterns of Love and Courtesy. Essays in memory of C. S. Lewis* (Edward Arnold. 45/-) which the Cambridge review describes as "Not unworthy of the great scholar to whose memory it is dedicated". I shall hang on before I order it in the hope that John will send me a copy. But after all why read it? There will be little there to remind me of the J I loved, if indeed I prove capable of understanding it. For a rather disconcerting discovery made in the *T.L.S.* is that to me English is rapidly becoming a foreign language. What for instance does "snazzy" mean, an adjective pejoratively applied to food? Elsewhere I noticed that undergraduates are now "swinging London". This I took to be an absurdly exaggerated way of saying that some circles in London were developing quite considerable interest in youth's opinions on some subject or other. Nothing of the sort; to "swing" in modern English means to dismiss an opinion, place, or person as something irrelevant in contemporary life and therefore of no interest.

---

278. From November 1940 until April 1941, Coventry, with its many important industries, suffered numerous German air raids. This resulted in almost total destruction of the city center, including the fourteenth-century cathedral. In 1954, work was begun on a new cathedral, contemporary in design; this cathedral was consecrated in 1962. The old ruins now serve as a precinct to the new cathedral, and as a Memorial Shrine of Reconciliation.

Saturday 21st October.

Amongst my letters was a charming little paper by Adam Fox[279] on the breakfasts in Magdalen Coll., SCR [Senior Common Room] in his time, thumb nail sketches of Benecke, JA[280] and J. I wish he had written at greater length. Amongst other good things is a delightful story, new to me, illustrative of J's ignorance of and contempt for the passing show. He invited Hone to dine at High Table and in the few uneasy minutes before dinner was announced, to set the conversational ball rolling asked H "if he played any games?" This was in the summer term in which Hone was Captain of the Varsity XI! . . . He has an interesting note on his own election to the Poetry Chair. One morning at breakfast when it was learnt that X was a candidate, Fox exclaimed, "Why they might as well make *me* Professor of Poetry!" to which J replied, "We will"—and probably it was his energetic canvassing which brought this about.

Wednesday 6th December.

David, after spending Monday night here, returned before lunch to Cambridge which he leaves next Monday for an extended stay in Jerusalem as a student. Every time I meet him I'm more and more astonished at the pleasant young man who has emerged from the really detestable boy from whom we suffered so much. This time he was as good company as last, and I enjoyed his visit. The only thing I now regret about him is his relapse into very strict Judaism; he fed himself out of supplies which he brought with him, and refused a drink.

Thursday 7th December.

In the evenings I've been reading Bowra's *Memories*[281] and finding them very entertaining; notes on several university people known to me. I get the impression that B is rather given to favourites among undergrads., and was interested in one of them, a man called Yorke who appears to have written novels under the name of Green. When

---

279. Adam Fox (1883-1977), Fellow of Magdalen College and Dean of Divinity since 1929, and elected Professor of Poetry at Oxford in 1938. In 1942, he became a Canon of Westminister Abbey. He was a member of the Inklings. For published version of Fox's paper, see the essay "At the Breakfast Table," pp. 89-95, in *C. S. Lewis at the Breakfast Table and Other Reminiscences,* ed. James Como (New York: Macmillan Publishing Co., Inc., 1979).

280. John A. ("J. A.") Smith, Fellow of Magdalen College and Professor of Moral and Metaphysical Philosophy at Oxford.

281. *Memories: 1898-1939* by C. Maurice Bowra, the Warden at Wadham College, Oxford.

he was up he read English and J was his Tutor, but he dropped the School—"he was irritated and bored by C. S. Lewis". I wonder can this have been the young cub who, when J made some severe criticisms on an essay, replied, "Whenever I read to you I feel I am casting pearls before (pause) an unappreciative audience".

Christmas Day.

Yesterday being Sunday I went to Highfield as usual and there was entertained with what J would have described as a gravity-dispelling incident. Before service Cooke was kerfuffling round the Church after his usual manner, making us otiose little speeches and delivering unwanted instruction. Finally, having transferred a number of urchins from one pew to another, he took his stance in the middle of the Choir, thumbs in the girdle of his cassock, and surveyed us after the manner of a Sergt. Major who has at last got a parade drawn up to his satisfaction. At this moment there appeared from somewhere in the central aisle a small boy carrying a cup and saucer slowly and carefully, and advancing into the Choir handed it to Cooke. I must admit he didn't carry off his ridiculous situation at all badly; giving a startled grin, he grabbed the cup and disappeared with it at top speed into the Vestry.

Wednesday 27th December.

Jean Wakeman[282] turned up at the characteristically inconvenient hour of 12.40, but none the less I was glad to see her again. Her chief news was to give me a digest of a long letter she has had from Douglas [Gresham]'s wife Merry in Tasmania. M says that those who only knew the D of the old days would not now recognize him as the same man. He has apparently at last resolved to face life and is working both hard and successfully: is liked and respected by the neighbouring farmers and the local bank has sufficient confidence in him to have made him a loan of £2,000 to "bridge" him while he gets into full production. His dairy herd is doing well, the cream realizes a good price, and the skim milk feeds his pigs which are flourishing. As a side line Merry herself keeps turkeys and this year has sold them well. Pray God that all this may be true!

Sunday 7th January, 1968.

Old age is not so much a sad as a humiliating business, all the more so because I don't usually feel old, and when I have the fact

---

282. Jean Wakeman, close Oxford friend of Joy Davidman Gresham Lewis, who helped Jack with the care of the Gresham boys after Joy's death.

brought before me sharply I resent it. Today has been the worst day of the winter, its badness aggravated by bright sunshine from a cloudless sky. Last night it snowed lightly, turning to heavy rain, and finally a hard frost with the result that when I set out for Church I found it like trying to walk on ice in ordinary shoes—or rather it *was* walking on ice. By the time I got as far as the Bell—feeling each step of the way—I'd already had a couple of ominous slithers and there I lost my nerve. Had to turn and pick my way home, and very glad I was to find myself safely back in the study with my slippers on. If only I'd been wearing gum boots I might have saved my amour propre!

Wednesday 10th January.

Another horrible day. When I got up at 6.30 there was ice on the inside of my bedroom windows, the hall temperature was forty and outside the kitchen door eighteen. When daylight came it disclosed the spectacle of the kindly earth still defiled and hidden by its loathsome white carpet. The morning paper screams with headlines about "Chaos"! However I managed to shuffle to 10 a.m. Communion, not unprofitably, where we were literally "three gathered together". When I got home the whim took me to look back through my diaries to see what I was doing on this day in past decades. Of only one is there any record, 10th Jan. 1937 which was the opening day of our Wiltshire walk. For some reason we started late, by train to Didcot, changed to a doubtless vanished branch line to Challow, lunched there, and completed the day by walking 5-1/2 miles into Wantage where we put up at the Bear. Afterwards I fell to idle musing as to what I would say if God gave me the option of moving my life back to this day thirty years ago. There was so much to be said both for and against expressing a wish of the sort that I could come to no decision.

Monday 15th January.

Today I read *Henry VIII* which I've enjoyed, and indeed which as a piece of Stagecraft I'm inclined to think Shakespeare's best play. . . . So now I can say I've "done" Shakespeare which has been a spare time stock job since 11th March 1967. And what of the harvest? Well, I've read the five "great" tragedies, and this decided me that for me it would be time wasted to attempt the "minor" ones. Of the great, I hope to re-read *Othello, Macbeth,* and *Romeo.* But as for *Hamlet* and *Lear* I would not do this for any less of a consideration than a fee of twenty five guineas for each play. There are half a dozen comedies to which I think I shall return; and probably none of the histories except *Falstaff*. So on balance I've regretfully confirmed my old opinion that Shakespeare is not for me. What a pity that circumstances forced him to become a playright instead of a poet! Of course the plays contain much splendid poetry, but this is crude ore which you have to smelt for yourself to extract the gold, and this can be a tedious process.

Sunday 31st March.

I've been reading *A Search for Rainbows*, reminiscences by Barbara Cartland, a romantic novelist I'd never heard of before, but well known to the Millers. An attractive character and much more than a mere romancer. A woman always ready to fight the Establishment as champion of the underdog, and often with considerable success. The reason I mention her here is for the extract from the book which follows:

I was annoyed in February 1946 when I lunched at the House of Commons and found an enormous and varied menu starting with hors d'oeuvre, thick or clear soup or spaghetti, and choice of five dishes for the main course— goose, wild duck, sole, lamb or tripe—with five different sweets to follow or cheese and biscuits, all for five shillings.

And no doubt if she had investigated the bar (open all day) she would have found it as plentifully stocked with wines, spirits, beer, and cigarettes in 1946 as it had been in 1936. But how these political scum must have laughed at us, their dupes! Coming out tight-bellied from their dining room to listen to and applaud the introduction of still further restrictions on our miserable diet than we had known in the six war years, and to cheer speeches exhorting us to pull our belts a hole tighter etc. And Cartland's story must be true for she would doubtless long ago have been severely punished for making it had it been a lie. But I must say I didn't imagine even Parliament could sink so low as this. Though it happened of 20 years ago, to read of it makes one feel like leading a mob to storm Westminster with the cry, "A la lanterne tous les politiques"!

Friday 12th April.

(Good Friday). In his later years J used to maintain that it was a duty to attend one's Parish Church and there make the best use of the spiritual nourishment offered whether it was to your taste or not. But I never could follow the force of this reasoning. There is of course a duty to fulfill one's financial obligation to one's own Parish, but why am I compelled to accept food which is ritualistically unsatisfying if I can assuage my hunger better elsewhere?

The question recurs every Good Friday more acutely than on any other day. It is now impossible to get a traditional service for the day anywhere within practicable distance so it becomes a question of finding the least unsatisfactory one.

Monday 6th May.

Mollie and Len got back at tea time after a flying visit to Rochdale to see the former's aunt and cousin, having left here after breakfast yesterday. I was glad to see them go and glad to have them back again. To go, in order to test my reaction to solitude, and to return because I find it no longer has much of its old charm. Odd how one changes. In my crowded mess life days a lonely cottage to myself somewhere in Ireland was my favourite pipe dream; and even after I retired I longed for a little place of my own to which I could make periodic retreats from the strain and friction of Kilns life. Yet now, when to secure such a life simply means to sign a cheque, I don't want to do it. I suppose the explanation is that when you feel life drawing to its close, you also feel that too much time for reflection on what awaits you would be intolerable.

Sunday 19th May.

The one thing I struggle more and more to free myself of as I grow older is *anxiety*. And I'm never free of it for more than a couple of days at a time—financial anxiety, health anxiety, anxiety about the impending national collapse, about the future life—all weigh heavily upon me. In short, it is only within recent years that it has been impressed upon me that I am truly my father's son!

Saturday 27rd July.

Last week New York Macmillan sent me two stout volumes, *History of Popular Culture*[283] Vol. I from the ancient Greeks to 1815, the other from 1815 to 1955. The title sounded forbidding and I was about to lay them aside as biblia abiblia. But having nothing on hand at the moment I decided to give them a trial. I was rewarded by finding them fascinating reading, for the title is [a] rather unfortunate one. In fact the book is an enormous snapshot album of the social and domestic life of a very large number of countries at different stages of their development drawn from the works of scores of modern writers. . . . I apparently owe my free copies to the fact that they have

---

283. *History of Popular Culture*, by Norman F. Cantor and Michael S. Werthman (New York: Macmillan, 1968).

used a couple of largeish chunks from *Splendid Century*. . . . One amusing surprise though in this section was nearly a whole page about Joy, her appearance ("chunky") and how she became a Communist. Poor woman, if she was still alive how furious she would be at having American readers informed of her youthful indiscretion!

Wednesday 14th August.

A doctor, or perhaps someone posing as such, is reported in to-day's paper on the problem of those who have reached an age at which so far contributing to the national income they have become a drain on it. There were 1-1/2 million such in 1900, today there are 6-1/2 million; and he goes on to say that the time is drawing near when the problem will be ripe for "the Final Solution". And in case you are so ill-informed as not to know what that means, he then says explicitly that he means a mass extermination of the aged on the same lines as Hitler's attempted "Final Solution" of the Jewish problem. Even if nothing worse happens, it is not pleasant to contemplate being unable to go for walks without encountering gangs of unemployed hooligans shouting "Yah, you useless old b—, why don't yer volunteer for the gas chamber"!

Monday 26th August.

By an odd coincidence this morning I get a letter from Owen Barfield informing me of the impending exhaustion of J's Charity Fund and asking my advice on the disposal of the money which remains. I recommended that the three most deserving in my opinion . . . should continue to be paid as long as funds permit, and payment to the others be stopped forthwith.

Saturday 26th October.

One of the books I bought for [the] Walberswick [holiday at June Flewett Freud's cottage], and of course didn't read there, was Edmund Gosse's *Father and Son;*[284] well written and showing more vividly than anything I can remember, the horrors of life in a mid-Victorian Evangelical home of the extremest type. . . . Toys, books, except his father's works of theology, and friends were forbidden him, for "the Elect" must be always on guard against the world's pollution. Fiction, even children's stories, were not allowed on the ground that these were tales of things which had never happened to people who had never existed. In fact they were *lies,* and

---

284. *Father and Son* (1907), a memoir by Sir Edmund Gosse.

the Elect must run no risk of blurring the line separating truth from falsehood by the absorption of printed untruth.

Thursday 21st November.

Letter from David announcing that he intends to settle in Palestine, has enrolled at Jerusalem University, and has cancelled his nomination to Magdalene [Cambridge]. A wise decision I think from his point of view.

Friday 22nd November.

It is five years ago today that I lost my dear SPB and it still hurts; not of course any longer a constant ache, but only rarely does a day pass in which I do not miss him acutely and momentarily—when I turn to call his attention to a yellowing tree or a good sunset, and above all when in my reading I come across something about which I long for his opinion. Well, I suppose this is just something I shall have to live with for the rest of my days.

Thursday 5th December.

Below is an excerpt from this month's Parish Magazine,[285] and I don't know which is the more amazing, the incident itself or the Bishop's comment on it. Did the thing ever happen? Phillips is a Christian, a theologian, and an honest man, so I impute no falsehood to him; but could he in fact have dreamt the whole thing? That J

---

285. Warren Lewis had carefully inserted the following account, "I Saw A Spirit" by Canon J. B. Phillips, into his diary entry of December 5th: "Many of us who believe in what is known as the Communion of Saints must have experienced the sense of nearness, at some time, of those we love after they have died. This has happened to me several times. But the late C. S. Lewis, whom I did not know very well and had only seen in the flesh once but with whom I had corresponded a fair amount, gave me an unusual experience. A few days after his death, while I was watching television, he appeared sitting in a chair within a few feet of me, and spoke a few words which were particularly relevant to difficult circumstances through which I was passing. He was ruddier in complexion than ever, grinning all over his face and positively glowing with health. The interesting thing to me was that I had not been thinking about him at all. And I was neither alarmed nor surprised. He was just there. A week later, when I was in bed reading before going to sleep, he appeared again, even more rosily radiant than before, and repeated to me the same message, which was very important to me at the time. I was a little puzzled by this, and mentioned it to a certain saintly Bishop. His reply was: 'My dear J, this sort of thing is happening all the time.' The reason I mention this personal experience is that although 'Jack' Lewis was real in a certain sense it did not occur to me to reach out and touch him. It is possible that some of the appearances of the risen Christ were of this nature, being known as versidical visions." This account, taken by Warren Lewis from his Parish Magazine, is also available in a slightly different version in J. B. Phillips, *Ring of Truth* (Wheaton, Illinois: Harold Shaw Publishers, 1967), pp. 117-118.

spoke is far more difficult than that he appeared, for so far as I can recollect it is contrary to all stories of revenants, except the Witch of Endor; speaking ghosts are normally to be found only in literature or on the stage. To me the whole episode brings very mixed feelings. It affords evidence of existence after this life which, assuming the story to be true, is irrefutable. But why, oh why, if able to do so, should SPB never have come to me in the lonely study some evening with a word of comfort and good cheer? Is it that I am of such an earthly nature that to make contact with me is impossible for him? Perhaps he has so far outstripped me that I shall never see him again—a horrible thought, against which I rebel, but I'm afraid not entirely a fantastic one. Whatever the communication it seems to have been relevant and sensible, not the sort of slush by any means which is dealt out by mediums. The only thing equally remarkable concerning revenants which I've ever heard was Pirrie Gordon's story of the meeting with the dead naval officer in the Malta Club.[286]

Tuesday 25th February, 1969.

Last night I finished [Dumas's] *Three Musketeers* once more, and find that it retains all its old magic. I don't remember how many times I've read it. Of all the cloak and rapier school it is, with the exception of the cream of Scott, the very best example; and indeed for one thing I put him above Scott, viz. that where there is melodramatic rant, Dumas's is the less unrealistic and stagey of the two. This must I think have been the first novel I ever read—not counting as novels the "prescribed reading" of my boyhood, T. B. Read, Henty and the like, which I would never have ploughed my way through without external pressure. And the time when I read it must have been the latter half of June 1906 at Wynyard of accursed memory. . . . 1906 was a hot summer, and in such, the Sunday evening programme was that we should walk round the garden "in crocodile", reading, or talking as we chose. One thing stamps these walks in my memory, namely that on these evenings, and these evenings only, did this duty walk carry us to the gate of our prison round the front of the house— a very doubtful privilege, for this meant passing and re-passing under Oldie's study windows. It was in these circumstances that I made the acquaintance of Dumas who has captivated me ever since.

Friday 14th March.

Here is a sentence from a novel which I'm reading that so perfectly

---

286. See diary entry for December 7, 1933.

describes a leading characteristic of the P'daita as to be worth preserving:

He was one of those for whom there was no reality without words, for whom a thing did not exist until it was verbal.

It put me in mind of something I had not thought of for fifty years at least. J and I were both at home and during the usual desultory evening conversation some one raised the old question of one's reactions on hearing that he had inherited a large fortune. What J and I said I have forgotton—nothing probably, for P was off at score immediately. For him no dawning realization that a castle in Spain had become a reality! He had, he said often played with the idea and what he saw was himself seated at his desk with a pen in his hand and a new note book, beginning to write, "It was at _____ on the evening of _____ that I received a letter from my lawyers. . .". In short, to become real, the news had to be translated into his own language and put on paper. And I can see only too well the rich, over-sentimental little essay which he would have turned out—indeed probably *had* turned out at some time or other as a jeu d'esprit.

Saturday 22nd March.
In bed I reflected on my extraordinary good fortune in never having married—or I suppose I should say, at being unmarried within two months of my seventy fourth birthday.

On April 8, 1969, the Millers drove Warren Lewis to Malvern for a visit with his friends, George and Moira Sayer. The following day, Warren and George took a brief holiday to the Black Mountains of Wales. On April 11, Len and Mollie arrived at Malvern to return Warren to The Kilns.

Wednesday 9th April.
A perfect summer day, by some happy choice transplanted into a cold and backward April, and we spent it in an expedition to the Black Mountains, tho' why so called I don't know, for they are green to their summits. . . . One o'c. found us in a narrow stream fed gorge containing a hamlet where it seemed unlikely that we would be able to get as much as a plate of bread and cheese—when low and behold round a bend we came upon the astonishing place shown overleaf.[287] How this pub. exists I can't imagine, yet appointments, service, food

---

287. The Skirrid Mountain Inn, North Abergavenny, Monmouthshire, Wales.

were as good as could be found in London. We had excellent soup, piping hot, and that rare thing, perfect steaks perfectly cooked. So fortified, we set out again, turning right up a very lovely valley with an unpronouncable mountain torrent on our right. After a steady climb we reach Llanthony Abbey, the object of our expedition and well worth seeing. It must have been a big place in its day, and even in ruin it is impressive, specially the shafting. But the oddest thing here is that, actually built into the west end of the abbey, is a little hotel! George tells me that once when he was here with J they were refused lunch in the dining room (owing to J's clothes?), but as a favour were given a meal by themselves in the housekeeper's room.[288] ... Pony trekking seems popular hereabouts; in the abbey were sixteen saddled and bridled animals awaiting their riders. From the Abbey to Gospel Pass at the head of the valley is a long, very beautiful climb, the valley not precipitous but very steep grassy slopes rising to around 2,200 ft. No rock showing, but green to the summits. Here and there I was surprised to see quite large patches of snow. The road left a good deal to be desired and indeed made me a trifle uneasy. No where in the latter stages was there room for two cars to pass and tho' there was a layby from time to time I could not help wondering what we would do if we met another car head on. George told me that J, when his passenger on this trip, insisted on getting out and doing the last half mile on foot—dear man, I quite sympathize with his feelings. ... A day to be marked with a white stone.

Tuesday 6th May.

This afternoon I got a Margery Allingham Omnibus from the library, with a foreword by her husband Youngman Carter from which I learnt with regret that the poor woman died of "a sudden and devouring cancer" on June 30, 1966. Pax cineribus. She'll be a great loss in the field of 'teccie [detective] writers. . . . Why, I wonder, does the 'teccie provide a medium for so many women writers, most of them too at the top of the field in this genre—Dorothy Sayers, Ngaio Marsh, Margery Allingham, Josephine Tey, Patricia Wentworth— and all of them outstanding.

Tuesday 27th May.

After breakfast we said goodbye to Paxford and started off on the highlight of the year, our annual summer holiday in Ireland.

---

288. See George Sayer's essay, "Jack on Holiday" (pp. 206-207), in *C. S. Lewis at the Breakfast Table and Other Reminiscences.*

Wednesday 11th June.

[Today we stopped at] our own beach, Killyhoey. Here I saw a horse and a young man—or rather was it the Horse and his Boy?[289] —swimming together, the horse up to his neck and the boy not mounted but swimming beside him. I mention it because the horse seemed to be enjoying himself as thoroughly as the boy.

Monday 16th June.

I read in the lounge until 11.30 when we set out for Drogheda via Collon and Ardee, and so on to the Mother House at Lourdes where we had a warm welcome from Sr. Ruth. The place has been much smartened up and inter alia now has a court with fountain and a rectangular pool. After the embarrassing habit of nuns Sr. Ruth did not eat with us but sat at the table and chatted whilst we ate the admirable lunch which she had provided. We were all easy together and had much merry talk. At the end of the meal an enormous cake appeared, decorated with enough coloured tapers to make the figures "74", this alas being my 74th birthday. I asked that the uneaten portion should be sent over to the children's ward.

Monday 21st July.

At breakfast this morning we watched the picture of the American astronauts disembarking on the moon, which they had done sometime around 3 a.m. The picture had been made possible because one of the first things unloaded had been a power operated cine-camera. We saw them plant the Stars and Stripes. The men's movements were slow, heavy, and can accurately be described as unearthly, and in appearance they were the Horrors from Outer Space of an old fashioned Science Fiction film. The whole business of course overwhelming, stupendous, epoch making, in fact almost any adjective you like to apply to it, but cui bono? It has left me with a curious feeling which I cannot analyse—sorrow? Regret? I don't know. But it sent me down to the study with an added and heightened sense of gratitude for the old familiar things the colours of light and shade on the trees and flowers, the sound of the wind and bird music. On further reflection I think that my feeling is one of sadness and its cause is the reflection that the enormous technical advances since the flight of Beriot in 1909 have been accompanied by an equally striking decline in *civilization*. Could not the thousands of billions of dollars spent to get a plastic bag

---

289. A reference to Jack's children's story, *The Horse and His Boy* (London: Geoffrey Bles, 1954).

of grit and pebbles off the moon's surface have been used for some more worthwhile purpose—as for instance a real fight to suppress the world wide crime wave?

Friday 25th July.

Len drove me in to the Randolph to keep a lunch engagement with Jock Gibb.[290] We had allowed time for a traffic block so of course there wasn't one, and I sat for ten minutes in the sun outside the Ashmoleum watching the passing traffic. . . . Jock turned up on time and it was pleasant to meet him again. . . . A good plain lunch in a room where all the waiters were Spaniards, and much good talk over coffee afterwards. . . . I was disappointed to learn that the project for the Boxonian Saga has, in Jock's words "been put on the ice". The reason he gave me was that several of the firm think that it would be regarded as the genesis of the Narnian Saga—with which, except for the dressed animals, it has nothing whatever in common. And even if it were to be so regarded, what harm would that do? I think the real explanation must be that others of the firm have convinced him that it would be a financial flop. Home by taxi at 3 p.m.

Tuesday 29th July.

Owen Barfield arrived at 6.30 to dine and spend the night, and it was pleasant to have a long chat with him again. Like the rest of us, and no doubt myself, he has aged a lot since I last saw [him], but is as mentally alert as ever, though he complains that he cannot remember names, worse still, cannot remember in the case of casual acquaintance whether they are people he has met before or not. In the course of our talk it emerged that he is that baffling thing, a practising Christian who is a believer in reincarnation; I objected that if there is reincarnation, the essential *me,* WHL dies, and therefore it amounts to the atheist belief that death ends everything. This he would not have, holding that in each life you add something fresh to the basic *you* from which you started. But what about the endless re-incarnation of your ancestors, from which you inherit? I doubt if either of us understood the other, but I found it an interesting evening. Owen now takes a glass of whiskey and hot water last thing at night—which made me congratulate myself on having bought a half-bottle this morning "just in case"!

---

290. Jocelyn E. ("Jock") Gibb (1907-), partner with Geoffrey Bles in the publishing house of Geoffrey Bles. Bles was the original publisher of many of Jack Lewis's books.

1969

Warren and the Millers take another Walberswick holiday at the cottage of June Flewett Freud from September 19 through October 3.

Saturday 20th September.

Up after a good night to find it another lovely day. I went down to the beach after breakfast, being stopped on the way by a friendly child who wanted to show me the note from her mother to the school mistress asking that her daughter might be excused [from] school on her birthday. I offered my congratulations and continued to the beach. . . . When I tire of the sight and sound of waves breaking on sand I'll know I'm tired of life.

Friday 10th October.

This wonderful weather continues. Yesterday was the last day of summer, today the first of the real autumn that fortells winter's coming. As J would have put it, Peter Ping is in evidence.

Monday 13th October.

A note from Ruth this morning—irritatingly undated—to say that Joey [Lewis] died "last night" which I deduce from the postmark to have been the night of the 8th. I wrote the usual futile note to Ida, then smoked a cigarette while old memories flooded over me—all of Larne oddly enough, not of Sandycroft—the "piers" on the freshne from which we used to fish for crabs: that really remarkable "steamship" Blackbird which Joey built in the back yard: the daily visit to the harbour to watch the arrival or departure of those graceful ships *Princess May* and *Princess Victoria:* Dick and his hobbledehoy flirtations with Yvonne Courvoisier: evening visits with Dick to pierrot shows on the Bank Heads: J's precocious flame Beth Thompson. Lord, how it all comes back to me! In those days our generation of the family numbered fourteen; today four of us survive. Lord, teach us so to number our days—.

Wednesday 7th January, 1970.

Roger [Lancelyn Green] with his wife and young son came to lunch today to carry off the *Lewis Papers* which I let go with something of a pang I admit. This is the first time I've met Mrs. Roger and she turned out to be one of those very rare women whom you regard as an old friend within a quarter of an hour of meeting her; so we were soon all merry and at our ease, with much good talk, mainly of books. Mollie gave us an excellent lunch and the wine went round merrily. I was much impressed with the sixteen year old boy—neither

[294]

a speechless lump nor a conceited youngling anxious to impress his elders, but taking his share (and no more) in the conversation modestly and with good sense. When I remembered what I myself must have been like in 1911, I blushed inwardly!

Wednesday 28th January.

Here is an interesting fact from a book I'm reading about [detective] writers and their methods of work. Dorothy Sayers and Josephine Bell were not only at the same school, Godolphin School, Salisbury, but were there at the same time. There may be other cases where two authors were contemporaries at school, though I admit I've never heard of one. But that there are two such who have both reached the first flight in such a specialized genre must I imagine be unique.

Thursday 5th February.

At breakfast this morning Len disclosed that he has a quite unsuspected streak of poetry in him. The talk had turned to how admirably the villages in the Cotswolds blend into their countryside. "They look" said Len "as if someone had dropped house seed there and it had sprouted". This can hardly be bettered I think.

Sunday 8th February [Death of Lady Jane].

We are a sad household this evening. At tea time poor Mollie in floods of tears came back from Snodgrass where they had taken the cat, Lady Jane, who had been restless all day and was obviously suffering from constipation. Snodgrass diagnosed her case as an incurable hemorrhage and advised her instant destruction, and this was at once done. Sic transit. Mollie I'm afraid will take it hard, she having had Jane ever since she was weaned, a matter of around twelve years ago. All very sudden for last night at television time she was with us stretched out in front of the fire looking the very picture of comfort. Not much use pointing out that few cats have had a happier and a longer life than our poor Lady Jane. I shall miss her myself.

Tuesday 24th February.

A letter from Ruth this morning—always interesting and now my sole link with a vanished world. She tells me inter alia that Gundred, now 82, is "still tall and lovely". Pleasant to think that my Helen of Troy has grown old with such grace. She must have been about twenty four when I first realized that she was the most beautiful woman I'd ever seen.

Monday 11th May.

Today we set out on the highlight of the year, the annual visit to Ireland [returning to The Kilns on June 3rd].

Tuesday 16th June.

My 75th birthday. The first I recorded in this diary was my 23rd and I now remember with amusement the faint uneasy feeling I had that life was moving all too swiftly. Those were the days when I thought a man of 40 elderly, and one of 50 definitely old. Had I then known that I would live to be 75 I would have viewed the fact with horror—seeing myself as a toothless, witless, shrivelled, nurse fed wreck whom it would be a kindness to knock on the head! We celebrated with a ramble through the eastern Cotswolds, coffee at our old friend Kirtlington, and an excellent lunch with wine at the Dorchester in Woodstock. And now the inevitable reflection—have I just celebrated my *last* birthday?

Sunday 21st. June.

I'm re-reading Angela Thirkell[291] and thinking about the handling of *weather* in English fiction and poetry. Where and how did the convention arise that the months either have anyway ought to have, each its fixed weather pattern? The tradition is as old as Chaucer and is carried on right through the Victorians, Dickens, Thackeray, Keats, Trollope, Surtees, though reference to contemporary letters and diaries shows that 19th Century weather was as unpredictable as that of today. . . . But generally speaking it's always "flaming June" or September's "mists and mellow fruitfulness" and so forth: But in Thirkell comes a break with tradition. One of her favourite scenes is half a dozen friends in a country house gathered round the blazing fire for tea on an August afternoon; and Rose Macaulay pinpoints an episode in one of her novels by saying that it happened "on the day that summer when one could sit out of doors".

Tuesday 7th July.

Today I finished [Wordsworth's] *The Prelude* for the fifth time since I first read it twenty eight years ago at J's instigation. The descriptive parts I found as exquisite as ever, but his obscure philosophizings just as dull. And his flashes of bathos! Certainly the most unequalled of any of the first rank poets we have produced.

---

291. Angela Thirkell (1890-1961), an English novelist who "continued" Anthony Trollope's Barsetshire saga.

Saturday 8th August.

By appointment at ll a.m. to see a surgeon, Tibbs, in Banbury Rd. to whom I had been sent by Turner at the Wingfield. A pleasant, soft spoken, youngish man with whom I was favourably impressed. He examined me very thoroughly and then announced that my left leg was in good condition but that in the right the pulse was very low, which means that there is an obstruction in the artery. I shall never get any better, and may get worse, though he thinks the latter unlikely—tho' I expect this statement is intended merely to boost my morale; if some part of a machine is functioning inefficiently, laissez-faire is surely unlikely to restore its efficiency! I am to do nothing about it unless the foot becomes painful, and in that case I must see him again with a view to his operating. Whether I shall do so or not I don't know. What are the prospects for a man over seventy-five? But my immediate reaction is sadness at the thought that I can never live to take a walk again. A love of walking is I think the only thing I inherited from my father, and since the days of the shepherded walk it has been one of my greatest pleasures. Many of my happiest and most vivid memories of J are associated with walks—not only walking tours, but the common or garden daily walks. This leg trouble may not be the herald of the last fatal illness, but it is a warning sign that I'm nearing the end of the course. Apropos of which, I read a Psalm the other day in which the author wishes that God had told him when he was to die, which is surely an odd wish even for a Jew or a Christian to entertain. We have been told so very little about the future life that even the believer must see it as a plunge into the unknown, and such abrupt changes in this life always bring apprehension with them. Would my fear of death be less or greater if I was told I would certainly die this day next month? It's pretty clear to me that, unlike the Psalmist, I should hate to know—though perhaps I should spend the next four weeks more profitably if I did. Quien sabe?

Thursday 10th September.

George Sayer has been doing some research into J's Malvern days as recollected by his contemporaries, and this has produced two remarkably interesting letters from Hardman with whom J shared a study when they were both "new boys". The first was written before Hardman had read *Surprised by Joy,* and in it he says:

He was a bit of a rebel; he had a wonderful sense of humour and was a pastmaster of mimicry. I think he took his work seriously, but nothing else; never took any interest in games and never played any so far as I can remember unless he had to. The quite extraordinary thing about Lewis is the complete transformation of character that took place after he left Malvern. I met him in Oxford after the war and noticed he had changed, but was staggered to find him the author of *The Screwtape Letters*. When I knew him, I can only describe him as a riotously amusing atheist. He really was pretty foul mouthed about it.

After reading *Surprised by Joy*, Hardman wrote to George again criticizing J's account of SH [School House] as he saw it in his day:

In a word it is in my view unbalanced and exaggerated. This is not to say that some of the practices and customs he complains of did not exist; they did, but Lewis has blown them up out of all proportion. . . . Lewis blames one of his prep. schools for the fact that he was no good at games. I blame both for a good deal more than that. I think that they, coupled with an inadequate home life (no mother and a curious father to say the least) made the abnormal boy he was when he went to Malvern. Even so, I am sure he was not unhappy all the time. I can remember going long walks with him on Sundays when he was in the gayest of moods. Story telling, and mimicking people, one of his chief butts being the worthy master in charge of the O.T.C. It is surprising that he should forget the happy times and remember only the unhappy ones.

Altogether a really valuable contribution to the history of J's early years.

Saturday 14th November.
Blackwells is certainly a remarkable firm. I had a note from them this morning to say that the book which I ordered on 13th December 1957 is now available if I still require it! I replied "yes" for it is Volume IV of the *New Cambridge History*, published at long last. Collecting the four vols. I want has been a long business—Vol. VII on 15th Nov. 1957, Vol. V, 10th June 1961, Vol. VI 15th July 1970, and now at last, Vol. IV in sight!

Wednesday 17th February, 1971.
I wonder where the "rage of innovation" is to cease? We have just swallowed, tho' not digested, decimalization and now have learnt on last night's TV that the thousand year old boundaries of the counties are to vanish. Judging from one of the new areas the cake has been cut up by someone with no historical knowledge, for I see that roughly a third of the old Yorkshire is to be incorporated in the new Lancashire. Rutlandshire ceases to exist completely swallowed by Leicestershire. I could not study the plan long enough to grasp anything else except that Scotland and Wales are to be drastically reconstructed. I'm sur-

prised that the planners have been sentimental enough to retain many of the old county names instead of cutting the island up into rectangles called Administrative Areas—so that our postal address would have become, say "Oxford OX38EY, Admin.4". The explanation given for the changes is the usual one, increased efficiency and economy, but I can't help feeling that the real one is give us a "new look", get away from the old fuddy duddy sentiment of county pride. But I'm cheered by remembering the despondent Communist pupil who told J that what was wrong with England was that "we had such a rotten proletariat". I feel that the Yorkshire man in the new Lancashire will continue to call himself a Yorkshireman, and the Rutlander will continue to talk of Rutland.

Saturday 10th April.

I don't look back over Lent with much satisfaction, though there have been years in which I've passed the season worse. I can take no credit for having drunk no spirits, for it must now be two years or more since I've tasted any; nor can I plume myself on my dieting, for this, such as it was, I did for merely physical reasons. I spent an hour each day in religious reading and during the last six weeks I've read Law's *Serious Call*, Lathom's *Pastor Pastorum*, Jack's *Reflections on the Psalms, God in the Dock, Screwtape*, and *Letters to Malcolm*, G. K. Chesterton's *Everlasting Man*, and Austin Farrer's *Is There a Science of God*—as well of course as my normal daily Bible reading; and I attended Evensong on the six Sundays as well as Mattins. Not much of an achievement I fear, but still, better than nothing.

Monday 3rd May.

The interesting map on the opposite [page] . . . was made by J for Pauline Baynes'[292] guidance. . . . It is now in Bodder [Bodleian Library, Oxford]. I'm rather surprised that I never heard of, or saw it whilst J was alive; but it is undoubtedly genuine.

Sunday 14th November.

All day a squad of Morlocks[293] has been at work destroying the hedge in the lane below the Community Centre, and with it goes the last reminder of the unmade country lane down which J and I would

---

292. Pauline Baynes (1922-), illustrator chosen by Jack Lewis for his seven children's stories, *The Chronicles of Narnia*. Her selection for the first of these stories, *The Lion, the Witch, and the Wardrobe* (1950), came after Jack saw her excellent illustrations for J. R. R. Tolkien's *Farmer Giles of Ham* (1949).

293. A race of underground monsters from H. G. Wells's science-fiction novel *The Time Machine* (1895).

trudge to the Chequers in the silent darkness of what could still pass for countryside. Mollie regrets its destruction, Len welcomes it. He is unique in my experience in being the only man I know of his age who is an enthusiastic modernist—welcomed the vanishing of steam from the railways, likes to see new buildings going up everywhere, rejoices in new roundabouts, and positively likes to see slabs of woodland and meadow being turned into wider and ever wider motorways. Yet with it all, has a genuine appreciation of such countryside as still remains.

Tuesday 30th November.

At the clinic this morning I picked up a copy of the *Telegraph,* a paper I never see these days, and almost the first thing I saw in it was the announcement that Mrs. Tolkien died yesterday in Bournemouth and is to be buried here in Wolvercote Cemetry, a burial ground I've never heard of. . . . I had only a nodding acquaintance [with her], but peace to her ashes. I must write to Tollers tomorrow; via Priscilla, for his address is a closely guarded secret.

Tuesday 21st December.

A letter card from Gundred this morning, firmly written, tho' she and Cherry Robbins who is now staying at Glenmachan, are both 83. So when I first realized that she was the most beautiful girl I'd ever seen, she must have been 23. Well, well. Len tells me that he has today put his name on the waiting list for a council house, which strikes me as a very prudent measure on his part—tho' it conveys to me the uncomfortable realization that I'm failing more rapidly to the onlooking eyes even more rapidly than my own sensations lead me to believe is the case!

In January 1972, Warren's recurring circulatory problems resulted in the installation of a heart pacemaker. This device seemed to accentuate his tendency to dizziness, and he never totally accepted it.

Friday 18th February, 1972.

Since I began writing in 1953 my earnings come a total of £9,766-10. Not so bad for a complete amateur who was over fifty eight when he turned author!

Wednesday 23rd February.

I'm still worried by attacks of dizziness when I stand up quickly, and though Richards tells me I have nothing to worry about I can't help worrying, wondering if it's a warning that the end is near.

Thursday 2nd March.

Head came at 10 a.m. and administered Communion to me in the front room, not I hope without profit; the first time this has befallen me in this house.

Monday 6th March.

After an early lunch and squired by Len I went in to the Radcliffe. By taxi because of the impossibility of parking anywhere near the hospital. When the girl on the counter produced a form and asked for the year of my birth, to which I replied 1895, she said "What"! and fixed me with a stare—which was gratifying. After a long and tedious wait in a very crowded reception room I saw the doctor at 2.30 instead of 2 as appointed. To my great relief he told me that my dizzy attacks were merely due to the pace maker adjusting itself to my rate of heart beat and there was nothing to worry about; and that in two years time I would need another operation to replace the run down battery in the pace maker. A nurse then came in and took out my stitches. We had a tiresome wait for the return taxi.

Friday 2nd June.

An odd little incident last night. I came into the front room just at the moment when the cast of a TV play was showing. One of the characters was called Warren and the name of the actor playing the part was *Jack Lewis!*

Wednesday 12th July.

"The Twalth" of glorious and immortal memory, but alas likely to be a sad one in Belfast. Recently I asked Sister Ruth if I could be admitted to Lourdes for the second half of August and yesterday got a warm reply to say that all had been fixed, how much they looked forward to seeing me again, and only regretted the shortness of my proposed visit—all with a warmth that gladdened me. Costella will be my doctor. I don't suppose they will be able to do anything for my complaint, but I yearn for a blessed fortnight away from this desk. The only year I wrote to my "regulars" asking them to stop writing during my holiday proved disastrous; one and all wrote proudly to say that "this letter is timed to reach you on the day you reach home"!

Warren planned his month-long convalescent rest at his beloved Our Lady of Lourdes Hospital in Drogheda, Ireland, for August 1972, in order to escape the pressures of tourist season in Oxford with its accompanying number of C. S. Lewis fans (as well as to take a break from his large and steady correspondence). Unfortunately, while at Drogheda, Warren's ever-increasing circulation difficulties resulted in the development of gangrene in both feet (which in turn necessitated minor surgery on the affected tissue). Thus it was not until the following April that Warren was able to return home to Oxford from the Hospital in Ireland.

Just a few days later, on April 9, 1973, Major Warren Hamilton Lewis died peacefully at home in The Kilns. He was buried at Headington Quarry Parish Church in the same grave with his brother Jack.

Sister Ruth of the Medical Missionaries of Mary, Drogheda, who was in attendance at the funeral, described it as a day full of sunlight, birds singing, and with the daffodils in bloom.

INDEX

NOTE: Because of the many references to C. S. Lewis, Warren Lewis, Mrs. Moore, and Maureen Moore, a list would overwhelm rather than inform. Therefore, in connection with these people, only major events, characteristics, and ideas are indexed.

INDEX

INDEX

INDEX